From

Nepal

by Karl Samson

Macmillan • USA

MACMILLAN TRAVEL

A Simon & Schuster Macmillan Company
1633 Broadway
New York, NY 10019

Copyright © 1995 by Simon & Schuster, Inc.

All rights reserved. No part of this book may be reproduced or transmitted in any form or by any means, electronic or mechanical, including photocopying, recording, or by any information storage and retrieval system, without permission in writing from the Publisher.

Macmillan is a registered trademark of Macmillan, Inc.

ISBN 0-02-860627-2
ISSN 1055-5439

Editor: Blythe Grossberg
Map Editor: Doug Stallings
Design by Michele Laseau
Digital Cartography by Jim Moore and Ortelius Design

SPECIAL SALES

Bulk purchases (10+ copies) of Frommer's Travel Guides are available to corporations at special discounts. The Special Sales Department can produce custom editions to be used as premiums and/or for sales promotion to suit individual needs. Existing editions can be produced with custom cover imprints such as corporate logos. For more information write to: Special Sales, Simon & Schuster, 1633 Broadway, New York, NY 10019.

Manufactured in the United States of America

Contents

List of Maps

For my father, Lyle, from whom I inherited my longing for travel and adventure.

An Invitation to the Reader

In researching this book, I discovered many wonderful places—hotels, restaurants, shops, and more. I'm sure you'll find others. Please tell me about them, so I can share the information with your fellow travelers in upcoming editions. If you were disappointed with a recommendation, I'd love to know that, too. Please write to:

Karl Samson
Frommer's Nepal, 3rd Edition
Macmillan Travel
1633 Broadway
New York, NY 10019

An Additional Note

Please be advised that travel information is subject to change at any time—and this is especially true of prices. We therefore suggest that you write or call ahead for confirmation when making your travel plans. The authors, editors, and publisher cannot be held responsible for the experiences of readers while traveling. Your safety is important to us, however, so we encourage you to stay alert and be aware of your surroundings. Keep a close eye on cameras, purses, and wallets, all favorite targets of thieves and pickpockets.

What the Symbols mean

✪ Frommer's Favorites

Hotels, restaurants, attractions, and entertainment you should not miss.

⑤ Super-Special Values

Hotels and restaurants that offer great value for your money.

The following abbreviations are used for credit cards:

AE	American Express	EU	Eurocard
CB	Carte Blanche	JCB	Japan Credit Bank
DC	Diners Club	MC	MasterCard
DISC	Discover	V	Visa
ER	en Route		

Getting to Know Nepal

1

For centuries, Nepal has intrigued the Western mind. Closed to the outside world from the mid-19th century until the early 1950s, Nepal was regarded as a mysterious land as shrouded in myths and legends as the Himalayas are shrouded by monsoon clouds. When this tiny Himalayan kingdom wedged between China and India finally opened its borders to the outside world, some of the very first visitors were mountain climbers headed for Mt. Everest, the highest peak in the world. By the early 1970s, Nepal had, however, been discovered by a very different sort of traveler—globe-trotting, backpack-toting hippies. The word had gotten out that in Nepal, hashish was legal and the cost of living was dirt cheap. Kathmandu became a Himalayan Haight Ashbury.

The hippies eventually headed home to Europe and North America when their funds ran low and began to speak about living among the peaceful people and snow-capped peaks of Nepal. Tales of the mystic East sent seekers of enlightenment to India and Nepal. Although the image of a Westerner asking the meaning of life from a holy man on top of a mountain has become a cliché, people really do journey to Nepal seeking spiritual guidance from Buddhist lamas and Hindu holy men. Sometimes, you really do have to climb a mountain to find a holy man, and sometimes that holy man is living among the most spiritually uplifting scenery on earth. For many visitors, it is enough merely to walk amid the inspirational scenery.

Today, adventure travel is no longer the exclusive realm of well-financed mountain-climbing expeditions, and Nepal has become a popular destination for people seeking active vacations. However, Nepal has far more to offer than just the chance to hike in the Himalayas. As overwhelming as they may be, Nepal's mountains are just a backdrop for the country's diverse and complex cultural landscape. The peoples of Nepal have been molded by their environment; their religions, agriculture, architecture, and very lives have been dictated by the mountains. The Nepali people make a trip to Nepal a truly unique experience.

Although Nepal is a fascinating travel destination, it is still one of the poorest countries in the world and is confronting the same problems faced by many developing nations—overpopulation, pollution, deforestation, and the lack of safe drinking water. Political and geographic isolation had combined to keep Nepal separate from the world until less than 50 years ago, so today the nation is rapidly trying to catch up with the rest of the developed world. At the same time, people from more developed countries are journeying to Nepal searching for glimpses of what life was like before the frantic pace of the late-20th century.

Himalayan villages still live by the rhythms of the seasons, and farming is still done by hand with oxen and buffalo. However, overpopulation has forced Nepal to decimate its forests both for firewood and for more arable land. In Nepal's capital of Kathmandu, sacred cows still sleep in the streets and ash-besmeared Hindu holy men still beg for alms outside temples dedicated to a seemingly endless pantheon of gods. In Kathmandu, there are also traffic jams and smog, computers and Coca-Cola. Nepal is not now and never was "Shangri-La," but the tiny country on the rooftop of the world has captured the collective Western imagination. Trekkers, mountain climbers, and spiritual pilgrims have all beaten a trail to Nepal, and what they have found is a country trying to strike a balance between the 19th and the 20th centuries.

1 Nepal Past & Present

THE LAY OF THE LAND

Nepal is a small, mountainous kingdom 550 miles long by 90 to 150 miles wide (about the size of Iowa) with a population of around 18 million people. Roughly rectangular in shape, the country follows the line of the Himalayas from southeast to northwest. Nepal is bordered on the north by the Tibetan Autonomous Region of China and on the east, south, and west by India, which makes it one of the few landlocked countries in the world. This precarious position between two of the world's political giants has dictated Nepal's history for centuries.

Though most foreigners associate Nepal only with the Himalayas, its elevation varies from 29,028-foot Mt. Everest, the highest mountain on earth, to a low of only 220 feet above sea level in the southern part of the country. Between these two extremes lies the midland, home to the majority of the population. Nepal is divided into 14 zones, which are further divided into 75 development districts. Though Nepali is the official language, there are 22 major languages spoken by different ethnic groups.

The Himalayas The Himalayas, the highest mountain range on earth, comprise approximately one third of Nepal's landmass. They form the country's northern border with Tibet and range in elevation from about 10,000 feet to 29,028 feet. They are some of the youngest mountains on earth and antedate several of the rivers that flow from Tibet. These rivers flow *through* the Himalayas not *from* the Himalayas, though they are considerably enlarged by the many streams and rivers flowing off the mountains. The Kali Gandaki is the

Dateline

- 7th or 8th c. B.C. The Kiranti settle in Kathmandu Valley.
- 563 B.C. Prince Siddhartha Gautama born in Lumbini.
- 250 B.C. Emperor Ashoka of India makes pilgrimage to Lumbini; visits Kathmandu Valley.
- ca. A.D. 200 Licchavi dynasty begins in Kathmandu Valley.
- 460 King Manadeva I records construction on Swayambunath Stupa and has Boudhanath Stupa erected.
- 879 End of Licchavi dynasty. Beginning of Thakuri dynasty.
- Late 10th c. Kathmandu founded.
- 1200 Start of Malla dynasty.

continues

best example of such a river: It flows between Dhaulagiri and Annapurna I, forming a valley nearly 4 miles deep—the deepest river valley on earth. This sparsely populated region of the country is the destination of most trekkers. One of the greatest surprises that most people have on their first visit to Nepal is that the Himalayas are not visible from most of Kathmandu, the country's capital. Kathmandu lies in a valley surrounded by high hills. It is necessary to ascend a bit from the valley floor before more than just the tips of a few peaks become visible.

The Midland   Located between 3,000 and 10,000 feet above sea level, the midland of Nepal is composed of the Mahabharat Hills (actually mountains) and numerous fertile valleys. It is in this region that most of Nepal's major cultural developments took place. The Kathmandu and Pokhara Valleys are the two most populous valleys of the region. The mountains are still heavily forested, though the valleys are entirely under cultivation, as are many of the less steep slopes.

The Lowland   Extending from 220 to 3,000 feet above sea level, the lowland includes both the fertile Terai region, part of the Gangetic Plain, and the Churia (or Siwalik) Hills. The Terai, which is hot and humid, comprises about 17% of Nepal's landmass and until the 1960s was sparsely populated due to malaria. Since controlling malarial mosquitoes with DDT, the Nepali government has turned the Terai into its main industrial and agricultural region. There are still large stands of hardwood forests here, and several national parks and preserves provide protection for the abundant wildlife.

HISTORY & POLITICS

Reality or Myth?   The early history of Nepal is inextricably interwoven with Hindu and Buddhist mythology, and consequently it is often difficult to discern what is historical fact and what is myth.

There is evidence that as early as 700 B.C., there were people living in the Kathmandu Valley. The two Indian epics *Ramayana* and *Mahabharata* both mention the Kirantis who lived in the mountains north of India—an area that would coincide with the Kathmandu Valley. A fifth-century inscription at Changu Narayan, a temple in the Kathmandu Valley, indicates that the Kiranti dynasty lasted from the eighth century B.C. to the third century A.D. The Kirantis may themselves have been descendants of an even older dynasty, the Ahirs, shepherds who supposedly were the first rulers of the Kathmandu Valley.

- **1346** Swayambunath Stupa destroyed.
- **Mid-17th c.** Swayambunath Stupa rebuilt.
- **1696** Temple built at Pashupatinath.
- **1769** Prithvi Narayan Shah unifies Nepal.
- **1792** Nepal loses war with Tibet.
- **1815** Nepal loses war with British.
- **1816** First British resident arrives in Kathmandu.
- **1846** Jung Bahadur Rana seizes power. Ranas rule the country until 1951.
- **1854** Nepal goes to war with Tibet.
- **1934** Earthquake shakes Kathmandu Valley, destroying temples and other sites.
- **1951** King Tribhuvan restored to the throne; declares Nepal a democratic country.
- **1956** Nepal joins the United Nations.
- **1959** First parliament elected; later the same year it is dissolved.
- **1962** New constitution and panchayat system of government introduced.
- **1972** King Birendra ascends the throne.
- **1975** King Birendra crowned.
- **1990** King allows political parties and democratic elections.
- **1994** Nepal's communist party forms coalition government.

Over the centuries of Nepal's early history, there were successive migrations into the mountains by refugees, nomads, and conquering armies from Tibet, India, and even Central Asia. Both the Ahirs and the Kirantis are likely to have migrated into the mountains.

The Enlightened One   From a global perspective, the most significant event in Nepal's history was the birth of Prince Siddhartha Gautama around 563 B.C. in the Shakya kingdom of Kapilvastu in the lowlands of Nepal (near present-day Lumbini). Siddhartha Gautama, at age 29, renounced his claim to the throne of his kingdom and became a wandering ascetic searching for a way to end all human suffering. After wandering for six years and practicing all types of accepted spiritual pursuits of the time, he sat down under a *bo* tree to meditate. From this meditation, the prince found the answer he had been seeking. From that time on, he was known as the Buddha (the Enlightened One). Within a few centuries, the doctrine of the Buddha had spread throughout much of India and Nepal.

In 250 B.C., the Indian emperor Ashoka, who had converted to Buddhism after conquering most of northern India, made a pilgrimage to Lumbini. There he erected a stone pillar with an inscription commemorating the birth of the Buddha. The pillar was not rediscovered until 1895, at which time its inscription led to the discovery of other ruins in the area. Legends hold that Ashoka continued to Kathmandu and erected four *stupas* (reliquary shrines) at the four corners of Patan, where the Buddha is said to have visited briefly. However, there is no record anywhere of either of these visits.

From the second century to the ninth century A.D., the Kathmandu Valley was ruled by the Licchavi dynasty. Many stone inscriptions, the earliest historical records in Nepal, date from this period. In A.D. 460, King Manadeva of the Licchavi dynasty is said to have erected Boudhanath Stupa and had construction done on Swayambunath Stupa. Whether these projects were actually carried out by Manadeva is still a matter of speculation.

By the end of the ninth century A.D., the Thakuri dynasty began. Under this dynasty, Kathmandu was founded at the confluence of the Vishnumati and Bagmati Rivers. Little is known about the Thakuri period, but around 1200, the first of the Malla kings came to power in the Kathmandu Valley. Under the Mallas, who ruled until the middle of the 18th century, architecture and the arts flourished in Nepal. Most of the temples and palaces on the valley's three Durbar Squares were built by Malla kings.

The Unification of Nepal   Prior to the 18th century, Nepal was a patchwork of tiny independent kingdoms, but in 1769 the Ghorkha (Gurkha) King Prithvi Narayan Shah conquered the tiny kingdoms of the Kathmandu Valley and completed his quest to unify Nepal. Part of his reason for uniting Nepal was to create a strong defense against the encroaching British, whom the king saw as a threat. The East India Company was firmly in control of India by this time, and British soldiers guarded the Nepal–India border. In 1767 Prithvi Narayan Shah's troops battled with a British regiment, defeating them and seizing a considerable number of weapons. A period of expansionism ensued during the latter part of the 18th century under the successors of Prithvi Narayan. However, their armies suffered a defeat at the hands of the Chinese in 1791 and again in 1792 after the Nepali army invaded Tibet.

In 1814, 39 years after the death of Prithvi Narayan, the Nepali army attempted to enlarge Nepal's borders into India. It took two years for the British troops

❷ Did You Know?

- Nepal has the only nonrectangular national flag of any nation, consisting of two crimson triangles one above the other, trimmed in blue. In the upper triangle is the moon, and in the lower one the sun.
- There is only one doctor for 100,000 people in parts of Nepal, and life expectancy averages less than 50 years.
- The Himalayas, which comprise about a third of Nepal's land area, are the highest mountains on earth.
- Mt. Everest, the tallest mountain on earth, is 29,028 feet tall and was first successfully climbed by Sir Edmund Hillary and Tenzing Norgay in 1953.
- Machhapuchhare, the Fishtail Peak, is a sacred mountain said to be the abode of gods and has never been climbed to the summit.
- There are at least 22 major languages spoken in Nepal. Even in the Kathmandu Valley many people speak only a smattering of Nepali, the national language.
- Nepal is the world's only Hindu country: 90% of Nepal's population is Hindu.
- Under Nepalese law, yetis, or abominable snowmen, are protected; hunting them is prohibited.
- The world's deepest river gorge is that of the Kali Gandaki River in central Nepal. This gorge is nearly 4 miles deep.

to defeat the Gurkha army, much longer than they had anticipated. The British developed such respect for the fighting abilities of the Gurkhas that they have recruited these rugged fighters ever since. The peace treaty signed with Britain at the end of this war effectively set the boundaries of present-day Nepal.

From the time of the unification, there was a great deal of struggle within Nepal between the various royal families who had been conquered by Prithvi Narayan. In 1846, Jung Bahadur Rana seized power from the reigning king and installed himself as prime minister for life. The position of prime minister became hereditary, and members of the Rana family ruled the country for the next century. During this time the Shah royal family was kept in place but without any real power.

The Nationalist Movement   During the 1930s and 1940s, there was growing discontent with the ruling Rana regime. When India gained independence in 1947, the Ranas lost the British support they had enjoyed for many years. The nationalist movement that had started in India spilled over into Nepal with the formation of the Nepali Congress party. In 1950, this party spearheaded a revolution against the Rana regime. At about the same time, the powerless King Tribhuvan Bir Bikram Shah sought refuge in India. In 1951, the Indian government helped negotiate a cease-fire, and the monarchy was restored to power with King Tribhuvan on the throne. A coalition Rana-Nepali Congress cabinet was also formed.

Over the next eight years various unsuccessful attempts were made at forming a democratic government. In 1959 a new constitution took effect, and in that year the Nepali Congress party won the majority of the votes. King Mahendra, who had succeeded his father King Tribhuvan in 1955, immediately came into conflict with

Nepal

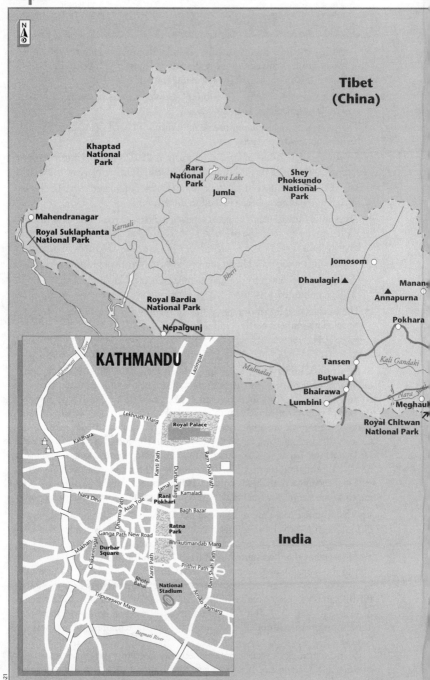

Tibet (China)

Khaptad National Park

Rara National Park

Rara Lake

Jumla

Shey Phoksundo National Park

Mahendranagar

Royal Suklaphanta National Park

Karnali

Bheri

Royal Bardia National Park

Nepalgunj

Jomosom

Dhaulagiri ▲

Manang

▲ Annapurna

Pokhara

Kali Gandaki

Tansen

Butwal

Bhairawa

Lumbini

Meghaul

Royal Chitwan National Park

Malnalai

Nara...

KATHMANDU

Vishnumati River

Laxmat

Lekhnath Marg

Royal Palace

Kaldhara

Kanti Path

Durbar Marg

Ram Shah Path

Nara Devi

Dharma Path

Jamal

Kamaladi

Asan Tole

Rani Pokhari

Bagh Bazar

Ganga Path New Road

Ratna Park

Chikanmugal

Makhan

Durbar Square

Bhrikutimandab Marg

Prithvi Path

Bhote Bahal

Kanti Path

National Stadium

Ram Shah Path

Tripureswor Marg

Arniko Rajmarg

Bagmati River

India

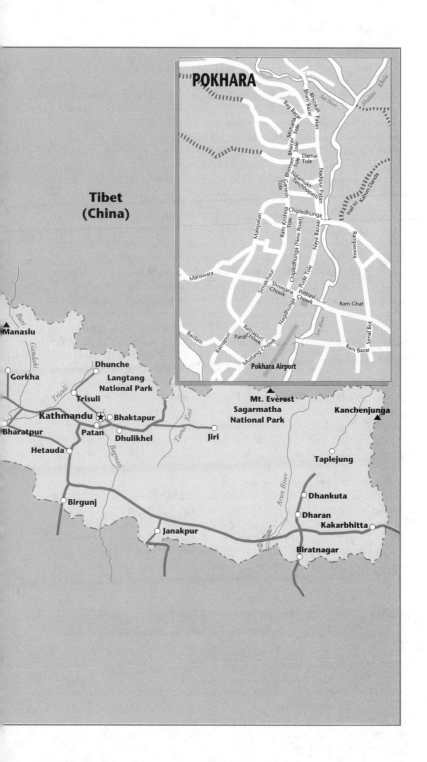

POKHARA

Seti River

Bhimkali Patan
Bhim Bazar

Bag Bazar

Bhairav Tole
Moharia Tole

Damai Tole

Bhimsen Tole

Nadipur Patan

Gairhi Tole
Kalamukh
Terchhopatti

Chipledhunga

trail to Kahun Danda

Ram Krishna Tole

Malepatan

Naya Bazar

Chipledhunga (New Road)

Ranipauwa

Manswara

Simalchaur

Pude Tole

Shreejana Chowk

Prithavi Chowk

Napdihunga

Ram Ghat

Baidam

Ratnapuri

Simal Bot

Ratnapuri Pardi Chowk

Mustang Chowk

Ram Bazar

Soti River

Pokhara Airport

**Tibet
(China)**

Buri Gandaki

▲
Manaslu

Gandaki

○
Gorkha

○ **Dhunche**

**Langtang
National Park**

Trisuli

○ **Trisuli**

Kathmandu ★ ○ **Bhaktapur**

○ **Patan**

Bharatpur ○ ○ **Dhulikhel**

○ **Hetauda**

Tama Kosi

○ **Jiri**

Bagmati

▲
**Mt. Everest
Sagarmatha
National Park**

Kanchenjunga
▲

○ **Taplejung**

Arun River

○ **Birgunj**

○ **Dhankuta**

○ **Dharan**

Kakarbhitta

○ **Janakpur**

Biratnagar

Sherpas

One of the many ethnic groups of Nepal, the Sherpas inhabit the Solu-Khumbu region and have become integrally associated with mountaineering and trekking in Nepal. Since the first Western expeditions to climb the high peaks of the Himalayas, Sherpas have led the way, carried the loads, cooked the food, and often climbed side by side with famous mountaineers. However, the most famous Sherpa of all, Tenzing Norgay, who accompanied Sir Edmund Hillary on the first successful ascent of Mt. Everest, is from India.

---

this popularly elected government and dissolved the cabinet in 1960. In 1962, the king introduced a new constitution and a new form of government called the panchayat. This system banned all political parties, prohibited organized opposition, and effectively consolidated all real power in the hands of the king.

In early 1990, widespread dissatisfaction with the panchayat system and the initiation of the democratic process throughout Eastern Europe brought about organized protests throughout Nepal. Banned political parties, with assistance from political parties of neighboring Asian countries, held a conference in Kathmandu. The result of this conference was the demand for a democratic form of government and an end to the ineffective panchayat system. Bloody protests and rioting broke out in early April 1990. On April 6, King Birendra Bir Bikram Shah announced that a new constitution would be drafted, and on April 8, after further protests, he agreed to the establishment of a multiparty democratic political system. The first elections were held in 1991. Today, Nepal is a constitutional monarchy with the king as head of state.

In 1994, Nepal's communist party, which had made a strong showing in the 1991 elections, gained a plurality of seats in parliament. Thus Nepal became the first post–Cold War country to elect a communist government. However, the communists did not gain a majority of parliamentary seats and consequently were forced to form a coalition government.

The election results were attributed by many Nepalis to a collective fear that India has been gaining too much control over Nepal and its politics through the Nepali Congress party, which has strong ties to India's Congress party. In addition, the Nepali Congress party had failed to improve the economy and the national infrastructure as it had promised. Nepalis in 1994 cast their vote for a government that they hoped would improve the country's standard of living. The new government faces a difficult job because Nepal remains one of the world's poorest countries.

2 Art & Architecture

ART

Virtually all of Nepal's art, except for works by a handful of little-known contemporary artists, is religious in nature and expresses both Hindu and Buddhist iconography. Religious expression in art has taken the form of stone, wood, terra-cotta, and metal statuary, as well as paintings on canvas and paper. Much of this artwork is on display in temples and palaces throughout the Kathmandu Valley and other parts of the country. There are also four museums in the Kathmandu Valley devoted to the art of Nepal.

The oldest existing works of art in Nepal are stone statues dating from the first century A.D. During the period of the Licchavi dynasty stone carving flourished. There are several fifth- and sixth-century statues and reliefs on display at the National Museum, and several others can be seen at Changu Narayan, a temple in the eastern part of the Kathmandu Valley. The massive statue of the Reclining Vishnu at Budhanilkantha, north of Kathmandu, dates from this period.

The Malla dynasty, which lasted from 1200 to 1769, witnessed a flowering of the arts, primarily in the 17th and 18th centuries. Sculptures of Buddhist and Hindu deities in bronze, wood, and terra-cotta from this period are on display at the National Museum. *Repoussé,* a style of metalworking in which sheets of brass or gilded copper are beaten into relief designs, reached a peak during the Malla period and is best represented by the Golden Gate in Patan. Arguably the most famous works of art in Nepal are the erotic roof struts on many of the country's pagoda temples. These carved wooden struts display men, women, and animals in various erotic poses.

Thangkas, painted scrolls used by Buddhist monks for meditation and religious ceremonies, are another art form that has become particularly popular. These colorful scrolls, often minutely detailed, depict Buddhist deities. Another prevalent motif is that of the wheel of life, depicting life on earth and in heaven and hell. Both the National Museum and the National Art Gallery have collections of thangkas. However, most of these 18th- and 19th-century thangkas are in a style different from those commonly sold in Kathmandu Valley shops. In Kathmandu, Patan, and Bhaktapur, there are shops where you can see thangkas painters at work.

The decorative arts have long been a part of Nepali culture, and almost no household item went undecorated until the recent advent of mass production. Water pots, vases, and pitchers were often decorated with simple patterns. The Brass and Bronze Museum in Bhaktapur has a representative collection of such items. Wood carving, which was centered in Bhaktapur, was used on everything from butter churns and knife scabbards to windows and door frames. Today, the roof struts and windows of the Malla period are among the main tourist attractions of the Kathmandu Valley. The peacock window on Bhaktapur's Pujari Math, a former Hindu priests' home and now the National Woodcarving Museum, is considered the finest example of the wood-carver's art, though the windows on the Kumari Bahal on Kathmandu's Durbar Square are even more beautiful in my opinion.

One unusual form of folk art still practiced today is the painting of bicycle rickshaws, trucks, and buses with colorful designs and sometimes even landscapes. Keep your eyes open for such rolling artwork as you walk the streets of Kathmandu.

ARCHITECTURE

Art and architecture overlap in Nepal, where temples and palaces are decorated with intricately carved windows, sculptural roof struts, and repoussé metalwork facades. Redbrick and dark hardwood construction of densely packed neighborhoods has led many Western visitors to compare the cities of the Kathmandu Valley to medieval European cities. This architectural style is characteristic of the Newars, the ethnic group that has traditionally lived in the Kathmandu Valley. Newari architecture is Nepal's most distinctive architectural style. The rosy glow of pink brick homes dotting the terraced fields of the Kathmandu Valley at sunset is one of the valley's most memorable images, especially when seen from a plane.

Newari architecture reached its zenith under the Malla kings in the 17th and 18th centuries, and it is from this period that most of the Kathmandu Valley's most important buildings date. Since palace architecture was based on standard home styles, with one or more courtyards, it was in temple architecture that Newari architects experimented. Temple architecture in Nepal embraces a number of styles, though the most notable and beautiful is the pagoda style. Nepali tradition holds that pagoda architecture originated in Nepal. The style was later copied in Lhasa, Tibet, from where it made its way to China. Pagodas in Nepal have between one and five roofs, though there are only three in the Kathmandu Valley with five roofs. The Nyatapola Temple in Bhaktapur, a five-roofed temple atop a five-tiered pyramid base, is considered the most beautiful, symmetric, and graceful temple in Nepal. The Basantapur tower, within the Hanuman Dhoka Palace on Kathmandu's Durbar Square, is the only pagoda that can be climbed, and in fact not all pagodas have floors to correspond to their many roofs.

Most pagodas, and in fact most Nepali buildings, are constructed from brick, the most common building material in the middle elevations of Nepal. However, a few temples are built in the *shikhara* style of architecture from north India. These temples are usually plastered and whitewashed or made of stone. The Mahaboudha Temple in Patan is the most ornate shikhara-style temple in the Kathmandu Valley.

Two of Nepal's most important architectural constructions are the *stupas* of Swayambunath and Boudhanath. Stupas are large hemispherical mounds that represent the Buddha and his teachings. They resemble the pyramids of Egypt or pre-Columbian America, though they have never been used as tombs. Smaller stupas credited to Indian emperor Ashoka stand at the four corners of Patan. *Chaityas* (small spires often found in courtyards) and *chortens* (medium-sized structures often found in Buddhist villages of the high mountains) are smaller than stupas but similar in shape.

Over the centuries, the Kathmandu Valley has been repeatedly hit by major earthquakes. In 1934 a devastating quake razed most of the temples and palaces in the valley. Since then most, but not all, of the valley's damaged historic buildings have been reconstructed. However, often reconstruction does not exactly duplicate the original architecture, as is the case with the Mahaboudha Temple in Patan. When reconstruction of this temple was completed, there were enough of the original bricks left over to build another small temple. The Bhaktapur Development Project, a German-funded program, has restored more than 100 buildings in Bhaktapur, making this city a showcase of Newari architecture. In Panauti, a small town in the southeast corner of the Kathmandu Valley, a joint French–Nepali project has been busy in recent years restoring an extensive temple complex.

Though Newari architecture predominates in the Kathmandu Valley, architectural styles vary from village to village outside the valley, depending on the ethnic makeup of the residents. In the lowlands of the Terai, the Tharu people build almost exclusively with grasses, using a mixture of mud and cow dung to seal the walls of their small houses. In the high elevations of Solu-Khumbu, home of the Sherpas, most homes are built of stone; even the roofs are made of slate. This ethnologic architectural diversity is one of the reasons that a trek through the hills and mountains of Nepal is so fascinating.

An architectural footnote worth mentioning is the dozens of European-style neoclassical palaces and residences in Kathmandu. The Gaddi Baithak on Durbar

Square is an example of this style, as is the Hotel Shanker and the old wing of the Hotel Yak & Yeti. All of these buildings were built during the Rana regime. During this time, various Ranas made several trips to Europe, becoming infatuated with everything European. The country's coffers were emptied to erect these stuccoed, pilastered, and shuttered architectural excesses. Today these buildings are nearly as fascinating as the Newari temples and palaces. A visit to the dining room of the Hotel Shanker or one of the Yak & Yeti's conference halls will almost convince you that you are in Europe.

3 Hinduism & Buddhism

Nepal calls itself the world's only Hindu kingdom. Nearly 90% of the population claims to be Hindu, though in Nepal there is a fine line between Hinduism and Buddhism. Many temples and shrines that are ostensibly dedicated to Hindu deities are frequented by Buddhists as well. Overlaying both of these religions is the practice of Tantrism, which in the West is often misconstrued as a religion based on sex. Tantrism is a set of prescribed formulas calling on physical and moral precepts such as meditation, yoga, and magic formulas to understand the interconnectedness of all spiritual and physical existence. It is Tantrism that has given Nepal many of its more frightening deities such as Bhairav and Kali.

HINDUISM

Hinduism is a polytheistic religion that had its origins between 4,000 and 5,000 years ago in northern India. It is based primarily on moral codes published thousands of years ago in the *Vedas,* as well as precepts set forth in other ancient books such as *Puranas, Upanishads, Bhagavad Gita,* and *Ramayana.* At the heart of Hindu beliefs are three major gods: Brahma (the creator), Vishnu (the preserver), and Shiva (the destroyer). With less power, but often of more personal significance for individuals, are the thousands of (some say one million) lesser gods.

Most Westerners find Hinduism infinitely confusing because of this plethora of gods. What causes much of this confusion is that many gods are worshiped in different incarnations (*avatars*). These different incarnations represent different valuable attributes, as do most Hindu gods. To further confuse matters, each god has his consort and vehicle (animal or being) upon which he travels.

With thousands of gods to choose from, it is not surprising that Hinduism has divided into numerous sects which focus on specific gods. The largest sects in Nepal are the Shaivites (followers of Shiva), Vaishnites (followers of Vishnu), Shaktas (followers of Shakti), and Ganpatyas (followers of Ganesh).

The caste system, though it is now officially illegal in Nepal, has been an integral part of Hinduism since its inception. This class system divides society into very rigid strata based on the types of work performed by members of the caste. Brahmans are the priest caste, Chhetris are the warrior caste, Vaisyas are the merchants and artisans, and Sudras are the farmers. Formally it was impossible for a person from a lower class to aspire to a job reserved for people of a higher class. Thus members of society were kept in their places. Today, though the caste system is not as rigid as it once was, people of lower castes are rarely able to improve their socio-economic status due to the deeply ingrained restrictions of the caste system.

Shiva In Nepal, Shiva is the most revered Hindu god. He is most commonly worshiped in the form of the Shiva *lingam,* a phallic symbol that is usually displayed atop a base called the *yoni,* which is symbolic of the female sexual organ. Shiva lingams sometimes have four or even five faces on them. Nepal's most famous Shiva lingam, which has five faces on it, is at Pashupatinath Temple in Kathmandu. Pashupati, the lord of the animals, is an incarnation of Shiva. Another of Shiva's incarnations, Natraj, also called the dancing Shiva, is rarely depicted in Nepal. More often, however, Shiva appears in his terrifying aspect as Bhairav. There are several famous images of Bhairav in Kathmandu, including the Kal Bhairav and Seto Bhairav of Hanuman Dhoka Square and the Akash Bhairav in Indrachowk. Parvati is Shiva's consort, and Nandi the bull is his vehicle. A statue of Nandi stands in front of nearly every temple containing a Shiva lingam.

The cult of Shiva is one of the largest Hindu cults, and wandering Shaivite ascetics known as *sadhus* are a common sight around Pashupatinath Temple. During the annual festival commemorating Shiva's birthday, pilgrims from all over Nepal and India visit Pashupatinath. Among these pilgrims are many holy men who paint themselves with ashes, perform yogic feats, and sleep on beds of nails. Shaivite sadhus can be recognized by the trident they carry, a symbol of Shiva.

Vishnu   Vishnu has appeared on earth in 10 incarnations. These include Krishna (well known in the West because of his followers, who are commonly called Hare Krishnas); Narayan (who embodies universal love); Narsimha (half-man and half-lion); Rama (hero of the epic *Ramayana*); the Buddha (there is frequent overlap of Buddhism and Hinduism in Nepal); and the king of Nepal. Vishnu has also appeared as a fish, a turtle, a boar, a lion, a dwarf, and a giant. Vishnu is often depicted with four arms holding a conch shell, a wheel, a club, and a lotus bud. Changu Narayan and Budhanilkantha, both in the Kathmandu Valley, are the two holiest Vishnu shrines in Nepal. Vishnu's consort is Laxmi, who is worshiped as the goddess of wealth in Nepal. Each year on Deepawali during the Tihar festival, usually held in October, Nepalis put candles in their doorways and windows to light the way to the family moneybox for Laxmi, who visits earth on that day. Vishnu's vehicle is the half-man, half-bird Garuda, who is often seen kneeling in front of temples dedicated to Vishnu.

Ganesh   Ganesh, the elephant-headed god of wisdom and good fortune, is the son of Shiva and Parvati. According to tradition, Ganesh was born a normal child while his father was away on a long journey. When Shiva returned, he suspected his wife of infidelity and chopped off Ganesh's head with such force that he was unable to find the head. When Parvati told him it really was his son, Shiva took the head of the first animal he spotted and affixed it to the body of his child. This figure is one of the most commonly worshiped gods in Nepal because he is credited with removing obstacles and protecting people on journeys. Ganesh shrines are seemingly everywhere in Kathmandu, though the most revered shrine is behind the Kasthamandap building just off Durbar Square.

Parvati   Shiva's consort has developed her own following of worshipers. She is depicted in both benevolent and wrathful incarnations, though the terrifying incarnation as Durga or Kali is much more common. The Dakshinkali Temple just outside the Kathmandu Valley is known for the animal sacrifices that are regularly performed there. The annual Dasain festival is dedicated to Parvati's terrifying aspects, and during the festival, many goats and water buffalo are sacrificed.

Hanuman   In the Indian epic *Ramayana,* when Rama's wife Sita is kidnaped, Hanuman the monkey king plays an important role in rescuing her from the evil Ravana. Because of his assistance, he is seen as an ever-faithful servant. A statue of Hanuman guards the old royal palace on Kathmandu's Durbar Square and even lends its name to the palace and square, which are both called Hanuman Dhoka (gate). Over the years people worshiping this statue have smeared it with red paste so that it is no longer recognizable as Hanuman. (Smearing red powder or paste is a standard form of showing respect or worshipping a deity.)

BUDDHISM

Buddhism, which is often called a philosophy rather than a religion, had its beginnings in southern Nepal and northern India about 2,500 years ago. It is based on the teachings of the Buddha, who was born Prince Siddhartha Gautama in present-day Lumbini, Nepal, around 563 B.C. The prince led a very sheltered life until he was 29 years old. At that time he saw for the first time in his life the suffering of old age and death. The sight of so much suffering deeply affected him, and he left his wife and family to become a wandering ascetic searching for a way to end all suffering. For six years the prince wandered, studying every contemporary religion and spiritual discipline without success. On the verge of giving up his search, he sat down beneath a *bo* tree (a banyan or pipal tree) and, during meditation, the way to end suffering came to him. From this time on he was called the Buddha, "The Enlightened One."

His realizations during meditation came to be known as the four noble truths and the eightfold path to enlightenment. The four noble truths are that life is full of pain and suffering, pain and suffering is caused by desires and attachments, there is a way to end pain and suffering, and the way to end pain and suffering is through the eightfold path of Buddhism. The eightfold path consists of right views, right intent, right speech, right conduct, right livelihood, right effort, right mindfulness, and right meditation.

Today Buddhism is divided into two main schools called Hinayana or Theravada and Mahayana. Hinayana Buddhism adheres more closely to the original teachings of the Buddha and emphasizes the quest for personal enlightenment (nirvana). Mahayana, on the other hand, emphasizes the individual's responsibility to help others to achieve nirvana. A person who follows this path becomes a *bodhisattva,* an enlightened being who remains on earth to help others to achieve nirvana. Mahayana Buddhism is the type followed by most Nepalis. Tibetan Buddhism is a form of Mahayana Buddhism and has as its spiritual head the Dalai Lama, who won the Nobel Peace Prize in 1989 for his 30 years of nonviolent protest against the Chinese invasion of his homeland of Tibet. Tibetan Buddhism is a synthesis of Buddhism and an older Tibetan religion called Bon. There are four major Tibetan Buddhist sects: Gelugpa, Nyingmapa, Kargyupa, and Sakyapa. All four sects are represented in Nepal by various monasteries, with the greatest concentration of monasteries in the vicinity of Boudhanath Stupa near Kathmandu. Tibetan Buddhism is also known as Vajrayana Buddhism and Lamaism. Among Nepal's ethnic groups that profess Buddhism as their faith are the Tamangs, Gurungs, Newars, and Sherpas.

4 Nepali Culture

The ethnic makeup of Nepal is as varied as its geography. Consequently, the country's cultural and social life is complex and diverse. There are 35 distinct ethnic groups and castes, each with its own specific customs. These groups are differentiated by dialect, region, traditional dress, religion, and more. Nepal, a natural barrier between two giant landmasses and countries—China to the north and India to the south—is a meeting point of races. The Indo-Aryan or Caucasoid peoples of India have moved up into the hills, and the Tibeto-Burman or Mongoloid peoples have crossed over the Himalayas and moved down into the fertile hills. The people of Nepal can be divided into three main categories: Hindu castes, ethnic groups of the lowlands and middle hills, and northern border people. The Hindu castes are Indo-Aryan, while the border peoples—Sherpas, Bhotiyas, and Tamangs—are purely Tibeto-Burman. The Newars, Rais, Limbus, Gurungs, and Magars, who inhabit the middle hills, are a mixture of the two races.

The Brahmans and Chhetris, high Hindu castes, tend to dominate politics. Brahmans have traditionally been the priests of Hindu society and can be recognized by the long thread they wear over their shoulders. Chhetris are the warrior class. Both the royal family and the Ranas, who ruled Nepal for more than a hundred years, are of the Chhetri caste. Lower castes tend to do various menial jobs.

The ethnic groups of the middle hills predate the Hindu castes, who migrated north from the plains of India. These groups inhabit different regions of the middle hills, and within a single region they may live at different elevations. The Newars live primarily in the Kathmandu Valley, where they originated. Much of the art and architecture that is identified as Nepali is more specifically Newari. The Gurungs inhabit the higher hills of central Nepal near Pokhara. They are primarily farmers and shepherds and practice both Hinduism and Buddhism, depending on where they live. Many Gurkha soldiers are Gurungs. The Magars, primarily Hindus, follow a similar lifestyle, farming the lower hills of the same parts of central Nepal. The Thakalis, who are Buddhists, live almost exclusively in the Thak Khola Valley near the upper reaches of the Kali Gandaki River, which flows down from Tibet. Though they once controlled the salt trade with Tibet, they are now international traders and innkeepers. The Rais and Limbus live in eastern Nepal, where they practice a mixture of Buddhism and Hinduism. The Tamangs are a primarily Buddhist ethnic group from the hills near Kathmandu. Today many of them work as porters.

The Yeti

Among the world's best loved and most persistent legends is that of the yeti—the abominable snowman. Stories of the yeti originated in the Solu-Khumbu region near Mt. Everest. Is the yeti fact or fiction? In the absence of a live specimen or verifiable remains of a yeti, no one is sure. The Nepali government is taking no chances, however, having passed a law protecting yetis in the early 1960s. Though the Sherpa people, who have frequently reported seeing or hearing yetis, have no doubt about the existence of the humanlike animal, scientists throughout the world are very skeptical. As recently as the mid-1970s a Sherpa woman was said to have been attacked by a yeti, and several yaks were reported to have been killed by a yeti in a separate incident. Several yeti expeditions have been mounted since the 1960s, including one led by Sir Edmund Hillary. None of these expeditions turned up anything more than questionable footprints. Two monasteries in the Khumbu region have what they claim are yeti relics—scalps and a skeleton of a hand. These have been examined by Western authorities and declared to be fakes, but the legend refuses to die.

In the lowland Terai region are a number of ethnic groups, the largest of which is the Tharu people. The Tharus are an aboriginal people who practice an animist religion with Hindu influences. They are subsistence farmers who rely on native grasses for house construction. The people in villages surrounding Chitwan National Park are Tharus. In the eastern Terai there are several more distinct ethnic groups, though their numbers are much smaller than those of the Tharus. There are also a few Muslims living along the Indian border.

In the high mountains of the northern border region live the Sherpas and the Bhotiyas, people of Tibetan stock who practice Buddhism. They are primarily shepherds and farmers who live in a very harsh environment where a single crop may be cultivated by irrigating rocky fields. There are also two small ethnic groups living in the Mustang region. The term "Bhotiya" means "people of Tibet" and is used to describe both the native ethnic groups and more recent Tibetan immigrants.

Dominating life for all these ethnic groups is religion. Buddhism, Hinduism, and the synthesis of the two dictate much of the cultural and social life of the country. Almost nothing is done without first making an offering to the appropriate god, and throughout the year religious celebrations and festivals are held to honor the various gods. Several Hindu festivals include animal sacrifices, and though to Western minds these sacrifices seem a bit barbaric, for many families it is one of the few times a year when there is meat on the table.

Among all ethnic groups and religions, arranged marriages are still the norm in Nepal. Marriages may be arranged as early as birth, or sometimes even earlier, though it is more common to arrange the marriage when the boy and girl are in their teens. Polygamy, though officially illegal, is still practiced by some ethnic groups. Polyandry, the taking of more than one husband (usually brothers) by a woman, is also still practiced by some people of the northern border regions. This tradition originated among the Tibetan peoples because men were often gone for many months on trading expeditions.

When it comes to sports, however, Nepali people are fully oriented to the Western world. Among the favorite recreational activities of young Nepali boys and men are soccer, volleyball, badminton, and table tennis. In Kathmandu, international soccer matches are followed with the same intensity that they are followed in Europe and Latin America. In fact, one of the few times that Nepali television extends its short hours is for the World Cup matches. While trekking once, I met dozens of people traveling many miles to the next village to watch an intervillage volleyball match. At any time of year, it is not unusual to see a side street in Kathmandu turned into an impromptu badminton court. Many times I have seen boys playing table tennis on the bases of temples, using a few bricks for a net.

In the mountains, ancient sporting events are still pursued. In the Annapurna region, there is an annual event pitting local villages against one another in a contest to see who can throw a heavy stone the farthest. The one time I had the opportunity to witness this sport, the stone split in half before the contest was settled.

5 Nepali Cuisine

MEALS & DINING CUSTOMS   Most Nepalis eat only two real meals each day. For breakfast they will have sweet milk tea and fried dough. The first significant meal comes around 10am. Dinner is usually eaten between 6 and 7pm. Lunch and dinner for most of the population consists of rice, lentils, and vegetables. However, in the higher elevations where rice does not grow, potatoes and barley are substituted.

Because cows are sacred, beef is not eaten in Nepal. In the absence of beef, water buffalo is the most popular meat, though it is expensive. Goat, chicken, and pork are eaten, but again these are all expensive. Most Nepalis are restricted to a vegetarian diet for financial reasons.

Do not throw garbage into any household cooking fire in Nepal. The flame is considered sacred by many of the country's people, and you would be committing an insult. Hindus consider food contaminated or polluted if it has been touched by a Westerner since Westerners are casteless. Do not offer to share your food if you have already taken a bite, and do not touch cooked food that is intended for other people. Wait to be served rather than serving yourself, as this would contaminate the meal for everyone else. Also, remember that you should use only your right hand for eating.

THE FARE   Nepali cuisine is similar to simple Indian cuisine in that it relies on chilies, garlic, and onions for flavoring. Few restaurants in Nepal serve Nepali food because it has developed a bad name due to the generally insipid renderings of dal bhat (rice and lentils)—the national dish—that get served to tourists and trekkers. However, Nepali dishes, including dal bhat when well prepared, are quite delicious. Tibetan food is slightly more common on menus partly because of the mysterious cachet that Tibet still enjoys.

Soups and Appetizers   Thukpa is a Tibetan vegetable-noodle soup. Momos and kothays are meat- or vegetable-stuffed dumplings similar to Chinese potstickers. Momos are steamed, and kothays are fried.

Main Dishes   *"Dal bhat, dal bhat, dal bhat"*—a trekker's mantra. Dal bhat, which is Nepali for lentils and rice, is the mainstay of the Nepali diet and can be good, bad, or mediocre. It is sometimes, but not always, accompanied by spicy fried vegetables and perhaps some pickled radish. After only a few days on the trail, most Westerners become infinitely tired of consuming heaping mounds of dal bhat and switch to such gourmet fare as boiled potatoes and fried eggs, which most people find infinitely preferable to dal bhat.

Desserts   In general, Nepalis eat desserts only on special occasions. However, many milk- and lentil-based sweets similar to Indian versions are available in sweetshops. Sikarni is an ambrosial yogurt dessert that shows up on menus in Nepali/Tibetan restaurants.

Water   Never drink water that you do not know for certain has been purified. This goes for ice as well. I always carry a water bottle and a small bottle of iodine so that I can make my own purified water whenever I need it. Bottled water is readily available in Kathmandu, Pokhara, and even on most trekking routes. When trekking, your main source of liquid is likely to be tea of one sort or another, and though the tea water has probably not been boiled long enough to sterilize it, this is the chance you take. Water must be boiled for 5 minutes (some say 20 minutes) to kill all harmful bacteria. Though portable water filters are effective against bacteria and protozoa (including giardia), most are not effective in filtering out viruses such as hepatitis. Therefore I do not recommend using a water filter as your sole means of purification, unless it also has an iodine matrix for killing viruses.

Soft Drinks   If you can handle the sugar and caffeine, such international soft drinks as Coke, Sprite, and Fanta are available throughout Nepal. Also available, and preferable in my eyes, are boxed juices, including a delicious mango juice. You can also get bags of soy milk in most places.

Beer and Wine   There are several brands of domestic beer, as well as locally brewed international brands such as Tuborg and San Miguel. All are quite reasonably priced. Wine as Westerners know it is not made in Nepal because of the lack of appropriate growing conditions. However, you may run across a menu that lists "Nepali wine" or "local wine." This means moonshine. The local name for moonshine is *rakshi*, and it is pretty terrible stuff and not much more potent than wine. It is often served warm. *Chang* is another local favorite. It is the equivalent of home-brewed beer, though it tastes more like hard cider. *Tongba* is another less common local brew, which tastes a bit like sake (Japanese rice wine).

6 Recommended Books & Films

BOOKS

General   Hardly a day passes in Nepal without some festival being celebrated somewhere in the country. *The Festivals of Nepal* (London: George, Allen and Unwin, 1971) by Mary Anderson will help you to understand the sometimes bizarre, often baffling, but always colorful festivals of Nepal.

Of the many coffee-table picture books about Nepal, *Kathmandu, The Forbidden Valley* (Time Books International, 1990) is one of my favorites. Stunning photos and plenty of historical and cultural information make this book a good memento of a trip to Nepal.

Fiction   Though it is not specifically about Nepal, James Hilton's novel *Lost Horizon* (Buccaneer Books, 1983) is inextricably interwoven with Western images of Nepal. This tale of a tranquil Himalayan valley is an endearing classic.

For more than 100 years, Nepal was ruled by a despotic line of prime ministers who kept the royal family under house arrest. The royal family was finally restored to power in the 1950s, and Nepal began to emerge from its isolation. Han Suyin's novel *The Mountain Is Young* (London: Jonathan Cape, 1971) is a love story set in Nepal during this time.

Readers of spy novels might enjoy *The Fever Tree* by Richard Mason (author of *The World of Suzie Wong*). A tale of love and espionage is woven around an attempt to destabilize Nepal. In *All the Grey Cats* by Craig Thomas (author of *Firefox*), the Soviet Union plots against Nepal, and a British spy becomes involved in an attempt to thwart Soviet plans. Neither of these novels has been published in the United States, but they are available in Kathmandu.

Escape from Kathmandu (Unwin Paperbacks, 1990) by Kim Stanley Robinson is a lighthearted romp through modern-day Nepal.

Natural History   *The Snow Leopard* (Penguin Books, 1987) by Peter Matthiessen combines science, religion, and philosophy in an extremely readable work. In this book Matthiessen writes of his trip to the Dolpo region of Nepal with George Schaller. Matthiessen's search for the elusive snow leopard parallels his own search for spiritual fulfillment.

If you are inspired to learn more about snow leopards after reading Matthiessen's book, you'll want to read *Vanishing Tracks* (Arbor House/Morrow, 1989) by Darla Hillard, who spent four years in the more remote reaches of Nepal studying snow leopards.

While Peter Matthiessen was busy writing about his spiritual pilgrimage and quest to spot a snow leopard, George Schaller was busy studying the rare blue sheep. His studies of the blue sheep, which are actually not sheep but goat antelopes, culminated in his own account of the trip to Dolpo in *Stones of Silence* (University of Chicago, 1988).

Honey Hunters of Nepal (Harry N. Abrams, 1988) is a large format coffee-table picturebook based on the National Geographic film about the daring honey hunters who scale cliffs with homemade ropes to collect large honeycombs produced by wild bees. In addition to the film, which is available on video, this was a *National Geographic* cover story.

With more than 800 species of birds found in Nepal, *The Birds of Nepal* (currently out of print) is an indispensable guide for the avid birder. A trip to Chitwan National Park alone is reason enough to have a copy of this book, which can help you identify the park's more than 450 species.

If *The Birds of Nepal* is unavailable, your best choice is *Collins Handguide to the Birds of the Indian Sub-Continent* (Collins, 1990) by Martin Woodcock. This book includes illustrations of only the most common birds.

Religion   If you are interested in learning more about Tibetan Buddhism as it is practiced in Nepal, read *Himalayan Pilgrimage* (Shambhala, 1981) by David L. Snellgrove. This book is similar to *The Snow Leopard* in that Snellgrove shares what he learns as he treks through Buddhist regions of Nepal. However, it is not quite as readable as Matthiessen's book.

Short Description of Gods, Goddesses and Ritual Objects of Buddhism and Hinduism in Nepal, published by the Handicraft Association of Nepal, is an indispensable illustrated guide to the myriad religious iconography the visitor will encounter in Nepal. You'll find this book in most Kathmandu bookshops. Make it one of your first purchases when you arrive. You'll get much more out of your trip.

Travelogue   In the late 1940s and early 1950s, H.W. Tilman, Nepal's first trekker, explored the hills and mountains of Nepal. *Nepal Himalaya*, Tilman's account of his explorations, was recently reprinted as part of *The Seven Mountain-Travel Books* (Mountaineers, 1991).

In the title essay from his insightful and incisive collection of essays, *Video Night in Kathmandu* (Vintage, 1989), Pico Iyer cuts through the surface of Kathmandu's mysterious image to find that Nepalis are crazy about Rambo and that the drugged-out hippies of the '60s have been replaced by trekking yuppies.

The quest for the perfect Buddha statue becomes an obsession with Jeff Greenwald in *Shopping for Buddhas* (Harper & Row, 1990), a travelogue that uses shopping as a metaphor for the spiritual quest that brings many travelers to Nepal. His shopping adventures help him to understand the teachings of the Buddha, especially the concept of nonattachment.

Music in Every Room: Around the World in a Bad Mood (Atlantic Monthly Press, 1984) is John Krich's account of a less-than-wonderful around-the-world trip. His three chapters on Nepal are full of astute observations made by budget travelers in Nepal as they wander through the Himalayan kingdom.

Himalayan Odyssey (Donald I. Fine, 1990) is Parker Antin's account of his six-month trek through remote sections of west Nepal that, at the time, were off-limits to trekkers. Antin's trek was filled with mishaps and misadventures. Hopefully your own trek will not be like his.

In *The Violet Shyness of Their Eyes: Notes from Nepal* (Calyx Books, 1993), Barbara J. Scott gives a woman's perspective on life and travel in Nepal. Scott's book is based on a year she spent living and working in Nepal.

Trekking and Rafting   Compact and concise, *Trekking in the Nepal Himalaya* (Lonely Planet, 1991) by Stan Armington is an easy-to-follow guidebook for independent trekkers doing teahouse treks. All the major trekking routes are covered by Armington, who has operated his own trekking company since 1971.

For many years the definitive trekkers handbook has been *A Guide to Trekking in Nepal* (Mountaineers, 1991) by Stephen Bezruchka. Extremely thorough, this book's only fault is that the trekking times listed are much faster than most independent trekkers tend to hike. Bezruchka is a doctor, and the health-care chapter of this book is particularly thorough.

With concise route descriptions and excellent photos of the mountains, the English translation of Toru Nakano's *Trekking in Nepal* (Allied Publishers, 1990) will look great on your coffee table if it isn't too badly battered by use on the trail.

For more in-depth regional trekking guides, check out *Trekking in the Everest Region* (Trailblazer Publications, 1993) by Jamie McGuinness and *Trekking in the Annapurna Region* (Trailblazer Publications, 1993) by Bryn Thomas. These books include suggestions for day hikes from various high-altitude locations and include detailed area maps.

If you have already done a few treks in Nepal and are looking for something more challenging, pick up a copy of *The Trekking Peaks of Nepal* (Cloudcap, 1989) by Bill O'Connor. This book provides route descriptions for most of Nepal's trekking peaks—mountains that can be scaled with a minimum of equipment.

Anyone serious about rafting or kayaking in Nepal should check out *White Water Nepal* (Menasha Ridge Press, 1992) by Peter Knowles and David Allardice. This book is full of detailed descriptions of Nepal's rivers and also includes all the information you'll need to mount your own paddling expedition.

Mountain Climbing   *Annapurna* (Paladin, 1986) by renowned climber Maurice Herzog is an account of the first ascent of Annapurna I, which was the first 8,000-meter (26,000-foot) peak to be scaled. The book is very readable and provides excellent background on the Annapurna region for anyone who plans to trek in this area. Incidentally, this expedition was mounted from the north side of the peak, not from Annapurna base camp in the Annapurna Sanctuary.

FILMS

In 1994, Italian director Bernardo Bertolucci released *Little Buddha,* which tells both the story of the Buddha's life and of a contemporary search for a reincarnate Tibetan lama. Filmed partly on location in the Kathmandu Valley, it includes many scenes shot in the city of Bhaktapur.

Though it is aimed at a teenage audience, the made-for-TV film *Night Train to Kathmandu* does offer some glimpses of what modern-day Kathmandu is like. There are also scenes of the mountains that will whet the appetites of would-be trekkers. Another film with little to recommend other than a few great location shots and a story loosely based on beliefs of Tibetan Buddhists is *The Golden Child* starring Eddie Murphy. James Hilton's novel *Lost Horizon* has been filmed twice, though the original version made in 1937 is infinitely better than the musical remake of 1973.

2 Planning a Trip to Nepal

Planning a trip to Nepal is not as easy as planning a vacation in Hawaii or Europe. Nepal is one of the most distant destinations on earth if you are starting your trip from North America, so it takes almost two days just to get there. A trip to this Himalayan kingdom requires a great deal of advance planning. You should set aside plenty of time to do all the necessary planning to make your journey as enjoyable as possible.

When should I go? How do I get there? Where should I stay? What kind of restaurants are there? What should I see? What do I need to pack? These are some of the questions that this chapter will answer. It will also answer equally important questions about immunizations and visas. Planning a trip can be exciting, especially a journey to somewhere as remote as Nepal. By reading through this chapter, you will be better prepared for Nepal; and hopefully have a much easier trip.

1 Information, Entry Requirements & Money

SOURCES OF INFORMATION

It is very difficult to get current information on Nepal before arriving there because the government of Nepal does not maintain any information offices outside of the country.

Your best source of information on Nepal before you arrive is likely to be this book. You could also take a look at some of the books listed under "Recommended Books & Films" in Chapter 1. Other possible sources of information are some of the adventure-travel companies listed under "Adventure Travel" in this chapter, below. These companies will be happy to send you information on their trips to Nepal, and from their brochures, you may be able to cull a bit of useful information.

Another possibility is to contact the nearest Nepali embassy and ask them if they have any brochures available, but don't count on it. In the United States, the **Nepali embassy** is located at 2131 Leroy Place NW, Washington, DC 20008 (☎ **202/667-4550**); in the United Kingdom the embassy is at 12A Kensington Palace Gardens, London W8 4QU (☎ **071/229-1594**).

Your local library is another good source of information. There are frequent articles about Nepal in travel magazines and travel sections of newspapers. Check back issues or look in the *Readers' Guide to Periodical Literature.*

The Internet has up-to-the-minute information, if you have a computer and are a member of this on-line service. Post a question about Nepal, and you're likely to get dozens of responses from people who have just been there.

Once in Nepal, the best sources of information are likely to be your hotel staff, travel agencies, and *Travellers' Nepal* magazine, which is sometimes available at hotels in Kathmandu.

ENTRY REQUIREMENTS
DOCUMENTS

Passport All foreign nationals need a valid **passport** (check its expiration date).

In the **United States,** citizens 18 or older who meet the requirements are granted a 10-year passport. For an application, go to a U.S. post office or the federal court office. In addition, there are federal passport agencies in 13 cities, which you can visit in person. These include New York, Washington, D.C., Stamford (Conn.), Seattle, Philadelphia, San Francisco, New Orleans, Boston, Honolulu, Chicago, Los Angeles, Miami, and Houston. Youths under 18 are granted a 5-year passport. Children under 13 must have their parents apply for their passport, and teenagers 13 to 16 must also have a parent's permission before applying for a passport. If your passport is 12 years old (or older), or was granted to you before your 16th year, you must apply in person at a passport agency, post office, or federal or state court office, otherwise, you can renew it by mail. Passports cost $65 for adults and $40 for children and teens.

To apply for a passport, you'll need a completed government passport application form, and you must provide proof of U.S. citizenship—a birth certificate or naturalization papers. An old passport (providing it's not more than 12 years old) is also accepted. You should also have identification with your signature and photograph, such as a driver's license. You'll also need two identical passport-size photographs. You'll wait the longest to receive your passport between mid-March and mid-September; in winter it usually only takes about 2 weeks by mail. Passports can sometimes be issued in an emergency, providing you present a plane ticket with a confirmed seat.

In **Canada,** citizens seeking a passport may go to one of the nearly two dozen regional offices in such cities as Ottawa or Montréal. Alternatively, you can mail an application to the Passport Office, Section of External Affairs, Ottawa, ON K1A 0G3. Post offices have application forms. Passports cost $35 Canadian, and proof of Canadian citizenship is required, along with two signed identical photographs. Passports have a 5-year validity.

In **Great Britain,** citizens may apply at one of the regional offices in Liverpool, Newport, Glasgow, Peterborough, and Belfast, or else in London if they reside there. Applications are available at main post offices. The fee is £18, and the passport is good for 10 years. Documents required include a marriage certificate, naturalization certificate, or a birth certificate. Two photos must accompany the application.

In **Australia,** apply at the nearest post office or passport office. Provincial capitals and all major cities such as Sydney or Melbourne have passport offices. The fee is $102 AUS for adults, $61 for children under 18. The passport is valid for 10 years.

New Zealand citizens may go to their nearest consulate or passport office to obtain an application and file in person or via mail. Proof of citizenship is required, and the passport is good for 10 years. The fee is $130 NZ for adults, $65 NZ for children under 16.

Visa   It is necessary to have a visa to visit Nepal. To obtain a visa you must present your passport, two passport-size photos, a completed visa-application form, and $15 for a 15-day visa, $25 for a 30-day visa, $40 for a 30-day double-entry visa, or $60 for a 60-day multiple-entry visa. A visa obtained in this way must be used within 3 months. If you do not happen to live near a Nepali embassy or consulate, first write and request a copy of the visa-application form, and then send this, your passport, and your two passport-size photos registered mail with a self-addressed stamped envelope for the return of the passport. Visas generally take from one to two weeks depending on the type of mail used.

The following are Nepali embassies and missions that can provide visas:

In the United States: 2131 Leroy Place NW, Washington, DC 20008 (☎ 202/667-4550 or 202/667-4551).

In the United Kingdom: 12A Kensington Palace Gardens, London W8 4QU (☎ 071/229-1594 or 071/229-6231).

At the United Nations: 820 Second Ave., New York, NY 10017 (☎ 212/370-4188 or 212/370-4189).

The following are Nepali honorary consulates general that provide information, visa applications, and sometimes visas.

In Canada: 310 Duport St., Toronto, ON M5R 1V9 (☎ 416/968-7252).

In Australia: 18–20 Bank Place, Suite 23, 2d Floor, Melbourne, VIC 3000 (☎ 03/602-1271); P.O. Box 1097, Toowong, Brisbane QLD 4066 (☎ 07/378-0124); Airways House, 4th Floor, 195 Adelaide Terrace, Perth, WA 6004 (☎ 09/221-1207); 377 Sussex St., 3d Level, Sydney, NSW 2000 (☎ 02/264-7197).

Alternatively, you can obtain a visa upon arrival in Nepal. Visa-application forms are usually found on one of the tables just inside the arrivals hall at the airport. If you are entering overland, the border immigration desk should have copies of the visa-application form. Obtaining your visa this way saves you the cost of postage, and you don't risk losing your passport in the mail. (Visas must be paid for in U.S. dollars even in Nepal.)

After 30 days, it is necessary to extend your visa. Visa extensions can be obtained for an additional 60 days past the original 30 days. Under extenuating circumstances it is possible to obtain a further 30 days' visa extension for a total of 120 days. However, 150 days is the longest you are allowed to visit Nepal in one calendar year. Visa-extension fees are $1 per day. To obtain a visa extension you will need to go to an immigration office and fill out the visa-extension form. You must then present your passport, one passport-size photo, and the visa extension form.

Customs   In addition to personal effects, each visitor to Nepal may bring into the country duty-free 200 cigarettes or 50 cigars, one bottle of hard liquor or 12 cans of beer, one still camera and 15 rolls of film, one movie camera and 12 rolls of film or one video camera, one radio, one tape recorder and 15 tapes, one sleeping bag, and one walking stick. When leaving the country, your bag may be inspected by Customs. It is illegal to remove most Nepali antiques from the country. If you have made any purchases that might be considered antique or that even look old, be sure to have them inspected and stamped by the Department of Archaeology (see "Shopping" in Chapter 4).

MONEY

CASH & CURRENCY   The Nepali rupee (abbreviated Rs) is divided into 100 paisa. There are coins of 5, 10, 25, and 50 paisa, and also of 1 rupee. Paper money comes in denominations of 1, 2, 5, 10, 20, 50, 100, 500, and 1,000 rupees. At press time, $1 was worth 50 rupees, and this was the exchange rate used throughout this book. By the time you reach Nepal, the exchange rate will likely have changed a bit, and you may get more rupees for each dollar. However, prices are likely to remain unchanged, because as the rupee is devalued, prices go up.

There are two things to remember when carrying out cash transactions in Nepal: Hang on to your small bills, and don't take torn notes. Merchants rarely have small bills, and even if they do, they don't want to relinquish them. Making a purchase or paying for a service in Nepal becomes a game of trying to see who will give up their small bills. You should always start by offering a note that is larger than your purchase and insist that you have nothing smaller. Very large bills are almost worthless for making small purchases. A 1,000- or 500-rupee note is only good for paying hotel bills or making large purchases. Ask the bank to give you 100-rupee notes or smaller. It is especially important to carry lots of small bills if you do a teahouse trek. There is an acute change shortage in the hills.

Torn notes are worthless. Even a tiny nick can make a bill unacceptable. However, a gaping hole through the middle of a bill does not make it worthless. It is a common bank practice to staple stacks of bills together and then rip them off the stack. Always check your change to make sure that someone is not slipping you

The Nepali Rupee & the Dollar

At press time $1 = approximately Rs 50 (or Rs1 = 2¢), and this was the rate of exchange used to calculate the dollar values given in this book (rounded to the nearest nickel). This rate fluctuates from time to time and may not be the same when you travel to Nepal. Therefore the following table should be used only as a guide:

Rs	U.S.	Rs	U.S.
1	.02	250	5.00
2	.04	300	6.00
3	.06	350	7.00
4	.08	400	8.00
5	.10	450	9.00
10	.20	500	10.00
15	.30	750	15.00
20	.40	1,000	20.00
30	.60	1,500	30.00
50	1.00	2,000	40.00
75	1.50	2,500	50.00
100	2.00	3,000	60.00
150	3.00	3,750	75.00
200	4.00	5,000	100.00

What Things Cost in Kathmandu	U.S. $
Taxi from the airport to the city center	2.00–3.00
Local phone call	.10
Double room at the Hotel Yak & Yeti (deluxe)	172.50
Double room at Hotel Marshyangdi (moderate)	66.70
Double room Hotel Excelsior (budget)	24.20
Lunch for one at Amber (moderate)	6.00
Lunch for one at Le Bistro (budget)	2.50
Dinner for one, without wine, at Gurkha Grill (deluxe)	25.00
Dinner for one, without wine, at Fuji (moderate)	8.00
Dinner for one, without wine, at Utse (budget)	4.00
Large bottle of beer	2.00
Coca-Cola	.40
Cup of coffee	.30
Roll of ASA 100 Kodacolor film, 36 exposures	3.20
Admission to the National Museum	.10
Movie ticket	.35
Ticket to Cultural Program	4.40

any bad bills. This is especially important to keep in mind if you change money on the black market. There are no ATMs (Automated Teller Machines) in Nepal at the current time.

TRAVELER'S CHECKS   Traveler's checks can easily be exchanged for Nepali rupees at banks and hotels. Even some shopkeepers will accept traveler's checks, though technically this is illegal, as is changing traveler's checks on the black market. Traveler's checks in U.S. and Canadian dollars and pounds sterling are the most easily exchanged. Don't count on being able to change a traveler's check in a small-town bank, though the banks in Jomosom and Namche Bazaar (on the two most popular trekking routes) will usually change them. It is always best to carry enough rupees for the duration if you are doing a teahouse trek.

CREDIT CARDS   American Express, MasterCard, and Visa credit cards are widely accepted in Nepal at tourist hotels and restaurants. In Kathmandu many shops that sell primarily to tourists also accept credit cards.

WHAT WILL IT COST?

Nepal is one of the world's greatest bargains. Whatever you wish to spend, whether it is $5 a day or $250 a day, you will find what you are looking for. A meal may cost as little as $2, and you just can't spend more than $25 on a dinner in Nepal. Though U.S. trekking companies charge more than $100 per day for an organized trek, it is possible to arrange your own trek once you are in Nepal for as little as $30 a day. If you want to set out on your own, you can even trek for less than $10 a day. Down in the lowlands at Chitwan National Park, you can stay at the famous Tiger Tops jungle lodge for $250 a night or at a very basic lodge outside the park for about $10.

What Things Cost in Pokhara	U.S. $
Taxi from the airport to Lakeside	1.00
Local phone call	.10
Double room at Fishtail Lodge (deluxe)	95.20
Double room Base Camp Resort (moderate)	60.50
Double room Ashok Guest House (budget)	22.00
Lunch for one at Hungry Eye (moderate)	4.00
Lunch for one at Rodee Lake View (budget)	2.00
Dinner for one, without wine, at Fish Tail Lodge (moderate)	12.00
Dinner for one, without wine, at K.C.'s (budget)	4.00
Large bottle of beer	2.00
Coca-Cola	.30
Cup of coffee	.30
Roll of ASA 100 Kodacolor film, 36 exposures	3.50
Admission to the Pokhara Museum	.10
Movie ticket	.35
Ticket to Cultural Program	2.00

2 When to Go

CLIMATE

Nepal ranges from an elevation of less than 600 feet above sea level in the Terai to 29,028 at the top of Mt. Everest. Between these two extremes, the rugged topography of peaks, ridges, and valleys creates a variety of climates and microclimates. Temperatures vary as much with elevation as with time of year. In the Terai days are warm even in January and December, while in the high Himalayas the snow remains year-round.

There are, however, two distinct seasons—the rainy monsoon season and the dry season. The monsoon begins as early as late April or early May in the Kathmandu Valley but as late as mid-June in the Terai. Rains, though not as torrential as farther south in India, are constant and steady. This is the main growing season in Nepal and the time of year with the fewest visitors. The rains continue until mid-October with a gradual slacking off beginning as early as late September. With the end of the monsoon, the cool dry season begins. From mid-October to mid-December is the prime time to visit Nepal, whether for trekking or simply for sightseeing. The sky is a clear blue, and the mountains are visible almost daily. Temperatures even at 13,000 feet rarely go below freezing during the day and in the Kathmandu Valley it can be warm enough for shorts and T-shirts. From mid-December to late January, there is a slight chance of frost in the Kathmandu Valley, and higher up in the mountains it can get well below freezing. Fewer people visit at this time, but there is still good trekking at lower elevations. This is my favorite time to visit, though the country is quite dry and brown by November. From February to March, the weather begins to warm up, and the skies are sometimes cloudy, although there are still quite a few clear days. March to April is the second most popular time for trekking, though haze often obscures the mountains and it can be much too hot to trek at lower elevations. In May the weather even in Kathmandu or Pokhara can be uncomfortably hot, and in the Terai temperatures can reach more than 110°F.

Average Monthly Temperature & Rainfall In Kathmandu

	Jan	Feb	Mar	Apr	May	June	July	Aug	Sept	Oct	Nov	Dec
Avg. High (F°)	64	71	78	86	85	85	83	85	84	83	75	69
Avg. Low (F°)	37	36	44	47	60	66	67	67	65	56	43	35
Rainfall (in.)	1.9	.4	.6	.2	5.8	5.3	12.9	8.1	7.8	1.7	0	0

HOLIDAYS

There are more than 35 days of official government holidays each year in Nepal; most are religious in nature. The sheer number of Hindu deities that must be honored is the cause of this holiday calendar. Add to the numerous Hindu holidays the Buddhist holidays and days of national significance, and hardly a week goes by without a major holiday or festival. Since most of these holidays are based on the phases of the moon, the date on which they fall changes from year to year. In addition, many shops close for several days on either side of the official holiday date.

Holidays include April 13 (New Year's Day), April or May (Buddha's birthday), July or August (Janai Purnima), August 11 (the Queen's Birthday), nine days in September or October (Dasain), October (Tihar), December 16 (Constitution Day), December 28 (the king's birthday), January 10 (King Prithvi Narayan Shah Day), January or February (Shree Panchami), February 19 (National Democratic Day), February (Shivaratri), February or March (Fagu Purnima), April (Ran Navami).

If you wish to plan your visit to coincide with a particular festival, contact a Nepali embassy or one of the tourist information centers in Nepal to determine the specific date for the year you are traveling.

NEPAL CALENDAR OF EVENTS

February
- **Tibetan New Year.** Boudha. Attended by Buddhists from Nepal and Tibet, the religious festivities include the raising of prayer flags, masked dances by lamas, prayers, and blessings.

March
- **Holi** (also called Fagu). All over Nepal. This festival is marked by the throwing of colored powders and colored water on everyone and everything in sight. Keep your camera covered. Full moon of March (sometimes late February).

April
- **Bisket.** Bhaktapur. This seven-day festival marks the beginning of the new year. A huge chariot containing statues of the gods Bhairav and Bhadrakali is pulled through the streets of the city and down to the bank of the Hanumante River.
- **Chaitra Dasain.** All over Nepal. A smaller version of Dasain, which is held in September or October, is marked by many animal sacrifices.

May
- **Mani Rimdu.** Thami, Solu-Khumbu Buddhist monks dance with masks at a monastery. Held at the time of the full moon.

September
- **Bada Dasain.** All over Nepal. Nepal's biggest festival, it lasts 15 days. On the ninth day, thousands of water buffalo and goats are sacrificed, and images of the goddess Durga are bathed in blood. On the last day of Dasain, the royal palace is opened to the public, and the king and queen place *tika* marks on people's foreheads.

October
- **Tihar** (also known as Deepawali or Diwali). All over Nepal. Called the Festival of Lights. Crows, dogs, cows, bulls, and brothers are honored on separate days. On the day of Deepawali, houses and businesses are covered with candles, and lights and paths are traced to the family moneybox so that the goddess Laxmi will bless the house and help it to prosper in the upcoming year. Early to mid-month.

November
- **Mani Rimdu.** Thangboche Monastery, Solu-Khumbu. Masked dances by monks at a remote Buddhist monastery.

KATHMANDU CALENDAR OF EVENTS

February
- **Shivaratri.** Pashupatinath. Devout Hindus come from all over Nepal and India to celebrate the birthday of the god Shiva. Many *sadhus* (mendicant ascetic holy men) make the pilgrimage to Pashupatinath, where they collect alms.

March
- **Seto Machendranath Jatra** (Rath festival). Kathmandu. Dedicated to the patron deity of the Kathmandu Valley, this festival features a giant chariot that towers over the heads of the people pulling it. The celebrations last four days. It begins in the market near Asan Tole. Each night when the chariot ends its day's journey, the image of Seto Machendra is taken out and bathed.

April
- **Rato Machendranath Jatra.** Patan. Lasting an entire month, this festival is highlighted by a huge chariot being pulled through the streets of Patan. Rato Machendra is the patron deity of the Kathmandu Valley, and this festival is held to ensure a good monsoon for the rice crop.

August
- **Gaijatra.** Kathmandu Valley. Called the Festival of Cows, Gaijatra is an eight-day-long celebration to honor dead relatives. People who have had a death in the family within the past year bring a cow (either real or someone in costume) to participate in the festival. Festivities take place on the valley's three Durbar Squares.
- **Krishna's Birthday.** Patan. An all-night celebration with much music and singing takes place at the stone Krishna Temple in Patan.
- **Teej.** Pashupatinath. This is a woman's festival during which women go to bathe in the holy waters of the Bagmati River at Pashupatinath Temple.

September
- **Indrajatra.** Kathmandu and all over Nepal. This four-day festival is in celebration of Indra, the god of rain. It marks the end of the monsoon and the beginning of the cool dry season. The Kumari is paraded through Kathmandu, and blessed homemade beer flows from the mouth of the giant mask of the White Bhairav on Hanuman Dhoka Square. Newari dances are performed in the Durbar Square area.

November
- **Ekadashi.** Budhanilkantha, Changu Narayan, and Pashupatinath. This festival celebrating Vishnu's awakening from a four-month nap is marked by pilgrimages to shrines and temples dedicated to this god. Eleventh day after the full moon.

December
- **Bala Chaturdashi.** Pashupatinath. People from all over the Kathmandu Valley visit this temple to light candles and scatter seeds. There is much singing and dancing by pilgrims late into the night.

3 Health, Insurance & Other Concerns

HEALTH PREPARATIONS

What follows is meant to be used for general guidance only; consult your doctor or local international health clinic for details.

Staying healthy in Nepal is many tourists' primary concern, and for some, it becomes an obsession. Perhaps the best thing you can do to keep yourself healthy is to get plenty of rest. Remember that Kathmandu is at around 3,500 feet, and most trekking is done at elevations from 6,000 to 16,000 feet. These elevations alone can put stress on your body. I suggest taking a multiple-vitamin supplement containing Vitamin C while you are here.

During the winter months, colds are probably the most common illness in Nepal. Kathmandu is the dustiest city I have ever been in. The dust can be very irritating to the eyes, nose, and throat and may be the cause of colds and allergies. Some people choose to wear aspirators (face masks) to keep out the dust. Masks are sold at many shops frequented by tourists. Though a cold is likely the worst thing that you'll come down with in Nepal, there are quite a few other illnesses you should know about and take precautions against.

Purifying Water   The majority of illnesses in Nepal are spread by unsanitary conditions and contaminated water. The best protection is not to drink any water unless you have purified it yourself. Avoid tap water; avoid unsealed or sealed bottled water with a screwtop; avoid raw salads that have been rinsed in water; avoid ice cubes or crushed ice in drinks, *even at the top-notch, most expensive hotels.* There are a number of ways that water can be purified for drinking, but boiling for 20 minutes is the most common. Be aware, though, that Nepal is suffering from severe deforestation, and anything you as a visitor can do to limit your use of precious firewood will be a step toward helping to preserve the Himalayas.

A much better method of purifying water is with iodine, though some people find the taste of iodized water to be too strong. Iodine, which is a poison and should never be taken internally at its full strength, comes in solutions of varying strengths. Use 8 drops of tincture of iodine (a 2% solution) or 4 drops of Lugol's solution (the most common form of iodine in Nepal) to sterilize a quart or liter of water.

Water-purification tablets are another option. There are two types available, but only one of them, tetraglycine hydroperioiodide, is effective for purifying water in Nepal. Chlorine tablets, which are the most common form of water-purification tablets, are *not* effective at killing amoebic cysts. Most water filters that have rapidly gained popularity among backpackers in the United States will filter out bacteria, amoebas and their cysts, and giardia and their cysts, but they are ineffective at filtering out the hepatitis virus. With such a limitation, these filters are of no use in Nepal, where hepatitis is prevalent. However, there are now two-stage water filters available that both filter and iodinize water, which means they are effective against the hepatitis virus. Look for these filters at a large camping-supply store.

Vaccinations   Nepal does not require any vaccinations for entry. However, Nepal is one of the poorest countries in the world, and consequently hygiene and medical-care standards are very low. In some areas of the country there is only one doctor for every 100,000 people. Diseases associated with poor sanitation, often considered tropical diseases, are commonplace in Nepal. At least six months before leaving home, you will need to begin taking the series of vaccinations needed to travel in this region. To find out what's recommended call the U.S. Department of Public Health or your county health department and ask what immunizations are needed for the regions to which you'll be traveling.

Alternatively, you can call the International Travelers' Hotline at the Centers for Disease Control in Atlanta (☎ 404/332-4559).

Once they have advised you about what vaccinations and health precautions are needed, call your state or county health department to find the international health clinic or doctor nearest to you where you can receive vaccinations.

For travel to Nepal, the following vaccinations are recommended: typhoid, tetanus, diphtheria, and polio. Also, if you were born after January 1, 1957, you should make sure you have been immunized against measles. Malaria tablets (if you are visiting the Terai), an immune serum globulin (gamma globulin) shot, and a vaccination against meningococcal meningitis are also advised.

In Kathmandu the best and most reliable sources of information are either the CIWEC Clinic or Nepal International Clinic; either will tell you which immunizations they currently recommend.

One problem with contacting your county health board for information is that, unless you live in a major metropolitan area, the chances of their having vaccinations for tropical diseases are slight. You might have to drive to the nearest city, pay an initial-visit fee to see a doctor, and then pay usually astronomical fees for the vaccinations. Although usually costly and time consuming, they may be necessary. Booster shots, for those who have traveled in the tropics before, can be had conveniently and relatively inexpensively in Kathmandu. The two clinics mentioned above, both staffed by Western or Western-trained medical staff, provide immunizations in Kathmandu. The Nepal International Clinic (☎ 977/1-412842) is located on Naxal near the current royal palace, and the CIWEC Clinic (☎ 977/1-228531) is off Durbar Marg near the Hotel Yak & Yeti. All of the immunizations listed below are available in Nepal at either of these clinics. Both of these clinics use disposable needles and vaccines manufactured in Europe or North America.

Meningococcal Meningitis   Outbreaks of meningitis have occurred in Kathmandu in recent years, and protection against this often-fatal disease is highly recommended. Meningococcal meningitis is a bacterial infection that affects the central nervous system.

Hepatitis A   Infectious hepatitis (Type A) is common in Nepal. It is characterized by extreme fatigue and jaundice (yellowing of the skin and eyes) and is spread by contaminated food and water. The efficacy of the immune serum globulin (gamma globulin) injection has been questioned in recent years by some Western doctors, but many still feel, as do the clinics in Nepal, that it provides protection against the disease.

Hepatitis B   This viral disease is spread primarily by sexual or blood contact with an infected person and is often fatal. A vaccine is available against this disease, though tourists' chances of contracting hepatitis B are quite low. The vaccine is taken in a series of three injections over 6 months.

Polio   Though it is no longer a significant threat in most developed nations, polio is still common in Nepal. Your childhood immunization series of three doses will need to be updated to provide protection against this disease. The oral vaccine is still commonly used. If you did not receive a series of polio vaccinations as a child, consult your doctor as far in advance of your departure as possible.

Typhoid Fever   Spread by contaminated food and water, typhoid is a bacterial infection characterized by high fever. Typhoid is common in Nepal, and vaccination against the disease is highly recommended. You'll need to have it several months before leaving for Nepal.

Tetanus-Diphtheria   Tetanus (lockjaw) can easily be contracted from cuts and scratches, especially puncture wounds. The immunization, which is generally given in conjunction with a diphtheria immunization, is good for up to 10 years.

Cholera   Cholera is a bacterial infection spread by contaminated water. The main symptom is severe diarrhea. Cholera is quite common in Nepal, especially during the monsoon season, although tourists rarely contract it. Cholera vaccinations are no longer recommended, but if you should develop severe diarrhea accompanied by nausea, vomiting, cramps, and dizziness, you should suspect cholera and seek medical attention immediately.

Malaria   Malaria is a mosquito-borne disease that occurs in the Terai region of Nepal, where Chitwan National Park is located. It is characterized by high fever, chills, and general malaise. The species of mosquito that transmits malaria is active only from dusk to dawn, so extra precautions against bites should be taken at these times. Wear a long-sleeve shirt, long pants, and socks to cover as much of your skin as possible. Use mosquito repellent on any exposed skin. If possible, sleep under a mosquito net, or burn mosquito coils, which are available at most general stores in Nepal. There is no immunization against malaria, but a prophylaxis can reduce or prevent the outbreak of the disease. Chloroquine is still the accepted prophylaxis in Nepal (in other countries the disease has developed resistance to chloroquine). If you should come down with malaria despite these precautions, the standard treatment is Fansidar. However, Fansidar can cause severe side effects, including death. You should consult your doctor before taking it. Another drug, mefloquine, has recently become available in the United States and is effective in chloroquine-resistant areas. However, this drug also has side effects, though not as extreme as those of Fansidar.

Japanese Encephalitis   This is another mosquito-borne disease found in the lower elevations of Nepal. It is most common during the monsoon season and the beginning of the dry season. You are at greatest risk if you spend more than three weeks in the Terai region of Nepal, especially in a rural area such as Chitwan National Park. The vaccine against this disease is given as a series spaced over several weeks.

Rabies   This fatal disease is endemic in Nepal and is commonly carried by dogs and monkeys. Extreme caution should be taken around these animals. Do not feed temple monkeys! If not treated within 24 hours, rabies is fatal. There is, however, a vaccine that gives partial protection against this disease. The vaccine will not prevent you from getting rabies if you are bitten by a rabid animal, but it will give you more time in which to seek medical attention and will eliminate the need for the series of five painful injections into the stomach muscles. This preexposure vaccine is given as a series of three shots spaced over one month. The shots are generally recommended only for people who plan to spend several months or longer in an area where they might be exposed to rabies.

If you have not had the preexposure vaccine and you are bitten by a possibly rabid animal, thoroughly rinse the wound with running water for 20 minutes. Immediately seek medical attention. If you are trekking, you must find the nearest two-way radio and request a helicopter evacuation to Kathmandu, where you should immediately begin the series of injections to prevent the onset of rabies.

Diarrhea   The best way to avoid developing diarrhea during your visit to Nepal is to avoid eating raw vegetables and unpeeled fruits and to drink only treated water or bottled drinks. Most restaurants in Nepal that cater to tourists include a note on their menu to the effect that all their vegetables are treated with a solution of sterilized water. This is an effective way to clean vegetables, but it isn't always reliable. Why take a chance on getting diarrhea just so you can eat a pile of shredded cabbage and a slice of tomato (this is what most salads consist of in Nepal)? Don't be tempted by the fresh guavas in the markets in October unless you are willing to sterilize them first or peel them with a knife. I stay away from ice water and any water that I have not purified myself. There are plenty of soft drinks available, as well as bottled water (mineral water), sparkling water (soda), beer, and juice. Tea is the most common drink in Nepal and is made with boiled water, though whether it has been boiled long enough to kill bacteria and other diarrhea-causing organisms is never certain. You are always taking a chance with tea, but this is a relatively low risk. Though you may be tempted, you should also avoid cheesecakes and meringue pies while in Nepal. Salmonella bacteria favor these two foods.

The next most important thing to remember is to wash your hands before you eat. This may sound simple, but it is not always easy, especially when trekking. Nepalis always wash their hands, or at least rinse them, before eating because they eat with their hands. Moist towelettes are a good thing to carry with you at all times, so you can clean your hands even when there is no water handy.

Unfortunately, what is commonly contracted in Nepal is not always the simple traveler's diarrhea that goes away after a few days. Doctors in Nepal clinics have found that a majority of cases of diarrhea seen here require treatment with antibiotics of one sort or another. The most important thing to remember if you develop diarrhea is to drink enough fluids to avoid becoming dehydrated. Packets of oral rehydration salts added to drinking water will help to replenish salts and electrolytes lost by the body. These packets are readily available for only a few cents per package all over Nepal. In the West, the same salts are difficult to find and are often very expensive. I suggest you buy them in Nepal should the need arise rather than bringing them with you.

There are a number of ways to deal with diarrhea, depending on its severity. The first line of defense should be Pepto-Bismol tablets, which are unavailable in Nepal, so be sure to bring some from home. If the diarrhea becomes so severe that it is difficult to stay hydrated, an antidiarrhea drug such as Imodium, Lomotil, or codeine can be taken. Such drugs are not antibiotics and only treat symptoms, but they're particularly helpful if travel is necessary. If diarrhea is due to food poisoning, though, these drugs can be harmful. Remember, too, that codeine is a narcotic and can become addictive if taken over a long period of time.

Bacterial Diarrhea   Of all the possible causes of diarrhea, bacterial infection is by far the most common. This is caused by a proliferation of a usually harmless form of bacteria. The most common way to treat such an illness is with the antibiotic sulfamethoxazole-trimethoprim (SMZ-TMP), marketed in the United States under the trade names of Septra and Bactrim. However, the Nepal International Clinic in Kathmandu has noticed a growing resistance to this drug, possibly due to overuse in Nepal. This clinic now recommends Norfloxacin and Ciprofloxacin (readily available in Nepal).

Amoebic Dysentery   Though this is one of the most dreaded of diseases among travelers to the tropics, amoebas can be easily treated if diagnosed. However, amoebas are often difficult to detect. If left untreated, they will migrate to the liver and cause damage, so it is very important that you let your doctor know that amoebic dysentery is a possibility should you develop diarrhea after leaving Nepal. Symptoms of amoebic dysentery include abdominal pain, diarrhea (frequently with blood or pus in the stool), lethargy, and fever. In Nepal, the recommended treatment for amoebic dysentery is tinidazole (marketed in Nepal as Tiniba). In the United States, where tinidazole is not available, Flagyl is the recommended drug.

Giardiasis   Another cause of long-term diarrhea, giardiasis is caused by a protozoan and is quite common in Nepal. Giardiasis is spread by water and food that has been contaminated with the cysts of the giardia organism and has an incubation period of seven days. Therefore, if you develop diarrhea on your second or third day in Nepal, giardiasis is not the cause. Giardiasis has been frequently associated with the passing of gas and burps that smell like rotten eggs. Though this is often true, it is not always the case, and in fact some bacteria will have the same effect. More common symptoms of giardiasis are a violent bubbling in the intestines accompanied by pain in the upper part of the abdomen. Diarrhea may come and go and often occurs only in the morning. Because the giardia protozoa live in the upper intestines, they are very difficult to detect in a stool test, and people often go undiagnosed for months because the symptoms can be similar to those of many other illnesses. Remember that the incubation period for giardia is about one week, and should you develop diarrhea after returning home, it is important that you tell your doctor that giardiasis is a possibility. In the United States, giardiasis is usually treated with the drug Flagyl, but in Nepal, the recommended treatment is tinidazole (marketed as Tiniba).

Blue-Green Algae   The first cases of this tiny one-celled plant causing diarrhea were diagnosed in Kathmandu in 1989. Prior to this time, blue-green algae had never been known to make people ill. Shortly after being identified as algae by the Centers for Disease Control in the United States, they were identified in several other cases among travelers to the tropics. However, there were eight times as many cases in Nepal as in the rest of the world combined. The symptoms of blue-green algae are frequent and watery diarrhea, fatigue, and weight loss. Fever and vomiting have not been associated with this type of infection. Fortunately for tourists, blue-green algae infections seem to occur only during the monsoon months from June to September, which is the least popular time of year for visiting Nepal. There is no known cure for blue-green algae. Infections generally last from two to eight weeks, with an average duration of three to four weeks. As of this time there is no known way to prevent blue-green algae infection: eating only cooked vegetables and drinking only treated water and bottled drinks should, however, help avoid it.

Food Poisoning   Salmonella is the most common food poisoning contracted in Nepal. It is caused by a bacteria that is common in chickens and therefore in egg products. Fresh-cooked eggs are rarely a problem, but such dishes as cheesecake and meringue pie commonly support the growth of the salmonella bacteria. It's best to avoid these two treats. The symptoms of salmonella are severe stomach cramps, diarrhea, vomiting, fever, and chills. Luckily these all pass within 24 hours. Antidiarrhea drugs such as codeine, Imodium, and Lomotil should *never* be taken if salmonella poisoning is suspected. The reason for the illness is the poison that is being secreted by the salmonella as this bacteria passes through your body. To slow its progress is to make yourself sicker. To treat salmonella, drink as much liquid as possible.

Altitude Sickness   Altitude sickness (also called acute mountain sickness or AMS) is an illness caused by the lack of oxygen at high altitudes. Anyone planning to go trekking in Nepal should become familiar with the symptoms, causes, and cures for this sometimes fatal illness. Though altitude sickness generally does not occur below 10,000 feet, some people may suffer minor symptoms as low as 8,000 feet. Symptoms of altitude sickness include headaches, fatigue, lassitude, coughing, shortness of breath, loss of appetite, nausea, reduced urine output, heavy legs, a drunken gait, and a generally lousy feeling. Being physically fit is no guarantee that you will not develop symptoms. Even people who have been above 12,000 feet previously without any difficulty may develop altitude sickness at the same elevation or even lower. There is just no way to predict who will and who will not be struck with this illness, but trekkers who are overexerting themselves and are panting and breathless may be more susceptible. Someone who staggers into camp far behind the rest of the group is also a likely candidate to develop altitude sickness. The best advice is to take it easy. Carry a light pack. Walk slowly.

Trekkers who spend several days hiking up to an altitude of 10,000 or 11,000 feet are less likely to develop altitude sickness than those who fly into such high altitude airstrips as those at Lukla, Jomosom, and Manang. It can be very dangerous to fly into an elevation higher than 10,000 feet, such as the airstrip at Shyangboche above Namche Bazaar. It is very important for trekkers who fly in to spend one or two days acclimatizing to the elevation. Acclimatization is best done by resting for part of the day and perhaps making a short hike to higher elevation before returning to the elevation at which you will be sleeping. This is the climb high, sleep low theory of acclimatization and should be used throughout high-altitude treks. The rule of thumb is not to ascend more than 1,000 feet per day when you are above 9,000 or 10,000 feet. Also, above 10,000 feet you should sleep for two nights at the same elevation for every 3,000 feet you ascend, which means that after every three days of trekking you should spend two nights at the same place.

The first warnings of impending altitude sickness are headache, extreme fatigue, shortness of breath, and loss of appetite. Should someone in your party develop these symptoms, that person should not continue climbing until after acclimatizing for one or two days. Once the symptoms disappear, it is safe to continue. If the symptoms do not disappear, or get worse, descending to lower elevation is advisable.

Symptoms of worsening altitude sickness include increasing tiredness, severe headaches, vomiting, and loss of coordination. These are symptoms of high-altitude cerebral edema (HACE), an extreme form of acute mountain sickness. Acute mountain sickness is a result of fluid collecting between cells in the body, particularly in the brain and lungs. HACE, the accumulation of fluid in the brain, can cause death within 12 hours if symptoms are ignored. Increasing shortness of breath, coughing (sometimes with pink sputum being coughed up), and tiredness are symptoms of high altitude pulmonary edema (HAPE), which is the accumulation of fluid in the lungs. If nothing is done to alleviate the symptoms of HAPE, the person suffering from this form of altitude sickness can drown in the fluid collecting in the lungs.

One very important symptom of acute mountain sickness is loss of coordination. If someone is seen to stagger or seems to be walking as if they were drunk, acute mountain sickness should be suspected. A good test of this is to ask the affected person to walk a straight line placing one foot directly in front of the other without staggering or losing balance. If the person cannot perform this simple task, he or she should descend immediately. If someone feels so bad or is so tired that he or she only wants to lie in their sleeping bag, that person should be made to perform this test; it could mean the difference between life and death.

If the symptoms of HACE or HAPE occur, the person must descend immediately, and never alone. Descent should continue until symptoms begin to decrease; this is usually in 1,000 to 1,500 feet. The affected person should descend slowly and not overexert. It is always best to recognize symptoms early and have the sick person descend while still able to walk. If the person is unconscious, a yak, pony, or porter can usually be hired to carry them to lower elevation.

Those people trekking with a group often have the hardest time dealing with altitude sickness. Group treks are usually on a tight schedule and no one wants to have to call their trek short because they are feeling a little bad. Don't let peer pressure get to you, and don't take chances. If you are feeling bad, stop climbing. Don't try to keep up with the others.

People with heart disease or respiratory problems are advised not to attempt to trek to high elevations. Pregnant women should also stay below 12,000 feet. Children are more susceptible to altitude sickness and should be watched closely for any symptoms. Infants, who can not tell you when they are feeling bad, should not be taken to high elevations. Also, sleeping pills and sedatives should not be taken at high altitudes because they decrease breathing and may lead to altitude sickness.

The Himalayan Rescue Association, Hotel Tilicho Building, Tri Devi Marg, Thamel (P.O. Box 495), Kathmandu (☎ 977/1-418755), is a nonprofit organization that is working to reduce the number of casualties among trekkers and mountain climbers in Nepal. Founded in 1973, the organization operates two rescue posts that are staffed by volunteer doctors during the main trekking seasons. One post is at Pheriche on the way to Everest Base Camp, and the other is in Manang at the foot of Thorong Pass. At the association's main office in Kathmandu (near the Department of Immigration office), you can find out more about altitude sickness. They also have a bulletin board that is used by independent trekkers looking for trekking companions.

INSURANCE

Health/Accident   Check your health insurance policy before you leave the country to make sure you are covered while traveling abroad. When traveling to Nepal, the most important type of insurance to have is a policy that pays for emergency evacuation. The hospitals in Nepal are frightfully far behind Western standards, and most foreigners living in Nepal go to Bangkok or Singapore when they need medical treatment. If there is enough time you should try to get to one of these cities before having any type of emergency surgery performed. Evacuation insurance is especially important for trekkers, and most major trekking agencies will not take you on a trek unless you can show proof that you have insurance to pay for emergency evacuation from the mountains. Helicopter rescue flights cost $600 to $1,400 per hour. Most helicopter rescues take two to three hours, so you are looking at a bill of $1,200 to $4,200. Before a helicopter will be sent to rescue you, you must usually prove that you can pay for the service. An insurance policy is sufficient proof.

International SOS Assistance, P.O. Box 11568, Philadelphia, PA, 19116 (☎ 215/244-1500 or 800/523-8930), is a travel-assistance company. They offer a 24-hour hotline, emergency evacuation, hospital admission, return of unattended minors, and return of remains; the cost is $55 for 1 to 14 days. There are special rates for couples and frequent travelers. This company now also offers trip cancellation and medical insurance for travelers.

Travel Guard International, 1145 Clark St., Stevens Point, WI 54481 (☎ 715/345-0505 or 800/826-1300), offers a policy that includes medical coverage, emergency evacuation, trip cancellation and interruption, baggage protection, legal assistance, return of an unattended minor, and life insurance. Supplemental trip cancellation, baggage loss, and life insurance may also be purchased.

Tele-Trip (Mutual of Omaha), Mutual of Omaha Plaza, Omaha, NB 68175 (☎ 800/228-9792), offers different travel insurance policies for any length of time. Coverage includes medical, baggage, trip cancellation or interruption insurance, and flight insurance against death, dismemberment, and loss of sight.

Wallach & Company, P.O. Box 480, Middleburg, VA 22117 (☎ 800/237-6615), and **Access America Inc.,** 6600 W. Broad St., Richmond, VA 23230 (☎ 804/285-3300 or 800/424-3391), offer policies similar to Tele-Trip's.

Loss/Theft   It can ruin your vacation if it happens, and no one wants to think about it, but loss and theft of baggage do happen. If you're taking expensive trekking equipment or cameras, you should be sure to check your homeowner's, condo, co-op, or renter's insurance policy to make sure that it covers theft of your belongings when traveling abroad. If it does, be sure you know what sort of documentation you'll need and how soon you will have to contact the insurance company after the theft occurs. If you do not have this kind of insurance, consider taking out insurance against loss, theft, or damage. **Tele-Trip (Mutual of Omaha),** Mutual of Omaha Plaza, Omaha, NB 68131-0618 (☎ 800/228-9792), offers reasonably priced insurance against loss, theft, or damage of your baggage.

Cancellation   If you feel that there is some possibility of your not being able to make your planned trip, think about trip-cancellation insurance. This can refund the price of your ticket or entire tour package should you have to cancel at the last minute. **Tele-Trip** (see above) also offers this type of insurance.

4 What to Pack

CLOTHING Nepal is a mountainous tropical country, which means that it experiences great climatic extremes. In October, which is one of the prime trekking months in Nepal, it can be hot enough to swim in Kathmandu or Chitwan while there are snowstorms raging in the high mountains. Be prepared for these extremes. Also keep in mind that your wardrobe is likely to be quite different depending on whether you are going trekking or are just sightseeing.

Among the necessary items, the most important is sturdy, enclosed walking shoes. The streets of Nepal are very bad and very dirty and there are rarely sidewalks. You'll want to keep your feet as well protected as possible. As far as clothing is concerned, you should probably bring at least three changes of clothes since it often takes more than 24 hours to have clothes washed. The only place you might want to wear dressy clothing is at an expensive hotel restaurant or a business meeting. Casual clothing is the norm. Silk or polypropylene long underwear is a necessity in winter months and when trekking, as are wool socks and a wool sweater, although beautiful wool sweaters are available in Nepal for around $15. A down jacket is compact, lightweight, and warm whether you are going trekking or not. A hat of some sort is a good idea in winter. When trekking, a hat and gloves or mittens can make the difference between being comfortable and freezing. If you are going to Chitwan in search of tigers and rhinos, remember to bring some khaki, brown, or green clothing so you won't be too conspicuous. A poncho or good rain jacket can come in handy any time of year.

OTHER ITEMS In addition to the clothing mentioned above, here are some other items you might want to bring:

Binoculars If you are a birdwatcher, you will want to bring along your binoculars and make a trip to Chitwan National Park, home to more than 400 species of birds.

Camera and Film Nepal is one of the most photogenic regions on earth. Film is slightly more expensive than in the United States, and Kodachrome is rarely available.

Dropper Bottle A small bottle with a built-in dropper is a good way to carry iodine, which is probably the best way to purify water in Nepal. Though iodine is available in Nepal, it comes poorly packaged in bottles that almost always leak.

Earplugs Barking dogs can ruin a night's sleep even in Kathmandu's most expensive hotels; consequently, earplugs are invaluable.

Flashlight The electricity is regularly shut off in Kathmandu, and out on the trail there usually isn't any electricity at all.

Lip Protection The winter climate in Nepal can be dry and cold, and up in the mountains, it is often very windy. It is good to have something to protect your lips from drying and cracking.

Moist Towelettes A container of disposable moist towelettes is great for cleaning hands when there is no soap and water handy when trekking.

Pepto-Bismol Unavailable in Nepal, these tablets are about the best thing you can take for a simple upset stomach and are considered invaluable by many.

Sleeping Bag Down is the best since it is lightweight, compact, and warm. If you are traveling on the cheap, you will find that budget hotels often don't provide enough blankets. If you are trekking, you will definitely want to have a warm sleeping bag.

Sunglasses   The sun is bright, and in the snowfields at high altitude the glare can cause snow blindness.

Sunscreen   Despite the cool weather, this is still the tropics, and the sun can be intense. Apply sunscreen on your face and hands, especially at higher elevations.

Swiss Army Knife   These all-purpose utility knives are invaluable.

Tampons   These are difficult to find in Nepal.

Umbrella   If you are visiting during the rainy season, an umbrella is an absolute necessity.

Water Bottle   With your own water bottle and iodine, you can make purified water no matter where you are.

5 Tips for Special Travelers

FOR TRAVELERS WITH DISABILITIES   Though a few of the more expensive hotels are becoming aware of the needs of travelers with disabilities, Nepal in general remains a difficult country for people with disabilities to get around in. Sidewalks, where they exist, sometimes have curbs more than a foot high. Streets are uneven, potholed, muddy, and crowded. Temples and other buildings of interest to visitors almost always have steps, if not a steep stairway.

This said, there is at least one company that offers tours to Nepal for travelers with disabilities. **Accessible Journeys,** 35 W. Sellers Ave., Ridley Park, PA 19078 (☎ 610/521-0339 or 800/846-4537), operates group tours to Nepal and India for the mobility impaired.

For more general information, contact **Mobility International USA,** P.O. Box 10767, Eugene, OR 97440 (☎ 503/343-1284; fax 503/343-6812), a membership organization that promotes international educational exchanges for people of all disabilities and ages. Although they do not offer trips to Nepal, this organization is a good source of general information and referrals. For a $20 membership fee, you receive a quarterly newsletter and access to a referral service.

Access: The Foundation for Accessibility by the Disabled, P.O. Box 356, Malverne, NY 11565 (☎ and fax 516/568-2715), can also provide recommendations and helpful information to people with disabilities who want to visit Nepal.

In the U.K., general information about travel for people with physical disabilities is available from the Royal Association for Disability & Rehabilitation (RADAR), 12 City Forum, 250 City Rd., London EC1V 8AF (☎ 071/250-3222; fax 071/250-0212). This organization publishes fact sheets and books that can be very useful to any person with disabilities planning a trip to Nepal or anywhere else.

FOR SENIORS   With each passing year, I have been meeting more and more older travelers in Nepal, and as is the case with younger travelers, most seem to be coming here with the specific goal of trekking. Though trekking is a strenuous activity, if you are in good health and accustomed to walking regularly, you may find trekking far less difficult than it sounds. If you set your own pace or opt for a group trek with others in the same age range, you should have no problem. However, there are still some things to be aware of before buying your ticket to Kathmandu.

Nepal is about halfway around the world from North America, which means that jet lag can be devastating. Since there are no direct flights to Nepal from the United States, you must stop for a night's rest en route. This can help combat jet lag, but the rule of thumb that it requires one day to recover completely from each hour of time change means that it will take more than two weeks to recover from a trip to Nepal if you are coming from the West Coast of the United States. For most Americans, that is as long as they may have in Nepal. It is essential therefore to take it easy. It is also a good idea to break up your travels, say by stopping in Thailand or Europe for a few days before continuing to Nepal.

Before heading to Nepal, it is a good idea to have a physical exam. Medical care is far from adequate in Nepal, and even a minor medical emergency could prove life-threatening here. Also, if you suffer from heart disease of any sort, consult your doctor before planning a trek that will take you to high elevations. Altitude sickness can be particularly dangerous for anyone with a prior heart condition.

Make sure you have an adequate supply of any medications you require, and be sure to bring the generic name of the drugs with you. If you should happen to lose your medication or run out, Nepali pharmacists are more likely to know the drug by its chemical name than by its U.S. trade name. Though many prescription drugs are available over the counter for much less than in the United States, you can't count on a Nepali pharmacy to carry the wide variety of medications available in the United States. It is also a good idea to carry a spare set of glasses and keep one pair in a safe place such as the hotel safe-deposit box, in case your first pair gets lost or broken.

When making an airline reservation, be sure to ask for any senior citizen discount the airline might offer. Many seniors visiting Nepal choose to come on an organized tour. Most of these tours are combined India and Nepal trips that tag a few days in Kathmandu and perhaps Chitwan National Park onto the end of the trip. **AARP Travel Services,** an American Express Travel Program, 400 Pinnacle Way, Atlanta, GA 30071 (☎ 800/927-0111), sometimes offers tours that include Nepal in their itineraries. This service can also provide independent travelers with a list of travel suppliers who offer discounts to members. If you are not already a member, the **American Association of Retired Persons (AARP),** 601 E St. NW, Washington, DC 20049 (☎ 800/424-3410), affiliated with the AARP Travel Service, is a good source of information for senior citizens. Membership is only $8 for two married people. **Grand Circle Travel, Inc.,** 347 Congress St., Boston, MA 02210 (☎ 617/350-7500 or 800/221-2610), specializes in tours for "mature Americans." Among many other tours and cruises, they offer an India and Nepal tour.

Seniors looking for a traveling companion have a couple of choices open to them. **Partners-in-Travel,** 11660 Chenault St., Suite 119, Los Angeles, CA 90049 (☎ 310/476-4869), includes around 400 travel personals ads in the classified section of its semiannual publication. Though this service is not restricted to older travelers, 90% of the subscribers are over 50. A one-year subscription costs $25. **Travel Companion Exchange,** P.O. Box 833, Amityville, NY 11701 (☎ 516/454-0880), provides listings of possible travel companions who often specify special interests, age, education, and location. It costs $99 for a six-month membership and subscription to the service. It is also possible to subscribe to the organization's bimonthly newsletter without becoming a member. The newsletter costs $48 per year (sample issues cost $5).

FOR SINGLE TRAVELERS Single travelers need never travel alone in Nepal unless that is truly what they want. The Thamel neighborhood, frequented by budget travelers, is a meeting ground for independent travelers who hang out in the cafés, restaurants, and pubs meeting other like-minded travelers. The most popular restaurants are often so crowded that single travelers are seated together at the same table—a great way to meet people. There are also a number of bulletin boards around Thamel that act as clearinghouses for people seeking trekking companions. The board just to the left of the Kathmandu Guest House's front entrance is a good one to check, as is the board inside the office of the Himalayan Rescue Association. The Pumpernickel Bakery also has a very popular bulletin board.

Trekking agencies in Nepal will often allow single travelers to join with groups that have already arranged a trek if it is agreeable with the trekking party. Other companies have regularly scheduled treks and white-water rafting trips that solo travelers can join. Still, other adventurous types set off for the trekking trails alone (not advisable) and meet up with fellow trekkers on route to the trailhead. I have done this myself and found trekking companions before ever setting foot on the trail. Solo U.S. citizens in Nepal often find themselves spending time with Canadians and other English-speaking folks from Britain, New Zealand, and Australia.

If you feel that you would rather arrange a traveling companion before leaving home, **Travel Companion Exchange,** P.O. Box 833, Amityville, NY 11701 (☎ 516/454-0880), can help you find someone who shares the same interests. This agency publishes a bimonthly newsletter. As a member you will receive the newsletter and listings of personal profiles of other members (see "For Seniors," above for details).

Nepal is still a very safe country for single travelers of either sex, and you should be generally quite safe anywhere in Kathmandu, Pokhara, or any other small town or village. The only exception is on the trekking trails. In the past few years, there have been increasing numbers of robberies and even occasional murders of lone trekkers. Do not trek alone! Always find a companion, whether it is another trekker, a porter, or a guide.

FOR FAMILIES   There are a lot of things to consider before bringing children to Nepal, but one consideration stands out above all others. Have your children had all their childhood vaccinations? If not, you could be risking your children's health and possibly their lives by bringing them to Nepal. Childhood diseases that have long been controlled in developed nations are still widespread in Nepal. See "Health, Insurance & Other Concerns," above, in this chapter for more information on which diseases are problems in Nepal. Children are also more susceptible to and more severely affected by gastrointestinal illnesses, which are very common in Nepal. Diarrhea is one of the main causes of child deaths in Nepal. Carry some moist towelettes at all times so you can clean your children's hands whenever necessary. This is a first line of defense against stomach bugs.

One of the hardest parts of a family trip to Nepal is the plane ride. It takes well over 24 hours of flying, plus an overnight stop somewhere, to reach Nepal. That's a long time for a child to be stuck in a plane. Be sure to bring plenty to entertain the young ones. It is also wise to bring your kids' favorite snacks, since airline food may not appeal to them. Some airlines have special meals for children; be sure to ask when making your reservation. A good idea is to have kids carry a little day pack of their own filled with books, crayons, paper, and small toys. They'll feel right at home once they arrive in Kathmandu, where virtually all visitors wear day packs everywhere they go.

Don't bother bringing a stroller to Nepal; it will only be an inconvenience on the uneven streets. A better choice is a child carrier that you wear on your back. Outdoor supply stores now sell very well-designed baby packs that combine storage space with a seat for the baby. These are an excellent idea if you plan to go trek-king with a child too small to walk all the time. Keep in mind, though, that chil-dren this young are more susceptible to altitude sickness.

You won't find disposable diapers in Nepal. In fact most children in Nepal don't wear diapers at all, or pants for that matter, until they are old enough to be toilet trained. You may have to rely on cloth diapers and have them washed daily.

Most hotels allow children under age 12 to stay for free in your room if you don't request an extra bed. Bring along sleeping bags and mats for the kids to sleep on. Only a few of the most expensive hotels in Nepal have any facilities for chil-dren, and there aren't any playgrounds around either. You might want to pick a hotel that has some sort of garden for the kids to play in. Tourists and trekkers, though, tend to have a lot of interaction with Nepali children because the children are much more likely to speak a little English than adults. With so many English-speaking children, your kids will likely find playmates wherever they go.

Be sure that your children always carry a photocopy of their passport so that if they should get lost, whoever finds them will know which local authorities to contact. Another good idea is to tie a whistle around a young one's neck so that if they get lost they can blow on their whistle. Many of the streets in Kathmandu are so crowded that a child could be only a few feet away from you and be unable to see you.

FOR STUDENTS   Though a student ID card won't get you any discounts in Kathmandu, it can save you a bundle on your air ticket. Be sure to ask about stu-dent discounts when you're making airline reservations. If you do not already have a student ID, you may be able to get one by contacting the **Council on Interna-tional Educational Exchange (C.I.E.E.)**, 205 E. 42nd St., New York, NY 10017 (☎ 212/661-1414 or 212/661-1450).

6 Alternative/Adventure Travel

OUTFITTERS, ADVENTURE TOUR OPERATORS & ACTIVE VACATIONS

Nepal is one of the most popular adventure travel destinations in the world, and there are hundreds of companies that specialize in trips to this tiny Himalayan kingdom. Nepal's adventures are of three major types—trekking, white-water raft-ing, and jungle safaris. Mountain-bike tours are just beginning to get organized, so if you are an avid cyclist, you might want to look into this as well. It is possible to combine all of these adventurous activities into one trip if you have enough time and stamina.

Companies offering trekking, rafting, and jungle safari trips to Nepal include the following.

IN THE U.S.A.

Above the Clouds, P.O. Box 398, Worcester, MA 01602-0398 (☎ 508/ 799-4499 or 800/233-4499; fax 508/797-4779).

Adventure Center, 1311 63rd St., Suite 200, Emeryville, CA 94608 (☎ 510/ 654-1879 or 800/227-8747; fax 510/654-4200). The center offers trekking, raft-ing, and jungle safaris.

InnerAsia Expeditions, 2627 Lombard St., San Francisco, CA 94123 (☎ 415/ 922-0448 or 800/777-8183; fax 415/346-5535). This organization offers trekking and jungle safaris.

Journeys, 4011 Jackson Rd., Ann Arbor, MI 48103 (☎ 313/665-4407 or 800/255-8735). Journeys has trekking, rafting, and jungle safaris.

Lute Jerstad Adventures International, P.O. Box 19537, Portland, OR 97280 (☎ 503/244-6075; fax 503/244-1349). They have trekking, rafting, and jungle safaris.

Mountain Travel•Sobek—The Adventure Company, 6420 Fairmount Ave., El Cerrito, CA 94530 (☎ 510/527-8100 or 800/227-2384). They organize trekking expeditions and jungle safaris.

Overseas Adventure Travel, 349 Broadway, Cambridge, MA 02139 (☎ 617/876-0533 or 800/221-0814). They offer trekking, rafting, and jungle safaris.

Wilderness Travel, 801 Alston Way, Berkeley, CA 94710 (☎ 510/548-0420 or 800/368-2794; fax 510/548-0347). They have trekking programs.

IN THE U.K.

Classic Nepal, 33 Metro Ave., Newton, Alfreton, Derbyshire DE55 5UF (☎ 01773/873497; fax 01773/590243). Classic Nepal offers trekking, rafting, and jungle safaris.

Exodus, 9 Weir Rd., London SW12 0LT (☎ 081/675-5550; fax 081/673-0779). They offer trekking, rafting, and jungle safaris.

Explore, 1 Frederick St., Aldershot, Hampshire GU11 1LQ (☎ 01252/319448; fax 01252/343170). Explore organizes trekking, rafting, and jungle safaris.

Himalayan Kingdoms, 20 The Mall, Clifton, Bristol BS8 4DR (☎ 0117/923-7163; fax 0117/974-4993). This organization has trekking, rafting, and jungle safaris.

Karakoram Experience, 32 Lake Rd., Keswick, Cumbria CA12 5DQ (☎ 017687/73966; fax 017687/74693). This outfitter organizes trekking expeditions.

Sherpa Expeditions, 131a Heston Rd., Hounslow, Middlesex TW5 0RD (☎ 081/577-2717; fax 081/572-9788). They have trekking, rafting, and jungle safaris.

Twickers World Limited, 20/22 Church St., Twickenham TW1 3NW (☎ 081/892-8164; fax 081/892-8061). They offer trekking, rafting, and jungle safaris.

TREKKING   The mountains and the recreational opportunities they offer are what attract many visitors to Nepal. About 10% of all visitors to Nepal go trekking. These treks can be anything from an overnight trip out of Pokhara or a three-month-long mountaineering expedition. However, mountain climbing should be in a class by itself since it requires massive amounts of money, special equipment, and expensive permits from the Nepali government. Trekking is a much less demanding activity, though some treks can be quite difficult. There are treks of all lengths and difficulties, so nearly anyone visiting Nepal can do a little trekking if they wish.

Mountain climbing is the granddaddy of trekking. When Nepal opened its doors to the world in 1951, mountaineers were the first outsiders to arrive. They had their eyes set on all those unscaled Himalayan peaks, and within 20 years, all of the 8,000-meter (26,000-foot) peaks had been scaled. These expeditions had the benefit of Sherpa guides and porters to carry their massive loads of equipment and supplies. Today a trekking group consists of the same basic support personnel as a major mountaineering expedition, though generally on a smaller scale. Trekkers who crave a bit more adventure can attempt one of the designated "trekking peaks." These are mountain peaks that can be scaled with a minimum of difficulty (relatively speaking) and equipment. Several of the top trekking agencies offer treks to various trekking peaks.

See Chapters 8 and 9 for information about specific treks and outfitters.

Spiritual Study & Yoga

For centuries, India, Nepal, and Tibet have been well known as mystical destinations for spiritual seekers. The Beatles made spending time in an *ashram* (center for religious studies) the in thing to do in the '60s, and ever since then people have been flocking to this part of the world to find enlightenment. The frequently seen cartoon of some poor lost soul climbing to the top of a mountain to ask a famous yogi the BIG QUESTION—what is the meaning of life?—may well have originated in Nepal. This country is a crossroads, a meeting ground of two of the world's great religions—Buddhism and Hinduism. There aren't any Hindu ashrams here that I know of (India has cornered the market), but those interested in studying Tibetan Buddhism, meditation, or yoga have come to the right place.

Kopan Monastery, P.O. Box 817, Kathmandu (☎ 977/1-226717 or 977/1-413094), is a Tibetan Buddhist monastery located a couple of miles north of Boudha in the Kathmandu Valley. Home to more than 150 young monks and nuns from Nepal and Tibet, it is also a center for Westerners seeking to learn more about the teachings of Buddha. Throughout the year the monastery offers many short courses on meditation and Buddhism. Every November, there is a month-long course that includes daily teachings and meditation instruction. The course is attended by people of all ages from all over the world; some fly in from the United States and New Zealand simply because it is cheaper than attending a similar course at home. The course costs $260, including teachings, all meals (vegetarian), and a bed in a dormitory. For those who prefer a more private room, there are a few available.

The **Himalayan Yogic Institute,** Maharajgunj (☎ 977/1-413094), is affiliated with Kopan Monastery and offers short courses and weekly teachings on Buddhism and·meditation. Bulletin boards around Kathmandu usually have notices for courses in Buddhist studies being held in Boudha, the center for Tibetan Buddhism in Nepal and home of many monasteries. **Kathmandu Buddhist Center** (fax 977/1-411933), also offers weekly teachings. For more information, stop by the Nepalese Kitchen Restaurant near Chhetrapati.

All over Thamel, Kathmandu's budget travelers' neighborhood, there are signs advertising yoga instruction. Any of these instructors should be able to teach you quite a bit of yoga in a short time, and fees are very reasonable. The **Patanjali Yoga Center,** Chhauni, Museum Road (☎ 977/1-270508), near the National Museum, offers daily classes. They welcome students at all levels.

If you would like to study Nepali music and dance, enquire at the **Hotel Vajra** (☎ 977/1-272719 or 977/1-271545). Weekly classes may be available.

WHITE-WATER RAFTING   Rafting in Nepal is today almost as popular as trekking. This is not surprising considering the number of rivers that flow down from the Himalayas. There is a wide range of rafting opportunities for everyone from novices to seasoned paddlers. Trips of 1 to 10 days are possible on several different rivers. All are led by experienced river guides and include food, life jackets, and waterproof bags. There is a wide range of rates depending on length, starting point, and mode of transportation to put-in point (buses are cheaper than private cars). Many companies in Thamel advertise very inexpensive rafting trips starting at $25 per day. Make sure you know exactly what you are getting before signing on. If you have to take the public bus, or even the deluxe tourist coach, you will spend most of your first day driving to the river, and catching a bus back to Kathmandu at the end of your trip can be frustrating and cut many more hours off your time on the river. Agencies that provide transportation by hired car will get you to the river sooner, but you will pay a higher price for this convenience. Also ask if helmets are provided.

One of the most popular raft trips is down the Trisuli River to Chitwan National Park. This trip includes several rapids and lots of leisurely floating, which makes it ideal for beginners. Rafting companies offer trips of 1 to 4 days on this river. For a longer trip with much more white water, there is the Sunkosi, lasting 10 days.

The following are some of the better rafting companies in Kathmandu:

Himalayan Encounters, Kathmandu Guest House Courtyard, (P.O. Box 2769), Thamel (☎ 977/1-417426; fax 977/1-417133); or contact **Encounter Overland Expeditions Ltd.,** 267 Old Brompton Rd., London SW5 9JA, United Kingdom (☎ 071/370-6845; fax 071/244-9737). A 3-day trip down the Trisuli costs $142. A 10-day trip down the Sunkosi River costs $450.

Equator Expeditions, Thamel (P.O. Box 8404), Kathmandu (☎ 977/ 1-416596; fax 977/1-414803), which has its office next door to the Kathmandu Guest House, is currently one of the most highly regarded rafting companies in Nepal. They offer trips on the Sun Kosi, Karnali, and Kali Gandaki; trip prices average between $45 and $55 per day. Their British office is at 125 Hook Rise South, Surbiton, Surrey KT6 7NA (☎ 081/391-0299; fax 81/391-5114).

Himalayan River Explorations, Tiger Tops Office, Durbar Marg (P.O. Box 170), Kathmandu (☎ 977/1-418491), is the pioneer river rafting company in Nepal. It is affiliated with Tiger Tops Jungle Lodge; consequently reservations can be made through any Tiger Tops affiliate or a travel agent. Trips offered are on the Trisuli, Karnali, Kali Gandaki, and Sunkosi. Rates range from $35 to $75 per person per day, depending on the number of people in the group and the length of the trip.

Ultimate Descents, across from Le Bistro, Thamel (☎ and fax 977/1-229389), or in Pokhara next door to the Hotel Snowland (☎ 977/61-20335), is based in New Zealand and may be the most popular rafting company in Nepal. They offer trips on the Kali Gandaki, Sun Kosi, and Karnali and charge between $45 and $50 per day. They also offer kayak trips and kayaking clinics. Their New Zealand office is at P.O. Box 208, Motueka, New Zealand (☎ 64/3528-6363; fax 64/3528-6792).

BIRDWATCHING   With numerous climatic zones from steamy lowlands to alpine aeries, Nepal is a birdwatcher's paradise. Royal Chitwan National Park alone has more than 450 species of birds. Any serious birder will want to pick up a copy of the book *Birds of Nepal* (if it is back in print) as soon as they arrive in Kathmandu. Armed with this excellent reference, you will quickly add dozens, if not hundreds, of bird sightings to your life list while you are in Nepal. Royal Chitwan National Park is the most popular birdwatching location, and all lodges provide experienced guides to help those unfamiliar with the birds of the subcontinent. For more information on Royal Chitwan National Park, see Chapter 7.

JUNGLE SAFARIS   The lowland forests of Nepal, though not really jungles, are full of rare wildlife, including the Bengal tiger and the one-horned Indian rhinoceros. There are several national parks and wildlife preserves throughout the lowland region called the Terai. The most popular and most easily accessible is Royal Chitwan National Park, which has numerous lodges both within and just outside the park. Here you can explore the park on the back of an elephant, by Land Rover, or by dugout canoe. For more information on Royal Chitwan National Park, see Chapter 7. Other parks include Royal Bardia Wildlife Reserve and Koshitappu Wildlife Reserve.

7 Getting There

BY PLANE
THE MAJOR AIRLINES

There are only four airlines that operate between the United States and Nepal, and there are no direct flights. **Thai Airways International** (☎ 800/426-5204) flies from Los Angeles via Bangkok. **Singapore Airlines** (☎ 800/742-3333) flies from Los Angeles, San Francisco, New York, and Vancouver via Singapore. **Lufthansa** (☎ 800/645-3880) flies from New York, Newark, Boston, Miami, Atlanta, Chicago, Dallas, Houston, Los Angeles, San Francisco, Vancouver, Calgary, and Toronto via Frankfurt. **Pakistan International Airlines** (☎ 800/221-2552) flies from New York via Karachi.

From outside the United States, you have a few more choices of airlines. **Royal Nepal Airlines** has the greatest number of flights to Nepal. These include departures from London, Frankfurt, Paris, Dubai, Delhi, Calcutta, Bombay, Bangkok, Hong Kong, and Singapore. (Royal Nepal flies twice weekly from Gatwick to Kathmandu.)

Airlines with service between London and Kathmandu include **Royal Nepal Airlines, Lufthansa, Biman Bangladesh Airlines,** and **Pakistan International Airlines.** Alternatively, you can fly to Delhi and then transfer to an airline with service to Nepal.

Airlines with service from Australia to Nepal include **Singapore Airlines** and **Thai Airways International.** You can also fly **Qantas** to Bangkok and then transfer to **Thai** or **Royal Nepal Airlines. Biman Bangladesh Airlines** flies from several European and Southeast Asian cities via Dhaka and has consistently low rates; consequently Biman is favored by budget travelers. **India Airlines,** Air India's domestic carrier, flies from Calcutta, Delhi, and Varanasi. Should you be exploring other parts of the Himalayas, you may wish to know that **China Southwest Airlines** flies from Lhasa, Tibet, and **Royal Bhutan Airlines** flies from Paro, Bhutan.

REGULAR FARES   Nepal is about as far away from North America as you can get; consequently it is expensive to fly there. If you have a few days to spare, you can usually schedule a stop in Europe or Southeast Asia at no extra cost, which is a nice bonus for flying so far and spending so much money. Keep in mind that tickets to Nepal have been getting steadily more expensive over the past few years, and you will probably avoid the next rate hike by paying for your ticket as far in advance as possible.

Advance-Purchase Excursion Fares (APEX) These are the lowest regular airfares and usually have restrictions on when you can fly and how far in advance you must pay for your ticket. APEX fares usually carry stiff penalties for cancellation, and departure dates may not be changed after paying for your ticket. However, for these restrictions, you can save several hundred dollars over the regular economy airfare. At press time an APEX fare was between $1,500 and $1,800 from either the East or West Coast of the United States.

Coach Coach fares are full-price tickets with no advance-purchase requirement. The tickets are refundable, and you can change your date of departure. However, these two slight advantages over an APEX fare do not outweigh the great cost difference that often applies. Currently full coach fares are around $3,800 from the West Coast and slightly more from the East Coast.

Business Class You get slightly larger seats, better meals, and more attentive service in business class, which might be just what you want on such a long trip. Currently business-class fares are between $4,000 and $4,500 from the West Coast and $500 to $1,200 *more* from the East Coast.

First Class If you need a large seat, gourmet meals, and personal service, you are going to pay considerably more on a flight to Nepal. At press time first-class seats from the West Coast were going for between $7,000 and $7,750; add $300 to $1000 more from the East Coast.

BUCKET SHOPS Bucket shops are discount ticket brokers who sell airline tickets at reduced prices. You can find ads for ticket companies in the travel sections of major-city newspapers. Their ads are usually just a list of destinations with prices accompanied by a name and a phone number. Pay attention to the fine print at the bottom of the ad. The list of prices is usually just a come-on and does not include numerous taxes and surcharges. However, when all the additional charges are added in, these tickets are often cheaper than what you will get by going directly to the airlines. On my last trip to Nepal, a bucket shop in San Francisco got me a ticket on Thai Airways that was almost $400 less than the lowest regular airfare. I have also booked tickets with companies in New York and Portland, Oregon, at equivalent savings. At press time, West Coast bucket shops were selling tickets for $1,250 to $1,450 from West Coast cities to Nepal.

Bucket-shop tickets are often nonrefundable or carry a $100 penalty for cancellation, and initial departure dates cannot be changed once the ticket is issued. Because of the limited number of such low-cost tickets, it is important to make reservations as much as six months in advance if you are planning a trip in the busy October-November trekking season.

THE CHEAP AIRLINES For flights into Nepal from Asian cities, there are a couple of cheap airlines frequently flown by budget travelers. **Biman Bangladesh Airlines** and **PIA** (Pakistan International Airlines, ☎ 800/221-2552) consistently offer lower-priced tickets, and both of these airlines fly to Europe as well.

BY BUS

It is possible to take a deluxe bus from Delhi, India, to Kathmandu. The trip takes 36 hours, but at only $25 for the whole trip, the price can't be beat (unless you take slower regular buses). The best place to find out about these buses is at the travel agencies around Connaught Place in New Delhi. This is a budget travelers' neighborhood, and numerous travel agencies sell tickets on these buses. There are six official border crossings with India, and at all of these there are usually Nepali buses to meet you. However, wherever you happen to cross the border, you still have a long and bumpy ride to Kathmandu or Pokhara. It is also possible to travel from Lhasa overland by bus or truck to the Nepal border crossing at Kodari. From here you can catch a Nepali bus for onward travel to Kathmandu. This trip takes from three days to one week.

PACKAGE TOURS

There are few package tours that go only to Nepal, unless they also happen to include a bit of trekking, rafting, or a jungle safari. If you simply want to do a bit of sightseeing and admire the Himalayas from afar, then you will probably have to visit Nepal as part of an India-Nepal tour. These tours are offered by quite a few companies, and your local travel agent should be able to find out about different tours best for you. Among the most reliable companies offering tours that include Nepal in the itinerary are the following.

IN THE U.S.A.

Abercrombie & Kent, 1520 Kensington Rd., Oak Brook, IL 60521-2141 (☎ 708/954-2944 or 800/323-7308).

Esplanade/Swan Hellenic, 581 Boylston St., Boston, MA 02116 (☎ 617/266-7465 or 800/426-5492).

Sita World Travel, Inc., 8127 San Fernando Rd., Sun Valley, CA 91352 (☎ 818/767-0039 or 800/421-5643).

Smithsonian Institution, Study Tours and Seminars, 1100 Jefferson Dr. SW, MRC 702, Washington, DC 20560 (☎ 202/357-4700; fax 202/633-9250).

Tours of Distinction, 5530 Wisconsin Ave., Suite 615, Chevy Chase, MD 20815 (☎ 301/215-9272 or 800/888-8634).

IN THE U.K.

Abercrombie & Kent, Sloane Square House, Holbein Place, London SW1W 8NS (☎ 071/730-9600; fax 071/730-9376).

Encounter Overland Expeditions Ltd., 267 Old Brompton Rd., London SW5 9JA (☎ 071/370-6845; fax 071/244-9737).

Explore Worldwide Ltd., 1 Frederick St., Aldershot, Hampshire GU11 1LQ (☎ 01252/319448; fax 01252/343170).

Twickers World, 22 Church St., Twickenham TW1 3NW (☎ 081/892-7606; fax 081/892-8061).

8 Getting Around

BY PLANE

Until a few years ago, Royal Nepal Airlines (RNAC), the national carrier, was the only airline operating in Nepal. RNAC was legendary for its inefficiency, and a trip to their office in Kathmandu was often a Kafkaesque nightmare. However, there is now plenty of competition from three airlines that fly to most of the destinations to which RNAC flies. It is easiest to make flight reservations through a travel agency in Kathmandu, but should you wish to contact an airline directly, here is the information. **RNAC,** corner of New Road and Kantipath (☎ 977/1-220757 or 977/1-226574); **Nepal Airways,** Maharajgunj (☎ 977/1-418494 or 977/1-418495); **Everest Air,** Durbar Marg (☎ 977/1-222290 or 977/1-228392); and **Necon Air,** Kamal Pokhari, Lal Durbar (☎ 977/1-418608). It is not usually possible for a foreign travel agent to book domestic flights. If you want to book a domestic flight before your arrival in Nepal, try contacting a Kathmandu travel agent such as **Natraj Tours & Travel,** Ghantaghar (☎ 977/1-225532), or **Nepal Travel Agency,** Ramshahpath (☎ 977/1-413188 or 977/1-412899). If you are unable to make a reservation before arriving in Nepal, do so as soon after your arrival as possible, especially in the busy months of October and November, when all the domestic flights get booked up quickly.

The most popular flights are those between Kathmandu and Pokhara ($61 one way). Also popular are flights to Lukla ($83 one-way) near Mt. Everest, bypassing a week's trekking. The flight to Jomosom from Pokhara ($50 one way) is another flight popular with trekkers who don't have much time or who prefer not to backtrack to Pokhara. Other flights used by trekkers include Kathmandu to Tumlingtar ($44 one way) and Kathmandu to Jumla ($127 one way). Those visitors headed to Chitwan National Park can fly into Bharatpur ($50 one way) or Meghauli ($72 one-way).

Flight schedules in Nepal change frequently, and flights are often canceled due to bad weather, especially in early October when the monsoon is still lingering. It is very common for flights out of Lukla to be canceled for several days in a row. This is one of the times when it is helpful to be on an organized trek; these groups generally have more clout and get on the planes before independent trekkers. Keep this in mind if you are planning to go trekking in the Everest region. Try not to make any reservations for a week after your scheduled return flight from Lukla just in case weather and a logjam of trekkers forces you to walk out or sit in Lukla for several days.

On several routes into the mountains, **helicopters** are now the preferred mode of travel because they can fly lower and slower than fixed-wing airplanes and in worse weather. This means that if you are scheduled to fly out of a remote mountain airstrip and cloudy weather sets in, you are more likely to get out on time if you have a reservation on a chopper. Helicopter flights from Kathmandu are offered by **Asian Airlines,** Bhatbhateni (☎ 977/1-417753), and **Nepal Airways,** Hattisar, Kamal Pokhari (☎ 977/1-418214). Both airlines fly to Lukla ($90 one way), Shyangboche ($120 one way), and Phaphlu ($80 one way).

BY BUS

In Nepal if there is a road, it is served by a bus or some other vehicle carrying paying passengers. Buses in Nepal are slow, crowded, cramped, dirty, smoky, decrepit, and frequently break down. The roads are potholed, winding, and frequently closed by landslides. This combination makes for some of the hardest traveling in the world. You might get the impression that I don't like traveling by bus in Nepal, and you are absolutely correct. If you can afford to avoid the buses, by all means do so. If your budget requires you to travel by bus, at least try to take the better buses when possible. There are several "deluxe tourist coaches" operating between Kathmandu and Pokhara. Any hotel or travel agency in either city will make a reservation on one of these buses. They are slightly more expensive than the regular bus service ($3 instead of $1.50), but they offer more legroom, wider seats, and take fewer hours to cover the 200 kilometers (say 7 or 8 instead of 10 or 12).

Regular buses throughout Nepal are incredibly cheap. You can get a 16-hour ride for less than $2 (although you will only cover 125 miles).

All local buses in Nepal make frequent tea stops at filthy roadside teahouses. Due to the lack of hygiene at these places, I don't recommend eating anything that doesn't come wrapped, bottled, or inside a peel (bananas and mandarins). These truckstops usually do not have any toilets other than the nearest bushes. I always bring my own snacks and a bottle of water when traveling by bus, and you'd be wise to do the same.

Trekkers will find that newer roads leading up into the mountains to trailheads are often served only by jeeps and trucks. These vehicles are always overloaded and can be extremely uncomfortable. If you have the time to take an alternative walking route, I recommend that you do so.

BY TAXI

Taxis, usually old Toyotas with a roof light, are plentiful in Kathmandu and Pokhara. In Kathmandu you'll find taxis waiting outside major hotels, around tourist sights, and around Thamel and Durbar Marg. In Pokhara they are easier to find at the bus station, the airport when planes are arriving, and in the Lakeside neighborhood. Taxi drivers will usually solicit your business, or you can flag them down. In Kathmandu taxis have meters, but it is almost impossible to get the taxi drivers to use them. In Pokhara, there are no meters. The bottom line is that you will have to bargain. For a price, taxis will take you from Kathmandu to Pokhara or vice versa. If you can get three people together, this can be a cost-effective way to travel between the two cities. It is faster than the bus and less expensive than by plane. To hire a taxi, car, or minivan to take you to Pokhara will cost between $60 and $80.

BY CAR

Rentals There are no self-drive car rentals in Nepal. All cars are rented with a driver, which has two benefits: You don't have to deal with the chaotic driving of Nepali bus, truck, and taxi drivers, and you can enjoy the amazing scenery. Almost every hotel, no matter whether it is a budget guesthouse or a deluxe hotel, will be able to arrange a hired car (or taxi) and driver for you. Rates don't vary much. In Kathmandu there is one rate for trips within the valley (Rs1,200 to Rs1,500; $24 to $30) and another for trips outside the valley (Rs2,000 to Rs3,500; $40 to $70). Be sure to find out whether gasoline is included when hiring a car. This is one of the only areas that varies from one car rental to another.

Gasoline Called petrol in Nepal, gasoline was selling for around $2.35 per gallon at press time. Because the price is so high, you may be expected to pay for gasoline when you hire a car and driver or taxi for a day or more.

Driving Rules In Nepal, as in India and other countries influenced by the British Empire, you drive on the left-hand side of the road with the steering wheel on the right. However, there are a few trucks and buses on the road with left-hand drive. These vehicles are usually marked as such to give other drivers a warning. Since you won't be driving yourself, most driving rules are of no concern. However, one rule bears mentioning. Do not hit a cow! Should you rent a motorcycle, this could be very important to you. Cows are sacred, and there are stiff jail sentences for anyone convicted of hurting or killing a cow in Nepal. And cows, for some reason, love to sleep in the middle of roads!

SUGGESTED ITINERARIES

Highlights

The following in order of importance are the main tourist destinations in Nepal.

- Kathmandu/Patan
- Bhaktapur
- Chitwan National Park
- Pokhara
- Nagarkot
- Dhulikhel
- Gorkha
- Lumbini

If You Have 1 Week

Days 1–3   Explore the Kathmandu Valley, including Bhaktapur, Patan, Boudha, and either Dhulikhel or Nagarkot. Stay in Kathmandu or Patan.

Days 4–6   Ride elephants and search for rhinos, tigers, and bears at Chitwan National Park. Stay at one of the many lodges in or near the park. Proceed to Pokhara on day 6.

Day 7   Explore Pokhara, returning to Kathmandu the next morning in time to catch a departing flight.

If You Have 2 Weeks

Days 1–7   See above.

Days 8–13   Take a 6-day trek out of Pokhara.

Day 14   Rest in Pokhara before returning to Kathmandu.

If You Have 3 Weeks

Days 1–7   See above.

Days 8–19   Take a 12-day trek based on your abilities and interests (Jomosom and the Everest region are two good choices).

Days 20–21   Rest in Pokhara before returning to Kathmandu.

FAST FACTS: Nepal

American Express   Nepal's only American Express office (☎ 977/1-226172) is in Kathmandu in front of the Hotel Mayalu, just around the corner from the south end of Durbar Marg on the road that leads to Kantipath.

Bookstores   In both Kathmandu and Pokhara, there are dozens of bookstores selling English-language books.

Business Hours   Banks: Sunday to Thursday 10am to 2:30pm in summer (10am to 2pm in winter), Friday 10am to 12:30pm; bars: closing time is 10pm or midnight; offices: Sunday to Thursday 10am to 5pm in summer (10am to 4pm in winter), Friday 10am to 3pm; stores: daily 10am to 7pm (tourist shops often stay open later). Many businesses and some shops close for an hour at lunch.

Camera and Film   Though it will cost you a bit more, most types of film are available in Kathmandu. Before coming to Nepal you might invest in a polarizing filter if your camera will accept one. At high altitudes and in snowy areas, a polarizer will eliminate glare, make blues richer, and reduce contrast. Before heading out on the trail be sure you have an extra battery (available in Kathmandu). When departing Nepal through Tribhuvan International Airport it is important to remember that the X-ray machines used on checked baggage are *not* film-safe.

Cigarettes   Imported cigarettes from the United States are available for about Rs100 ($2) per pack. Locally made cigarettes are about Rs25 (50¢) per pack.

Climate   See "When to Go," above in this chapter.

Crime   See "Safety," below.

Currency   See "Information, Entry Requirements & Money," above in this chapter.

Customs   See "Information, Entry Requirements & Money," above in this chapter.

Documents Required   See "Information, Entry Requirements & Money," above in this chapter.

Driving Rules   See "Getting Around," above in this chapter.

Drug Laws   Though marijuana and hashish were once legal in Nepal, today you can be jailed for possession of even small amounts. Many drugs that are available only by prescription in the West are available over the counter in Nepal, and you can save a substantial amount of money by purchasing anything you need for a first-aid kit here instead of at home.

Drugstores   Known as pharmacies, chemists, and dispensaries, drugstores in Nepal are usually tiny shops stocked floor to ceiling with boxes and bottles. Tell the proprietor what you need, and he will get it for you.

Electricity   The current in Nepal is 220 volts/50 cycles, and is not very reliable. There are regular blackouts in Kathmandu.

Embassies and Consulates   If you lose your passport or have some such emergency, the consulate can usually handle your individual needs. An embassy is more often concerned with matters of state between Nepal and the home country. **U.S. Embassy,** Pani Pokhari, Maharajgunj (north of Thamel on an extension of Kantipath), Kathmandu (☎ 977/1-411179 or 977/1-412718); **British Embassy** (handles Canadian and New Zealand citizens also), Lainchaur, Lazimpat (on the road to the left of the Hotel Ambassador, which is north of Thamel on an extension of Kantipath), Kathmandu (☎ 977/1-410583 or 977/1-414588); **Australian Embassy,** Bansbari (north of Ring Road on an extension of Maharajgunj), Kathmandu (☎ 977/1-411578).

Emergencies   See the individual chapters for phone numbers to call in the event of an emergency. Since medical facilities in Nepal are far below Western standards, most Westerners who need major medical attention fly to Bangkok or Singapore.

Etiquette   It is customary to remove one's shoes before entering a Nepali household or temple. You should walk clockwise around Buddhist temples, stupas, mani walls, and chortens. Many Hindu temples are off-limits to non-Hindus. When giving or receiving something, use your right hand or both hands. It is also customary to eat with your right hand only. Do not point your finger or your feet at people or religious objects. Do not throw garbage in cooking fires, which are considered sacred. Do not offer a Hindu a bite of food if you have already taken a bite yourself. Likewise do not touch food that is meant for someone else.

Gasoline   See "Getting Around," above in this chapter.

Hitchhiking   See "Getting Around," above in this chapter.

Holidays   See "When to Go," above in this chapter.

Information   See "Information, Entry Requirements & Money," above in this chapter and the Kathmandu and Pokhara chapters for local information offices.

Language   Though Nepali is the national language, more than a dozen other languages are spoken. The *Nepal Phrasebook* published by Lonely Planet is a useful and readily available phrasebook.

Laundry   There are no self-service laundries in Nepal and few washing machines. Laundry is done by hand in rivers and at bathing fountains. Nearly all hotels offer laundry service.

Legal Aid   Your embassy or consulate can provide you with a list of local attorneys and information on Nepali laws. Embassies cannot, however, get you out of jail if you have broken a Nepali law.

Liquor Laws   Liquor laws are lax in Nepal. If you look old enough, you'll get served.

Mail   Letters take anywhere from two to six weeks to get to the United States; a postcard to the United States costs Rs10 (20¢), and letters start at Rs13 (26¢). You can get stamps at post offices, bookshops, and often at hotel reception desks, though you'll pay a little extra at the latter two. There are main post offices in Kathmandu and Pokhara offering all services, and even in small towns and villages you will usually find a post office or someone who acts as the local postal agent. Though there are mailboxes in major cities, they should not be used; always take your letters and cards to the post office, and make sure that the stamps are canceled. Otherwise you run the risk that someone might remove the stamps from your letters. Parcels can only be shipped from the Foreign Post Office in Kathmandu (adjacent to the G.P.O.). To ship a package from Nepal, you must show your passport, have your package inspected by Customs, and then have the package sealed. This all takes time and money at every step. In fact you will have to buy an empty cardboard box to put your package in and then have it sealed in muslin. It is much easier and only slightly more expensive to let a reliable shipping agent take care of your shipping. There is a 20-kilogram (44-pound) limit per package. Sea mail takes at least 3 months, while airmail takes from two to six weeks.

Maps   Bookshops in Kathmandu and Pokhara have a wide variety of maps in a range of prices. For Kathmandu and Pokhara, the yellow maps are the best. The tourist office in Kathmandu sometimes has free Nepal and Kathmandu maps available, and the tourist information center in Pokhara hands out free maps to that city. The best trekking maps are the German-made Schneider maps; however, these are expensive and hard to find in Kathmandu. But they may be available from a good map store in your home country. The best commonly available trekking maps are those of the Nepa Maps series, which are designed by an Italian mapmaker. These maps are only slightly more expensive than other maps and are readily available in bookshops in the Thamel district of Kathmandu.

Newspapers and Magazines   *The Rising Nepal* and *The Kathmandu Post* are Nepal's English-language daily newspapers and cover international and national news. *Nepal Travellers'* is a very informative monthly English-language magazine for tourists. In addition, the *International Herald Tribune* and *USA Today* are available daily. Asian editions of *Time* and *Newsweek* are also available. You'll find that their news coverage varies slightly from their U.S. editions.

Passports   See "Information, Entry Requirements & Money," above in this chapter.

Pets   Rabies is rampant in Nepal, and for this reason it is best that you leave your pet home.

Police   Police are rarely in evidence outside cities in Nepal. Should you need the police while traveling between cities, go to the nearest town or village and ask for the local police officer (who will likely not speak English).

Radio and TV   There is only one television station and one radio station in Nepal. English-language news is broadcast over the radio at 8am and 8pm, and over the TV at 9:40pm daily. However, satellite cable television is now available at many hotels.

Restrooms   You won't find many public restrooms in Nepal. To the Nepali people the entire world is one giant public toilet, and you are expected to follow suit. This can be very inconvenient for women when there is no convenient shrubbery to hide behind. I suggest always wearing a long skirt when traveling long distances by bus or car. This will provide a semblance of modesty should you need to relieve yourself en route. In cities such as Kathmandu and Pokhara, there are toilets in all restaurants and in the lobbies of more expensive hotels. The Nepali word for toilet is *charpi,* and in English you should ask for the toilet, not the restroom.

Safety   Nepal is relatively safe. However, the crime rate has been rising in recent years. Therefore, you should never trek alone. Take extra precautions with your valuables when traveling on crowded buses where you are easy prey to pickpockets. I suggest always keeping your money (preferably traveler's checks), passport, and airline tickets in a moneybelt or neck bag worn under your clothes. Try to avoid displaying large amounts of money in public. Also, backpacks and items from backpacks do sometimes get stolen off bus roofs (especially on the bus to Jiri). Make sure your bag is securely fastened to the luggage rack, and don't leave anything of value in it.

Taxes   Hotels in Nepal charge a different percentage of tax on room rates depending on the number of stars the hotel has been given by the Hotel Association of Nepal. Hotels with no stars charge 10%, one-star hotels charge 11%, two-star hotels charge 12%, three-star hotels charge 13%, four-star hotels charge 14%, and five-star hotels charge 15%. The tax on meals served in restaurants is 10% unless the restaurant is in a hotel. In this case meals are also taxed based on the number of stars the hotel has. There is a Rs700 ($14) international departure tax levied at the airport.

Telephone, Telex, and Fax   The telephone system in Nepal is surprisingly good. The dial tone is a bit lower and softer than that heard on U.S. telephones, but otherwise it is similar. Rapid beeps mean that the line is busy. In Kathmandu, all phone numbers now have six digits; in Pokhara they have five digits. Elsewhere the number may be less than five digits. When dialing Nepal from another country, you must dial the country code (977) and the city code (Kathmandu—1; Pokhara—61), and then your number. When dialing long distance within Nepal, you must first dial zero, then the city code, and then the number you are trying to reach. Many hotels now offer international direct dialing. For the international operator and for making collect calls, dial 186.

Time   Nepal is one of the few countries in the world that does not base its clock on an even-hour difference from Greenwich mean time. Instead, Nepal takes its time from the number of hours and minutes difference there are between Greenwich and Kathmandu. Thus the country is 5 hours and 45 minutes ahead of Greenwich mean time, 10 hours and 45 minutes ahead of eastern standard time, and 15 minutes ahead of India. Nepal is 1 hour and 15 minutes behind Thailand, 2 hours and 15 minutes behind China (except between April and September, when it is 3 hours and 15 minutes behind).

Tipping   Tipping was not common in Nepal until introduced by Western tourists, and still it is only done in hotels and restaurants frequented primarily by tourists. Airport porters expect Rs20 to Rs25 (40¢ to 50¢); hotel staff (in more expensive hotels), Rs5 to Rs10 (10¢ to 20¢) per day (look for a tip box on the reception desk); waiters, 10% (but only in expensive restaurants such as those at luxury hotels); service personnel, 10%; taxi drivers, nothing.

Tourist Offices   See "Information, Entry Requirements & Money," above in this chapter and also the Kathmandu and Pokhara chapters.

Visas   See "Information, Entry Requirements & Money," above in this chapter.

Water   Water in Nepal is not safe to drink unless purified in some way. See "Health, Insurance & Other Concerns," above in this chapter for details.

Yellow Pages   There are no yellow pages per se in Nepal, and even if there were, it would be in the Devanagri script of the written Nepali language. There are, however, a couple of telephone directories that can usually be found at hotel reception desks.

3 Introducing Kathmandu

To arrive in Kathmandu at dusk on the night of a power outage is to enter a world apart. With the sunset painting the snowy tips of distant Himalayan peaks in shades of rose and mauve, oil lamps and candles begin to flicker in dark alleyways. Kathmandu is a city of alleyways leading into the unknown, and in the darkness of a night without power, the magic and mystery are magnified. Strange odors—a mélange of incense, cow dung, and rotting garbage—drift through the dank streets. Eerie discordant music—a tinny jangling of cymbals, the drone of a harmonium, the pulse of drums—fills a nearly deserted square. The musicians sit hunched over their ancient instruments on the floor of a tiny temple. In the market, vendors swaddled in woolen shawls place candles in their baskets of mandarins and radishes. In the darkness, it is easy to stumble over cows sleeping contentedly in the streets.

Kathmandu has been called a medieval city, and it is hard not to think of it as such. The streets are narrow and in the oldest parts of town, there is little traffic (though the few cars and motorcycles that venture into these ancient alleys make frequent use of their horns). People do the heavy work here, not vehicles. They carry heavy-laden baskets on their backs or slung from poles across their shoulders. The streets are filled with garbage, often thrown from the balconies of precariously leaning brick buildings that are one, two, or even three hundred years old. In the daytime little light reaches the floor of old Kathmandu, where the balconied buildings nearly close out the sun.

For more than a hundred years Kathmandu was nearly completely cut off from the outside world by a government that wished to keep the country isolated. When the royal family was restored to power in the mid-1950s, Nepal opened its borders to the world, and the painful process of entering the 20th century began. Today Kathmandu has much of the Western world's technological advances and many of its environmental and social woes. There are cars and computers, facsimile machines and factories. There are also smog and a heroin problem, traffic congestion, and deforestation. However, with the help of developed nations in the West, Nepal is working to overcome these problems. Kathmandu is certainly no Shangri-La, but it *is* one of the world's most fascinating cities, nonetheless.

1 Orientation

ARRIVING

BY PLANE   The **Tribhuvan International Airport** (☎ 977/1-470537) is located less than four miles east of downtown Kathmandu. When you arrive, the very first thing to do is to change money. Because Nepali rupees are not available outside of Nepal, you cannot avoid this step. Be sure to hang onto your receipt; you're probably going to need it later in your visit. Next, if you do not already have a visa, you must get one. It will cost you $15 for a 15-day visa. There should be visa application forms on the table behind the currency exchange counter. You'll also find embarkation cards on this table; you'll have to fill out one of these also if you did not already do so on the plane.

When you have completed these formalities, proceed downstairs to baggage pickup. Customs will then inspect your bag. You must have all your bags, even carry-on bags, marked with a piece of chalk before you can leave the terminal.

Just through the doors after passing through Customs, you will be assaulted by taxi drivers, hotel touts, and porters. A tout, for those who have never encountered one, is a person who is paid on a commission basis to take you to a particular hotel, shop, taxi, or wherever. Be prepared. Know how you want to get into town and what hotel you are going to before you step through the airport door.

If you can fend off the touts and porters for a few minutes, you can visit the tourist information desk and pick up a free Kathmandu map and other tourist brochures. If you don't have a room reservation, the folks here will call around for you.

There are only two alternatives for getting into town from the airport. You can try to get a taxi at the official rate of Rs100 ($2), though you are likely to have to pay more than this, or you can walk down to the main road and cram yourself into one of the overcrowded public buses that pass by the entrance to the airport. I highly recommend taking a taxi.

Should you choose to take a taxi to the airport when you leave Kathmandu, be aware that most taxi drivers refuse to use their meters. If you can, by some strange fluke, get one to use his meter, it will cost around Rs75 ($1.50) to the airport. If you can negotiate a price of Rs100 ($2), you'll be doing well.

If you know where you will be staying, write, fax, or phone the hotel to let them know when you will be arriving, and they will gladly send a taxi, car, or van to pick you up. Likewise, when departing ask first at your hotel if they offer airport taxi service. Some hotels offer this service free of charge, while others charge slightly more than a regular taxi.

BY BUS   Dozens of different bus lines operate in Nepal, though if you are arriving in Kathmandu for the first time by bus, you are probably coming from either India or Pokhara. If coming from India, your bus will more than likely let you off at the new bus station north of Thamel on the Ring Road. From the new bus station it's a 10-minute taxi ride to Thamel or Durbar Marg.

If you happen to be coming into town on a tourist bus from either Pokhara or Chitwan, you will likely be let off at the intersection of Kantipath and Tridevi Marg. The latter street leads into Thamel.

BY CAR   The likelihood that you will be arriving in Kathmandu by car is slight, unless you happen to be living in India or another part of Nepal. The road from

What's Special About Kathmandu

Living Gods
- The Kumari is venerated as a living goddess.
- The king of Nepal is considered an incarnation of the Hindu god Vishnu.

Natural Spectacles
- The Himalayas, the highest mountain range in the world, can be glimpsed from many parts of the city.
- Nagarkot and Dhulikel, villages on the rim of the Kathmandu Valley, afford stunning panoramas of the Himalayas.

Architectural Highlights
- Durbar Square has dozens of temples of all different sizes.
- There are equally rich Durbar Squares in Patan and Bhaktapur.

Hindu Temples
- Pashupatinath is the holiest Hindu temple in Nepal.
- Nyatapola Temple in Bhaktapur is the most beautiful pagoda temple in Nepal.

Buddhist Temples
- Boudhanath Stupa is the largest stupa in Nepal.
- Swayambunath Stupa is said to have been built more than 2,000 years ago.

Shopping
- Carpets, curios, and outrageous fashions are just some of the amazing buys in this shoppers' paradise.
- Patan's metalworkers produce exquisite figures of Buddhist and Hindu deities.

Great Neighborhoods
- Kathmandu's old city, surrounding Durbar Square, is an area of medieval streets and Eastern temples and shrines.
- The area around Boudhanath Stupa is filled with Tibetan Buddhist monasteries.

Great Nearby Towns
- Patan, once a separate kingdom, has its own Durbar Square that is almost as richly endowed with temples as Kathmandu's.
- Bhaktapur, another former kingdom with its own Durbar Square, is the most medieval city in the Kathmandu Valley.

Offbeat Oddities
- There is a toothache god in Kathmandu—an old tree stump that over the years has had thousands of coins nailed to it to relieve toothaches.
- Every Saturday and Tuesday there are animal sacrifices at the temple of Dakshinkali on the edge of the Kathmandu Valley.

Pokhara and India comes into town from the west by way of Kalimati and Tripureswor. To reach Thamel and Durbar Marg, turn left at the traffic circle in front of the National Stadium. Should you be coming from Tibet, you will come into town on Baneswor, which will eventually lead you to the Tundikhel, a large open field in the town center. On the far side of the Tundikhel, turn right on Kantipath. When you come to a small lake on your right, take the next right and then the first left to reach Durbar Marg. To reach Thamel, continue past the lake for one long block and turn left.

TOURIST INFORMATION

The **Department of Tourism** operates two information centers in Kathmandu: at the airport (☎ 977/1-470537) and just off Durbar Square on New Road (☎ 977/1-220818). They are both open Sunday to Friday from 10am to 5pm (4pm in the winter). You are more likely to find brochures and maps at the airport information desk, though the downtown office does manage to have brochures during the peak seasons. Either of these desks can help you with general questions, but for more specific questions on times and prices and such, you'll do better to ask questions at your hotel or at a tour agency.

CITY LAYOUT

MAIN ARTERIES & STREETS   There are two distinct sections to Kathmandu—old Kathmandu and new Kathmandu. Old Kathmandu is a maze of narrow streets and even narrower alleys. The best way to get around in old Kathmandu is on foot. Not even a bicycle is very successful at negotiating these crowded streets. New Kathmandu, on the other hand, consists of many wide avenues, most of which are one-way.

At the center of things is **Ratna Park** and the **Tundikhel,** a vast expanse of grass that is used primarily as a military parade ground. A small part, however, is used by the general public, including grazing goats, children flying kites, and teenagers playing soccer. The Tundikhel is divided by only a few streets and, consequently, it is difficult to get from one side to the other. Down the east side of this green area runs an extension of **Durbar Marg,** the city's upscale shopping street. The extension has no name as far as I know and is one-way heading south for nearly a mile without any way of getting to the other side of the Tundikhel. On the opposite side of the Tundikhel, with northbound one-way traffic is **Kantipath.** Farther to the north Kantipath becomes **Lazimpat.** About midway up the Tundikhel on Kantipath, **New Road** comes off to the west and continues for half a mile to **Durbar Square.** The famous **Freak Street** is to the left just before you get to Durbar Square.

This is the heart of old Kathmandu, and streets here rarely have names and are never marked. The road that angles toward the northeast from Durbar Square starts out being called **Makhan** and then begins changing names every block as it becomes the main market street of Kathmandu. This road terminates at Kantipath. If you angle to the left at the first intersection north of Durbar Square, you will be on a nameless road that leads to the **Thamel** neighborhood. From the main square (really just an intersection) in Thamel, **Trideyi Marg** leads east to the top of Durbar Marg.

Circling the two cities of Kathmandu and Patan is a ring road. From this ring road, main roads lead off to other towns and cities. The road to Bhaktapur, Dhulikhel, Nagarkot, Tibet, and Jiri (trailhead for the Everest trek) begins in the southeast corner of the city. The road to Pokhara and Chitwan National Park starts in the southwest part of the city. The road to Budhanilkantha is an extension of Lazimpat, which is an extension of Kantipath. The road to Boudhanath begins in the northeast corner of the city, and the road to Balaju, Kakani, and Trisuli Bazaar begins in the northwest.

   Finding an Address   In most of Kathmandu, there are no street addresses; in fact, most streets aren't even named. If you look at a business address, you will see what appears to be a street name, and it may be just that, but it could refer to an entire neighborhood. Thamel is a good example of this. I have never figured out if there is an actual Thamel street, but Thamel is the address given for dozens of hotels, restaurants, and businesses located on different streets all over this tourist neighborhood. In places where a street does have a name, it might change every block. More often than not you will be given the general vicinity a business is in, and it will be up to you to keep asking directions as you get closer to your destination. To help you out, I have tried to refer to easily recognizable reference points when locating a hotel, restaurant, or shop.

   Street Maps   The tourist information desk at the airport hands out free maps of Kathmandu. This is the same yellow **Kathmandu/Patan** map for sale at every bookshop in Kathmandu for about Rs25 (50¢) and is the best map of the city.

NEIGHBORHOODS IN BRIEF

   Thamel   This is Kathmandu's primary budget-accommodations neighborhood, and nearly every street is lined with interesting shops, trekking agents, and cheap hotels and restaurants. It begins one block west of Kantipath on Tridevi Marg near the Department of Immigration. From Jyatha on the south to Lekhnath Marg on the north and over to Paknajol on the west is all considered Thamel, though the neighborhood seems to extend its boundaries every year.

   Durbar Marg   This is Kathmandu's upscale shopping and hotel street. You'll find expensive restaurants, deluxe hotels, and shops selling Tibetan antiques and fine Nepali handcrafts. This is also where many airline offices are located. Durbar Marg begins at the gates of the Royal Palace.

   Durbar Square   The heart of old Kathmandu, Durbar Square is home to one of the greatest concentrations of temples, shrines, and old palaces anywhere in the world, and by day it is overrun with tourists, taxis, curio sellers, and cycle rickshaws. It is at the western end of New Road, which has its start at the Tundikhel.

   Freak Street   Well known in the days when Kathmandu was the hippie capital of the world, Freak Street is no longer the budget traveler's main lodging area in Kathmandu. However, there are still shops and very cheap guesthouses lining this street just off Basantapur Square, which is just east of Durbar Square.

   Lazimpat   This is Kathmandu's embassy row and one of the city's upscale residential neighborhoods. There are several good hotels located here. Lazimpat is a continuation of Kantipath, which runs up the west side of the Tundikhel and Ratna Park.

   Kupondole   This is another of the city's upscale neighborhoods and is across the Bagmati River on the edge of Patan. There are a few hotels here as well as private residences, and the views of the mountains are excellent. Kupondole is west of Kandevta, the main road from Kathmandu to Patan.

   Patan (Lalitpur)   Though it is actually a separate city, Patan, which is also known as Lalitpur, is divided from Kathmandu only by the Bagmati River. Patan has its own Durbar Square and old city area, as well as the Patan Industrial Estate and the Tibetan Refugee Camp. The city is known for its metalworkers, and their shops abound in the area near the Temple of 1,000 Buddhas.

2 Getting Around

BY PUBLIC TRANSPORTATION

BY BUS   Public buses in Kathmandu, with the exception of the electric buses to Bhaktapur, are best avoided. There are two types of public buses: full-size blue buses and minibuses of different colors running the same routes. However, they are all rolling sardine cans, especially the minibuses, which are built for people with an average height of about five foot, two inches. It is nearly impossible to get a seat on one of these buses. Even a short ride can be a traumatic experience. They are, however, very cheap (less than 10¢). The electric buses to Bhaktapur, on the other hand, are rarely crowded except in rush hour. These buses leave from just east of the traffic circle near the National Stadium. They are about the same price as the regular bus.

BY TAXI   Taxis can be found in front of all major hotels, in Thamel, and along Durbar Marg, among other places. They are easily hailed on any major street. Though taxis do have meters, it is almost impossible to get taxi drivers to use them. You will be forced to bargain for the price of a ride. Be sure to settle on a price before getting into the cab. Whatever price the taxi driver asks, offer about half. The price you settle on will still be above what you would pay on the meter, but there is not much you can do about this. If you should convince a driver to use his meter, you will almost certainly be taken on the most circuitous route to your destination. On my last visit, taxi drivers were asking as much as Rs250 ($5) from Thamel to the airport. On the meter, this trip would cost about Rs75 ($1.50), and in an official airport taxi into town from the airport, the fare would be Rs100 ($2). Rates go up after dark. Also most of the major hotels have their own private taxis, though these are more expensive than regular cabs.

If you aren't going too far, an alternative is to flag down a tempo. These are the three-wheeled windowless scooters that look a bit like giant black eggs. Tempo drivers are more likely to use their meters than taxi drivers but you must insist on it before getting in. A short trip across town will cost Rs10 to Rs20 (20¢ to 40¢). Tempos are not very spacious or comfortable, but for short trips they're fine. In some parts of town there are tempos that operate as minibuses on a fixed route. These tempos have two bench seats behind the driver and are not black.

BY CYCLE RICKSHAW   Though the traditional pulled-by-hand rickshaw long ago disappeared from most of Asia, the bicycle rickshaw is alive and well. For many people, riding in these human-powered vehicles is the essence of traveling in Asia. In Kathmandu, they are an excellent means of making short trips around the city's older neighborhoods. Because they are narrower than a taxi, they can negotiate many streets that a taxi would have difficulty getting through. A cycle rickshaw can carry two people and baggage (if the bags aren't too heavy). Rates are negotiable, and you must be sure to agree on the fare before getting in. Bargain hard—drivers know that tourists can pay more and charge accordingly. A trip between Durbar Square and Thamel will cost about Rs30 (60¢).

BY CAR   A car is not the way to get around Kathmandu. Most of the places you will want to visit are in areas that a car will not be able to go. However, if you want to make an excursion outside the city, say to Bhaktapur or Nagarkot, a car is a good idea. Regardless, you will not be doing the driving since there are no self-drive car rentals in Kathmandu. See "Getting Around" in Chapter 2 for more information.

Rentals There are many ways to rent a car and driver in Kathmandu. In Kathmandu, **Avis** is represented by Yeti Travels/American Express office (☎ 977/1-227635), at the Hotel Mayalu, which is around the corner to the west at the south end of Durbar Square. A car and driver for a 9-hour day will cost $66 to $83. **Natraj Tours & Travels,** Kamaladi, Durbar Marg (☎ 977/1-222014 or 977/1-220001), just off the south end of Durbar Marg past the traffic circle, also hires out cars and drivers. They charge around $20 for an 8-hour day within the Kathmandu Valley. In addition, almost any hotel, even those in the budget category, can arrange a car and driver for you at reasonable rates. Another option is simply to hire a taxi for the day. You should be able to get a taxi for around Rs900 to Rs1,200 ($18 to $24).

For trips outside the valley, expect to pay a bit more than the above-mentioned rates. You can hire a hotel car or van to drive you to Pokhara and back for around Rs4,000 ($80).

BY MOTORCYCLE For the young and adventurous, a motorcycle is a great way to see the Kathmandu Valley outside the city, in particular Nagarkot or Dhulikel. Just be sure you get helmets and have a functioning horn on the motorcycle. Also keep in mind that it is a criminal offense to injure a cow, and you are likely to encounter quite a few cows in the roads as you travel around the valley. **Moto de Location,** Narsing Gate, Thamel (☎ 977/1-225593 or 977/1-223569), right on the main square in Thamel, rents motorcycles for Rs350 to Rs550 ($7 to $11) per day. A tank full of gasoline will cost around Rs400 ($8).

BY BICYCLE Bicycles are one of the best and most popular ways of getting around Kathmandu and the rest of the valley. For only Rs30 (60¢) you can rent a single-speed bicycle made in either China or India. These sturdy bikes are lousy on hills, but the rest of the time they're fine. The most important thing to look for when renting a bicycle is a good bell. If the bell isn't loud and easy to ring, find another bike. Bells are the only way of clearing the streets in front of you. They work especially well on children playing in the street, but are totally ineffective in moving sleeping cows. If the bell is in good working order, check to see if other important features—such as the brakes—are functioning. Give the bike a test ride; if the seat isn't right, have it raised or lowered.

It is also possible to rent 10-, 12-, and 18-speed mountain bikes for Rs80 to Rs100 ($1.60 to $2). A few of these are quality Taiwanese or Japanese bikes, but the majority are less-than-rugged rip-offs from India. My wife prefers a mountain bike because its many gears make it easier to climb hills. However, few rental mountain bikes come with bells (no place to mount them), and consequently I deem them too dangerous.

If you are a regular cyclist at home, you should find Kathmandu a stimulating challenge. If you haven't been on a bike since you got your driver's license, you might find cycling in Kathmandu a terrifying experience. However, be assured that despite the chaotic appearances of traffic, drivers are looking out for you. Cows and children, however, couldn't care less.

ON FOOT In Kathmandu's old city, your feet are often the only feasible means of getting around. In the market area north of Durbar Square, the crowds of people are usually so dense that it is impossible to even get a bicycle through the streets. If you are in reasonably good health, you should be able to walk to most of the interesting sights in Kathmandu. From Durbar Marg or Thamel to Durbar Square is about a 20-minute walk. Swayambunath is a 30- to 45-minute walk.

Pashupatinath and Boudhanath are best visited by bicycle or some other means of transportation.

The streets of Kathmandu are rough, uneven, and often filled with garbage and cow dung. I suggest sturdy walking shoes.

FAST FACTS: Kathmandu

American Express   The American Express office (☎ 977/1-227635 or 977/1-226172) is located in front of the Hotel Mayalu just around the corner from Durbar Marg at the opposite end from the Royal Palace. Open Sunday to Friday from 10am to 5pm.

Babysitters   Major hotels in Kathmandu offer babysitting services, but other than that, you'll have to take the little ones with you.

Bookstores   Bookstores selling English-language books abound in Kathmandu, especially small shops selling secondhand books. Thamel has the greatest concentration of bookstores, followed by Freak Street. See "Shopping," in Chapter 4, for details.

Business Hours   See "Fast Facts: Nepal" in Chapter 2.

Car Rentals   See "Getting Around" in this chapter.

City Code   If you are calling Kathmandu from elsewhere in Nepal, the city code is 01. If calling from outside Nepal, drop the 0 and just dial 1.

Climate   See "When to Go" in Chapter 2.

Country Code   When phoning Kathmandu, or anywhere else in Nepal, from another country, it is necessary to first dial 977 (the country code), the city code (see above), and then the phone number.

Currency   See "Information, Entry Requirements & Money" in Chapter 2.

Currency Exchange   Officially you can change foreign currency only at a hotel, bank, or currency exchange office. Unofficially, a black market flourishes and offers a slightly higher rate, especially for large-denomination U.S. dollars. Changing money on the black market is, however, illegal, even though many people do so. Your hotel is likely to be the best place to change money, since there won't be a line, and you will get an official receipt.

The next best place to change money is at the currency exchange windows in Thamel. The few banks around town that do change money usually have long lines (it can take several hours to change money during the busy trekking season). Convenient banks include the Nepal Grindlay's Bank across from the Hotel Star in Thamel, the Nepal Bank on Kantipath, and the R. B. Bank currency-exchange window at the supermarket on the corner of New Road and Sukrapath (one block from Durbar Square). Banks are open Sunday to Thursday from 10am to 3pm (2:30pm in winter), and Friday from 10am to 1pm. The Kantipath bank is also open on Saturday from 9am to 1pm. Always be sure to get your receipt so you can change rupees back to foreign currency upon leaving Nepal. You will be allowed to change back only 15% of the money you converted into rupees.

Dentist   For the names of English-speaking dentists in Kathmandu, contact your embassy or consulate.

Doctor   For the names of English-speaking doctors, contact your embassy or consulate.

Drugstores   Drugstores in Kathmandu are known as chemists or pharmacies. They are usually little hole-in-the-wall places crammed with prescription medicines. Most drugs that you might need for your trekking first-aid kit are available here at much lower prices than in the United States and without a prescription. There are two on the corner of Kantipath at Rani Pokhari (the square pond with the temple on an island). More are located along New Road. If you are staying in Thamel, there is a pharmacy on the street leading north from Thamel's main square (where the taxis and rickshaws gather). There is another about a third of the way between Thamel and Durbar Square.

Embassies and Consulates   United States Embassy, Pani Pokhari (☎ 977/1-411179 or 977/1-412718), open Monday, Wednesday, and Friday from 2 to 4:30pm and Tuesday and Thursday from 8:30 to 11:30am; **British Embassy,** Lainchaur (☎ 977/1-414588 or 977/1-410583), open Monday to Friday from 9am to noon; **Australian Embassy,** Bansbari (☎ 977/1-411578), open Monday to Thursday from 10am to 12:30pm; **Indian Embassy,** Lainchaur (☎ 977/1-410900 or 977/1-414913), open Monday to Friday from 9am to 12:30pm; **Thai Embassy,** Jyoti Kendra Building, Thapathali (☎ 977/1-213910 or 977/1-213912), open Monday to Friday from 9am to 12:30pm; **People's Republic of China Embassy,** Baluwatar (☎ 977/1-411740), open Monday, Wednesday, and Friday from 10 to 11:30am.

Emergencies   Fire: ☎ 977/1-221177. **Police:** 977/1-226998 or 977/1-226999. **Ambulance:** 977/1-211959 or 977/1-228094.

Eyeglasses   Optic Palace, Jamal, Ranipokhari (☎ 977/1-226673), open Sunday to Friday from 10am to 7:30pm, can replace or repair your glasses in 2 or 3 days. It is a good idea to bring along a spare pair of eyeglasses to avoid the possibility that yours cannot be replaced. Contact lenses can be problematic if you are planning a long trek. Fingers tend to stay dirty, and the risk of eye infections is great.

Hairdressers and Barbers   There are barbers and women's hair salons at the Soaltee Holiday Inn Crowne Plaza, the Hotel de l'Annapurna, the Everest Hotel, and at the southern end of Durbar Marg (women only).

Holidays   See "When to Go" in Chapter 2.

Hospitals and Clinics   Should you become seriously ill while in Nepal, the recommended procedure is to get yourself to Bangkok or Singapore as quickly as possible. Both of these cities have many excellent hospitals where quality of care is equal to that in any Western hospital. If it is an emergency that precludes evacuation, then the next best choice is the Patan Hospital, Lagankhel, Patan (☎ 977/1-521034 or 977/1-522266), which is under the supervision of Western doctors. For less serious illnesses there are two excellent clinics: CIWEC, Durbar Morg near Hotel Yak & Yeti (☎ 977/1-228531), is staffed by American doctors and nurses and is open Monday to Friday from 9am to noon and 1 to 4pm; Nepal International Clinic, Naxal (☎ 977/1-412842), located a block and a half past the main entrance to the current Royal Palace, at the top of Durbar Marg, open daily from 9am to 5pm. The latter clinic is operated by a U.S. board-certified internist and is staffed by Westerners.

Information   See "Information, Entry Requirements & Money" in Chapter 2.

Laundry and Dry Cleaning   Your hotel is the place for having laundry or dry cleaning done, since there are no self-service laundries in Kathmandu. If your hotel doesn't offer dry cleaning services, try Band Box, Sukrapath (on New Road near Durbar Square). They're open Sunday to Friday from 9am to 8pm, and Saturday from 10am to 6pm. However, I don't recommend bringing any clothes that have to be dry cleaned; if you do, it's better to wait and have whatever it is cleaned back home.

Libraries   The British Council Library, Kantipath (☎ 977/1-223000), has current international publications. Open November 15 to February 14, Monday to Friday from 10am to 5pm; February 15 to November 14, Monday to Friday from 9:30am to 6pm.

Lost Property   Your only hope to recover lost items is to post notices in restaurants around town and hope that your lost item was recovered by another tourist who reads English. Should you need to report a lost or stolen wallet or purse to the police, try to get someone who speaks English and Nepali to go with you to the police station. Few police officers in Kathmandu speak English.

Luggage Storage   Virtually all hotels in Nepal offer luggage storage while you go off trekking. I have found that even in budget hotels items left in storage will be safe. Usually there is no charge for storing luggage.

Newspapers and Magazines   Kathmandu's English-language daily newspapers are the *Rising Nepal* and *The Kathmandu Post*. Both papers carry a surprising amount of international news, along with extensive national coverage. The *International Herald Tribune* and *USA Today* are available at bookstores and newsstands in Thamel, Freak Street, and at major hotels. Asian editions of *Time* and *Newsweek* are also available at the same locations.

Photographic Needs   Most common films, with the exception of Kodachrome, are readily available in Kathmandu at prices only slightly higher than at home. Be sure to check the expiration date on the box before purchasing a roll. You can also find most camera batteries at photo shops in Thamel. In Thamel there are also shops offering one-hour film processing, though quality may not be as good as you would like. It's better to wait until you get home to have your film processed.

Police   Dial 977/1-226998 or 977/1-226999.

Post Office   The Kathmandu G.P.O. is on Sundhara beside the Bimsen Tower (easily spotted minaretlike tower in the middle of town) on the corner of Kantipath one long block south of New Road (☎ 977/1-223512). Open Sunday to Friday from 8am to 7pm and Saturday from 11am to 3pm for stamps. If you want to receive mail while in Nepal, have it sent: c/o Kathmandu G.P.O., Kathmandu, Poste Restante. The Poste Restante room is open summer, Sunday to Friday from 10:15am to 4pm; winter, Sunday to Thursday from 10:15am to 3pm, Friday from 10:15am to 2pm. To mail a package out of Nepal, you must send it from the Foreign Post Office, Sundhara (☎ 977/1-211760), beside the G.P.O. Open: Sunday to Friday from 10am to 1:30pm.

Radio   The one Nepali radio station broadcasts on several frequencies and has English-language news daily at 8am and 8pm.

Religious Services   The International Protestant Congregation of Kathmandu holds English-language services Sunday at 9:30am at St. Mary's School in the Jamshikel area of Patan (☎ 977/1-522687 for directions). Roman Catholic services are held at St. Francis Xavier Church, Jawalakhel, Patan (☎ 977/1-522599 for directions), on Sunday at 9am and 5:30pm.

Restrooms   Public restrooms are few and far between in Kathmandu. You'll find them in restaurants and some hotel lobbies. Don't be surprised if an otherwise very Western-looking establishment has only an Asian-style squat toilet. The common term for a restroom in Nepal is toilet (or *charpi* in Nepali).

Safety   Kathmandu is still a surprisingly safe city, even at night. However, this does not mean you can be careless with your money, passport, and other valuables. I suggest always carrying tickets, money, and passport in a moneybelt or neck bag that can be worn under your clothing. Carry only as much cash as you expect to spend during any foray out of your hotel. Keep this money separate from your moneybelt so that you don't reveal the location of your valuables to curious eyes.

Shoe Repairs   Shoe repairmen set up shop on sidewalks all over town. Ask at your hotel for the location of the nearest shoe repairman.

Taxes   Nepal's hotel tax varies with the number of stars a hotel has been awarded by the Hotel Association of Nepal. There is also an international departure tax of Rs700 ($14) charged at the airport, so be sure to save that much in Nepali rupees, or you'll have to change more money. Restaurants also charge a 10% tax.

Taxis   See "Getting Around" in this chapter.

Telephone/Telegrams/Telex   International phone calls can be made and telegrams and telexes can be sent from the Central Telegraph Office on Kantipath south of the General Post Office. Open daily from 7am to 7pm. A three-minute phone call to the United States will cost about Rs360 ($7.20). The rate for a telegram ranges from Rs6.50 (13¢) to Rs15.50 (31¢) per word. A telex will cost Rs255 ($5.10) for three minutes. Unfortunately, this office is not very convenient. On the other hand, there are dozens of communications centers conveniently located in the Thamel neighborhood. At one of these offices, you can make a phone call or send a fax for around Rs170 to Rs200 ($3.40 to $4) per minute. See "City Code" and "Country Code," above, in "Fast Facts: Kathmandu" for information about using the telephone in Nepal.

Television   There is one Nepali television station. English-language news is broadcast daily at 9:40pm. However, many hotels, even budget hotels, now get satellite cable television (if not in the rooms, at least on a lobby television) that includes the BBC World News.

Useful Telephone Numbers   Local operator (English-speaking)—180; international operator—186 or 187; English-speaking directory assistance—197.

Weather   For the day's weather forecast, check the *Rising Nepal,* Kathmandu's daily English-language newspaper.

3 Accommodations

In the very expensive and expensive range, you will be paying for the sort of standards you would expect in top-notch hotels. These hotels usually have a swimming pool and other exercise facilities, as well as several restaurants and bars. However, conditions in Nepal conspire to confound hoteliers, and you may be slightly disappointed in the quality of even the most expensive rooms in Kathmandu. Trust that regardless of any shortcomings you might encounter, you are still experiencing the best that Nepal has to offer. You won't find very many rooms in the moderate range listed here. I have found that most Kathmandu hotels in this price range are rather shabby and highly overpriced. If you want the sort of comfort you would expect in the moderate price range, try a deluxe room in an inexpensive or budget hotel. In the inexpensive and budget ranges, I have found that one of the most important factors is a quiet location. I have chosen hotels with this in mind so that your sleep will be as undisturbed as possible.

Because hotel bills (except in the cheapest of budget accommodations) must be paid with foreign currency, I have listed rates in U.S. dollars only, which is how you will be billed.

Hotel taxes in Kathmandu vary with the number of stars that have been awarded by the Hotel Association of Nepal. A five-star hotel is required to charge a 15% room tax; a four-star hotel, 14%; a three-star, 13%; a two-star, 12%; a one-star, 11%; and those with no star, 10%. Because this can amount to a rather substantial chunk of money and can be a bit confusing to calculate, I have included the tax in room rates quoted below. Therefore the rates listed here will not be the same as those you might find listed in a hotel brochure. Also keep in mind that although I have tried to compensate for the steady inflation rate in Nepal, rates are likely to continue to climb and may be a bit higher when you arrive in Nepal.

Because of the torrential rains that occur during the monsoon season, carpets are often musty with mildew even in the most expensive hotels. Also, you should be aware that barking dogs are a problem throughout Nepal and often keep people awake even at Kathmandu's most expensive hotels. Bring earplugs even if you are normally a heavy sleeper.

Phone numbers listed here include both the Nepal country code and the Kathmandu city code. When calling from within Kathmandu, it is only necessary to dial the last six digits.

In the listings below, the "Very Expensive" category includes hotels charging more than $130 per night for a double room; the "Expensive" category includes hotels charging between $90 and $130; the "Moderate" category includes hotels charging $50 to $90; the "Inexpensive" category includes hotels charging $25 to $50; and the "Budget" category includes hotels charging less than $25 per night. Unless otherwise noted, all rooms have private bathrooms.

AROUND DURBAR MARG
VERY EXPENSIVE

Hotel de L'Annapurna
Durbar Marg (P.O. Box 140), Kathmandu. ☎ **977/1-221711.** Fax 977/1-225236. 159 rms, 4 suites. A/C TV TEL. $138–$155.25 double; $230–$345 suite. AE, DC, JCB, MC, V.

A longtime favorite with tour groups, the Annapurna is situated in the middle of Durbar Marg, Kathmandu's upscale shopping street that leads to the gates of the Royal Palace. The three-story building looks deceptively small from the front, but inside you'll find several restaurants and all the amenities of a world-class hotel. One of the largest *thangkas* (Buddhist religious paintings) in Nepal is also in the hotel, just inside the front door on the left. Also in the marble-floored lobby you'll find an unusual brass model of a Nepali pagoda-style temple, and throughout the hotel, there are other works of traditional art, including more thangkas, on the walls.

Rooms are a bit of a disappointment, unless you spring for one of the newer deluxe rooms, which have televisions, good lighting, marble bathrooms with telephones and plenty of counter space, and window seats with bolsters. The standard rooms, with older carpets and furnishings, are a bit of a disappointment. The best of these overlook the hotel's minimal gardens. Be sure to specify whether you want a double bed; otherwise, you may end up with two twin beds. The suites, though quite large and furnished with Tibetan carpets and thangkas, are permeated with the smell of the mothballs that fill the bathrooms' bidets.

Dining/Entertainment: Overlooking the hotel's pool is the Juneli Bar, and in the lobby lounge there is live jazz music nightly except Monday. Across the parking lot from the hotel's front door is the Casino Anna Ghar-e-Kabab, on the second floor of a building in front of the hotel, serves some of the best Indian food in Nepal (see "Dining," below, for details). Downstairs from Ghar-e-Kabab is a coffee shop and a pastry shop. The Arniko Room, down the hall leading back from the lobby, serves excellent Szechuan Chinese meals in a dark and cozy atmosphere, and the Arch Room, serves Nepalese and continental meals.

Services: 24-hour room service, laundry and dry cleaning service, travel agency, car rental.

Facilities: Swimming pool, shopping arcade, health club, tennis courts, billiard room, barbershop, beauty salon, business center.

✪ Hotel Yak & Yeti

Durbar Marg (P.O. Box 1016), Kathmandu. ☎ **977/1-413999.** Fax 977/1-227782. 270 rms, 19 suites. A/C MINIBAR TV TEL. $172.50–$230 double; $241.50–$345 suite. Children under 12 stay free in parents' room (maximum two children per room). AE, DC, MC, V.

This is by far the best of Kathmandu's downtown hotels and is situated down a lane off busy Durbar Marg. The six-story hotel is composed of three very distinct buildings—two newer wings housing the guest rooms and an older wing that was once the palace of a Rana prime minister. This older wing has a couple of restaurants and several very grand banquet halls that are well worth seeing. Ask someone at the reception desk; I'm sure they'll be glad to give you a tour.

Central air conditioning keeps the hotel pleasant no matter what the weather and has helped the Yak & Yeti avoid the mildew problems that plague many of Kathmandu's other luxury hotels. Granite floors, carved wood pillars, and gleaming brass and copper make the lobby a fine place for lounging. A wall of glass looks out onto the extensive garden and pool area.

Most, but not all, rooms are very attractively decorated with interesting details that reflect the cultural heritage of the Kathmandu Valley. Bathrooms have long marble counters set with a basket of toiletries. There are even slippers for you to wear so you won't have to endure the cold marble bathroom floor. You have your choice of a king-size bed or a pair of twins. Suites are just as nice and considerably roomier. Ask for a room facing the garden. The deluxe rooms in the new wing are by far the hotel's most comfortable and up-to-date. If you crave modern conveniences and comforts, these are the rooms for you. There is also a club floor designed for business travelers.

Dining/Entertainment: In the lobby is the Yak & Yeti Bar, a comfortable and convenient place for a drink. For before- or after-dinner drinks, try the Chimney Bar. The Chimney Room restaurant, adjacent to the Chimney Bar, is a popular continental restaurant known for its Russian dishes (see Kathmandu "Dining,"

Kathmandu Accommodations

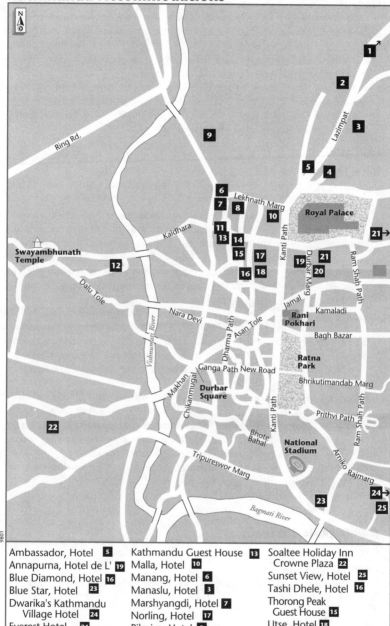

Ambassador, Hotel **5**	Kathmandu Guest House **13**	Soaltee Holiday Inn Crowne Plaza **22**
Annapurna, Hotel de L' **19**	Malla, Hotel **10**	Sunset View, Hotel **25**
Blue Diamond, Hotel **16**	Manang, Hotel **6**	Tashi Dhele, Hotel **16**
Blue Star, Hotel **23**	Manaslu, Hotel **3**	Thorong Peak Guest House **15**
Dwarika's Kathmandu Village Hotel **24**	Marshyangdi, Hotel **7**	Utse, Hotel **18**
Everest Hotel **24**	Norling, Hotel **17**	Vajra, Hotel **12**
Excelsior, Hotel **14**	Pilgrims Hotel **8**	Yak & Yeti, Hotel **21**
Garden Hotel **9**	Shangri-la, Hotel **2**	
Garuda, Hotel **11**	Shanker, Hotel **4**	
Kathmandu, Hotel **1**	Sherpa, Hotel **20**	

below, for details). Naachghar is a fabulously ornate dining room in a section of the hotel that was once a Rana palace. There are cultural performances of Nepali music and dance here daily at 8pm, and Indian food is served. For casual dining and buffet meals, there is the Sunrise Café, which overlooks the gardens. Also in this old palace building is the hotel's Casino Royale.

Services: 24-hour room service, 24-hour currency exchange, babysitting, laundry and valet service, doctor on call, safe-deposit box, tour and travel counter.

Facilities: Swimming pool, tennis court, sauna, massage room, business center, shopping arcade, drugstore and, beauty parlor.

EXPENSIVE

Hotel Sherpa

Durbar Marg (P.O. Box 901), Kathmandu. ☎ **977/1-227000.** Fax 977/1-222026. 85 rms. 7 suites. A/C MINIBAR TEL TV. $124.30 double; $214.70 suite. AE, DC, JCB, MC, V.

Located on Durbar Marg amid the shops and restaurants of Kathmandu's upscale shopping street, the Sherpa's stone-and-brick facade and roof lines reflect traditional architectural styles of Tibetan and Sherpa temples and monasteries. The Himalayan character continues in the lobby, where there are interesting copper plaques and carved wooden reproductions of Bhaktapur's ornate peacock window. However, beyond the lobby, the regional influence disappears completely, and the best thing the Sherpa has going for it is its location.

Guest rooms are all nondescript, and carpeting throughout rooms and halls is worn. The rooms, most of which have twin beds, tend to be cramped. Rooms with double beds have more space, but space is also pretty tight in the rooms with king beds. Bathrooms, done in tile and marble, vary in size, and have bathtub-shower combinations. If you're lucky, you may find a fruit basket and fresh flowers in your room when you check in.

Dining/Entertainment: The Sonam Bar is set off from the lobby by the reproduction of the peacock window. Café de la Paix is a bright, casual coffee shop. In the Sherpa Grill, continental and Indian cuisine are the specialties. This restaurant features a cultural show nightly. When the weather is good the Namche Garden, a second-floor terrace restaurant, serves light meals and snacks.

Services: 24-hour room service, laundry and dry cleaning service, doctor on call, currency exchange, babysitting, safe-deposit boxes, travel agency.

Facilities: Health club, sauna, swimming pool, shopping arcade, conference rooms, business center.

DIPLOMATIC DISTRICT
EXPENSIVE

Hotel Kathmandu

Maharajgunj (P.O. Box 11), Kathmandu. ☎ **977/1-410786** or 977/1-418494. Fax 977/1-416574. 82 rms, 2 suites. A/C TV TEL. $123.15 double; $216.60 suite. Extra bed $30.80. AE, MC, V.

Located in the heart of the Kathmandu's diplomatic neighborhood north of the city center, the Hotel Kathmandu is convenient to many embassies and is only a 20-minute taxi ride from Durbar Square. The hotel boasts some very attractive architectural touches. The low brick building is set back from the road across a flagstone driveway that is overflowing with greenery during the rainy season. Brass-and-bronze lions guard the front door. A sunken seating area in the middle of the lobby is a cozy place to relax, and a large traditional Tibetan carpet and gleaming copper-and-brass pots add warmth and sparkle to the room.

The medium-sized rooms have either a double bed or twin beds. Large windows let in plenty of light and sometimes noisy air conditioners keep rooms cool in the warmer months. Unfortunately, the monsoons have not been kind to the carpets here. Many have become worn, and some rooms are extremely musty from the mildew in the carpets. If you should be given one of these musty rooms, immediately ask for a different room. Bathrooms have tubs and marble floors.

Dining/Entertainment: The Basantapur Bar is very formal with a soaring ceiling and brick walls. The Ilam Tea Lounge, only open for afternoon tea, is just off the lobby. Baithak, which is up a wide flight of marble stairs, serves international meals and is open for breakfast, lunch, and dinner. The tables of this dining room look across the stairs to an impressive wall mural of Patan's Durbar Square. The Café Royal is a more formal dining room, open for dinner only. Bagaincha is an open-air garden dining area where daily lunch barbecues are held in the winter.

Services: Complimentary city shuttle, babysitter, laundry and dry cleaning service, doctor on call, secretarial services, car rental, 24-hour currency exchange, safe-deposit boxes.

Facilities: TV lounge, newsstand, shopping arcade, travel desk, business center.

✪ Hotel Shangri-la

Lazimpat (P.O. Box 655), Kathmandu. ☎ **977/1-412999.** Fax 977/1-414184. 82 rms, 4 suites. A/C MINIBAR TV TEL. $125.40 double; $228 suite. AE, DC, MC, V.

Located north of downtown, the Shangri-la is one of Kathmandu's best hotels in any price category. Set amid beautiful gardens, the three-story brick building is hidden behind a high wall that protects it from the noises on busy Lazimpat. The lobby is bright and sunny with floor-to-ceiling windows looking, unfortunately onto the front driveway and gardens. However, the favored public area for relaxing is the back garden, which is almost always sunny and warm during the winter months. A four-headed-snake fountain is the focal point of the garden, while shocking-pink bougainvillea climb the wall, adding color even in the driest months. Nepal's most unusual swimming pool is off to one side of the garden. The pool is modeled after a traditional bathing fountain known as a *hiti.*

Rooms are attractive, with slightly worn brown carpeting and carved wooden lattices in some windows. Each room has a pair of comfortable chairs and a marble-topped table set with fresh flowers and a fruit basket at check-in time. Bathrooms are small but come with tubs and have green-marble counters. Be sure to request one of the rooms facing the garden.

Dining/Entertainment: The Lost Horizon bar, just off the lobby, is a good place to relax. Shambala Garden, where there are regularly scheduled luncheon barbecues, is an outdoor dining area serving three meals daily. The Shambala Garden Café is a cheerful, sunny coffee shop open 24 hours a day. Kokonor, only open for dinner, serves continental and French cuisine, and Tien-Shan, open for lunch and dinner, serves some of the best Chinese meals in Kathmandu.

Services: 24-hour room service, babysitting, courtesy airport transfer, courtesy city shuttle, secretarial services, 24-hour currency exchange, laundry and dry cleaning service, doctor on call, safe-deposit boxes, 24-hour taxi service.

Facilities: Conference hall, swimming pool, fitness center, sauna, shopping arcade, business center, beauty salon.

Hotel Shanker

Lazimpat (P.O. Box 350), Kathmandu. ☎ **977/1-410151** or 977/1-410152. 94 rms, 10 suites. A/C TV TEL. $119.70 double; $142.50 suite. Extra bed $34.20. AE, JCB, MC, V.

If you have ever had fantasies of living in a palace, this is the place to make your dreams come true, if only for a few days. Located just north of the present Royal Palace, the Hotel Shanker was built during the rule of the Rana prime ministers, who erected many European-style palaces. This is only one of many such architectured excesses around town.

Set back from busy Lazimpat in a large neatly manicured garden (the best in the city), the Shanker is an imposing white structure with lush green vines cascading from the roof of the portico. The building's arched windows, stately columns, and ornate cornices will all remind you of Europe.

Inside, a long narrow lobby with a low ceiling suddenly dispels the feeling of grandeur produced by the facade. Because the hotel is in an old building, rooms vary. Several front rooms have low arched windows and painted plasterwork moldings. These rooms were obviously created when an extra floor was constructed in a grand high-ceilinged hall. Other rooms have sleeping lofts (called double-decker rooms). Still others have attractive old plasterwork molding. Many have been recently redecorated and have new carpets, beds, and other furnishings. However, some rooms are permeated with the smell of mothballs.

Dining/Entertainment: Be sure to eat at the hotel's Kailash restaurant. Down a flight of stairs from the lobby, the restaurant is in one of the old palace's grandest banquet halls. Ornate plasterwork abounds, with Oriental dragons winding across the walls and ceilings. Crystal chandeliers sparkle high above the white linen of the table settings. Nepali, Indian, Chinese, and continental meals are served. The One-Eye Bar, above the lobby, is a dark, warm bar with a cozy, antique feel. Another lounge, the Kunti Bar, is up a few steps from the lobby.

Services: Room service, currency exchange, laundry and dry cleaning service travel agency.

Facilities: Shopping arcade.

INEXPENSIVE

Hotel Ambassador

Lazimpat (P.O. Box 2769), Kathmandu. ☎ **977/1-414432** or 977/1-410432. Fax 977/1-413641. 38 rms. TV TEL. $33.60–$44.80 double. Extra bed $10. Discounts for longer stays. AE, JCB, MC, V.

This aptly named hotel is located on Kathmandu's embassy row north of downtown. Rooms vary in size and quality, with those on the west side of the hotel being quieter since they are farther from busy Lazimpat. Though the rooms are usually clean, some are a bit more worn than others. Larger, more expensive rooms have bathtubs, while less expensive rooms have only showers. Some rooms have balconies.

Dining/Entertainment: There is a beer garden for sunny days and an Indian restaurant.

Services: Laundry service, babysitting, currency exchange, bicycle rentals, safe-deposit vault, luggage storage, travel agency.

Facilities: Beauty parlor, business center, health club, gift shop.

⊗ Hotel Manaslu

Lazimpat, Kathmandu. ☎ **977/1-413470** or 977/1-410071. Fax 977/1-416516. 53 rms. TEL. $31.40 double. Extra bed $9. Children under 5 stay free in parents' room when not using an extra bed. Special rates for diplomatic corps and employees of international aid organizations. AE, MC, V.

If you don't mind being a bit out of the tourist mainstream, the Hotel Manaslu makes a very good, economical choice. Located down a long, winding dirt lane in a quiet residential neighborhood, the Manaslu has a peaceful front garden that's great for a quiet lunch or afternoon tea. The low prices, quiet setting, and comfortable rooms make this a good value.

Rooms all have wall-to-wall carpeting and plenty of windows. Many rooms are quite large, and some have tubs in the bathroom while others have only a shower. My favorite rooms are those with Tibetan styling, including unusual paper lampshades and colorful block-printed bedspreads.

Dining/Entertainment: The restaurant and bar, decorated in traditional Newari style, serves Indian and continental cuisine.

Services: Room service, currency exchange, laundry and dry cleaning service, bicycle and car rentals and luggage storage.

THAMEL
VERY EXPENSIVE

Hotel Malla
Lekhnath Marg (P.O. Box 787), Kathmandu. ☎ **977/1-410320,** 977/1-410620, 977/1-410966, or 977/1-410968. Fax 977/1-418382. 142 rms, 6 suites. A/C TEL. $134.55–$148.20 double; $174.45–$217.75 suite. Extra bed $42.20; crib $26.25. Children under 10 stay free in parents' room without extra bed. AE, DC, MC, V.

Located on the northern edge of the Thamel neighborhood favored by budget travelers, the Malla is a quiet and convenient choice. The hundreds of shops and crowded streets of Thamel are only five minutes' walk away, but when you take a seat in the sunny garden across from the hotel's own miniature *stupa* (Buddhist shrine), you can easily forget that you are in the city at all. Rooms, with large windows and individual air conditioners, are comfortable, though cramped; they were recently remodeled with contemporary furnishings.

Dining/Entertainment: The Explorers Bar is popular with trekking groups for get-togethers before and after trekking. There's also a second bar to one side of the lobby. The Apsara, up a flight of stairs from the lobby, looks out over the hotel's attractive gardens. The cuisine is continental primarily. For Italian food, try Tara Restaurant. Across the parking lot from the hotel's main entrance is Mountain City Chinese Restaurant, which serves good Szechuan food. A tea lounge and garden luncheon barbecues complete the hotel's dining facilities.

Services: 24-hour room service, laundry and dry cleaning service, currency exchange, travel agency, trekking agency, car rental.

Facilities: Conference hall, shopping center. There are plans to add a swimming pool, health club, beauty parlor, barber shop, business center, and VIP lounge.

MODERATE

☉ The Garden Hotel
Naya Bazar, Thamel (P.O. Box 5954), Kathmandu. ☎ **977/1-411951,** 977/1-411131, or 977/1-415690. Fax 977/1-418072. 50 rms. TV TEL. $61–$89 double. AE, DC, JCB, MC, V.

Although the appearance of this hotel's garden is not yet up-to-par, the hotel has a small swimming pool which makes the Garden Kathmandu's best deal in this price range. Unfortunately, the hotel is a 10-minute walk down a steep, and usually very muddy, road from the heart of Thamel. However, if the weather's warm, the pool and garden make a good escape from the chaos of Kathmandu's streets. The standard rooms are cramped and have small bathrooms which have bathtubs but no counter space. In the deluxe rooms, you get air conditioning (which is rarely necessary), slightly more space, and a marble counter in the bathroom.

Dining/Entertainment: The hotel's restaurant is rather plain and serves standard Kathmandu international cuisine. However, with its glass walls, it's a bright spot for lunch. Behind the reception desk in the lobby, there is a small bar with Tibetan-inspired decor.

Services: 24-hour room service, safe-deposit boxes, laundry/valet service, airport transfers, babysitting, baggage storage, business center, travel and tour desk, currency exchange, bicycle rentals.

Facilities: Outdoor swimming pool, newsstand, shopping arcade.

Hotel Manang

Paknajol, Thamel (P.O. Box 5608), Kathmandu. ☎ **977/1-410993** or 977/1-419247. Fax 977/1-415821. 55 rms. A/C TEL. $55.50–$83.25 double. Extra bed $11.10. AE, DC, JCB, MC, V.

Located up on the north end of Thamel, the Manang is a six-story hotel offering simple, though moderately comfortable, accommodations. Though you can find similar guest rooms and lower rates in Thamel, you won't find the same array of restaurants and bars unless you spend a bit more. The marble-floored lobby is a showcase of Newari wood carving with an eye-catching front desk of brick and wood. Rooms are fairly standard, though the deluxe rooms have satellite television and minibars.

Dining/Entertainment: The Lotus Café is a coffee shop just off the lobby. For a view with your meal, there is the Swayambhu Garden Terrace up on the top floor, though only light meals and drinks are served up here. Across the parking lot from the hotel, you'll find the entrance to the Jewel of Manang restaurant, which offers live traditional music several nights a week.

Services: 24-hour room service, babysitting, travel desk, currency exchange, laundry/valet service, safe-deposit boxes, airport transfers, secretarial services, doctor on call.

Facilities: Shopping arcade, business center.

Hotel Marshyangdi

Paknajol, Thamel (P.O. Box 5206), Thamel, Kathmandu. ☎ **977/1-414105** or 977/1-412129. Fax 977/1-410008. 55 rms. A/C TV TEL. $66.70–$83.25 double. Extra bed $13.35. Children under 12 stay free in parents' room without extra bed or crib. AE, JCB, MC, V.

Charging slightly more for a room than its next-door neighbor, the Hotel Manang (see above), the Marshyangdi provides the same amenities—restaurants, bars, elevator, deluxe rooms with air conditioning and satellite television.

Rooms are clean, comfortable, and attractively decorated. There are large tile bathrooms with marble sinks, and big picture windows for taking in the elevated views. However, you may find that other hotels in the area offer the very same accommodations (sans elevator) at lower rates. On the other hand, if you want a view and don't want to climb stairs, this is a good choice.

Dining/Entertainment: The Khukuri Bar and Palace Restaurant on the hotel's roof offer splendid views of the mountains and valley. On the first floor, just off the lobby, is the more casual Lumbini Café.

Services: 24-hour room service, laundry/valet service, safe-deposit boxes, travel counter, currency exchange, airport transfers, concierge desk.

INEXPENSIVE

Hotel Blue Diamond

Jyatha, Thamel (P.O. Box 2134), Kathmandu-29. ☎ **977/1-226392** or 977/1-226320. 100 rms. TEL. $9–$30.25 double. AE, MC, V.

You'll find the Blue Diamond down the first road to the left as you walk from the Department of Immigration into Thamel. Though it is an older hotel, the Blue Diamond was recently remodeled and is still a decent place. It benefits from being set back a bit from the street, and almost all the rooms have large windows. As at other budget hotels, there is no elevator, so you'll have to walk up several flights of stairs if you want a room with a view. Bathrooms, though basic, are large and have tubs. There is a restaurant across the courtyard from the hotel. Services include room service, laundry service, currency exchange, and travel arrangements.

✪ Hotel Excelsior

Narsingh Camp Thamel (P.O. Box 4583), Kathmandu. ☎ **977/1-411566.** Fax 977/1-410853. 51 rms. TEL. $24.20–$39.60 double. MC, V.

By far the best deal in the inexpensive range of hotels, the Excelsior is located in the heart of Thamel behind the popular Pumpernickel Bakery restaurant. When you walk up the marble stairs and into the marble-floored lobby, you won't believe that a hotel this attractive could be so inexpensive. The staff are all very friendly and stay busy keeping the hotel in tip-top shape. Rooms have parquet floors, large windows, twin beds with wool blankets, large wardrobes, desk and chairs, and large bathrooms. The bathrooms, in Asian style, have the shower in the middle of the room, and there is no shower curtain. Room-service breakfasts and light meals are available, and there is a breakfast room in the basement. What keeps the hotel's rates down is the lack of an elevator, and of course the best views are a steep climb up to the fourth or fifth floor. The deluxe rooms are slightly larger than the standard rooms and have balconies, bathtubs, and telephones. There are also a few rooms with air conditioning. Services include laundry, currency exchange, luggage storage, safe-deposit box, and airport transfers.

Hotel Tashi Dhele

Thamel (P.O. Box 7247), Kathmandu. ☎ **977/1-217446.** 24 rms. $27.50–$33 double. No credit cards.

Located down an alley just south of Thamel's main square, the Tashi Dhele is partially hidden behind a row of shops and is thus somewhat protected from the noise of the street. The noise insulation is one of the hotel's greatest assets. Most rooms are also quite large, some have balconies, and all are carpeted. The more expensive rooms have telephones and televisions. Marble floors in the halls and arches in some doorways give the hotel a bit of character. Hotel services include laundry service, safe-deposit boxes, airport transfers, luggage storage room, free local phone calls, and free bicycle rentals.

BUDGET

✆ Hotel Garuda

Thamel (P.O. Box 1771), Kathmandu. ☎ **977/1-416776** or 977/1-416340. Fax 977/1-413614. 34 rms. $19.05–$24.65 double. AE, JCB, MC, V.

A couple of hundred feet north of the entrance to the Kathmandu Guest House, the road curves to the left. You'll find the Garuda on the curve. The Garuda offers surprising quality at low rates. Rooms are clean and comfortable and have daily maid service. There are good views from the roof of this five-story hotel, and many of the rooms also have nice views from their large windows. Some rooms even have balconies. Try to get a room on the north side. There is a restaurant, just off the lobby, that serves standard Thamel international food at very reasonable rates. Room service, laundry service, luggage storage, and safe-deposit boxes are all available.

✪ Kathmandu Guest House

Thamel (P.O. Box 2769), Kathmandu. ☎ **977/1-413632** or 977/1-418733. Fax 977/1-417133. 120 rms (90 with private bath). $3.35–$11.20 double without bath, $13.45–$33.60 double with bath. Extra bed $4.50. AE, MC, V.

Among Kathmandu's budget hotels and guesthouses, the Kathmandu Guest House is legendary. It is almost always packed, and getting a room here can often entail a wait of a day or two (long-distance reservations are often lost). Part of the hotel is housed in an old palace, but several new wings have been added over the years, creating a hodgepodge of rooms, many of which have been renovated in recent years. The main attraction here is the atmosphere. The hotel lobby, which was recently remodeled and is now very elegant for a hotel in this budget range, and quiet courtyard garden seem to be always filled with interesting people, many of whom are on long trips around the world or have spent years exploring the East. Conversation is lively. Services include laundry service, currency exchange, travel agency, luggage storage, and doctor on call.

Hotel Norling

Jyatha, Thamel (P.O. Box 9192), Kathmandu. ☎ **977/1-230734.** Fax 977/1-226735. 31 rms. TEL. $17.60–$27.50 double. No credit cards.

This Tibetan-run hotel is located next door to the ever-popular Utse restaurant and very close to the Department of Immigration (the trekking-permit office). Because the hotel is fairly new, the furniture and carpets are still in good shape, and the mattresses are still firm. In the center of the hotel there's an unusual atrium courtyard with a few tables and a garden, and in the lobby there is a TV lounge area. Rooms are a bit small but comfortable and have wall-to-wall carpeting. In every room you'll find a fan or heater depending on the season, and in the most expensive double rooms, there are bathtubs. There is a small dining room serving international dishes, and up on the roof there's a garden area where you can order drinks and meals while enjoying the view. Services include luggage storage, room service, safe-deposit boxes, and free airport transfers. If you are heading into Thamel, you'll find the hotel midway down the first street to the left after you pass the Department of Immigration.

Pilgrims Hotel

Thamel (P.O. Box 3872), Kathmandu. ☎ **977/1-416910.** Fax 977/1-229983. 18 rms (13 with bath), 1 suite. TEL. $11 double without bath, $16.50–$22 double with bath; $33 suite. AE, MC, V.

You'll find the Pilgrims Hotel up the road that leads north out of Thamel's main square. Operated by the owners of the popular Pilgrims Book House, this hotel offers clean, carpeted rooms. The rooms with private baths are slightly larger than those without, and some feature unusual octagonal windows. However, what makes this hotel truly special is the management's interest and dedication to the arts—visual, literary, and performing. There is a plethora of old photos, old prints, modern posters, and other framed artworks all over the hotel. There is a standing invitation to authors, poets, artists, musicians, photographers, philosophers, and all other performers to appear at the hotel. Surprisingly, quite a few folks who are just passing through town stop by to perform. There's no telling what sort of entertainment you might find on the schedule while you are in town. In addition to the lobby restaurant, there is a garden dining area.

Thorong Peak Guest House

Thamel (P.O. Box 1657), Kathmandu. ☎ **977/1-224656.** Fax 977/1-229304. 27 rms. 12 with private bath. TEL. $13.45 double without bath. $20.20 double with bath, MC, V.

Just down from Thamel's main square on the road to Durbar Square is a quiet and inexpensive hotel set back a hundred feet from the main road. Look for the sign. With a sunny patio by the entrance and a pleasant rooftop terrace, the Thorong Peak is a peaceful spot amid the noise and crowds of Thamel. With six floors and no elevator, though, it is definitely for those who are in good shape. Rooms with common bath are the best bet. They are clean and large, and the bathrooms down the hall even have bathtubs. The Tibetan owners are friendly and helpful.

Hotel Utse

Jyatha, Thamel, Kathmandu. ☎ **977/1-228952** or 977/1-226946. Fax 977/1-226945. 52 rms. TEL. $22–$31.90 double. MC, V.

For more than 20 years, Utse was one of Thamel's most popular restaurants, so when the owners opened a hotel, they met with almost instant success. One of the highlights of the hotel is a roof garden complete with lawn, a refuge when Kathmandu's noise and dust start getting you down. The standard rooms are of medium size and have parquet floors and either twin beds or a double. The deluxe rooms have carpeting and television and a tub in the bathrooms. For solo travelers, there are even tiny single rooms. The restaurant off the lobby is well known for its Tibetan meals and is packed most nights. Services include free airport transfers, room service, luggage storage, safe-deposit boxes, and laundry service.

ELSEWHERE IN THE CITY
VERY EXPENSIVE

The Everest Hotel

New Baneswor (P.O. Box 659), Kathmandu. ☎ **977/1-220567.** Fax 977/1-226088 or 977/1-224421. 162 rms. 6 suites. A/C MINIBAR TV TEL. $149.50–$161 double; $288–$460 suite. Extra bed $34.50. Children under 17 stay free in parents' room without extra bed. AE, DC, JCB, MC, V.

On a hilltop between the airport and downtown stands the Everest Hotel, Nepal's tallest hotel at eight stories. This hotel has everything you would expect of a first-class hotel anywhere in the world. A sweeping driveway leads to the entrance, where doormen salute you and hold the door for you. Inside you climb a wide flight of steps to enter the green-marble lobby with its sparkling red-glass chandelier and glass wall looking onto the garden and swimming pool. Bhutanese textiles, Buddhist pennants, hanging oil lamps, and plenty of potted plants make this one of the most attractive lobbies in Kathmandu. Plenty of couches and comfortable chairs set around plush Tibetan carpets also make the lobby a great place to meet friends or relax.

The large guest rooms come with two double beds and unusual and attractive carved-wood furniture, though the bedspreads and carpets are old and worn.

Bathrooms are done in marble and tile. Rooms all have large windows, most of which provide excellent views of the mountains. Ask for a room on the north side of an upper floor for the best possible view. The Bhaktapur and Patan suites are very attractive and are decorated with handcrafts from their namesake cities. Other nice touches in the suites are fresh flowers and fruit baskets, windows on two sides, king-size beds, and windows over the bathtubs.

Dining/Entertainment: The Himalayan Tavern Bar off the lobby has a comfortable homey feel with a warm fireplace to sit around. The Café features a continental and Chinese menu and is open daily for breakfast, lunch, and dinner. For more elegant dining, try Far Pavilions, a rooftop Indian restaurant specializing in tandoori food. Wednesday through Monday there is live Nepali and Indian music here beginning at 8:30pm. It's open for dinner only. Also on the roof are the Sherpaland Tibetan restaurant and Bugles & Tigers, a small and elegant bar with a men's club atmosphere. Reputations, above the shopping arcade in the lobby, is a casual coffee lounge. There is also a nightly barbecue in the hotel garden during the dry months. In the basement is the Disco Galaxy, one of Kathmandu's few discos. There is also a modest casino, the Casino Everest, on the premises.

Services: Room service, laundry and dry cleaning service, currency exchange, complimentary airport transfers, courtesy city shuttle.

Facilities: Health club, tennis court, swimming pool, beauty parlor, conference halls, shopping arcade.

✪ Soaltee Holiday Inn Crowne Plaza
Tahachal (P.O. Box 97), Kathmandu. ☎ **977/1-272550** or 977/1-272555. Fax 977/ 1-272205. 300 rms, 17 suites. A/C TV TEL. $184 double; $402.50–$776 suite. Children under 12 stay free in parents' room without an extra bed. Extra bed $34.50. AE, DC, EU, MC, V.

Kathmandu's largest hotel is located 15 minutes southwest of Durbar Square in a quiet residential neighborhood. The five-story redbrick building is surrounded by neatly manicured gardens with a separate building for suites. The hotel entrance doubles as a spacious open-air lounge overlooking the gardens. Just before you enter the hotel, notice the several prayer wheels set into the walls on either side of the doors. Give these wheels a spin, and you will send thousands of prayers heavenward. Inside, statues of Hindu and Buddhist deities and colorful traditional thangkas decorate the lobby.

Though the older rooms are a bit worn, they provide a bit more Nepali atmosphere than the newer guest rooms, which feature generic international decor. There are intricately carved dark-wood lattices framing the large windows, many of which have excellent views of the mountains. The tile baths have plenty of counter space. Central air conditioning assures that rooms will be not only the right temperature, but also quiet. You have a choice of two twin beds, a double, or a king bed. Rooms in the renovated wing are brighter, with beige carpet and blond wood furniture and come with a minibar and television. Bathrooms in these rooms all have hairdryers and telephones as well as marble counters and floors.

Dining/Entertainment: The Rodi Bar, just off the lobby, is an intimate bar with smoked glass walls. There is live piano music in the evenings. Al Fresco is the hotel's popular Italian restaurant, located in the basement of the small building by the swimming pool. The Garden Terrace is a bright and cheery coffee shop. Himalchuli serves Indian and Nepali cuisine, with a nightly cultural program of music and dance. The Gurkha Grill serves French cuisine. The Casino Nepal rounds out the hotel's entertainment.

Services: 24-hour room service, babysitting, currency exchange, car rental, travel agency, laundry and dry cleaning service, courtesy city shuttle, complimentary airport transfer.

Facilities: Swimming pool, putting green, driving range, shopping arcade, health club, sauna, steam bath, tennis courts, business center, barbershop, beauty parlor, newsstand, video room, children's playground.

EXPENSIVE

Hotel Blue Star

Tripureswor (P.O. Box 983), Kathmandu. ☎ **977/1-228833.** Fax 977/1-226820. 87 rms, 1 suite. A/C TEL. $110.75 double; $169.50 suite. Extra bed $22.60. Children under 12 stay free in parents' room without extra bed. AE, MC, V.

Hidden behind a shopping mall and office building on a rather dismal-looking avenue near the bridge to Patan, the Blue Star is a surprisingly good, though over-priced, hotel. The lobby has marble floors and walls and plenty of seating for those who like to socialize. You will have to put up with some scuffed-up walls, but in general the hotel is clean and well maintained.

Rooms vary in size from comfortable to huge. Room 614 is particularly large and is made even more spacious by a gigantic marble balcony with great mountain views. You have a choice of two twin beds or one double. Older rooms now have new carpeting, while rooms in the new wing have parquet floors. Bathrooms have marble floors and bathtubs. Some rooms here are a bit musty, so be sure to give your room a good sniff before settling in.

Dining/Entertainment: The Mandala Bar serves inexpensive drinks and snacks in casual surroundings and is separated from the lobby by a wall of prayer wheels. Rattan furniture and lattices give the hotel's Lumbini Coffeeshop the feeling of a garden restaurant. Menu offerings range from quick snacks to full meals. Vaishali, a traditionally elegant restaurant, serves well-prepared Indian and Nepali meals in fabulous surroundings modeled after a Tibetan *gompa* (temple).

Services: 24-hour room service, safe-deposit boxes, luggage storage, travel agency, car rental.

Facilities: Indoor swimming pool, shopping arcade, beauty parlor, business center, department store, health club, squash court, TV lounge.

✪ Dwarika's Kathmandu Village Hotel

Battisputali (P.O. Box 459), Kathmandu. ☎ **977/1-470770** or 977/1-473725. Fax 977/1-471379 32 rms. $97.90 double. Extra bed $23.10. AE, MC, V.

Located near Pashupatinath, Nepal's most sacred Hindu temple, on the east side of Kathmandu, Dwarika's is by far Nepal's most interesting and unusual hotel. If you are the type of person who stays in bed and breakfasts back home, then Dwarika's is for you. No two of the 32 rooms are the same, and all have incorporated antique architectural details into their design, construction, and decor. In addition, the several two-story buildings that house the guest rooms are built in traditional Newari style.

Though furnishings in some of the older rooms are showing signs of age, there are plenty of beautiful new rooms that are filled with works of art. Among the interesting details incorporated into various rooms are block-printed bedspreads and curtains, a 16th-century carved window, beamed ceilings, basket lamps, bronze statues, thangkas, brick-tile floors; there are also carved wooden chairs, mirror frames, ceiling light fixtures, windows, and doors. All have modern bathrooms with solar-heated hot-water showers. Newer rooms also have marble and parquet floors, double sinks, and built-in electric heaters.

Dwarika's is a repository for architectural antiquities, and as such, has quite a few piles of unused doors, windows, pillars, and the like. Consequently, the grounds are not the immaculately manicured gardens you might hope for, but I think the rooms more than make up for a bit of clutter in the yard.

There's a small dining room that features a huge antique carved window displayed against one wall, a bar, and a sunny lounge. Services include currency exchange and laundry service.

MODERATE

✪ Hotel Sunset View

New Baneswor (P.O. Box 1174), Kathmandu. ☎ **977/1-229172** or 977/1-211524. Fax 977/1-220049. 30 rms, 1 suite. TEL. $66 double; $82.50 suite. MC, V.

Operated by a Nepali-Japanese family, the Sunset View is one of the most peaceful moderately priced hotels in Kathmandu. Set down a dirt lane only a few hundred yards from the Everest Hotel, the Sunset View lives up to its name with an excellent western view across the valley. Surrounded by beautiful Japanese gardens, the hotel is built in the style of a contemporary home. A marble lobby with rattan furniture and a library of paperback books by the fireplace is the perfect spot to sit and read on a winter evening. There are several styles of rooms, but all are decorated with attractive block-printed fabrics. The suite is a real bargain. It has a high ceiling, large patio, a huge marble bath, and other amenities such as a refrigerator. Some rooms have sleeping lofts that make them ideal for families, and others have televisions. There is a tearoom across the garden from the main house and a terrace dining room that faces the sunset sky.

INEXPENSIVE

✪ Hotel Vajra

Bijeswori (P.O. Box 1084), Kathmandu. ☎ **977/1-272719**, 977/1-271545, 977/1-271819, or 977/1-271824. Fax 977/1-271695. 52 rms, 43 with private bath, 3 suites. $17.95 double without bath, $42.60–$68.35 double with bath; $100.80 double suite. AE, MC, V.

Located on the west side of the city on the road to Swayambunath Stupa, the Vajra is one of those rare finds in Nepal—a hotel that reflects Nepali culture, arts, and crafts. Set amid lush and shady gardens, the brick buildings of the hotel reflect the vernacular architecture of the Kathmandu Valley, and throughout the hotel's many buildings there are wall and ceiling murals by famous local artists and ornately carved wood details. The Vajra is a veritable cultural center and houses an art gallery, a theater, and a library filled with books on Tibetan Buddhism, Nepali ecology and natural history, Himalayan art, Himalayan exploration, and other subjects.

There are a number of different types of rooms, each with its own unique decor. My favorite are the mid-priced "super rooms," which come with twin beds, wicker chairs and table, Tibetan carpet, unusual tile floors, marble sink and bathroom floor, and Indian print bedspreads. The most expensive rooms are those in the new wing. These rooms are very elegant, with carved-wood lattice ceiling, exposed brick walls, and marble floors (three also have balconies).

Dining/Entertainment: The Rooftop Gardens, Sunset Bar, and Pagoda Bar are great places for lunch or a drink. The tiny Pagoda Bar, with walls of windows, has a beautifully painted ceiling based on traditional Tibetan Buddhist temple designs.

The Explorer's Restaurant on the ground floor is a spacious dining room with a diverse menu of international favorites. A large copper fireplace keeps the restaurant warm and cozy.

Services: Laundry service, currency exchange, bicycle rentals, safe deposit, luggage storage.

4 Dining

Though you won't likely return from Nepal raving about the meals you had, there is quite a bit of good food at very reasonable prices. In fact, you will have a very hard time spending more than $15 or $20 on dinner. For $10 you can dine in the best restaurants in the country, and for as little as $2 or $3 you can get a steak dinner at a budget restaurant. In my opinion, the city's best meals are served at its many Indian restaurants, one or two of which serve meals as delicious as you're likely to find anywhere in the world. Service, on the other hand, leaves much to be desired at even the best restaurants. Please be patient.

For visitors with a sweet tooth, Kathmandu is the cake-and-pie capital of Asia, and it is very tempting to sample your way through the desserts of Thamel. Be forewarned; those outlandishly iced cakes and mountain-peak meringue pies are usually a disappointment unless you have been traveling through India for a few months. Also, keep in mind that salmonella bacteria grow very well on meringue and cheesecake.

DURBAR MARG
EXPENSIVE

✪ Ghar-e-Kabab
Durbar Marg. ☎ **977/1-221711.** Reservations recommended for dinner. Vegetable dishes Rs95–Rs115 ($1.90–$2.30); main dishes Rs155–Rs300 ($2.10–$6). AE, DC, MC, V. Lunch daily noon–2:30pm; dinner daily 7–10:30pm. INDIAN.

Upstairs from the Hotel de l'Annapurna's coffee shop and bakery, which are located on Durbar Marg across the parking lot from the hotel, is Kathmandu's best Indian restaurant. Some claim that you can't get better Indian food in London or New York, and most nights I find it difficult to disagree. The ambience is elegant,with Moghul miniatures on the beaten-copper walls. On a hot afternoon the restaurant's air conditioning is a welcome relief.

In my opinion, the test of a good Indian restaurant is its chicken tikka, a more refined version of tandoori chicken (no bones to get in your way). Ghar-e-Kabab serves the most succulent chicken tikka I've ever tasted, and you can watch it being prepared in the restaurant's tandoor ovens, which are housed in a glass-enclosed viewing room. The different *nans* (tandoori-baked breads) and *parathas* (fried breads) should not be missed either. In the evenings, when the restaurant is usually packed, there is live Indian music beginning at 7pm. Unfortunately, service here can be glacially slow, and the kitchen does occasionally have a bad night.

MODERATE

Amber Restaurant
Durbar Marg. ☎ **977/1-225938.** Reservations recommended for dinner. Main dishes Rs90–Rs200 ($1.80–$4); vegetable dishes Rs3–Rs80 (70¢–$1.60). AE. Lunch daily noon–3pm; dinner daily 6–10pm. INDIAN.

At the south end of Durbar Marg, on the second floor of a row of shops and travel agencies, is another of Kathmandu's best Indian restaurants. Among the most flavorful dishes on the menu here are the chicken shahi korma and the chicken butter masala. Accompany your main course with one or more delicious vegetable dishes such as the malai kofta or shahi paneer and the Kashmiri pullao for a very filling and memorable meal. As at many Indian restaurants in Kathmandu, there is live traditional Indian and Nepali instrumental and vocal music nightly.

✪ Bhanchha Ghar

Kamaladi. ☎ **977/1-225172.** Reservations recommended. Main dishes Rs45–Rs150 (90¢–$3); set menu Rs605 ($12.10). AE, MC, V. Lunch daily noon–3pm; dinner daily 6–10pm. NEPALI.

There are very few restaurants in Kathmandu that specialize in Nepali cuisine, and only one other that serves Nepali cuisine in such elegant and unusual surroundings. Bhanchha Ghar utilizes a 100-year-old Rana residence that has been fully restored. Locally made wool felt rugs on the floor and colorful block-printed tablecloths and seat cushions brighten up what must have been a very dark home. Up on the top floor is a room where you'll think you are walking into a huge shepherd's tent when you see how the ceiling is draped with colorful block-printed fabrics. Low tables surrounded by brightly colored pillows further add to the exotic atmosphere. A round fireplace keeps the room warm on cold nights. While you wait for your dinner, lounge around on the floor like a Moghul potentate imbibing heady drinks and appetizers of venison and wild boar. Though there is an à la carte menu, most people order the fixed menu, which includes three flavorful and spicy meat dishes, rice, lentils, two fragrant vegetable dishes, Nepali-style pickles, dessert, tea or coffee, and a glass of *rakshi* (local moonshine).

✪ Fuji Restaurant

Kantipath. ☎ **977/1-225272.** Reservations recommended. Soups Rs30 (60¢); main dishes Rs50–Rs320 ($1–$6.40); set meals Rs230–Rs550 ($4.60–$11). AE, MC, V. Tues–Sun 11:30am–9:30pm (lunch 11:30am–3pm). JAPANESE.

One of my favorite restaurants in Kathmandu, Fuji should not be missed. The restaurant is located far back from Kantipath behind a row of offices. Dedicated in 1905, the building that houses Fuji was once a Rana gambling hall and dance pavilion. The redbrick facade with its white trim seems transported directly from Europe. To reach the restaurant, you must walk across a wooden bridge over the pond that surrounds the restaurant. When it's warm enough for al fresco dining, there is a large terrace built over the water, and for a truly unique dining experience, one table is set on its own private island. Inside, amid the high ceilings and painted plasterwork of past grandeur, there is a small bar, a teppanyaki bar, and a main dining area with large French doors opening onto the pond. The food is light and flavorful with many dishes served in fragrant broths. You'll find all your favorites on the menu with the exception of sushi and sashimi; it just isn't possible to get fish fresh enough for these dishes. The most popular menu offerings are the set lunches and dinners that come with appetizer, vinegar dish, braised vegetables, yakitori, steamed egg custard, tempura, sukiyaki, rice, miso soup, pickles, and fruit.

Koto Restaurant

Durbar Marg. ☎ **977/1-226025.** Reservations recommended for dinner. Soups Rs48–Rs170 ($1–$3.40); main dishes Rs50–Rs170 ($1–$3.40). MC, V. Lunch daily 11:30am–3pm; dinner daily 6–9:15pm. JAPANESE.

Kathmandu Dining

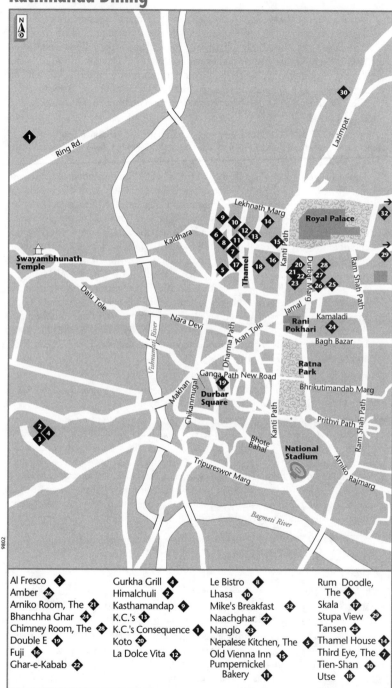

Al Fresco ③	Gurkha Grill ④	Le Bistro ⑧	Rum Doodle, The ⑥
Amber ㉖	Himalchuli ②	Lhasa ⑩	Skala ⑰
Arniko Room, The ㉑	Kasthamandap ⑨	Mike's Breakfast ㉜	Stupa View ㉙
Bhanchha Ghar ㉔	K.C.'s ⑬	Naachghar ㉗	Tansen ㉕
Chimney Room, The ㉘	K.C.'s Consequence ①	Nanglo ㉓	Thamel House ⑭
Double E ⑲	Koto ⑳	Nepalese Kitchen, The ⑤	Third Eye, The ⑦
Fuji ⑯	La Dolce Vita ⑫	Old Vienna Inn ⑮	Tien-Shan ㉚
Ghar-e-Kabab ㉒		Pumpernickel Bakery ⑪	Utse ⑱

9802

Down a dark alleyway near the entrance to the Hotel de l'Annapurna and up a flight of stairs is another of Kathmandu's Japanese restaurants. With only nine tables, the Koto is frequently full, so be sure to call and make a dinner reservation. Two of the tables are traditional low with cushions on the floor instead of chairs. Try the miso soup, made with locally prepared miso—it's especially warming on a cold night. The *yakitori don* (chicken barbecue on a bed of rice) is always good, or for an unusual twist try *tempura udon* (tempura on top of noodle soup).

ⓢ Nanglo

Durbar Marg. ☎ **977/1-222636.** Reservations recommended for dinner. Soups Rs40–Rs55 (80¢–$1.10); vegetable dishes Rs45(90¢); main dishes Rs35–Rs450 (70¢–$9). AE, MC, V. Daily 11am–9:30pm. CHINESE.

The first time I stopped in at Nanglo, I met an older British gentleman who swore that Nanglo served the best Chinese food in Kathmandu and that he would eat nowhere else. He had been visiting Kathmandu regularly for 17 years and for most of that time had been taking his custom to Nanglo. Though originally just a small Chinese restaurant, Nanglo has grown into a veritable dining complex at the south end of Durbar Marg near the Hotel Woodlands. There is a Chinese restaurant on the ground floor. It's a dark and traditional place with Chinese lanterns and red-and-black decor. The kitchen prepares excellent Cantonese and Mandarin dishes. For a light meal, try one of the noodle dishes, which feature homemade noodles. Then there is the pub in a separate room entered through a door to the left of the Chinese restaurant's door. Behind the pub is a bustling courtyard cafe that extends to a second-floor terrace overlooking Durbar Marg and the Himalayas. In the cafe the menu is mostly popular continental dishes, all for between Rs30 and Rs110 (60¢ and $2.20).

Tansen

Durbar Marg. ☎ **977/1-224707.** Reservations recommended. Main dishes Rs60–Rs225 ($1.20–$4.50). AE, MC, V. Daily 1:30am–9:30pm. INDIAN.

Under the same management as the ever-popular Nanglo Chinese restaurant across Durbar Marg (see above), Tansen serves good Indian food at reasonable prices. With copper plates, bowls, and cups, the table settings are as memorable as the meals themselves. You can sit at either Western tables or low Nepali-style tables on pillows on the floor. The white-jacketed waiters offer service that is usually a cut above what you can expect at most Kathmandu restaurants. For an unusual starter, try the *papri chat*—lentil chips in a spicy yogurt sauce. On the whole, sauces here are thick and rich, ideal for sopping up with any of the many interesting breads on the menu.

THAMEL & THE DIPLOMATIC DISTRICT
EXPENSIVE

Old Vienna Inn

Thamel. ☎ **977/1-419183.** Reservations recommended. Main dishes Rs95–Rs2.60 ($1.90–$5.20); desserts Rs65–Rs110 ($1.30–$2.20). Daily 6am–10pm. AUSTRIAN.

The Old Vienna Inn is a Kathmandu institution, and when the noise and dirt and crowds get to you, slip through the swinging glass door into Old Vienna to leave the stresses of Kathmandu behind. Inside, Old World decor and classical music set the tone. The menu is, as you would expect, heavy on the meat and potatoes, with such favorites as schnitzel and goulash, as well as less familiar dishes such as bacon dumplings and dumplings with sauerkraut. A tempting assortment of dessert crêpes will surely tempt you, but opt for the chocolate cake—it's the best in Nepal! When you're just hungry for a snack or want a quick lunch, the deli counter sells various imported sausages and salads.

✪ Thamel House

Thamel Tole. ☎ **977/1-410388.** Reservations recommended. Fixed-price dinner Rs400 ($8). MC, V. Daily 2–9:30pm. NEPALI.

Upscale restaurants serving Nepali food are proliferating in Kathamandu, and most have the same interior design and offer almost identical menus. This is the most convenient place if you are staying in Thamel, and it also happens to be the least expensive. It's housed in a 100-year-old brick home, one of Kathamandu's only buildings of this style and vintage which has been restored. You can choose to eat at a traditional low table surrounded by pillows rather than chairs. The fixed-price meals, though expensive by Thamel standards, are a bargain when you consider that they are all-you-can-eat and include a tiny clay cup of local rice liquor poured from a pitcher held three feet above your table. The set dinner includes an appetizer of spicy peanuts followed by rice served with bamboo-shoot and vegetable curries, mutton kebabs, wild boar, chicken curry, and pickled vegetables. For dessert, there is rice pudding and tea or coffee.

MODERATE

La Dolce Vita

Thamel. ☎ **977/1-419612.** Reservations recommended for groups. Main dishes Rs100–Rs165 ($2–$3.30); desserts Rs50 ($1). No credit cards. Daily 11am–10pm; bar 2–10pm. ITALIAN.

Located on the second and third floors of the building opposite the Kathmandu Guest House entrance, La Dolce Vita is an ode to old films, and there are movie posters hung on the walls throughout the restaurant. The emphasis of course is on the Italian classic *La Dolce Vita*. Everything inside seems to be done in black and white and bright red and yellow. La Dolce Vita serves very passable Italian meals considering the difficulty of getting ingredients here. The restaurant makes its own pastas, breads, and gelati and uses imported spices in their cooking. Try the gnocchi made with different local cheeses or the meat scallops in lemon sauce.

⑤ Kasthamandap Restaurant

Hotel Mandap, Thamel. ☎ **977/1-413321.** Reservations not necessary. Main dishes Rs50–Rs185 ($1–$3.70). AE, DC, JCB, MC, V. Daily 7am–10pm. INTERNATIONAL.

A budget traveler's version of the famous (and expensive) Chimney Room at the Hotel Yak & Yeti, Kasthamandap has the same type of high beamed ceiling and shiny copper chimney. However, it also has a brick-tile floor and redbrick walls, which give it a very Nepali feeling. Two walls of windows bathe the room in warm light during the day, or if you would rather be out in the sunshine, there are a few tables on the patio. Tables inside are set with linen and fresh flowers, and in one corner there is a small bar. Although the menu features shasklik and chicken Kiev (two of the Chimney Room's specialties), I like the Indian dishes best. The menu also includes pizzas and Mexican food.

BUDGET

⑤ Le Bistro

Thamel. ☎ **977/1-411170.** Reservations recommended for large groups. Breakfast Rs35–Rs75 (70¢–$1.50); vegetarian dinners Rs75–Rs80 ($1.50–$1.60); meat dinners Rs50–Rs140 ($1–$2.80). Daily 6:30am–10pm. INTERNATIONAL.

A longtime favorite with budget travelers, Le Bistro is only steps away from the entrance to the Kathmandu Guest House in the heart of Thamel. During the day, the restaurant's brick-paved garden is a popular meeting point. At night, when the weather gets cold, there are several small dining rooms decorated with interesting black-and-white photos of Nepal and Tibet. Service is very friendly but can be lackadaisical at times. Meals come with generous portions of bread, potatoes, two vegetables, and a salad of sterilized vegetables. The chocolate cake is addictive.

K.C.'s Restaurant

Thamel. ☎ **977/1-416911.** Reservations recommended for groups. Main dishes Rs80–Rs195 ($1.60–$3.90), desserts Rs50–Rs55 ($1–$1.10). No credit cards. Thurs–Tues 6am–9:30pm. INTERNATIONAL.

Always crowded, hot, and noisy, K.C.'s is one of Thamel's old standby restaurants. If you have a group and don't mind the noise level, the main dining room has two large, round, Japanese-style low tables surrounded by pillows. The menu, though it doesn't often change, is written on several blackboards around the restaurant. Steaks and pizzas are the most popular dishes, although the quiches are generally good (except for the spinach). The French onion soup makes a delicious and warming starter. Before or after dinner, you can hang out in the Bambooze Bar on the second floor.

Lhasa Restaurant

Thamel. ☎ **977/1-413841.** Reservations not accepted. Main dishes Rs16–Rs65 (35¢–$1.30). No credit cards. Daily 9am–10pm. TIBETAN/INTERNATIONAL.

The Lhasa is small and hot, and there's hardly enough room to walk between the tables. It also happens to be the best place in town for cheap Tibetan food, and one of the only tourist restaurants that serves *tongba*, a local alcoholic beverage made from fermented millet. What makes this drink so unusual is the way it is served. You get a stein full of millet and a thermos full of boiled water, which you pour over the millet. The hot water extracts the alcohol from the grain, and you ingest this hot brew through a crimped straw that prevents you from sucking up the millet. Want another glass? Just refill your stein with more hot water. To accompany your brew, order some momos and kothays (steamed and fried dumplings, respectively), and one of the numerous Tibetan noodle dishes.

The Nepalese Kitchen Restaurant

Chhetrapati. ☎ **977/1-211435.** Reservations not required. Soups Rs32–Rs45 (65¢–90¢); main dishes Rs50–Rs145 ($1–$2.90); set meals Rs72–Rs156 ($1.45–$3.15). No credit cards. Daily 8am–9:30pm. NEPALI.

Nepali food *is* more than just dal bhat, and at this restaurant on the road leading from Thamel to Swayambhunath, you can sample such unusual dishes as seven-bean soup or soup made with fermented bamboo shoots. Gundruk, another soup, is made with fermented and dried vegetables that are a staple in rural Nepal. These preserved veggies give the soup a unique flavor. To save yourself the trouble of making a decision, you can order a set meal that includes rice and black dal, local pickled vegetables, two types of vegetable curry, and dessert. If you have a dessert choice, always opt for the *sikarni,* a heavenly yogurt dish. There is live traditional Nepali music nightly on the restaurant's patio.

✪ Pumpernickel Bakery & Restaurant

Thamel. No phone. Reservations not accepted. Sandwiches Rs35–Rs38 (70¢–80¢). No credit cards. Daily 8am–6pm. INTERNATIONAL/BREADS.

With a large shady garden containing wicker tables, the Pumpernickel is popular with the sort of folks who frequent European cafes. A large and cluttered bulletin board gives an idea of how much cross-cultural exchange takes place here. What draws people of all nationalities to the Pumpernickel is good whole-wheat bread, rolls, bagels, and croissants. The menu is mostly a list of the different types of bread and toppings (yak cheese, egg, jam, honey, peanut butter) available. You get to mix and match. I suspect more coffee and tea are consumed here than at any other restaurant in town.

The Rum Doodle

Thamel. ☎ **977/1-414336.** Reservations not necessary. Main dishes Rs55–Rs130 ($1.10–$2.60). JCB, MC, V. Daily 6am–10pm. INTERNATIONAL.

Rum Doodle, whose name is a parody of old British mountaineering books, has long been the most popular bar in Kathmandu. Since moving a few years ago, it has also become quite popular for its food. The walls are covered with climbing, kayaking, and mountaineering gear, as well as big cutouts of yeti footprints that have been signed by various mountain-climbing and river expeditions. The menu includes such Kathmandu standards as chicken Kiev, beef stroganoff, and borscht, as well as chicken, buffalo, and tofu kebabs. The steaks and burgers are also popular with trekker just returned from their expeditions. In warm weather, you can dine in the garden, and when it's cold, you can sit by the fire in the main dining room.

Skala

Chha, Thamel. No phone. Reservations not required. Breakfast Rs45–Rs65 (90¢–$1.30); main dishes Rs70–Rs95 ($1.40–$1.90). No credit cards. Daily 8am–9pm. VEGETARIAN.

Down the lane to the left of the entrance to Le Bistro and tucked back behind a row of shops is a peaceful garden set with a few tables. Eclectic musical tastes control the stereo here and you might find yourself listening to Louis Armstrong or Sam Cooke. One reason I enjoy eating here is that this is one of the few places in town where you can get brown rice. The best meal on the menu is the Nepali dinner, which comes with rice, dal, and three vegetables for Rs90 ($1.80). The various vegetable dishes are all spicy and flavorful. This is certainly not the insipid dal bhat that trekkers become accustomed to on the trail.

The Third Eye

Chha 3-358, Thamel. ☎ **977/1-227478** or 977/1-229187. Reservations recommended for groups. Soups/salads Rs50–Rs80 ($1–$1.60); main dishes Rs80–Rs180 ($1.60–$3.60). AE, DC, MC, V. Daily 9am–10pm. INDIAN/INTERNATIONAL.

Though the Indian food here is quite good and the steaks and continental dishes are both filling and inexpensive, it is the unusual back dining room that has made this one of the most popular restaurants in Kathmandu. This back room features several tiers of low tables and has a very exotic, almost theatrical appearance. Diners leave their shoes out in the hall before entering this room and sit on pillows on the floor. The Third Eye stays packed every night, so if you want to have a seat in the back room, try to make a reservation, or arrive early. You'll find the restaurant almost across the street from the Blue Note Bar and the Maya Pub. The Third Eye's cappuccinos, though made with instant coffee, are covered with a thick layer of cinnamon.

Utse

Jyatha, Thamel. ☎ **977/1-228952.** Reservations not accepted. Main dishes Rs35–Rs150 (70¢–$3). MC, V. Daily 7am–9:30pm. CHINESE/TIBETAN.

For many years, Utse occupied a low building on Thamel's main square, but the restaurant has now moved to this new location in the lobby of the hotel of the same name. Utse stays packed at night, so come early, or try to make a reservation. I like the traditional low tables and Tibetan-rug–covered couches, but there are also plenty of Western-style tables as well. The menu is primarily Chinese, but it is the well-prepared Tibetan dishes that are the main draw here. Dishes worth trying are the *kothays* (fried dumplings), *momos* (steamed dumplings), and the thukpa soup. If you give the kitchen two-hours' notice, they can prepare a *gyakok* or *kadug dhayshey*, two special Tibetan dinners. It takes four to six people to polish off one of these special meals.

ELSEWHERE IN THE CITY
EXPENSIVE

✪ K.C.'s Consequence Restaurant & More

Balajutar. ☎ **977/1-272274.** Reservations recommended. Soups Rs110–Rs200 ($2.20–$4); main dishes Rs260–Rs295 ($5.20–$5.90). No credit cards. Tues–Sun 12:30–10pm. CONTINENTAL.

Owned by the same family that brought Kathmandu the ever-popular K.C.'s Restaurant in Thamel, K.C.'s Consequence is north of the city off the Ring Road. You'll need to take a taxi to get here, and if the taxi isn't familiar with the restaurant, have the driver head north out of Thamel to Ring Road, turn west, and then watch for the restaurant's small sign that points north up a narrow dirt road. The restaurant is a tranquil retreat surrounded by vegetable gardens and fruit orchards. Much of the food served here is organically grown on the property, and there is even a beehive producing honey for the kitchen's sweets. The gates to the property are decorated by a crazy quilt of welded scrap-iron objects, from pots and pans to sewing machines and old fans. Much of the restaurant is made up of sprawling terraces that allow you to enjoy the garden setting, but the indoor dining rooms, in an old house that has been expanded with salvaged architectural details from around the valley, are full of antiques and have wood stoves for warming you on winter nights. If you happen to have children with you, there is a supervised play area for them. When I last visited, K.C.'s Consequence was closed for renovations and expansion but planned to reopen by the 1995 trekking season. Be sure to call before heading out there.

BUDGET

✪ Mike's Breakfast

Naxal. No phone. Reservations not accepted. Breakfast Rs85–Rs175 ($1.70–$3.50); lunch Rs90–Rs175 ($1.80–$3.50). No credit cards. Daily 7am–9pm. INTERNATIONAL.

For many years Mike's Breakfast has been the most popular breakfast spot in Kathmandu. Local expatriates, middle-class Nepalis, and tourists all appreciate the flower-filled garden, huge portions, bottomless cups of coffee, and classical music on the stereo. I can think of no better way to start a day in Kathmandu. The restaurant is housed in a restored European-style minimansion a 10-minute walk east of the Royal Palace (located at the top of Durbar Marg). A previous incarnation of Mike's Breakfast was housed in a similar building and garden one block over from Durbar Marg, but that building was bulldozed in 1994 to make way for a modern office building. Mike's also serves other meals besides breakfast. When I last visited the restaurant, owner Mike Frame, who hails from Minnesota, was

working on a new project—the Northfield Café and Jesse James Bar—which will
be located a few doors up the street from the Kathmandu Guest House.

Double E Restaurant & Bar

Ratna Plaza, Dharma Path (New Road). ☎ **977/1-214085,** ext. 17. Reservations not
necessary. Main dishes Rs45–Rs190 (90¢–$3.80). DC, MC, V. Daily noon–10pm. INDIAN/
INTERNATIONAL.

Located atop a modern (by Kathmandu standards) shopping mall only two long
blocks from Durbar Square, this restaurant makes a good between–temples lunch
stop. You can dine inside or out on the terrace; in either area, you may have a view
of the Himalayas if the weather is clear. In the evenings and sometimes at lunch,
there is live Western music. Popular primarily with Nepalis and Indians, Double
E serves mostly Indian food with a selection of simple Chinese dishes as well. There
are also a few sandwiches on the menu.

Stupa View Restaurant

Boudha. ☎ **977/1-471368.** Reservations not required. Main dishes Rs45–Rs190 (90¢–
$3.80). No credit cards. Daily 9am–9:30pm. VEGETARIAN.

This German-run restaurant is Kathmandu's best vegetarian restaurant and also has
one of the best views in the city—it looks directly into the eyes of Boudhanath
stupa. A perusal of the menu turns up dishes with such unusual names as elephant
feet, crocodile tears, buffalo's nightmare, and monkey love affair. No, these dishes
aren't made with endangered species; they're all meat-free and include brown rice,
curried veggies, vegetable schnitzel, and Greek salad. There is a daily special that
goes for Rs165 ($3.30).

SPECIALTY DINING
HOTEL DINING

Be aware that hotels charge the same tax on food that they do on rooms. The fan-
cier the hotel the higher the tax (as much as 15%), whereas a restaurant that is not
part of a hotel charges only 10%.

Al Fresco

Hotel Soaltee Holiday Inn Crown Plaza. Tahachal. ☎ **977/1-272550.** Reservations recommended for dinner. Pastas Rs220–Rs595 ($4.40–$11.90); main dishes Rs365–Rs695 ($7.30–
$13.90); desserts Rs95 ($1.90). AE, DC, EU, MC, V. Daily 11am–10:45pm. ITALIAN.

Al Fresco, located in the basement of the suite wing, is a very fashionable (and
overpriced) little trattoria and Italian deli. Large glass windows look out onto the
hotel's neatly manicured lawns, and plenty of potted plants around the dining
rooms bring the greenery inside. White stucco walls are festooned with strings of
chili peppers and garlic braids. Wrought-iron chandeliers hang from the ceiling,
and European ceramics decorate the walls adding dashes of color. Waiters are
friendly and efficient. Among the memorable dishes are cold cream of pimiento
soup, veal scallops with parma ham and mozzarella, and smoked salmon with
capers and onion rings. The Italian-trifle is a perfectly decadent way to finish a meal.

The Chimney Room

Hotel Yak & Yeti, Durbar Marg. ☎ **977/1-413999.** Reservations recommended. Main dishes
Rs255–Rs680 ($5.10–$13.30). AE, MC, V. Daily 7:30–11pm. RUSSIAN/CONTINENTAL.

Originally known as the Yak & Yeti Restaurant and located in another hotel, the
Chimney Room was founded by a famous Russian expatriate, Boris Lissanevitch,
who resided in Kathmandu for many years. With brick walls and high ceilings, the

restaurant has the feeling of a rathskeller and takes its name from a large copper and brass chimney over a circular hearth in the middle of the restaurant. In the winter roaring fires and stiff drinks help keep the chill away as you wait to be seated. Though some say meals aren't up to their old standards, the Russian specialties introduced by Boris are still popular. Start with a bowl of thick rich borscht, and follow with chicken Kiev, beef Stroganoff, or jumbo prawn shashlik. You'll find all of these dishes on other menus in town, but nowhere are they prepared better than here. Follow up your meal with a rich baked Alaska à la Sagarmatha (the Nepali name for Mt. Everest) and a special coffee laced with liquor.

✪ Gurkha Grill

Soaltee Holiday Inn Crowne Plaza, Tahachal. ☎ 977/1-272550. Reservations recommended. Soups Rs95 ($1.90); main dishes Rs350–Rs795 ($7–$15.90); desserts Rs145–Rs300 ($2.90–$6). AE, DC, EU, MC, V. Tues–Sun 7pm–12:45am. FRENCH.

The Soaltee Holiday Inn Crowne Plaza seems to have cornered the market on great restaurants. I guess it goes along with being the most luxurious hotel in the country. The Gurkha Grill would be my first choice among the hotel's restaurants. Kathmandu's best French and continental cuisine is served here amid casual surroundings that draw on classical Kathmandu Valley architectural themes for inspiration—red brick and carved wood. You might start out with the escargot bourguignon and follow with the chateau-briand or rack of lamb. Since many of the hotel's Indian guests are vegetarians, the restaurant also offers some very innovative meatless dishes such as cottage cheese steaks with mushrooms and coriander sauce served on a bed of tomatoes and ginger with a honey glaze. For dessert, try the mango cheesecake with chocolate mousse and Benedictine sauce.

Himalchuli

Hotel Soaltee Holiday Inn Crowne Plaza, Tahachal. ☎ 977/1-272550. Reservations recommended. Soups Rs95 ($1.90); main dishes Rs150–Rs395 ($3–$7.90); vegetable dishes Rs85–Rs125 ($1.70–$2.50); desserts Rs95 ($1.90). AE, MC, V. Daily 7–10:45pm. INDIAN/NEPALI.

Through the large carved wood doors to the left of the reception desk is the Soaltee's venue for regional cuisine. With a menu that features Nepali, Indian, and a few Tibetan dishes, Himalchuli is an excellent restaurant to try if you want to sample a little bit of each. All the food is well prepared, though the Indian dishes tip the scales a bit. The yakhni shorba, a spicy almond soup, is both delicious and unusual. Momos, the popular Tibetan dumplings similar to something you might have for dim sum, are served with spicy tomato chutney. The tandoori chicken is always well done and is best accompanied by hot nan and a rich vegetable dish. Traditional Nepali music and dances are performed Wednesday through Monday from 7 to 9pm followed by *ghazals* (a traditional form of Indian and Nepali vocal music).

✪ Naachghar

Hotel Yak & Yeti, Durbar Marg. ☎ 977/1-413999. Reservations recommended. Main dishes Rs90–Rs375 ($1.80–$7.50). Daily 7:30–11pm. INDIAN/NEPALI.

Located in the old palace wing of the Yak & Yeti Hotel, Naachghar is perhaps Kathmandu's most elegant restaurant. The high-ceilinged palace room now occupied by the restaurant has a marble floor and classical pillars supporting the roof. Along the walls are shallow arched alcoves. Ornate plasterwork and a mural of the signs of the zodiac on the ceiling hint at the tastes of the Rana prime minister who had this palace constructed. A stage at one end is used for a cultural program of Nepali music and dance that is staged nightly from 8:30 to 9:30pm. The dishes emanating from the tandoor oven here are the real gems. Try the tandoori platter, which includes chicken tikka, seekh kebabs, tandoori fish, and *nan* (tandoor-baked bread). Accompany this with the creamy *birbal malai kofta* (a cheese dumpling made with nuts) for an exceedingly rich meal. If you still have room, in fact be sure to save room, try the *sikarni,* a sweet and spicy yogurt-based dessert.

Tien-Shan

Hotel Shangri-la, Lazimpat. ☎ **977/1-412999.** Reservations recommended. Soups Rs90–Rs105 ($1.80–$2.10); main dishes Rs75–Rs300 ($1.50–$6). AE, DC, MC, V. Lunch daily noon–2:30pm; dinner daily 7–11pm. CHINESE.

Popular with locals, expatriates, and tourists alike, Tien-Shan is arguably the best Chinese food in town. Located upstairs from the hotel's lobby, Tien-Shan is small and elegant with Chinese chairs, fresh flowers, and linens on the table. The staff is helpful and attentive. Szechuan- and Cantonese-style dishes are available for fire-eaters and those with tamer palates. I like the Szechuan spiced pork, but I recommend the chicken with hot garlic sauce and hot-and-sour soup as well. The hot candied banana is an unusual dessert that you're not likely to find on many other Kathmandu menus.

DINING WITH A VIEW

Several of the major hotels in Kathmandu have fine views from one or more of their restaurants, and even many budget hotels have rooftop gardens where you can order a meal through room service. My favorite view is that offered from the Hotel Himalaya's (see "Patan" in Chapter 5) **Chalet,** a continental restaurant open for lunch and dinner only. At the Everest Hotel, the **Far Pavilions** and **Sherpaland** restaurants, both on the top floor, offer outstanding mountain and valley views to accompany their Indian, Tibetan, and Chinese food. The **Explorers Restaurant** at the Hotel Vajra serves lunch and snacks up in the hotel roof garden where there is an excellent view of Swayambunath stupa. Over at Boudhanath stupa, there is the **Stupa View Restaurant,** which specializes in European vegetarian meals. In Patan, the **Café Pagode** provides equally memorable views. In Bhaktapur you can enjoy the views from either the **Café de Peacock** or the **Nyatapola Café.**

A LOCAL FAVORITE

Nirula's Hot Shoppe, Durbar Marg (☎ 977/1-211711), near the south end of Durbar Marg, is one of Kathmandu's most popular restaurants with the younger set. Nirula's is one of Nepal's only fast-food-type restaurants. Though it isn't all that fast, it certainly has the look and feel. Young Nepalis in blue jeans and denim jackets crowd into the booths and stuff themselves with hot dogs, pizza, burgers, and ice cream. Lots of homesick Westerners do the same. Reservations are not accepted. Pizzas and burgers cost Rs32 to Rs75 (70¢–$1.50); ice cream Rs20 to Rs41 per scoop (40¢ to 85¢). It's open daily from 10am to 10pm.

4 What to See & Do in Kathmandu

Kathmandu resembles a medieval city. Similarities, both living and preserved, to medieval cities of Europe can be seen everywhere. One of the greatest thrills is simply to wander through the narrow alleys of the old city. Getting lost in Kathmandu can lead to some of the most memorable sights and experiences. It is easy to imagine that you're the first foreign visitor ever to lay eyes on some tiny shrine tucked away down a muddy alley. Kathmandu is a living museum where lifestyles long since vanished from the Western world continue. It's a city of temples and shrines and living gods, where worship of gods and goddesses is an integral and public part of daily life. It is here, legend has it, that the pagoda was invented and later exported to China and Japan. Pagoda temples, each housing a different god, abound throughout the city. Keep your eyes open as you wander the streets, and you will likely find the daily life of the people of Kathmandu fascinating as any temple, palace, or museum you may visit.

SUGGESTED ITINERARIES

If You Have 1 Day

Head first to Durbar Square and spend the morning exploring the many temples and palaces. Then stroll up through the market area northeast of the square. In the afternoon, visit Swayambunath, Pashupatinath, and Boudhanath—three important religious sites in the valley. If you have only 1 day, though, it might be best to book two half-day tours of the city—an inexpensive way to see a lot of the city in 1 day. You could also hire a car, driver, and guide for the day.

If You Have 2 Days

Spend your first day as outlined above. On your second day visit Bhaktapur, considered the most medieval of the Kathmandu Valley's three cities. From Bhaktapur, continue to either Nagarkot or Dhulikel for a stunning panorama of the Himalayas. The best time of day for a visit to either of these towns on the rim of the valley is at sunrise or sunset.

If You Have 3 Days

See above outline for your first 2 days. On day 3, you might take a 1-hour mountain flight for a close-up view of the Himalayas (that is, if you don't plan to fly into one of the remote airstrips as part of a trek). Later in the day go to Patan and see this city's Durbar Square and its other beautiful temples. If you are interested in buying a carpet, visit the Tibetan Refugee Camp. For brass, bronze, and copper statuettes, visit the Patan Industrial Estate or the small shops around Durbar Square and the Temple of 1,000 Buddhas (Mahaboudha Temple).

If You Have 5 Days or More

If you are spending more than 3 days in Kathmandu, then you will probably want to spend an entire day shopping. This will also allow you to revisit your favorite sights. A visit to Budhanilkantha to see the Sleeping Vishnu statue is well worthwhile. For those with a taste for the macabre, or whose curiosity gets the better of them, a trip to Dakshinkali to witness the animal sacrifices is certainly a different sort of holiday experience. The town of Panauti, with its recently restored temple complex, is also worth a visit and makes an interesting combination with a half-day hike to the Namobuddha shrine. I strongly recommend spending one of your last 2 days on a long day hike somewhere in the Kathmandu Valley. The hikes down from Nagarkot are particularly interesting because they can lead through villages to different temples.

1 The Top Attractions

KATHMANDU'S DURBAR SQUARE

Durbar Square is the heart of Kathmandu and encompasses not only Durbar Square but also Hanuman Dhoka Square, Basantapur Square, Hanuman Dhoka, and Maru Tole. With more than 50 temples and shrines within a few blocks of one another, the square contains one of the most concentrated groupings of historical structures in the valley. Durbar means "king," and it was from the Royal Palace on the square that the kings of Nepal once ruled. Because there is so much to see in the square, it is best to be systematic in your peregrinations. The following are the highlights of the Durbar Square area. There are dozens of other temples and shrines in the neighborhood that you might also find interesting. The following walk around Durbar Square begins at the New Road entrance to the square, just past Freak Street.

Kumari Bahal   As you enter Durbar Square, you will see on your left two colorfully painted stone lions guarding the doorway of a beautiful house built in 1757. The Kathmandu Valley has long been known for the skill of its wood-carvers, and this house is one of the finest examples of the art. Intricately carved wooden lattice windows cover the facade of the three-story brick building. On the second floor are two peacock windows that, in my opinion, surpass the famous Bhaktapur peacock window in workmanship and beauty. On the third floor there are two circular windows set inside square frames and three shallow latticed balconies. The central third-floor window is the most attractive of all with gilding and two repoussé statues of Tantric deities. Over every window is a semicircular carved wood panel called a *torana*. Each torana depicts different Hindu deities and symbols.

Be sure to watch your head as you step through the low, open door that leads to a courtyard. Notice the human skulls carved into the wooden door frame and lintel. Inside the courtyard there are intricately carved windows even more beautiful than those on the exterior facade. Even the low stone wall that surrounds the sunken courtyard is carved with interesting images. In the middle of the courtyard are a tiny stupa similar to Swayambunath and two *mandalas* symbolizing the universe.

However, it is not the craftmanship or the architecture of this building that fascinates visitors; it is the person who lives here—the *kumari*. The kumari is a living goddess, and no other figure in Nepal captures the mystery of this isolated Himalayan kingdom better than this dark-eyed little girl. Since the first kumari was installed in this temple house more than 200 years ago by the then-king of Kathmandu, there has been a long succession of kumaris.

One legend claims that the first kumari was installed after King Jaya Prakash Malla exiled a young girl who was said to be possessed by the spirit of the goddess Kumari. This so outraged the king's wife that he brought the young girl back and locked her up in a temple. Another legend holds that the king had sex with a prepubescent girl who later died. To atone for his sins, he enthroned a young girl as a living goddess and worshipped her chastely. Once a year he would take her from her temple and parade her around the city. Yet another legend states that the king, who frequently played dice with the human incarnation of the goddess Taleju (herself an incarnation of Shiva's consort Parvati), angered the goddess by lusting after her. In response to his inappropriate advances, she promised to return only as a chaste virgin.

Some people believe that the kumari is an incarnation of the goddess Taleju, while others hold that she is an incarnation of Durga (another incarnation of Parvati). Still others claim she is one of the *asta matrika,* the eight mother goddesses. Regardless of which goddess she represents, she is highly revered. Several times a year she is paraded through the streets of Kathmandu in a massive wooden chariot, part of which can be seen through the yellow gate to the right of the main entrance to the Kumari Bahal. During the festival of Indra Jatra, held in late August or early September, the kumari blesses the king of Nepal by placing the *tika* mark on his forehead.

The kumari is not born into goddesshood. She is chosen, and the process is a grueling and frightening one. First a number of four- to five-year-old Newari girls of the Shakya goldsmithing and silversmithing caste are chosen as candidates. A likely candidate must bear 32 specific traits, among which are freedom from any deformities, black eyes, long slender arms, graceful hands and feet, straight black hair that curls to the right at the bottom, and a beautiful voice. Also important is that she must never have shed blood prior to her being chosen as a candidate. The likely candidates are then subjected to a terrifying test intended to determine which is the real kumari. The girls are locked in a dark room where men in horrifying masks try to scare them. Freshly severed water buffalo heads are displayed, and frightening noises are made. The girl who shows no fear is chosen, since a goddess would have no fear. After this test, an astrologer is called in to determine whether the kumari's horoscope is compatible with the king's. If so, she is enthroned during the Dasain festival.

The kumari is considered a living goddess only as long as she never shows sign of her mortality by bleeding. Many kumaris have been replaced when they lost a tooth, but often they retain their position until they reach puberty and begin menstruating. After giving up their goddesshood, kumaris are supported with an allowance until they marry, at which time a dowry is provided.

There are actually several kumaris in the Kathmandu Valley, but this one is by far the most famous and is called the royal kumari. If you are lucky, you may catch a glimpse of her in one of the upstairs windows of the Kumari Bahal. However, it is forbidden to photograph her.

Narayan Mandir To your right as you face the Kumari Bahal is a three-story pagoda temple atop a six-tiered platform. If you walk around to the far side of the temple, you will see a large and beautiful stone statue of Garuda, the half-man, half-bird vehicle upon which the Hindu god Vishnu travels. The presence of Garuda kneeling before this temple indicates that the temple is dedicated to, and contains a statue of, Vishnu. In this case Vishnu is in his aspect of Narayan, which is the most commonly encountered aspect of Vishnu in Nepal. Unfortunately the temple is not open to the public, and you will not be able to see the statue inside.

Kasthamandap Just behind the stone Garuda statue, Durbar Square abuts a smaller square known as Maru Tole, where vendors sell produce and vibrant marigold garlands to be used as offerings at the nearby Ganesh shrine. Hulking over Maru Tole is one of the most unusual buildings in Kathmandu. The Kasthamandap, meaning "Wooden Pavilion," is an imposing three-story pagoda-style building that legends say was built from a single tree in the 12th century. On each of the four corners of its first floor there is a viewing platform surrounded by low carved wooden railings. In the dark recesses there is a tiny statue of Guru Goraknath, a revered Hindu saint. Today it is a temple of sorts and is frequently used as a gathering spot.

Maru Ganesh While exploring the Kasthamandap, it is impossible to miss the bustle of activity surrounding a closet-sized shrine across the alley that runs behind the old pavilion. This is the Maru Ganesh, also known as the Kathmandu Ganesh or the Ashok Binayak. The gilded roof of this small shrine was erected by King Surendra Bir Bikram Shah Dev in 1874, and to this day all kings come to worship here as part of their coronation ceremony. Ganesh, the most popular of the Hindu gods, is the god of good luck and a bringer of good fortune to new homes and to people going on journeys. People constantly drop by the shrine to leave offerings of food and flowers and mornings are especially busy. On holidays there are usually two lines of worshipers—one for men and one for women—waiting to get into the tiny room that holds the small statue of Ganesh. The clanging of the temple bell is nearly constant at this time.

Maju Deval (Shiva Mandir) As you reenter Durbar Square from Maru Tole, you'll pass by a small Shiva temple, the first floor of which contains little shops. Behind the temple is the Maju Deval, or Shiva Temple, a favorite with people who want to just sit and soak up the passing scene on Durbar Square. Perched atop a 10-tiered pyramid is a three-roofed pagoda. Unfortunately, the view of the temple is interrupted by a badly whitewashed temple of the *shikhara* style (an Indian style of architecture). Inside this temple is a Shiva *lingam,* the phallic symbol commonly used to represent Shiva. If your eyesight is good, or if you can strain your neck without falling off the uppermost tier of this temple's base, you will see some of Kathmandu's famous erotic carvings on the roof struts. The carvings on the nearby Jagannath temple are, however, much easier to see.

Shiva-Parvati Temple With so many pagodas on the square, it would be easy to overlook this 18th-century house-style temple were not for the two figures gazing down from a second-floor window. This attractive couple is the Hindu god Shiva and his consort Parvati. The garish paint jobs allow them to fit right into the colorful scene of the square. The lions guarding the entrance to this temple indicate that the temple houses a goddess, in this case it is a black stone image of Asta Yogini. The base of the temple and the wide patio in front are popular spots with vendors who set up portable kitchens and cook snacks and tea (I advise staying away from such street foods).

The Big Bell, Stone Temples, and Giant Drums　Behind the Shiva-Parvati temple and on the same side of the street are several small temples and shrines. First is a big bell that was erected in the 18th century. Past the bell on the same side of the street are two small stone temples, the first dedicated to Vishnu and the second to Saraswati, the goddess of learning. Past these is an unusual octagonal stone temple dedicated to Krishna. Past this temple and before you reach the gates of the police station is a pair of giant drums that are played once a year during the Dasain festival after a goat and a water buffalo are sacrificed.

Kal Bhairav　Across the street from the giant drums is a high-relief image of Kal (Black) Bhairav, the Lord of Destruction. This fearsome 10-foot-tall stone figure is another of the many aspects of Shiva. Atop his wide-eyed face is a crown decorated with human skulls, and on his back is a human skin. The prostrate figure upon which Kal Bhairav is standing represents human ignorance. It is also said that the prone figure is Kal Bhairav's father-in-law, who insulted Shiva and caused his own daughter, Kal Bhairav's wife, to commit suicide. Kal Bhairav has six arms, and in one of his hands he holds a skull cup that worshipers often toss coins into—and there are always a few boys around to quickly snatch them up.

Erected in the 17th or 18th century, the statue was supposedly used as a lie detector. Someone suspected of committing a crime would be brought before the statue, made to touch its feet, and then forced to say whether or not they committed the crime. It was believed that if they lied, they would immediately bleed to death. The mere threat of being brought before Kal Bhairav was often enough to elicit a confession.

Taleju Temple　Located behind the walls of Hanuman Dhoka Palace, this massive temple is only open to the Hindu public once a year, during the Dasain festival. It is by far the largest temple in the Durbar Square area and dominates the horizon as you enter from the north. Its three gilded roofs and ornate spire glimmer in the sun, and bells that hang from each of the three roofs can often be heard when the wind blows.

The innermost room of the temple holds a statue of Taleju Bhawani that was brought from India and is off limits to everyone but the royal family. The temple is dedicated to Taleju Bhawani, also known as Durga, who is an aspect of Shiva's consort Parvati. Taleju was the tutelary goddess of the Malla kings who ruled Kathmandu from the 14th to the 18th century. The current building dates to the mid-16th century, though the temple was founded in the 14th century. Old legends say that human sacrifices were once performed here.

Opposite the gate leading into the Taleju temple complex is a very unusual temple. Erected in 1681, the Kakeshwar Mahadeva Temple incorporates both Nepali and Indian temple architecture. The bottom half of the structure is in the style of a Nepali pagoda, but the top half is a whitewashed stucco shikhara-style building.

Stone Inscription　Along the wall to the right of the entrance to the Taleju Temple is an inscription carved in stone. It is written in 15 different languages and several different alphabets. From the English version of the inscription, you will learn that the stone was erected on January 14, 1664, by King Pratap Malla, who prided himself on his mastery of languages.

Jagannath Temple   The larger of the two temples across from the stone inscription is the 17th-century Jagannath Temple. This pagoda is known for its colorfully painted erotic carvings, the best in Kathmandu's Durbar Square, on the wooden struts that support the lowest roof. Some say that the erotic carvings were meant to instruct young people. Others contend that the erotic carvings are there to test the powers of concentration of the devout—only inches away from the erotic scenes are beautiful carvings of Hindu deities. The most popular explanation is that the erotic carvings are there to protect the temple from the goddess of lightning who is quite prudish and shies away from such graphic depictions of sexual union. No temple so decorated has ever been struck by lightning.

Hanuman Statue   Across from the Jagannath Temple is the most revered statue in Nepal. It is this statue of the Hindu monkey god Hanuman that gives its name to both this square and to the adjacent palace. Hanuman Dhoka means "Hanuman Gate" and is a reference to the statue and the entrance into the old royal palace. Hanuman is a character from the Hindu epic, *Ramayana,* which tells the story of Prince Rama and his wife Sita, who is kidnapped by the evil Ravana. Hanuman, a white monkey, becomes Rama's most loyal ally and helps to rescue Sita. Hanuman is symbolic of unquestioned loyalty, and that is why his statue guards the gate of the old royal palace.

Erected in 1672, the statue stands atop a low pillar and is protected from the sun by an umbrella. Over the years, devout worshipers of Hanuman have covered the figure with a thick layer of orange paste that completely obscures the features of the statue. For the uninformed it is quite curious to see people lining up to leave offerings at the foot of a colorfully cloaked orange blob.

Hanuman Dhoka Palace   The oldest sections of this palace were built in the 17th century, but from that time until early in this century, there were frequent additions. The king no longer lives here (his new palace is at the top of fashionable Durbar Marg), but coronations are still held here. You enter the palace compound (there is a Rs10 [20¢] admission fee) through the lavishly decorated Golden Door beside the statue of Hanuman. A colorfully painted stone lion stands on either side of the doorway. Atop one lion sits Shiva and atop the other sits his *shakti* or consort, Parvati. On either side of the door are painted numerous Hindu and Buddhist symbols. Above the door are several statues and bas-reliefs of different gods. Just inside on the left is a stone statue of Narsimha, a half-man, half-lion god, who is shown devouring the evil demon Haranyakashipu. To the right of this statue is a portrait gallery of the Shah kings of the current dynasty.

This first of many palace courtyards is the largest and most historic. Called the **Nasal Chowk,** it is here that kings are crowned. Of the many towers within the palace, only the Basantapur Tower is open to the public, but it is this tower that makes a visit to Hanuman Dhoka Palace a necessity. Unless you are curious to see the royal bicycle, the royal typewriter, the royal boxing gloves, the decorative ornaments of the royal tusker, and other memorabilia of the late King Tribhuvan, then I would skip the Tribhuvan Museum, which is to your right as you enter the palace compound, and head straight for the tower. If you do visit the museum, you will have to lock up your camera, and since the museum leads into the tower, you will have to come back across the courtyard to get your camera before ascending to the top. This stately pagoda is four stories tall, but because it is built atop the roof of the four-story palace, the top floor is actually eight floors above the ground. Latticed windows look down from every floor and admit only filtered light into the brick-walled interior. Supposedly Malla kings were born on the first floor, granted public audiences on the second floor, observed dances and dramatic productions from the third floor, and surveyed the city from the fourth to make sure that there was smoke coming from every house, thus assuring that no one was going hungry. This is an excellent vantage point from which to observe the activity in Basantapur and Durbar Squares; the whole of Kathmandu spreads out below you with green hills and snowy peaks off in the distance.

Basantapur Tower, also called the Kathmandu Tower, is one of four towers erected at the four corners of the very ornate Lohan Chowk, the small courtyard adjacent to Nasal Chowk. These four towers were built by King Prithvi Narayan Shah, who unified Nepal. The towers represent the four cities of the Kathmandu Valley—Kathmandu, Patan, Bhaktapur, and Kirtipur.

With its circular roofs and very ornate roof struts, the five-story Pancha Mukhi Hanuman tower stands at the northeast corner of Nasal Chowk. To the left of this tower is a golden fish mounted on a pole, a symbol of the Hindu god Vishnu. Down in the courtyard there is a raised stage upon which the present king was crowned in 1975.

Seto Bhairav   If you walk straight ahead as you leave the palace, you will find a large lattice screen at the far corner of the building on your left. You may have walked right past this screen before without noticing that there was anything behind it, but if you peer through, you, will see a giant mask of a terrifying visage. This is Seto (White) Bhairav, another aspect of Shiva. The gruesome gilded mask with its huge fangs was erected in the late 18th century to protect the royal palace from evil spirits. Today, the mask is associated with an entirely different sort of spirit—home-brewed rice beer. Once a year, during the festival of Indrajatra, the lattice screen is opened to reveal Seto Bhairav. From a long straw sticking out of the mask's mouth, beer that has been blessed by this god flows into the mouths of eagerly waiting men. To drink this sanctified beer is considered a great blessing.

Above and to the right of the mask is a beautiful three-sided balcony. The wood carving is intricately detailed, and the overall effect very delicate. Decorating this balcony are gilt repoussé *toranas* (semicircular decorated panels) and *nagas* (protective snakelike animals). Only as recently as 1975 was it discovered that two of the adjacent windows are made of carved ivory and not wood.

King Pratap Malla   Facing the mask of Seto Bhairav and Hanuman Dhoka Palace is a statue of this famous Malla king. The king sits cross-legged atop his stone pillar and gazes over the square. Many of the temples and monuments in the Durbar Square area, including the statue of Hanuman and the stone inscription, were erected by this king. His statue faces the Degu Taleju Temple, the largest temple on Hanuman Dhoka Square.

Gaddi Baithak   Looking entirely out of place in the otherwise medieval tableau of Durbar Square, the whitewashed stucco facade of the Gaddi Baithak reflects neoclassical and European influences. This palace annex was built in 1908 by one of the ruling Rana prime ministers, whose family had seized power from the royal family in the mid 19th century. The Ranas were well known for their infatuation with European culture and emptied the kingdom's coffers constructing European-style palaces. The building is still used for state functions, and, during religious celebrations, the king sometimes observes festivities from a throne that is kept here.

Kathmandu's Durbar Square Area

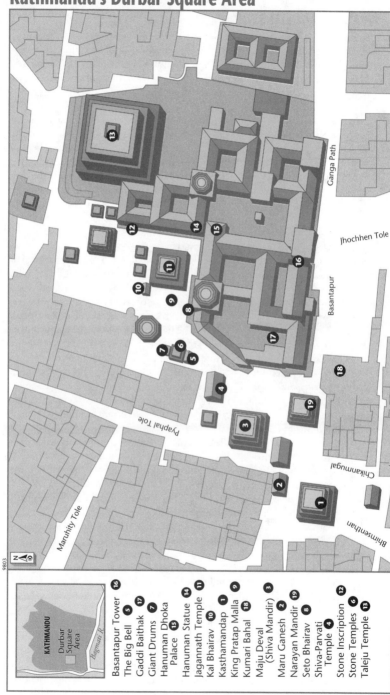

Ganga Path

Jhochhen Tole

Basantapur

Pyaphal Tole

Chikanmugal

Bhimsenthan

Maruthity Tole

9803

KATHMANDU

Durbar
Square
Area

Bagmati R.

Basantapur Tower 16
The Big Bell 5
Gaddi Baithak 17
Giant Drums 7
Hanuman Dhoka
Palace 15
Hanuman Statue 14
Jagannath Temple 11
Kal Bhairav 10
Kasthamandap 1
King Pratap Malla 9
Kumari Bahal 18
Maju Deval
(Shiva Mandir) 3
Maru Ganesh 2
Narayan Mandir 19
Seto Bhairav 8
Shiva-Parvati
Temple 4
Stone Inscription 12
Stone Temples 6
Taleju Temple 13

SWAYAMBUNATH STUPA

A long time ago, so the story goes, the Kathmandu Valley was a vast lake upon which floated a giant lotus flower glowing with the light of Swayambhu, the primordial, self-born Buddha from whom all creation emanated. The Tibetan god Manjushri heard of the existence of this Buddha and journeyed from Tibet to witness the sight. When he arrived, he could not get a close look at the lotus-flower Buddha because it was too far out in the lake. So, Manjushri used his sword to cut a slice out of a mountain on the south side of the lake, draining the lake and creating the Kathmandu Valley. The lotus came to rest on a hill in the western part of the valley, and here Manjushri built a shrine to honor this Buddha. The eerie part of this legend is that researchers have learned that the Kathmandu Valley was once a huge lake, but that the lake existed long before people inhabited the area. Chovar Gorge, the gorge that was supposedly cut by Manjushri on the south side of the valley, is a deep narrow canyon that actually looks as if it had been cut by a giant sword.

The earliest record of the stupa's existence is from a fifth-century stone inscription. However, scholars and archaeologists believe that there was probably a shrine here as long as 2,000 years ago. Regardless of how old it is, Swayambunath has an ancient feel that is accentuated by approaching it on foot as pilgrims do. Riding in a taxi up the road on the back side of the hill is less dramatic. The pilgrim's route is a steep stone staircase of more than 300 steps. Some claim that there are 365 steps to the top, but I have never been able to arrive at that number. At the base is a large, brightly painted gateway. To the right of the gate is a long row of copper prayer wheels, inside of which are thousands of Tibetan Buddhist prayers. It is believed that when the prayer wheel is spun, all the written prayers inside are recited and sent heavenward. Buddhists gain a better standing in their next life by saying as many prayers or *mantras* as possible. Within the gatehouse there is a massive prayer wheel nearly 12 feet tall that requires two hands to turn. Each time it goes around, it strikes a bell. Be sure to give it a spin before beginning the climb to the top of the hill.

Just inside the gate are three large statues of Buddha, all brightly painted. In early morning, there are often Tibetan women doing prostrations in front of these statues, another way that Tibetan Buddhists gain better standing in their next life. As you start up the hill, keep your eyes open for monkeys, for this stupa also goes by the name of the Monkey Temple. It is best to give the monkeys a wide berth and try not to feed them. They can be bad tempered and are carriers of rabies. Should you be bitten by one, wash the wound thoroughly and then see a doctor immediately.

About midway up the hill, where the stairs start to get steep, you are likely to see one or two young men sitting beside the steps carving *mani* stones—stones that have been covered with prayers and serve the same devotional purpose as a prayer wheel. The small ones are strictly tourist trade, but larger mani stones are scattered about the hillside.

If you haven't already lost your breath from the climb up, the sudden sight of the stupa and all its shrines and temples will certainly take your breath away. Immediately in front of you is a giant *vajra,* the thunderbolt that destroys all ignorance, an important symbol in Tibetan Buddhism. Behind this is the stupa itself, a large hemisphere that looks as if it has been coated with white cake icing. The mysterious eyes of the Buddha gaze out over your head from the gilded cube surmounting the white hemispheric body. Prayer flags, new and old, flutter in the breeze, sending their prayers heavenward on the wind. They serve the same purpose as prayer wheels and mani stones.

If you have just walked up the steps, step around to the observation area on the left and take in the hilltop scene before you. Swayambunath Stupa, a white dome crowned with a gilded spire, is easily seen from all over Kathmandu. This is one of the two holiest Buddhist shrines in Nepal, and the mysterious eyes that stare out from its spire are one of the most readily recognized symbols of Nepal. Painted on all four sides of the stupa's spire, these eyes, which represent the eyes of the Buddha, face the four cardinal directions—east, west, north, and south. Between each pair of eyes, where the nose would be, is what looks like a question mark. This is actually the Nepali character for the number one, which symbolizes unity and the "one" way to reach enlightenment—through the Buddha's teachings. Above this is the third eye, symbolizing the all-seeing wisdom of the Buddha. The upper part of the spire consists of 13 gilded disks tapering up to a gilded umbrella hung with a colorful skirt. The 13 disks represent the 13 steps to enlightenment, which is represented by the umbrella. Between the eyes and the lowest of the 13 disks are four toranas, one for each of the cardinal directions. The toranas each include an image of the Buddha and other important deities.

Facing the steps, which climb the hill from the east, is the first of five ornate shrines set into the base of the stupa. Behind heavy iron gates, each shrine contains one of the Dhyani Buddhas and their consorts. These Buddhas preceded the historic Buddha who was born near the present-day city of Lumbini in the Terai region of Nepal. Each of the Dhyani Buddhas faces one of the cardinal directions, with a fifth, slightly to the left of the east-facing Buddha, representing the Buddha at the center of the compass. Each of the five shrines is surrounded by exquisite gilded copper done in the repoussé style of metalworking, for which Kathmandu is well known. Between these shrines facing the subcardinal directions are shrines containing the consorts of four of the Dhyani Buddhas. Linking the nine shrines is a long wall of prayer wheels and butter lamps.

Surrounding the stupa is an odd assortment of temples, shrines, monasteries, and curio shops. On the east side of the stupa, flanking the stairs that lead up from the bottom of the hill, are two shikhara-style temples, and on the west a museum, a *gompa* (monastery prayer room), and a library for Buddhist studies. It is possible to climb the stairs to the gompa and then take a flight of stairs up to the gompa roof from which there is an excellent view of the stupa with the Kathmandu Valley in the background. From this height, you are looking directly into the eyes of the Buddha. Beneath the gompa is a large open room that is always bustling with people on Saturdays, the only day Nepalis have off. Women stir pots of stew, boil rice, and fry bread. They are not, however, cooking for themselves. Their meals will be given as offerings to the goddess Hariti Devi, whose temple stands just outside this cooking area.

The **Temple of Hariti Devi** is a small brick pagoda with a very ornate facade. Hariti is the goddess of smallpox, and though there is no longer any smallpox, her temple is still very popular both with Hindus and Buddhists. On Saturdays, a priest is often on hand to perform *pujas* (religious rituals) for those who have come with special requests. Rice, flowers, and colored powder get thrown every which way as prayers are said. Monkeys, stray dogs, and pigeons fight for the food offerings that get left at the temple, and there is a general sense of chaos about the premises.

Between the impromptu kitchen area and the stupa there is a shrine dedicated to the goddesses Jamuna and Ganga, who are housed inside an ornate cage surrounded by butter lamps. A flame symbolic of the Adhi Buddha, the primordial Buddha, burns in this shrine. There is also a beautiful bronze statue of a peacock. Behind the Hariti Devi Temple are dozens of small whitewashed *chaityas,* which are sort of miniature stupas. Also in this area of curio shops are a bas-relief image of a standing Buddha and the Temple of Agnipur, which symbolizes fire.

BOUDHANATH

Across the valley from Swayambunath, east of Kathmandu, is Boudhanath, the largest stupa in Nepal. The best ways to get here are either to take a taxi or ride a bike; the buses are overloaded and slow. Legend has it that this stupa was built after an old woman asked her king for enough land to build a shrine to the Buddha. The king agreed to give her only as much land as she could cover with the skin of a water buffalo. The woman cut the buffalo hide into thin strips, and, laying them end to end, formed a large circle that became the circumference of the stupa. An entire village inhabited primarily by Tibetan emigrants has sprung up around the stupa, so now it is completely encircled by shops, houses, and monasteries.

Boudhanath is built in the form of a *mandala,* a symbol of the universe that is often used in Buddhist meditations, with three square tiers surrounding the central circle of the dome. The stupa also symbolizes the five elements within its design. The base symbolizes earth; the dome, water; the spire, fire; the crescent atop the spire, light; and the flame-shape topping the spire, ether. A low wall set with hundreds of prayer wheels circles the base, and Tibetan pilgrims are often seen circling the stupa while spinning these prayer wheels.

You enter the stupa grounds through a colorfully painted gateway that leads off the busy bazaar street that runs through the town of **Boudha.** Opposite this gate, on the north side of the stupa, is the entrance to the stupa itself. Lamas often set up low tables and perform *pujas,* special rituals, beneath a tent just inside the stupa entrance. You will often hear them ringing their bells and chanting in the hypnotic drone of the Tibetan language. From this antechamber, a wide staircase leads up to the base of the stupa dome, where niches containing images of the Buddha can be seen. In the middle of the day, the whitewashed stupa can be absolutely blinding, but in late afternoon it takes on a warm glow.

Since the Chinese invaded Tibet in the late 1950s, Boudhanath has become an important center for Tibetan Buddhist studies. Several monasteries have been built near the stupa in recent years. One, on the west side of the stupa, is easy to reach and is open to visitors, who are requested to take off their shoes before entering the main prayer room. Don't miss the huge prayer wheel in a room on the left as you step through the gateway to this gompa.

The most beautiful of the Boudha monasteries is **Dilgo Kyentse's Gompa,** the gold-roofed building 150 yards northwest of the stupa. The monastery is richly endowed with beautiful Buddha statues, murals, painted pillars, and roof beams. During the Buddhist New Year's festivities each February, traditional masked dances are held in the garden.

Boudhanath is also a fascinating place to spend a morning or an afternoon. Tibetan pilgrims, many looking as if they have never seen a city before, circle the stupa in wide-eyed wonder. Often the men wear long braids wrapped around their heads. The women wear heavy dark cloaks and large chunks of turquoise and coral. Many of these pilgrims carry their own prayer wheels, which they spin incessantly. Others prostrate themselves on the ground with every step they take around the stupa. This form of worship is said to bring great benefits to a person in a future life and also serves as penance for past wrongs.

The shops and vendors around the stupa have many interesting items for sale, and their prices are often quite good. Many pilgrims, low on funds, sell off their valuables to these shopkeepers. Consequently this is a great place to buy old Tibetan artifacts and jewelry. Bargaining with these Tibetans is never likely to save you much money, but you can try.

On the north side of the stupa, on the third floor of one of the shophouses is the **Stupa View Restaurant** (see "Dining" in Chapter 3 for details).

PASHUPATINATH

Located on the banks of the Bagmati River, which is considered a sacred river because it eventually flows into the holy Ganges, Pashupatinath is Nepal's holiest Hindu temple. Dedicated to the god Shiva in his aspect of Pashupati, the Lord of the Animals, this imposing two-story pagoda contains a giant Shiva *lingam* (phallus) that is the object of great worship. Unfortunately, the temple's surrounding compound is off-limits to non-Hindus. Despite this restriction, the extensive temple complex is a fascinating place to visit. The streets leading up to the temple are lined with tiny shops selling brightly colored powders, holy beads, Shiva linga, and offerings to be taken into the temple. If you walk up to the open gate, you should be able to get a glimpse inside. Mostly what you will see is the hind end of a large statue of Nandi the bull, Shiva's vehicle. You should also be able to see the silver and gilded lower-level facade of the temple.

Perhaps of greatest interest to tourists are the cremation *ghats* (platforms) that are built below the temple on the banks of the river. For the best view of the temple complex and cremation ghats, walk down to the river from the parking area on the south side of the temple. There are two stone bridges across the river at this point, and on the far side, you will find high walls forming terraces on the bank of the river. Built on one of these terraces is a line of large shrines dedicated to Shiva. Inside each shrine is a stone Shiva lingam. Find a spot along here and have a seat.

Directly across from here are the ghats used by royalty and other people of high birth. Hindus consider it very auspicious to die with their feet in the waters of a holy river, so you may see someone being stretched out on the temple steps as they near their last breath. After death, cremation takes place on the banks of the river with Hindu priests officiating. The body is piled on a stack of firewood and covered with straw. The mourners dress in white and have their heads shaved after the cremation as a symbol of their mourning. During the seemingly haphazard cremation ceremony, priests are constantly throwing articles of the deceased person's clothing into the river. These are usually collected a few yards downstream by some enterprising soul. When the cremation is completed, the ashes of the deceased are sprinkled on the waters of the Bagmati River. If you glance downstream from the main ghats, you may see meager funeral pyres burning on the sandy banks of the river. These are the cremations of poorer people and people of low caste who are not allowed to be cremated within the temple complex itself.

If you walk up to the north end of the terrace with the Shiva shrines, you will see in the steep wooded river banks above the temple many small caves and ramshackle huts. These are the homes of Hindu ascetics known as *sadhus*. These wandering holy men are followers of Shiva who have renounced their former worldly lives to take a path of self-denial. They are often emaciated, have long matted hair and dirty beards, and carry tridents, a symbol of Shiva. Many sadhus wear nothing but a loincloth and smear their bodies with ashes. Some spend their days smoking marijuana and hashish, which for centuries have been smoked by followers of Shiva to help them gain greater spiritual attainment. During the festival of Shivaratri, held in February or March, thousands of pilgrims from all over Nepal and India descend on Pashupatinath. Among these pilgrims are hundreds of sadhus, many of whom display their agility in yoga. Others sit or lie on beds of nails as they meditate or beg for alms.

At the opposite end of this terrace is a famous seventh-century statue of the Buddha half buried in the grass. If you follow the stairs that lead up from the river, you will pass through a shady wood. At the top of the hill are several more temples and buildings occupied by pilgrims. If you continue following this path over the hill, you will come to the **Guheshwari Temple,** dedicated to Shiva's consort in the aspect of Kali. This temple is also off-limits to non-Hindus. There is very little to see, but it is a pleasant walk.

Good days to visit include the 11th day after a full or new moon, when many local people visit the temple. In August, during the Teej festival, thousands of women visit the temple to bathe in the holy waters of the Bagmati River. Because this ritual is meant to bring a long and happy marriage, many women dress in red saris, which are traditionally worn for wedding ceremonies.

Warning: You will probably be approached by very insistent young men offering to be your guide. They are very difficult to shake off once they have attached themselves to you and will go on explaining things about the temple complex whether you are listening or not. They are frequently very helpful, so you might as well let them join you. However, when it comes to paying them (they always say, "Pay what you want."), you must not give in to their demands for more money. Keep in mind that you can take a four-hour organized guided tour of Pashupatinath and a couple of other important sites for around Rs175 ($3.50).

BUDHANILKANTHA

This beautiful 15-foot-long stone statue of the god Vishnu is between 900 and 1,400 years old and is said to have been found by a farmer plowing his fields. The statue, which rests in the middle of a small rectangular pond, depicts Vishnu reclining in a bed of snakes. One of the largest sculptures in Nepal, it almost seems to be alive. The god is tranquil, quite content to lie prostrate and gaze up the sky as worshipers pile flowers, rice, and colored powders at its feet. On special holidays, a priest officiates at the offerings, and a small boy carries special offerings from Vishnu's feet, where pilgrims gather, up to his head. The main festivals at Budhanilkantha take place at the beginning and end of the monsoon season. Vishnu is said to sleep during the four months of the monsoon.

It is believed that if the king of Nepal ever sets eyes on this statue, he will fall down dead because the statue is of the god Vishnu, and the king is considered an incarnation of Vishnu also. However, on Vishnu's two main festival days each year, the king pays his respect by visiting a replica (actually a similar statue) at the Balaju Water Gardens.

DAKSHINKALI

Located in a dark wooded valley 12 miles south of Kathmandu is a shrine dedicated to the terrifying goddess Kali. The best way to get here if you do not come on a tour is to hire a taxi. The image of the goddess is not very big, but Hindus believe it possesses great power. Every Saturday and Tuesday, hundreds of people visit the shrine to offer animal sacrifices, primarily young male goats and chickens, to the bloodthirsty Kali. After their blood is sprinkled on Kali, the animals are taken down to the nearby stream and butchered for the evening meal. Most

Nepalis cannot afford much meat, so any sacrifice is seen as an opportunity to eat well. These ritual sacrifices, though gruesome, are a very popular tourist excursion. All tour companies in Kathmandu offer trips on Saturday to view the activity.

On the way out most tours also include a stop **Pharping** where there is a temple dedicated to Vishnu, who is depicted here as the dwarf Vaman. Beside the temple is a small pond full of fish that are considered holy because Vishnu once appeared on earth in the form of a fish. Some of the stone carvings date to the seventh century. A little bit farther back toward town the road passes **Chovar Gorge,** the only outlet for the rivers draining the Kathmandu Valley. Legends say that the Tibetan god Manjushri cut this gorge with his sword so that he could get a better glimpse of the primordial Buddha. This Buddha floated as a lotus flower on the surface of a lake that filled the Kathmandu Valley. When Manjushri drained the lake, the lotus came to rest on Swayambunath hill. It is easy to believe such a myth when you see the narrow chasm of Chovar Gorge. There is a pagoda nearby that was first erected by the Licchavis around A.D. 600.

2 More Attractions

The National Museum

Chhauni, near Swayambunath. ☎ **977/1-271504.** Admission Rs5 (10¢); Rs10 (20¢) more if you bring a camera. Wed–Thurs, Sat–Mon 10:30am–4:15pm (3:15pm in winter), Fri 10am–2:30pm. Closed all national holidays.

Nepal's National Museum contains three separate collections in three buildings. The building on your left as you enter the compound is of the greatest interest to foreign visitors because it houses the country's finest collection of ancient religious art. The works on display are primarily sculptural with different rooms devoted to different materials. The first room on the left is full of stone sculptures dating as far back as the first century, with the most recent carvings dating to the 13th century. The next room contains terra-cottas. It is in the next two rooms, containing metalwork, that the skill of past Nepali artists and craftspeople is truly evident. Just to the right as you enter the first metalwork room is a statue of the god Viwarupa with hundreds of arms. The next room has a 6-foot-tall, 19th-century statue of Hayagriva Lokeshwara that is quite beautiful. The next room contains wood carvings, mostly from the 18th and 19th century. Among the interesting pieces here are several toranas that you can inspect close up. The last room on the first floor exhibits thangkas from the 18th and 19th centuries. Spend a little time examining these paintings so you will know what to look for if you go shopping for a thangka. The second floor has a display on the lost-wax process for casting statues.

In the building directly across from this one, there is a weapons exhibit on the second floor. Among the many old weapons used by various Nepali armies over the years, there is a rare leather cannon captured during a war with Tibet in 1792. The third building in the compound is dedicated to the life of King Mahendra, the father of the present king.

The Tribhuvan Museum

Hanuman Dhoka Palace, Hanuman Dhoka Square. ☎ **977/1-215613.** Admission Rs10 (20¢). Feb–Oct, Wed–Mon 10:30am–5pm; Nov–Jan, Wed–Mon 10:30am–4pm. Closed all national holidays.

Dedicated to King Tribhuvan, who restored power to the Shah family after more than 100 years of rule by Rana prime ministers, this museum includes such

⭐ Frommer's Favorite Kathmandu Experiences

Getting Lost in Old Kathmandu   By far the best way to see the medieval side of Kathmandu is to get lost. Just pick any narrow lane, start walking, and then take the first left turn. There, now you're lost. The best time for this activity is just after sunrise, before the traffic takes to the streets. In winter a thick fog hangs over the valley early in the morning, making a walk at this time a thoroughly mysterious adventure.

Absorbing Swayambunath at Sunset   Any time of day, Swayambunath Stupa, high on a hill overlooking the entire Kathmandu Valley, is a fascinating place. Sunset, however, is especially magical. The sun lights up the gilded top of the giant shrine, old monks circumambulate the stupa, and the whole of the valley takes on a rosy glow as the shadows lengthen.

Taking in the Sunrise or Sunset at Nagarkot   The view of the Himalayas from Nagarkot encompasses more than 200 miles of snowcapped peaks, from Annapurna in the west to beyond Everest in the east. At sunrise and sunset (if the weather is clear), the mountains perform a light show unrivaled by any other mountain range.

Carpet Shopping in Patan   Shopping for a carpet near the Tibetan Refugee Camp in Patan is truly an Eastern experience. The stately Tibetan ladies who run the shops will bid you have a seat at a low stool and perhaps ask if you would like tea. Then they will begin unrolling their carpets for you to inspect. If you don't see anything you like, no problem; move on to the next shop and start all over.

Cruising the Bookshops   The bookshops of Kathmandu's Thamel neighborhood have the most fascinating collections of books, and there is no telling how they might be arranged on the shelves. One shop has them arranged by author's first name, another by title. Shopkeepers give you 50% back if you return a book, and they pay excellent prices for used books.

Hiking in the Valley   Kathmandu is the largest city in Nepal, but only a few minutes outside of town are villages that can only be reached by narrow trails through the rice paddies. The walk from Bhaktapur to the Changu Narayan temple complex is one of my favorites, and there are several equally interesting trails down from Nagarkot to the floor of the valley. If you prefer to be alone in a forest, try walking to the top of Nagarjun Hill; the view from the top is spectacular.

displays as the king's office, gym, hunting room, and one very enigmatic room simply called "Death," which contains the king's tomb. Also within this museum is the royal throne of Nepal, a numismatic museum, and a display on the techniques used to restore the palace. No cameras are allowed.

Balaju Water Gardens
Balaju. No phone. Admission Rs2 (4¢). Daily 8am–6pm.

Located northwest of Kathmandu in the town of Balaju at the foot of Nagarjun Hill, these unusual gardens contain a bathing fountain with 22 dragon-headed waterspouts carved from stone. There are also other fountains, fish ponds full of huge carp, and a swimming pool. However, the most interesting feature of the park is a copy of the Sleeping Vishnu statue located at Budhanilkantha a few miles northeast of here. The king of Nepal, who is considered to be an incarnation of the god Vishnu, is forbidden to view the statue at Budhanilkantha, so when it is time to pay respects to Lord Vishnu, the king visits this copy of the statue.

Jawalakhel Zoo

Patan. No phone. Admission Rs20 (40¢) adults, Rs10 (20¢) children; Rs10 (20¢) more if you bring a camera, Rs50 ($1) if you bring a video. Daily 10am–5pm.

This is an old-fashioned zoo with animals kept in small, dirty, cement-floored cages. However, if you want to see a snow leopard or Bengal tiger in their home country, you might want to stop by. A better reason to visit is to ride an elephant around the zoo. Of all the places in Nepal where you can ride an elephant, this is the cheapest at only Rs100 ($2) per ride. You can even hire an elephant for Rs1,000 ($20) per hour.

Godawari Royal Botanical Gardens

Godavar. No phone. Admission Rs2 (4¢). Daily 10am–5pm.

Though these gardens are not well marked nor well cared for, they make a pleasant morning or afternoon excursion if you are exhausted from seeing temples. The focus is on Himalayan and south Asian species of trees, shrubs, and flowers. An herbarium and an orchid house contain many varieties of the Himalayas' more delicate plant species. There is excellent birdwatching on the surrounding hillsides if you come early enough (before the official opening). Located about 12 miles from Kathmandu, the gardens are best reached by taxi. You should arrange to have the cab wait for you.

ELEPHANT RIDES

There isn't much at all in Kathmandu that is expressly for children, and you may find it difficult to keep your children entertained as you tour the temples, squares, palaces, and museums that are the main attractions of the Kathmandu Valley. However, there is one activity that children of all ages will enjoy and that is a ride on an elephant. These are available at the zoo in Patan (see above for details) and at Gokarna Wildlife Refuge near Boudhanath Stupa. Gokarna is located a mile or two beyond Boudhanath Stupa, and the rides here are far more interesting because they last longer and take you through a forest park, where you are likely to see deer wandering freely. Hour-long elephant rides are available from 9:30am to 4:30pm and cost Rs550 ($11).

WALKING TOUR
Durbar Square & the Market

Start: Durbar Square.
Finish: Thamel.
Time: Four hours, including museum visit and stop for lunch or a snack.
Best Times: Beginning early in the morning when the streets are still quiet.
Worst Times: Saturday when the market is particularly crowded.

Though the best way to experience old Kathmandu is simply to wander off down a few alleys until you are completely lost, first-time visitors will probably want to take in many of the highlights before attempting more adventuresome explorations. Since there are no street names in Kathmandu, be sure to stay oriented to the accompanying map.

Start at:

1. **Basantapur Square.** This wide-open square beside the old royal palace may still be empty if it is early in the morning, but by midmorning, it will be filled with dozens of vendors selling all manner of Kathmandu curios. If you buy something, remember to bargain hard. Running south from this square is the famous:

2. **Freak Street,** Kathmandu's counterculture hangout back in the 1960s and 1970s. Today the street still has many small shops and cheap restaurants and lodges. From Freak Street, backtrack to Basantapur Square and continue to the:

3. **Durbar Square Area.** Comprising both Durbar Square and Hanuman Dhoka Square, this is the heart of old Kathmandu and is the site of dozens of temples, shrines, old residences, and a former palace (see "The Top Attractions," above). It will probably take you at least two hours to thoroughly explore this fascinating square.

☕ **TAKE A BREAK**   Aside from the cheap restaurants on Freak Street, there are few places to eat in the Durbar Square area. My favorite spot is the **Double E Restaurant,** which is located on the roof of a shopping mall one block east of Freak Street on New Road.

Return to the north side of Hanuman Dhoka Square. A wide road lined with modern buildings angles out of the square to the northeast leading to Kathmandu's main market area, which is divided into three small squares. Head up this street to Indrachowk, the first square, where you will find the:

4. **Akash Bhairav Temple.** A house-style temple with large green, burgundy, and white tiles covering the first-floor facade, the Akash (Sky) Bhairav Temple is one of the most colorful temples in the city. On the balconied second floor stand four rearing bronze griffins that ward off evil spirits. Akash Bhairav, a small silver mask similar to the mask of Seto Bhairav in Hanuman Dhoka Square, gets its name from the way its eyes gaze heavenward. Only Hindus are allowed to enter this temple. To the left of the temple, in the middle of the street leading to Hanuman Dhoka Square, is a small brass shrine dedicated to Ganesh. From the way the brass has been polished and smoothed over the years, it is evident that this shrine is much revered.

Across from the temple begins:

5. **Indrachowk,** the area of the market devoted to cloth and carpet merchants, many of whom display their wares on the terraces of an old pagoda on the north side of the square. The naturally colored shawls, called *pashmina*, are made from the belly wool of a goat. This wool is similar to cashmere, and the shawls are surprisingly warm. Unfortunately most of the shawls for sale here are the more colorful and less expensive synthetic ones. Don't get ripped off. While here, ask one of the rug merchants to show you a *rari*, traditional Nepali felt rugs that have been overshadowed by the Tibetan rugs that are so readily available. Also across the square from the Akash Bhairav Temple is:

6. **The Bead Bazaar,** where you will find strands and strands of shiny imported beads hanging in tiny stalls. The vendors, most of whom are Kashmiris, will gladly put together a necklace to your specifications. Continue into the market on the same road that you took out of Hanuman Dhoka Square to the:

7. **Seto Machendranath Temple,** on Kel Tole (the next square), dedicated to a rain god who is particularly popular in the Kathmandu Valley. The temple is through a doorway on the north (left) side of the street just before the square.

Outside the entrance are two brass lions and, atop a short pillar, a small statue of Buddha. Inside, there are several statues and chaityas surrounding the main temple. Among the statues of Buddhas and Taras, there is a classical Greek statue of a woman balancing a lamp on her head. This statue was added during the Rana period of rule, when all things European were in vogue among the gentry. The temple itself is incredibly ornate with roofs of gilded copper and a gilded and embossed facade. The statue of Machendra is taken out of the temple once a year during the Seto Machendranath Jatra festival, bathed, and paraded around the city in a huge chariot. Machendra, who is an aspect of the bodhisattva Avalokiteshwara (also known as Chenrezig in Tibet), is worshiped by Hindus and Buddhists alike.

Outside the temple there are shops piled high with brass household goods and statuettes of various gods. The shops leading up to Kel Tole are old and small and offer a wide variety of goods. Between here and the next square is the first house in Kathmandu to have glass windows. It is on the left and is recognizable from the bas-relief frieze of marching soldiers between the first and second floors. Continue heading up the street in the direction you have been traveling since leaving Hanuman Dhoka Square. At Asan Tole, the next square, you will see the:

8. **Annapurna Temple.** Asan Tole is the heart of the market area you have been walking through since Indrachowk and is also the site of three small temples, the largest of which is the Annapurna Temple. With its three-roofed metal pagoda, this temple is dedicated to the goddess whose name means "Full of Grain." There is no image of Annapurna, only a *kialash* (holy water pot). The adjacent two-story pagoda temple is dedicated to Ganesh, who in this image has four arms. In the middle of the square is a small temple to Narayan, who is an aspect of Vishnu. The square is almost always packed with shoppers searching for deals on fruits and vegetables that are displayed in baskets or on sheets spread open on the street. Somewhere amid this chaos is the:

9. **Fish Memorial.** You may not be able to find this obscure little memorial, but I'm sure you would want to know the story behind it. In a shallow hole in the pavement of Asan Tole, there is an almost unrecognizable stone carving of a fish. This little statue was supposedly placed here to commemorate an event that long ago transpired between a father and son, both of whom were astrologers. In a contest to determine who was the greater astrologer, the two men made predictions about where a fish falling from the sky on a certain rainy day would land. The son's prediction proved correct when the father failed to account for the distance the fish would bounce before coming to a stop.

Six roads radiate out from Asan Tole. If you take the wide road leading almost due east, you will come in another long block to busy Kantipath, across which is a large square pond called:

10. **Rani Pokhari** or Queen's Pond. In the middle of the pond, connected to the shore by a long bridge, stands a whitewashed Moghul-style temple dedicated to Shiva. The lake is said to be haunted, and the temple is only opened once a year during Tihar. The rest of the year, the lake is locked behind a fence. If you walk to the northwest corner of the lake, you can turn left on a road that will take you back to Asan Tole. This is the road that you followed for most of the way from Hanuman Dhoka Square. From Asan Tole, take the road that heads due west and continue along this road to the next intersection while noticing the

overhanging balconies. Here on the southeast corner of the intersection is the strangest shrine in Kathmandu:

11. The Toothache God. You may have difficulty recognizing it as a shrine, but the strange amorphous shape is a tree trunk into which have been nailed thousands of coins. Nailing a coin on this shrine is supposed to relieve toothache pain. You may see someone touch it as they walk past and then touch their own forehead, just in case. Nearby are several dentists' offices.

If you continue one block down this narrow, shop-lined lane, you will come to a pagoda temple, the steps of which are covered with vendors preparing snacks and tea on portable kerosene stoves. In front of this temple and down the alley to the left are:

12. Stuffing Fluffers and shops specializing in quilts and cotton-stuffed mattresses. The men in long plaid skirts (called *longis*) lounging around the neighborhood and leaning against strange-looking single-stringed "musical instruments" are mattress-stuffing fluffers. They twang their musical instruments in a pile of matted cotton and return it to its original fluffy loft. Head back in the direction of the toothache god, and after passing that shrine, walk 200 yards or so north and watch on the left side of the street for the entrance to:

13. Kathesimbhu, a 15th-century stupa that, though much smaller than those at Swayambunath or Boudhanath, fills a large courtyard. The sudden sight of the Buddha's eyes staring down an alley between two shopfronts stops many wandering visitors dead in their tracks. Surrounding this whitewashed stupa are dozens of smaller shrines. Continue up this road and you will come to:

14. Thahiti, site of yet another stupa, this time in the middle of a traffic-filled square. Numerous prayer wheels are set into the low wall protecting this stupa. If you head east two blocks from the north side of this square, you will come to the 17th-century Chusya Bahal, a sadly dilapidated former monastery that has two stone lions guarding its front door. Backtracking to Thahiti, you can turn northward and be in the Thamel tourist district in a few minutes' walk.

3 Organized Tours

There are basically two types of organized tours available in Kathmandu. You can go on a half-day group tour, usually in a van, to various valley sights, or you can hire a car, driver, and guide to show you around to whichever sights you are most interested in seeing. The former is, of course, the less expensive option, though the commentary by the guide may not be too informative.

Virtually every hotel, tour company, and travel agency can arrange a spot in a group tour for you. The Nepal Travel Agency, below, offers several tour pickup points around Kathmandu. When making a reservation, be sure to ask for the pickup point nearest to your hotel.

Nepal Travel Agency, Ramshahpath (☎ 977/1-413188 or 977/1-229013), is Kathmandu's Gray Line representative. These are the best organized city tours available. Half-day tours cost between Rs175 ($3.50) and Rs250 ($5) and include Bhaktapur, Boudha, and Pashupatinath; or Patan and Swayambunath; or Dakshinkali, Chovar Gorge, and Shesh Narayan Temple; or Nagarkot; or Dhulikhel. Tours start either at 9am or 2:30pm.

Personal tours, including a car, driver, and guide, cost between $20 and $34 for two people for 3 hours. The advantage to these tours is that you can stay as long

Walking Tour—Durbar Square & the Market

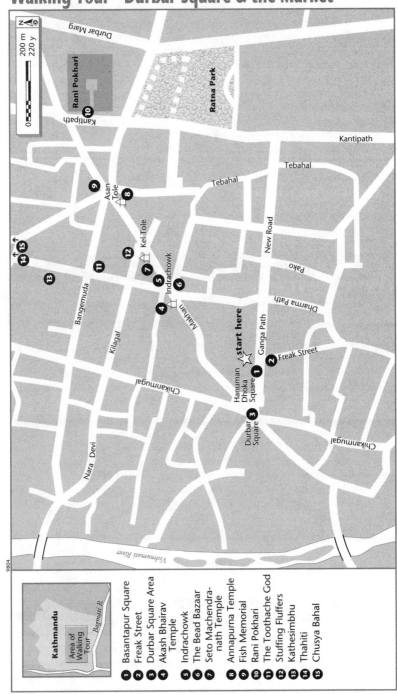

Kathmandu
Area of Walking Tour
Bagmati R.

① Basantapur Square
② Freak Street
③ Durbar Square Area
④ Akash Bhairav Temple
⑤ Indrachowk
⑥ The Bead Bazaar
⑦ Seto Machendra-nath Temple
⑧ Annapurna Temple
⑨ Fish Memorial
⑩ Rani Pokhari
⑪ The Toothache God
⑫ Stuffing Fluffers
⑬ Kathesimbhu
⑭ Thahiti
⑮ Chusya Bahal

as you like at any sight, though your guide will probably want to hasten you along. **Adventure Travel Nepal,** located in the Tiger Tops office on Durbar Marg (☎ 977/1-223328), is one of the best companies to contact for such personalized tours. **Natraj Tours & Travel,** Kamaladi, Durbar Marg, (☎ 977/1-220001), offers similar personal city tours. If there are more than three people in your group, the per-person price drops a little bit.

Kathmandu's most interesting organized tour is the daily "flightseeing" trip offered by **Royal Nepal Airlines** (☎ 977/1-220757). These one-hour flights provide a close-up aerial glimpse of the Himalayas, including Mt. Everest. The cost is $99 per person, and the flights are offered daily from September to May, weather permitting. You can make reservations for this flight through any local travel agency or directly through the airline. I recommend using a travel agent.

Everest Air (☎ 977/1-224188) offers a similar flight that heads straight for Mt. Everest, gives you a close-up view of that mountain, and then returns to Kathmandu. This flight is done in a small plane in which everyone gets a window seat. The price for this hour-long flight is also $99.

4 Sports

BICYCLING Bicycles are one of the most popular ways of getting around Kathmandu and the rest of the valley. (For rental information, see "Getting Around" in Chapter 3.) As anyone can see after doing a bit of exploring around Nepal, the country is ideal for mountain bikes. Over the years individuals and small companies have offered organized mountain-bike tours, but unfortunately none of these people or companies has been able to make a go of such an endeavor. However, there always seems to be someone offering such trips. Just look around on the bulletin boards in Thamel, and you are certain to see an ad for mountain-bike trips.

GOLF The **Royal Nepal Golf Club,** reached by the south entrance to Pashupatinath temple (☎ 977/1-472836), is Kathmandu's most accessible golf course. The greens fees are Rs350 ($7), club rental is Rs150 ($3). A caddie is another Rs75 ($1.50). It's open Sunday to Friday from 7am to 6pm. Out at **Gokarna Safari Resort** beyond Boudhanath a mile or two, there is another nine-hole course. Here you might even see deer on the fairways since this is also a wildlife preserve. The fee is $20, including greens fee, club rental, and caddie. Open daily.

WHITE-WATER RAFTING Though there is no white-water rafting in the Kathmandu Valley, this is where you should make your arrangements if you decide to take on the turbulent waters of one of the Himalayas' many rivers. See "Alternative/Adventure Travel" in Chapter 2 for details.

5 Shopping

After trekking, shopping is probably the most popular tourist activity in Nepal. The streets are literally covered with fascinating souvenirs, works of art, relics, curios, and religious statuary. Street vendors and shopkeepers have set up businesses around virtually every tourist attraction in the Kathmandu Valley. Wherever you go sightseeing, you will be accosted by people trying to sell you all types of trinkets and curios.

BEST BUYS   Among Kathmandu's best buys are nearly anything made of wool, including Tibetan carpets, sweaters, jackets, shawls, and handbags. Silver jewelry and semiprecious stones such as turquoise, red coral, and lapis lazuli are other good buys. Casual cotton clothes for men, women, and children are exceptionally good deals, though most of the ready-made clothes are in styles that look best in Kathmandu or on the beaches of southern Thailand. Metal religious figurines in brass, bronze, or copper sell for much less here than they do in the West, though prices can be quite high for those of good quality. Old copper pots with beaten designs are attractive and inexpensive, though quite heavy.

BARGAINING   Bargaining is an absolute necessity in Nepal, especially when it comes to tourist souvenirs and curios. Street vendors tend to charge the highest prices. How well dressed you are and whether you are wearing an expensive watch or flaunting an expensive camera will determine how inflated prices might be.

There are several rules you need to follow in order to play the Nepali shopping game. First and foremost is never pay the asking price for anything without first trying to bargain. You are expected to bargain for nearly everything in Nepal (Nepalis even try to bargain for the price of bus tickets, though it never works). Bargaining is most effective when you're buying something from a street vendor. Quoted prices are sometimes as much as four times the going price. However, it is difficult to know this until you have become familiar with what others are charging for the same item. As a rule of thumb, offer a third to a half of the asking price and work your way up from there. If you pay more than three-quarters of the asking price, you aren't doing too well. There are exceptions to the bargaining rule. Tibetan shopkeepers rarely discount their merchandise and will give you the cold shoulder if you try to bargain with them.

Second, never ask the price of something unless you are prepared to fend off a ravenous vendor. Asking the price of something means you are interested, and a vendor will rarely let you get away without buying whatever it is you asked about. This makes comparison shopping very difficult. However, with a little practice, it can be done. To get away without buying something, you must ignore the vendor as he/she follows you down the street demanding a price from you. This may sound cruel, but there is no other way to deal with Kathmandu's kings and queen of the hard sell. On more expensive items, it is much easier to ask prices and not be subjected to the hard sell.

Third, look around before buying anything. Prices, and especially quality, vary widely on all items. What may seem like a great price may actually be rather high when you realize that the merchandise is of inferior quality.

HOURS   Shop hours vary considerably and are rarely as fixed as they are in the West. Street vendors tend to set up around 9am and pack up their wares at dusk. Shops in Thamel open around 9am and usually stay open until 9pm. Shops around tourist attractions such as Swayambunath, Boudhanath, and the Durbar Squares tend to open around 9 or 9:30am (when the first tour buses arrive) and close around 6pm. Upscale shops on Durbar Marg generally open at 10am and close at 6pm (these are the only shops I know of that stay closed on Saturday, the Nepali weekend).

SHIPPING IT HOME   If at all possible, I recommend that you carry your purchases with you when you leave the country. The Nepali mail system is notoriously slow and unreliable. However, since most people flying out of Kathmandu receive a baggage allotment of only 20 kilograms (44 pounds), it is not always feasible to take all purchases onto the plane as baggage. Should you decide to mail a package home, you can either go to the **Foreign Post Office** (☎ 977/1-211760) on Kantipath beside the main post office and deal with it yourself (a time-consuming and often frustrating process), or you can pay a shipping company a little bit extra to deal with it for you. I prefer the latter. **Sharmason's,** Kantipath (☎ 977/1-222709), is the company used by foreign diplomats living in Kathmandu and claims never to have lost a single package they shipped. **Atlas Packers and Movers,** Durbar Marg (☎ 977/1-226916), is another reliable company that ships air freight only.

SHOPPING AREAS

Though curios and souvenirs can be purchased at every tourist attraction in the Kathmandu Valley, certain areas are better for shopping for certain items. The main shopping areas include the following:

Durbar Marg   On Kathmandu's upscale shopping, restaurant, and hotel street, prices are the highest in town, but the quality is also tops. This is where to head if you are looking for Tibetan antiques or the best that Nepal has to offer in the way of fine cast-metal figures of Tibetan Buddhist and Hindu deities.

Thamel   This is the budget traveler's neighborhood and has a little bit of everything for sale. Of particular interest are Kathmandu fashions, silver and turquoise jewelry, and books.

Indrachowk, Asan Tole, and Kel Tole   Kathmandu's main market area is a narrow street that runs from Durbar Square to Rani Pokhari and that changes names about every block. Along this street you'll find fascinating household goods, the uses of which you may only be able to guess at; sari shops; a produce market; shawl and carpet vendors; brass merchants; basket sellers; and much more.

Durbar Square, Basantapur, and Freak Street   Surrounding Kathmandu's Durbar Square, this area also has a little bit of everything for sale either on the street or in tiny shops in ancient buildings. Be sure to bargain hard here; vendors have been weaned on tour buses.

Patan   Known for its metalworkers, Patan is the place to go for cast-metal figures of Buddhist and Hindu deities. All around Patan's Durbar Square and on the narrow streets leading to the Golden Temple are dozens of shops offering quality bronze, brass, and copper figurines at good prices. Within the courtyard of the Temple of 1,000 Buddhas, there are several more metalworkers' shops.

Bhaktapur   Known as the wood-carving capital of Nepal, Bhaktapur still produces the carved windows that you have admired in old palaces and temples around the valley. Bhaktapur is also a good place to shop for old (not antique) copper and brass household pots and utensils.

Boudhanath   This huge Tibetan Buddhist shrine is surrounded by shops selling all types of religious curios, antiques, objets d'art, and goods of Tibetan origin. Vendors seem to acquire a lot of old Tibetan pieces from pilgrims who journey here from Tibet in the winter, making this a good place to find things you won't see anywhere else in town. I have found that prices for many items frequently sold by street vendors in Kathmandu are lower at Boudhanath.

Pashupatinath   Most vendors at these holiest-of-holy temples are in business to sell to Hindu pilgrims, not tourists (though there are a few selling tourist souvenirs). Interesting buys include holy beads and stone Shiva *linga.*

Swayambunath   Lots of little shops around this ancient Buddhist stupa sell Buddhist religious relics and souvenirs. On the steps leading up to the stupa, there are usually a couple of stone carvers selling tiny *mani* stones (prayer stones). These are inexpensive and make unique paperweights.

ANTIQUES

There are dozens of shops along Durbar Marg, in Thamel, at Boudhanath Stupa, and in Patan that sell antiques, near-antiques, and fake antiques. However, it is illegal to remove any genuine Nepali antiques from Nepal. The government is especially concerned that the country's religious art and antiques do not disappear since, in the past 20 to 30 years, Nepal has been raped by antiques collectors. Active temples all over the country have been plundered, and even a few of the most venerated statues in Nepal have disappeared. The wholesale theft of religious works of art has gotten so bad that many precious objects are now chained and bolted down.

It is, however, legal to export Tibetan, Bhutanese, Indian, and Ladakhi antiques (if you get an export stamp), all of which show up in Kathmandu shops. Keep in mind, though, that theft of religious antiques is not limited to Nepal. Just because an antique is from Tibet does not mean that it wasn't stolen from a temple in Tibet. Any object that looks even remotely antique and in fact any religious curio, which includes bells, masks, thangkas, and metal statuettes, could need to be cleared with the Department of Archaeology, Ram Shah Path (☎ 977/ 1-215358). Clearance usually takes only a few minutes if you do it yourself. Most shops will take care of this for you if you are making a large purchase, but they will probably require a day or two. It costs only a few rupees per object, and after being passed, a wax seal will be affixed to the object. When leaving the country, there are sometimes very thorough Customs inspections of baggage. These inspections are primarily for antiques and drugs. Should you be carrying something that could be deemed antique and does not have the archaeology department's wax seal, you will have to leave the piece in Nepal or miss your flight and take it to get the stamp.

This said, there are a couple of stores selling old and antique Tibetan and Bhutanese artifacts other than those of religious significance. Prices are generally quite high, though somewhat less than you would pay in the United States for the same piece.

Karma Lama Ritual Art Gallery

Durbar Marg. ☎ **977/1-226409.** Sun–Fri 10am–6pm.

Located about midway down Durbar Marg one flight up from the street, this store specializes in Tibetan ethnographic art and antiquities. There's an excellent collection of old Tibetan carpets and many beautiful iron and gold pieces such as horse stirrups and knives. The Ritual Art Gallery has long been one of Kathmandu's most respected dealers of Tibetan antiquities.

ART

Most art in Nepal is religious in nature, and both Hindu and Buddhist iconography is represented in paintings, metal statues, wood carvings, and terra-cotta figures. Of course there is good art and there is bad art. To get an idea of what to look for in a thangka or bronze statue, go into a store that appears to sell quality pieces and ask to see the most expensive piece in the shop. Then ask to see the least expensive comparable piece. If you cannot readily see the differences in quality, ask the proprietor to tell you why one is so expensive and the other is not. Shopkeepers in Kathmandu are usually very friendly and willing to explain their merchandise to you.

THANGKAS

Thangkas, Buddhist religious scrolls painted on canvas, are very popular with tourists. The scrolls commonly depict Buddhist deities and the Buddhist wheel of life. They may be very simple, depicting a single deity, or they may be incredibly detailed with hundreds of figures, some painted with single-hair brushes, covering the canvas. There are thangka shops on Durbar Marg and in Thamel, Patan, and Bhaktapur. In many shops, you can see the artists at work. Several thangka shops around Bhaktapur's Durbar Square have open studio areas.

METAL STATUES

Bronze, copper, and brass statuettes of Hindu and Buddhist deities are among the most beautiful works of art in Nepal. They come in a wide variety of sizes from tiny figures less than half an inch tall to giant statues weighing hundreds of pounds. There is an equally wide range of qualities so no matter what your budget, you should be able to find something to your liking. Just remember to have it stamped by the Department of Archaeology if it looks even vaguely antique.

These statues are made by the lost-wax process of metalworking. In this process the figure is carved in a piece of wax which is then covered with clay. The wax is then melted, and the cavity is filled with molten metal. After the metal cools, the clay is removed, the figure is cleaned, and fine details are added. You can see metal statues being made at the **Patan Industrial Estate** southwest of Patan's Durbar Square on Sat Dobato where there are small factories making statues. These factories also have showrooms where you can buy pieces. However, prices and selection are not as good as in the shops around Patan's Durbar Square and outside the Mahaboudha Temple in Patan. Shops on Durbar Marg in Kathmandu sell the highest quality pieces, which sell for hundreds to thousands of dollars.

CONTEMPORARY ART

Nepal Association of Fine Arts Art Gallery
Naxal. ☎ **977/1-411729.** Sun–Fri 10am–5pm (10am–4pm in winter).

This gallery exhibits and sells works by contemporary Nepali painters and sculptors. Call for directions.

The October Gallery
Hotel Vajra, Bijeswari, Swayambhu. ☎ **977/1-271545.** Daily 9–11am and 4–8pm.

This gallery features works by local and international artists and mounts changing exhibits of contemporary and traditional Nepali arts.

BOOKS

Kathmandu is a book-lover's paradise. In Thamel there are dozens of small bookshops, some of them no larger than a closet, where you can find an astounding array of new and used books from around the world. You'll find books in English, French, German, Italian, Spanish, Japanese, Swedish, Dutch, and other languages.

Most bookshops will buy your used paperback books for $2 or more depending on resale value. Also, you can usually return a book and get 50% of the price back. I like to take a stack of unwanted books with me to Kathmandu and swap them for new ones, which I read and return for my 50% rebate.

Though best-sellers and general fiction are the mainstays of the Kathmandu bookshops, they also have the largest selection I've ever seen of books on the Himalayas, including titles focusing on Nepal, Tibet, Bhutan, Ladakh, mountain climbing, trekking in the Himalayas, wildlife, and other subjects. Dozens of picture books are available and, though expensive, are well worth the expense if you didn't happen to get any award-winning photos while you were here. There is also one of the world's widest selections of books on religion and esoteric subjects.

Tiwari's Pilgrims Book House
Thamel. ☎ 977/1-231040. Daily 8am–10pm.

Located just a few doors up from the Kathmandu Guest House gate, this bookstore specializes in books on Hinduism, Tibetan Buddhism, yoga, Eastern medicine, and spiritual quests. It also has a wide selection of books on other topics and is one of the largest bookstores in Kathmandu. On the road leading to the Hotel Yak & Yeti is **Kailash Book Distributors,** another large bookstore under the same management.

CARPETS

Carpets are one of Nepal's best shopping deals, but it pays to know a bit about the carpets available. The most important bit of advice, as far as I'm concerned, is to stay away from the Kashmiri carpets that first showed up in Kathmandu a few years ago. These have quickly become very popular because they look like classic Persian carpets, seem to be made of silk, and sell for much less than a Tibetan carpet. A Kashmiri carpet is easily identified by its finely detailed arabesques and floral motifs. They are thin (less than one-quarter inch) and very shiny. Vendors will tell you that they are made of silk, but this isn't always true, as you will find out when they wear out within a few years.

The carpets that are a genuine value in Nepal are those known as Tibetan carpets. These thick wool carpets are based on designs that originated in Tibet. The hand-knotted carpets have traditionally served a number of purposes. Some are made into pony saddles, while others are used as cushions on the long low benches favored by Tibetans for seating. In the mountains, where homes are unheated, carpets are taken outside and spread on the ground as a seating area on warm days. Still others are used as wall hangings. The standard size for Tibetan carpets is 1 by 2 meters or roughly 3 by 6 feet.

There are basically three different grades of Tibetan carpet—60 knot-, 80 knot-, and 100-knot carpets. These numbers refer to the number of knots in 1 square inch. The more knots there are, the more time went into making the carpet and thus the more expensive the carpet will be. The best 60-knot carpets are made with wool that has been spun on a spinning wheel. This type of yarn is usually so bulky that it is not possible to get any more than 60 knots to the square inch. Sixty-knot carpets from hand-spun wool are increasingly hard to find because wool production in Nepal and Tibet has not been able to keep pace with the demand for carpets. Eighty-knot carpets are the most common and are usually the least expensive. They are made with machine-spun wool, usually from New Zealand, and are not as durable (or as heavy) as the 60-knot carpets. You won't see many 100-knot carpets because they are about double the price of a 60- or 80-knot carpet. They are, however, the most durable and are usually made from yarn that has been spun by hand with a drop spindle. This technique produces a tighter yarn that allows the greater number of knots. If you want the best quality rug, ask if a shop has any 100-knot rugs. The best way to check knots is to flip the carpet over and look at the back. If the pattern is very sharply defined, it is probably a 100-knot carpet. Carpets of fewer knots will have a much less definite pattern on the back.

The other factor to consider is the type of dye used on the yarn. Less expensive carpets tend to be made with chemical dyes that produce bright colors. Natural vegetable-derived dyes produce subtler colors that Westerners generally prefer. Carpets made with vegetable dyes tend to be a bit more expensive.

Tibetans themselves tend to go for the bright colors, especially dark blue, deep red, and orange. Old and antique carpets made in Tibet are available at many of the carpet shops around town. These carpets tend to be made with a finer grade of wool (supposedly lamb's wool), which is often mixed with silk to produce a very soft, smooth carpet with a natural shine to it. These carpets are always in traditional designs that are not to everyone's tastes and tend to be two to three times the price of a new made-in-Nepal carpet.

Once you have decided which grade of carpet you would like to buy, there are a few other things to keep an eye out for. Is the color uniform throughout the carpet? Often a different batch of yarn (and consequently a slightly different color) is incorporated into a carpet halfway through production. Are the knots tight? Loose knots are a sign of a poorly made carpet that will not last many years. Is the design straight? On a well-made carpet the design will remain even from one end to the other without developing a slant to it. Is the trimming well defined? The designs in Tibetan carpets are traditionally defined by trimming around the edges of any change in color. Also the surface should be of an even height so that the carpet appears very smooth. Are design details complete and symmetrical? Often if you don't study a carpet carefully you don't notice until too late that a design detail has not been completed as the pattern would indicate it should have been—a flower might not be connected to its stem or a square may be missing a side.

In the Kathmandu Valley, the best place to shop for Tibetan carpets is near the Tibetan Refugee Camp (☎ 977/1-521305) in Jawalakhel, Patan. I suggest that you take a tour of the refugee camp (open Sunday to Friday 8am to noon and 1 to 5pm) so that you can see how the carpets are made. All the steps from dying to knotting to trimming can be observed. The camp also has three large showrooms full of carpets. The designs range from traditional to contemporary. You'll find better prices in the shops just up the street from the camp. Prices have remained stable for quite a few years now. A good 60-knot carpet costs between $60 and $90; an 80-knot carpet around $80; and a 100-knot carpet between $135 and $250 (usually around $200). An old carpet from Tibet will usually cost between $235 and $270. If you don't want to carry your carpet home, you can have it shipped by sea mail for about $50 to the U.S.

FASHION

One unusual Kathmandu fashion bargain that should not be passed up is the machine-embroidered T-shirt. Though there are several standard designs you see in every store, shops selling such T-shirts are more than happy to embroider your own design onto a shirt. They'll even put designs on your clothes for you. It usually takes no more than a day or two to have something custom embroidered.

CHILDREN'S CLOTHING

Colorful children's clothes in all the popular Kathmandu styles can be found in Thamel and on Freak Street. These clothes are usually 100% cotton or wool and are an exceptional deal if the child you are dressing doesn't mind looking a bit like a hippie. Wool sweaters are one of the better buys for children, as are multi-colored jackets and overalls.

MEN'S CLOTHING

Attractive all-cotton button-down shirts are available. Wool sweaters, heavy wool coats, and casual jackets are also good buys. Try the shops in Thamel and on Freak Street. If they don't have something in your size, they'll make it up for you over-night. You will undoubtedly have noticed the jaunty little caps the Nepali men wear. These caps, called *topes,* look a bit like fezzes that have been punched in on one side. You'll find topes for sale in the main market near Indrachowk. Another type of hat derived from a Tibetan men's hat is available in tourist fashion shops in Thamel and Freak Street. These wool hats are warm and comfortable and have flaps that can be pulled down over the ears when it gets really cold. They are great trekking hats.

WOMEN'S CLOTHING

Though the dress shops of Kathmandu aren't as well known as those in Bangkok, many do good work, and it takes only a day or two to have a pair of pants, skirt, or dress made. Every year fashions change in Kathmandu, but they do not follow Western trends. Kathmandu fashions are in a world all their own. If your fashion tastes lean toward conservative, you may not find anything you like.

Among the best fashion buys in Kathmandu are sweaters, jackets, and coats. The clothing shops in Thamel have a wide variety of colorful wool sweaters, heavy wool jackets, and quilted cotton coats. Shawls made from pashmina (cashmere) wool, the soft underbelly wool of a mountain goat, are also available. They're wonder-fully soft and extremely warm. You'll find stacks of pashmina shawls for sale at tourist shops throughout Kathmandu.

Wheels Boutique

Durbar Marg. ☎ **977/1-224554.** Sun–Fri 10am–7pm.

Located on the second floor of a building about halfway down Durbar Marg, Wheels Boutique offers custom-designed women's fashions. Locally made raw silk in rich colors is the primary fabric used in the blouses, jackets, and coats that are the shop's most popular creations.

Dark Horse

Thamel. ☎ **977/1-217703.** Daily 10am–7pm.

South about a hundred yards from the entrance to the Kathmandu Guest House, you'll find a shop that sells ready-to-wear fashions that are better made and better designed than the majority of fashions in Thamel.

Durga Design

Thamel. ☎ **977/1-610048.**

Though most of the clothing for sale around Thamel is not very well made and looks good only on backpacking Asia travelers, the jackets, skirts, and dresses in this shop could easily be worn to work in even dressy offices back home. Heavy cotton block-printed by hand is used in these stylish and contemporary designs. If they don't have a piece you like in your size, they'll gladly make it up for you at no extra charge. You can even pick the material you want. Durga Design is across from the Potala Guest House on the street that leads to Chhetrapati.

GIFTS & SOUVENIRS

Gifts and souvenirs are available almost anywhere in Kathmandu. However, the best selections are in Thamel and around Durbar Square. In spots frequented by tourists, you will often have vendors follow you around trying to sell you trinkets. Should you buy from one of these vendors, be sure to bargain.

In recent years Kandevta, street leading from Kathmandu to Patan, has become a center for craft shops that are supported by international aid organizations. Profits from these shops go directly back to the craftspeople, primarily women. In these shops you'll find not only traditional crafts, but also modern applications of traditional techniques visible in such items as handwoven place mats. Many of these craft items are not available anywhere else in Kathmandu.

Sana Hastakala

Ga 1/113 Kupondole. ☎ **977/1-522628.** Sun–Fri 9:30am–6pm, Sat 10am–5pm.

Located directly across from the Hotel Himalaya, this craft shop is supported by UNICEF and has a wide assortment of interesting and inexpensive craft items. Specialties include handmade paper, pillow covers, and ceramics.

Mahaguthi

Durbar Square, Patan. ☎ **977/1-521493.** Sun–Fri 10am–6pm. Lazimpat and Kupondole shops open Sat 11am–4:30pm also.

Profits from this shop support the Tulasi Mehar Ashram, a refuge and training center for destitute women and children. When you buy here, you know that your money is going directly to the women who produced the handcrafts. Among the attractive well-made items are beautiful hand-printed note cards, colorful pillow covers, embroidered napkins and place mats, and stylish clothes made from local textiles. There are other Mahaguthi shops on Kupondole in Patan and on Durbar Marg and Lazimpat in Kathmandu.

Dhukuti Shop

Kopundole, Patan. ☎ **977/1-523147.** Mon–Fri 9am–7pm, Sat–Sun 11am–7pm.

This is another craft shop that serves as an outlet for various development projects. Proceeds from sales of the shop's pillow covers, bedspreads, leather bags, lamps, baskets, placemats, and other items go directly to the craftspeople themselves.

JEWELRY

Silver jewelry is another of Nepal's good buys and is sold primarily in shops in Durbar Marg, Thamel, and Freak Street. Much of this jewelry is made with turquoise and coral, as well as a few other semiprecious stones. All types of bangles and baubles are available, with traditional Tibetan designs predominating. Particularly attractive are bead necklaces strung on black cord. You'll find this type of necklace at several shops in Thamel. Antique Tibetan jewelry is also readily available, though prices are quite steep for these pieces.

MARKETS

Kathmandu's main market area is a long narrow street that cuts diagonally through the old city from Hanuman Dhoka Square to Rani Pokhari (Queen's Pond) on Kantipath near Ratna Park. With each block the market street changes name, and in fact it is better known by the names of the squares through which it passes.

Starting with **Makhan Tole** at the northeast corner of Hanuman Dhoka Square, you pass by shops selling thangkas, clothes for tourists, and saris. At Indrachowk, the next square, you will find flower sellers making garlands from marigolds and poinsettia bracts. Married Nepali women traditionally do not wear a wedding ring but several strands of shiny beads passing through a gold tube called a *tilhari*. The bead bazaar opposite the tiled temple is where many of these traditional necklaces are made. There are dozens of stalls hung with shimmering strands of beads. You can design your own necklace and have it made up on the spot. At the base of the temple on the north side of this square, sellers of pashmina shawls and felt rugs display their wares in colorful stacks.

As you continue along this road away from Indrachowk, you will pass shops selling carpets, brass and copper pots and household items, baskets, plastic kitchenwares, and saris. Down a side street to the left are numerous shops selling thin mattresses and quilts. The men in long skirts leaning against what seem to be single-stringed musical instruments are stuffing fluffers. Their instruments are used not for music but to fluff up the cotton or kapok stuffing of mattresses that have become matted down.

Asan Tole, the next square, is one of Kathmandu's main produce markets, and the crowds can be absolutely daunting. *Be especially careful with your valuables here.* If you happen to be here anytime between November and January, be sure to buy some mandarins. They're the best I've ever tasted. Remember to bargain.

METAL HOUSEWARES

Until very recently, Nepali housewares such as pots, pitchers, bowls, glasses, water jars, and oil lamps were made from brass, bronze, and copper and were often ornately decorated. Today, these items are rapidly being replaced by plastic and aluminum products, and as a result, the beautiful old pieces are slowly disappearing. However, shops selling new housewares often receive old pieces in exchange. As you wander the streets of Kathmandu, Bhaktapur, and Patan, keep your eye out for old copper pots in market shops. Though they are heavy, they are quite inexpensive.

Chainpur Brass
Pulchowk, Patan. No phone. Sun–Fri 10am–6pm.

The Kathmandu Valley has for centuries been a center of metalworking. In addition to the religious statuary (see "Metal Statues," above), household items have traditionally been made from brass and bronze. This store across from the Hotel Narayani specializes in old and high-quality, newer brass and bronze pots, lamps, urns, pitchers, cups, and other pieces of traditional housewares.

WOOD CARVINGS

Bhaktapur has been known as the wood-carving center of the Kathmandu Valley for centuries, and this ancient art is today continued by several wood-carving shops in this city. If you have become enamored of the intricately carved wooden lattice windows that decorate the temples and palaces of the valley, you might want to take one home with you. Small versions of these windows are available and will easily fit in a suitcase or backpack. They make interesting wall decorations. The scaled-down replica of the famous Bhaktapur peacock window is particularly popular. If you feel this is too ornate for you, perhaps a simple picture or mirror frame will be more to your taste.

Himalayan Wood Carving Masterpieces
Dattatreya Square, Bhaktapur. ☎ **977/1-610754.**

Right next door to the National Woodworking Museum, Himalayan Wood Carvers has its showrooms on the second floor. They usually have a few full-size windows on display for those planning an architectural undertaking. A large window can cost as much as $2,500, but a small one can be had for around $400.

6 Kathmandu After Dark

If you are a culture vulture, a disco diva, a pub crawler, or any other sort of night owl, you might want to reconsider spending your vacation in Nepal. The evening entertainment scene here is almost nonexistent, and cultural activities are often restricted to expatriates living and working in Nepal. There are few discos, bars close between 10pm and midnight and movie theaters show only Hindi musicals. However, no one seems to mind this lack of nightlife. Most visitors are either too jet-lagged to want to stay up late, are saving their energy for a trek, or are recovering their energy after a trek.

Despite these dire warnings, you don't have to go directly to bed when the sun goes down. Walking the streets of Kathmandu after dark (especially during a blackout when everything is lit by candles and oil lamps) is more dramatic than any film or play could ever be. As you wander the streets at night, listen for traditional Nepali music. In the evenings impromptu bands often perform at small temples all over the city. Night is also a good time to do your shopping since many shops catering to tourists stay open until 9pm.

Check in the *Travellers' Nepal* magazine (usually available at hotels) for information on new pubs or restaurants that might have live music. This magazine also lists information on special events at local hotels and schedules of cultural performances.

THEATER & DANCE

In addition to the companies listed here, you will also find cultural performances at the Hotel Yak & Yeti, the Hotel Sherpa, and the Soaltee Holiday Inn Crowne Plaza.

New Himalchuli Cultural Group

Hotel Shanker Compound. ☎ **977/1-410151.** Admission Rs220 ($4.40).

This group performs nightly traditional Nepali folk dances and music. The show includes dances that are performed during various festivals, as well as village courtship dances and shaman's dances. This company also offers dance classes. Performance time is daily at 6:30pm in winter, 7pm in summer.

The Everest Cultural Society

Hotel de l'Annapurna. ☎ **977/1-220676.** Admission Rs220 ($4.40).

Located in a small hall tucked away to the right of the hotel's main entrance, these shows present a variety of different dances from around Nepal. Performance time is daily at 7pm.

Naga Theater

Hotel Vajra, Bijeswari, Swayambhu. ☎ **977/1-272719.** Admission Rs200 ($4).

The Hotel Vajra is a regular cultural center with a theater, art gallery, and library of books on Eastern subjects. The Naga Theater includes the International Actors' Ensemble Studio 7 and the Institute of Classical Nepalese Performing Arts. During the peak tourist seasons there are regular performances, several evenings each week at 7pm. These performances might be classical Nepali music and dance, or they might be the latest avant-garde production. Be sure to check on the hotel lobby's bulletin board to see if anything is scheduled here during your visit.

BARS & DISCOS

Nepal is still an early-to-bed-early-to-rise kind of country, even in the bustling metropolis of Kathmandu, and bars tend to close between 10pm and midnight. All of the major hotels have classy little bars, many of which feature live Western (meaning English-language) music six nights a week. If you are searching for a comfortable place to have a drink and a bit of conversation, you need go no further than your own hotel's bar (see Chapter 3 for details on hotel bars).

Among my favorite hotel bars are **Bugles and Tigers,** which is designed to resemble a bastion of the British empire and which is located on the top floor of the Everest Hotel; the **Pagoda Bar,** a sort of miniature *gompa* on the roof of the Hotel Vajra; and the **Explorers Bar,** a popular post-trek gathering spot at the Hotel Malla.

In the Thamel neighborhood there are numerous pubs where rock music is played very loud and beer is cheap (or at least relatively cheap). A large locally brewed beer or a mixed drink made from domestic spirits will cost between Rs60 ($1.20) and Rs120 ($2.40). All bars are open daily. The **Rum Doodle,** Thamel (☎ 977/1-414336), has mountaineering and kayaking gear strewn all over the room and attracts casual trekkers and serious adventurers. This has long been Kathmandu's most popular bar. Plastered on the walls, there are cutout yeti footprints signed by famous adventurers and wannabes alike. Grab a stool at the bar here, and you may find yourself rubbing shoulders with someone just back from bagging Mt. Everest. You'll find Rum Doodle in Thamel north of the Kathmandu Guest House. Go around the curve and to the left at the T intersection.

GAMBLING CASINOS

Casino Nepal, Holiday Inn Crowne Plaza, Tahachal (☎ 977/1-270244 or 977/1-271011) is the oldest casino in Nepal and is very popular with wealthy Indians who cannot gamble legally in their own country. All bets are in Indian rupees. The games played include flush, poker, baccarat, paplu, roulette, pontoon, blackjack, and jackpot. Hourly from 8 to 11pm, the casino operates a complimentary shuttle bus between the city's major hotels and the casino. The bus stops at the Hotel de l'Annapurna, Hotel Yak & Yeti, Hotel Sherpa, Hotel Woodlands, Hotel Malla, Hotel Shanker, Hotel Kathmandu, Hotel Himalaya, Hotel Narayani, and the Everest Hotel. Admission to the casino is free. It's open 24 hours a day.

The **Hotel de l'Annapurna** and the **Hotel Yak & Yeti,** both in Durbar Marg, also have casinos. These two newer casinos offer the same gambling options, free hotel pickups, and similar enticements to get you to stop by and lose some money. Because their casinos are located on Durbar Marg in the heart of the city, they are more convenient than Casino Nepal. Out at the Everest Hotel near the airport, you'll find yet another casino—the **Casino Everest.**

5 Excursions from Kathmandu

The Kathmandu Valley is the heart of Nepal. Within the fertile valley are two cities that are as fascinating as Kathmandu. Patan (also known as Lalitpur) and Bhaktapur (also known as Bhadgaon) were once independent kingdoms as powerful as the kingdom of Kathmandu. An intense rivalry existed among the three cities, and each royal family built its own palace on its own Durbar Square, so today there are three equally beautiful Durbar Squares in the Kathmandu Valley. Kathmandu's Durbar Square has its towering temples but seems to lack cohesion because of the whitewashed European facade of the Gaddi Baithak. In Patan, the Durbar Square is long and narrow facade of the royal palace facing numerous temples built in different styles. Bhaktapur's Durbar Square is spacious and open, but some people say it lacks the impact and focus of Patan's Durbar Square. I'll leave you to decide which is the most beautiful. However, one thing that is agreed on by all who visit the Kathmandu Valley is that Bhaktapur is the most medieval of the three cities and is worthy of being explored at leisure.

When the crowded, narrow streets of medieval Nepal become too much for you, it is time to head for the hills. Dhulikhel and Nagarkot are two villages on the rim of the mountains surrounding the Kathmandu Valley. From these two spots it is possible to view almost 200 miles of snowy Himalayan peaks. Sunrises and sunsets from these vantage points are truly remarkable and should not be missed. You can even do a bit of hiking using one of these villages as a base. A day hike along these ridges will give you an idea of what trekking in Nepal is all about.

Some of the treks from Dhulikhel and Nagarkot lead to famous Kathmandu Valley temples. Changu Narayan and Bajra Jogini are two such temples that are worth a visit not only for the priceless works of art they hold but also for their remote and tranquil locations.

1 Patan

3 miles (4.8 kilometers) S of Kathmandu

GETTING THERE

BY CAR   You will have to hire a car and driver for the day for about Rs750 to Rs1,500 ($15 to $30). Trip time from Kathmandu is 20 minutes.

BY TAXI   A taxi from Kathmandu will cost around Rs100 ($2) one way and take about 20 minutes.

BY BUS   Blue tempos leave regularly from near the main post office on the west side of the Tundikhel and take 20 minutes. The fare is Rs3 (6¢).

ESSENTIALS   Patan is no longer a distinct city. Though it is separated from Kathmandu by the Bagmati River, urban sprawl has caused the two cities to grow together. Tempos will drop you at Patan Gate, from which you must walk another 10 minutes to Patan's Durbar Square.

WHAT TO SEE & DO
PATAN'S DURBAR SQUARE AREA

Sundari Chowk   The entrance to the ornate courtyard is guarded by a statue of the monkey god Hanuman that is almost as unidentifiable as the Hanuman statue guarding the royal palace in Kathmandu's Durbar Square. The same red paste has been smeared on the statue as an offering. The entrance to the Sundari Chowk is through the second door from the end of the building. This doorway is flanked by statues of Ganesh, the elephant-headed god, and Narsimha, the lion-headed god.

In the center of the courtyard is the **Tusha Hiti,** once the royal bath of King Siddhi Narsimha Malla. The bath's rich stone carvings of *nagas* (snakes) make it the most amazing *hiti* (bathing fountain) in Nepal. Stone steps lead down into the almost 5-ft-deep bath. Positioned along the lip and set in niches around the walls of the bath are more than two dozen 1-foot-tall carved stone statues of various gods and goddesses, including the eight Bhairavs, the eight nagas, and the eight Astha Matrikas. The water spout itself is a masterpiece of repoussé metalwork depicting Vishnu and his consort riding on the back of Garuda. At the top of the steps that lead into the bath is a highly detailed miniature replica of the Krishna Temple that is diagonally across the square from the Sundari Chowk. In front of this miniature temple is a statue of Hanuman and behind it is a large rectangular slab of stone. This is considered a very holy stone, and non-Hindus are requested not to touch it.

Set into the brick a around the inside walls of the Sundari Chowk are many niches, each of which contains a carved wooden figure of a god. Intricately carved and gaily painted lattice windows and balconies look onto the courtyard; the balconies are supported by colorful carved wooden struts. Note the excellent wood carving of the *toranas* over the doorways.

Royal Palace   Though parts of the royal palace were constructed as early as the 14th century, most of it was built in the 17th century. However, in the mid-18th century, the palace suffered much damage at the hands of King Prithvi Narayan Shah, who invaded Patan during his campaign to unify Nepal.

Taking up nearly the entire east side of Patan's Durbar Square, the palace is a sprawling complex of courtyards and temples. To the left of the Sundari Chowk, through a doorway carved with intertwined snakes and flanked by two stone lions, is the **Mul Chowk.** The roof struts depicting many-armed deities on the outside of this building are particularly attractive. The courtyard houses two large brass repoussé statues of the Hindu goddesses Jamuna (atop a turtle) and Ganga (atop a crocodile mythological creature called a *makara*). These statues, created in 1662 and restored in 1936, flank the entrance to the **Taleju Bhawani Temple,** also known as the small Taleju Temple to distinguish it from the towering Taleju Temple to the north of the courtyard. This smaller temple is considered much more sacred than the larger temple. The beautiful torana over the entrance to the temple was carved in 1715. Several images from this torana have disappeared, probably due to theft. In the center of the Mul Chowk is a gilded shrine called the **Bidya Mandir,** which looks like a temple finial. In the northeast corner of this courtyard, you can see an unusual octagonal temple built on the roof of the palace. This temple is also dedicated to the goddess Taleju.

Taleju Temple   To the left of the Mul Chowk and towering over Durbar Square, is the large Taleju Temple. Though the temple itself has only four stories, it is built atop the three-story palace, making it an imposing seven stories. Built by King Siddhi Narsimha Malla in 1640, it's dedicated to the Malla's tutelary goddess, Taleju, who looks over the Kathmandu Valley. The temple is only opened to the public once a year, during the Dasain festival, but only Hindus are allowed to enter. During the earthquake of 1934, the Taleju Temple was razed to the ground.

The Golden Door   To the left of the Taleju Temple is the exquisite entrance to the Mani Keshar Chowk. Though it is neither as large nor as ornate as the Golden Gate in Bhaktapur, Patan's Golden Door is certainly a testimony to the wealth of the Malla kings and the skill of Patan's craftspeople. Flanked by two stone lions, the gilded door is crowned by an intricate repoussé torana depicting the Hindu god Shiva and his consort Parvati. Above the doorway is a finely carved triple window. The central panel is gilded, while the two flanking panels are of carved and painted ivory. The palace behind this Golden Door is currently in the process of being renovated for use as a museum.

Krishna Temple   Opposite the entrance to the Sundari Chowk is an octagonal temple dedicated to the god Krishna. Constructed in the early 18th century by the daughter of King Yoganendra Malla, the temple is one of the few stone temples in the Kathmandu Valley and is designed in the shikhara style of India. Two stone lions guard the steps of this temple. Beside the Krishna Temple is Patan's **Big Bell.** Each of the valley's three Durbar Squares contains a similar large bell. This bell was used during worship at the nearby large Krishna Temple (not the small one beside which it stands) and to warn people of danger.

Nari Shankar Temple   A three-roofed pagoda dedicated to either Shiva or Vishnu and Shankar depending on who you ask, this temple is not worthy of close inspection. For some strange reason the tiers of the temple base are used as an open-air toilet by local residents. The smell can be quite overpowering. If you stand back to look at the temple, you'll see artful roof struts depicting scenes of murder and mayhem. Every arch around the first floor of the temple is decorated with an ornate torana. Around the base of this first floor are stone carvings. Two kneeling elephants flank the steps leading up to the temple.

Narsimha Temple   To the right and slightly behind the Hari Shankar Temple is a temple dedicated to Narsimha, the half-man, half-lion incarnation of the Hindu god Vishnu. Built in the 16th or 17th century, this temple is a simple, shikhara-style structure that is plastered and whitewashed. Flanking the steps are two small stone lions and a pair of deities that includes Garuda, the half-bird, half-man creature upon which Vishnu rides.

Statue of King Yoganendra Malla   Directly in front of the Narsimha Temple is 20-foot-tall stone pillar topped by a gilded bronze statue of King Yoganendra Malla. The king kneels with his hands clasped together in prayer facing the Taleju

The Kathmandu Valley

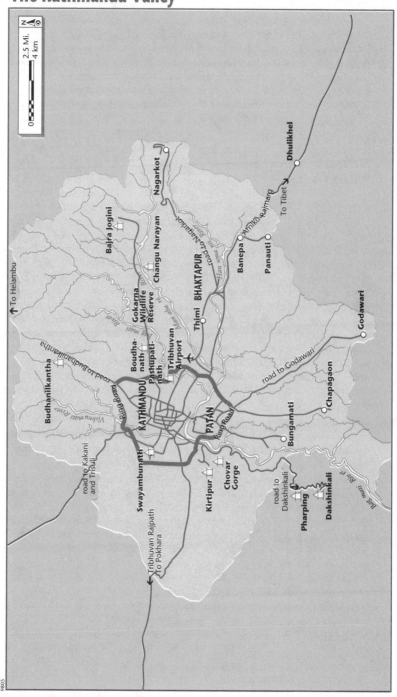

Temple that houses the tutelary goddess of the Malla Kings. A cobra with its neck flared rears up behind the king, and atop the cobra sits a tiny bird. Erected nearly 300 years ago, the statue is the source of numerous legends. My favorite claims that the king, who was said to be able to converse with gods, never died. He disappeared one night saying he would not die until the little metal bird on his statue flew away. Supposedly a window of the palace is left open and a door left unlocked each night so that the king will be able to enter his palace should he ever choose to return.

Charnarayan Temple　To the right of the statue of King Yoganendra Malla is a large pagoda-style temple dedicated to Charnarayan. The temple may have been built as early as 1565, which would make it the oldest temple on the square. The roof struts of this temple feature erotic carvings.

Krishna Temple　This is the most ornate of the temples on Durbar Square and one of the most beautiful temples in Nepal. Dedicated to Krishna and his consort Radha, the temple is constructed from stone and integrates a number of different traditional Indian architectural styles. Built in the mid-17th century by King Siddhi Narsimha Malla, the temple is considered extremely holy and is almost always bustling with reverent worshipers. Set atop a three-stage plinth, the temple is four stories tall. Around the second and third floors are profusely decorated pavilions topped with gilded finials. The uppermost floor is a central shikhara-style tower. Bas-relief friezes around the exterior of the temple on each floor depict scenes from the Hindu epics *Mahabharata* and *Ramayana*. Unfortunately it is not possible to get close enough to these friezes to make out any of the details. Each year on Krishna's birthday, which falls sometime in August or September, a huge crowd gathers here for a nightlong celebration filled with music. Kneeling atop a stone pillar in front of this temple is a bronze statue of Garuda erected in the mid-17th century. Though statues of Garuda are usually found outside temples dedicated to Vishnu since Krishna is an incarnation of Vishnu, this statue is not out of place.

Bishwanath Temple　Dedicated to the god Shiva, this two-story pagoda-style temple contains a Shiva lingam similar to the one housed in the Vishwanath Temple in Varanasi, India. The temple is guarded by two large stone elephants.

Bhimsen Temple　To the right of the Bishwanath Temple is a temple dedicated to the god Bhimsen, a character from the *Mahabharata* who was said to have been the strongest man who ever lived. The three-story pagoda-style temple has been restored three times since it was built sometime prior to 1682, and during the reign of the Rana prime ministers, a marble facade was added to the first floor. There is an elaborate gilded balcony on the second floor above the entrance and silver-painted doors. On the back side is an equally elaborate balcony that has not been gilded. The deities depicted on the roof struts have many arms and are accompanied by their *shaktis* (consorts). Hanging from the front of the temple is a metal ribbon—a symbolic pathway for the god to descend to earth. Over the doors and windows are ornately carved toranas, and in front, atop a stone pillar, stands a bronze lion.

Manga Hiti　Directly across the square from the Bishwanath Temple is a large public *hiti* (bathing fountain). Water pours from the carved stone waterspouts, and people can be seen bathing and washing their clothes here throughout the day. At the top of the steps leading into the hiti are a pair of *pathis* (pilgrims' resting pavilions).

Patan's Durbar Square Area

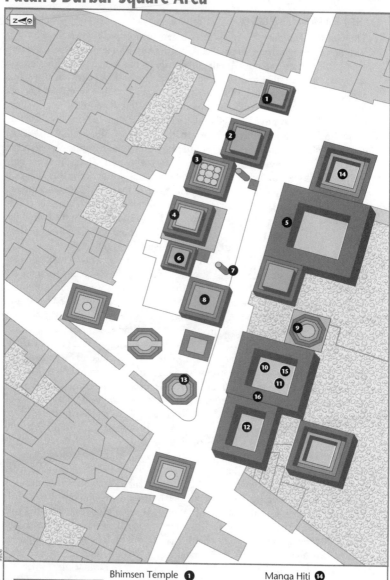

Bhimsen Temple ❶
Bidya Mandir ❿
Bishwanath Temple ❷
Charnarayan Temple ❹
Golden Door ❺
Hari Shankar Temple ❽
Krishna Temple
  (18th century) ⓭
Krishna Temple
  (17th Century) ❸

Manga Hiti ⓮
Mul Chowk ⓯
Narsimha Temple ❻
Royal Palace ⓫
Statue of King
  Yoganendra Malla ❼
Sundari Chowk ⓬
Taleju Bhawani
  Temple ⓰
Taleju Temple ❾

OTHER PATAN TEMPLES

The Golden Temple   To reach the Golden Temple walk down the alley that leads down the right-hand side of the Bhimsen Temple for about 100 feet and turn right at the first intersection. About 200 feet down this road on the right you will see signs to the entrance to the Golden Temple. Also known as the Hiranya Varna Mahavihar and Kwa Bahal, this temple is an active Buddhist monastery. Watch for the pair of large, colorfully painted stone lions that flank the door. Over the entrance are several carved stone Buddha statues. Through the first door is a tiny courtyard from which you can see the ornate golden roof of the temple. Over the doorway leading from this small courtyard into the main courtyard are more carved stone figures of various Buddhist deities. The narrow entry from the street does not prepare the visitor for the ornateness of the temple's inner courtyard. Beneath shimmering gilded roofs, children squeal and shout as they chase each other around the temple courtyard. From a second-floor room comes the faint drone of chanting monks. Old women carry their offerings of food and flowers to the foot of the main temple. Turtles, released by devout Buddhists hoping to gain merit in their next life, wander about the courtyard searching for a way out.

When you step through the door, you will be standing on a raised walkway separated from the flagstone courtyard by a low fence of prayer wheels. Two repoussé elephants with riders on their backs flank the inner doorway as it opens onto the main courtyard. A sign here informs visitors that no leather (on shoes, belts, etc.) is allowed in the temple, but it is OK to stay on the raised walkway if you don't feel like taking off your shoes. Directly in front of the door is a raised mandala surmounted with a large gilded *vajra*. Behind this Buddhist symbol of the thunderbolt that destroys all ignorance is a small temple dedicated to Swayambu, the primordial Buddha. On the two nearest corners of this temple are metal statues of rearing griffins. On the gilded roof there is an ornate finial consisting of a multitiered miniature umbrella (a traditional Buddhist symbol) held up by the tails of four cobras that stream sinuously down the gilded ribbons hanging from the finial. Unfortunately, this richly decorated little temple only detracts from the nearly completely obscured main temple behind it.

According to tradition, the temple was built in the 12th century, though the earliest records of its existence date to the early 15th century. With three gilded roofs and a facade covered with embossed and gilded metal and exquisitely detailed repoussé images of various deities, the temple is perhaps the most ornate in Nepal. The main door itself is covered with silver repoussé, and the gilded torana over this door is as beautiful and elaborate as the torana over Bhaktapur's Golden Gate. Above this torana are seven bas-relief images of the Buddha in different poses. Gilded lattice windows flank the entrance to the temple, and numerous gilded metal ribbons stream down from the roof, assuring any god who wishes to visit the temple plenty of paths to follow. At either end of the walkway that surrounds the courtyard is an unusual metal statue of a monkey holding a jackfruit in its hands. At the back of the small Swayambunath Temple and facing the main temple are two stone figures and two metal figures, all praying. If you are lucky, you might even catch a glimpse of the tiny statue that is housed in this ornate temple, though worshipers usually crowd the statue's tiny room, obscuring it from view. A door on the right side of the courtyard leads to a prayer room on the second floor where Buddhist monks are often found chanting and playing bells.

Kumbheshwar Temple   If you continue down the lane that leads to the Golden Temple, you will come to Patan's oldest temple after another 200 feet or so. Built in 1392, this temple is one of only three five-roofed temples in the Kathmandu Valley (the other two are the Nyatapola Temple in Bhaktapur and the circular Panch Mukhi Hanuman Temple in Kathmandu's Hanuman Dhoka Palace). Lacking a terraced base, the Kumbheshwar Temple is not as well proportioned or balanced as the Nyatapola Temple, but it is quite beautiful nonetheless. Devout Hindus believe that this temple is the winter residence of the god Shiva, who spends his summers on Mt. Kailash, a mountain in Tibet that is sacred to both Hindus and Buddhists. North of the temple, within the large temple compound, is a covered water tank that is said to be filled by a spring originating at the holy Gosainkund Lake high in the Himalayas, an eight-day walk north of Kathmandu. There are many beautiful stone carvings of different gods within the temple compound. As you walk through the front gate of the temple, you will be facing the hind end of a statue of Nandi the bull, the animal upon which Shiva is said to travel.

This is another perpetually active temple with children playing in the numerous pools of water, teenage girls rubbing their hands across rows of Shiva linga, and old men and women bathing at the waterspouts of the temple's fountains.

During the festival of Janai Purnima in July or August, pilgrims gather at the temple complex to worship a silver and gold Shiva lingam that is erected in the middle of one of the water tanks. During the Kumbheshwar Mela festival, also in August, Hindu shamans known as *jhankris* gather here to heal the sick by dancing and drumming away the evil spirits.

In a small temple to the right of the Kumbheshwar Temple you will probably see people lined up to leave offerings. This temple is dedicated to the crane-headed goddess Baglamukhi who is depicted in a gilded doorway framed by a canopy of silver snakes.

Mahaboudha   Known in English as the Temple of the 10,000 Buddhas, this temple is about a mile from Durbar Square. To find it, continue along the main bazaar road that passes the south end of Durbar Square. About 15 minutes down this road at the second major street, you will come to a wide square with a bathing fountain at the near end of the square. Turn right and in another 5 minutes you'll come to the Mahaboudha Temple.

A Buddhist temple designed in the Indian shikhara architectural style, Mahaboudha takes its name from the thousands of terra-cotta plaques covering it. Each plaque contains an image of the Buddha, and it is said that every brick used in the construction of the temple depicts the Buddha. The bricks used are of an ocher color rather than the usual red so prevalent in the Kathmandu Valley. Razed by the earthquake of 1934, the temple was rebuilt; with the leftover bricks, a shrine to the Buddha's mother, Maya Devi, was erected.

The small courtyard that houses this tall temple is at the end of a narrow, dark alley lined with shops selling well-made statues of various deities. If you are interested, prices here are usually quite good. Because the temple nearly fills the courtyard in which it stands, visitors must crane their necks to see more than a few feet of the temple's base. There is a flight of steps that leads to the second floor of the building surrounding the courtyard, and from here you can get a much better view.

The streets around this temple are home to metalsmiths who create all manner of religious statuary. You will hear them hammering away and might even catch a glimpse into one of their workshops.

Rudra Varna Mahavihar   If you turn right as you come out of the Mahaboudha Temple and then take the first left, you will see the entrance to the Rudra Varna Mahavihar across the street. In the sunny, open courtyard of this 19th-century monastery, there is an amazing array of metal and stone statuary, including two European-style lions, a king, two garudas in metal and one in stone, two Asian lions, two rearing griffins, two rearing goats, and eight repoussé high-relief icons. There is also a miniature replica of Swayambunath Stupa with a gilded canopy shading it from the sun. Two vajras are mounted atop mandalas.

Rato (Red) Machendranath Temple   Hidden from the main street down a lane lined with shops, this is one of the most important temples in Patan. Though the temple, which is surrounded by an unkempt garden, is said to date to the early 15th century, it more likely was built sometime in the late 17th century. Machendra, also known as Avalokiteshwara and Lokeshwar, is the same god as Chenrezig, the patron saint of Tibet, and Hindus consider him to be an aspect of Shiva. As Machendranath, this god is revered in the Kathmandu Valley as a god of rain. The strangely childlike figure of Machendra is roughly carved from dark wood and painted bright red. The statue is kept in this temple for only half the year; the other half it resides in the nearby village of Bungamati. Each year in April or May, during the festival of Machendranath Jatra, the image is taken out of its temple and paraded through the streets of Patan in a huge chariot pulled by devoted worshipers. Once every 12 years, the chariot is pulled all the way to Bungamati, about 3 miles away. This long chariot ride will next be undertaken in the year 2003. To find the temple, walk south on the road that begins to the right of the Sundari Chowk on Durbar Square. Take the first lane you come to on your right and walk through the gate at the end of the lane.

WALKING TOUR
Patan

Start: Patan's Durbar Square.
Finish: Patan's Durbar Square.
Time: Five hours, including lunch but not including shopping.
Best Times: Saturday when Nepalis have the day off and visit the temples.
Worst Times: Any day around 9:30am when the tour buses arrive.

Though Patan is now merely a district of greater Kathmandu, it was once a separate kingdom and consequently has its own Durbar Square, royal palace, temples, and fascinating streets and alleys.

  Start your walking tour at the south end of:
1. **Durbar Square,** at the Sundari Chowk in the royal palace. (See "What to See & Do," above in this chapter for details on all of the square's major temples and buildings.) After exploring the square, walk down the alley on the right side of the Bhimsen Temple, which is at the north end of Durbar Square. When you come to the first intersection, turn right. At the next intersection there is an interesting little Ganesh shrine in which poor Ganesh is almost unrecognizable. If you continue through the intersection in the same direction you have been walking, you will see just ahead of you on the left:
2. **The Golden Temple,** an exquisitely adorned temple within the confines of a Buddhist monastery (see above in this chapter for more details). Continuing down the same street another five minutes, you will come to an open area in which stands:

3. **Kumbheshwar Temple,** one of only three five-roofed pagodas in the Kathmandu Valley. It is set within a compound filled with smaller temples and water tanks that are supposedly fed by a sacred lake far to the north in the high mountains (see above in this chapter for more details). If you turn right after the Kumbheshwar Temple and then take your first major left, you will come to the:

4. **Ashoka Stupa,** one of four such ancient stupas that were built at the four ancient corners of Patan. Legend has it that the stupas were erected by the Indian emperor Ashoka when he visited the Kathmandu Valley around 250 B.C. You may have seen another of the stupas on your way from Kathmandu since there is one diagonally across from the Hotel Narayani. Another of the stupas is southeast of Durbar Square between the bus stop and the Patan Industrial Estate. If you continue north from the Ashoka Stupa, you will walk downhill to the bank of the Bagmati River, which is the site of the 1-km-long:

5. **Sankhamul Ghat.** Because the Bagmati River no longer flows past this stone embankment, it is no longer used much for cremations or other religious rituals, as it once was. However, it still retains a certain grandeur that hints at how powerful Patan was in years past as an independent kingdom. Head back the way you came and, after passing the Ashoka Stupa and Kumbheshwar Temple, you will reach a section of street lined with old brick homes. Along this stretch on the left is the two-story:

6. **Uma Maheshwar Temple,** which houses a stone bas relief of Shiva and Parvati seated side by side. This carving dates to the Licchavi period, which ended in the 9th century. A bit farther along this street, you will come to a square with:

7. **Three Temples.** The temple on your immediate left is dedicated to Vishnu and has a beautiful stone statue of Garuda in front. Within this temple is a stone bas relief of Vishnu, and in the paving stones in front of the temple, there is carving of a snake.

☕ **TAKE A BREAK** There aren't too many places in this area that you would probably want to patronize for more than a bottled drink, but the **Café Pagode,** facing the Bhimsen Temple on Durbar Square, is an exception. If you have worked up a big appetite, try the set Nepali lunch of dal bhat and vegetables. It's an all-you-can-eat affair that will fuel you up for more exhausting touring.

From Café Pagode, walk back to the large road at the south end of Durbar Square and turn left. Continue away from Durbar Square on this street until you come to the second major intersection, which has a temple on your immediate right and a bathing fountain across the intersection on the right. Turn right here and almost at the far end of this narrow street, you will come to:

8. **Mahaboudha,** a Buddhist temple built in the shikhara-style of architecture from northern India (see above in this chapter for details). Be sure to have a look inside the shops in the temple courtyard. This area is known for the skill of its craftspeople, who fashion metal statues of various Buddhist and Hindu deities using the lost-wax method. Turn right as you leave this temple, walk to the end of the street, and turn left. Diagonally across the street is the entrance to the:

9. **Rudra Varna Mahavihar,** which is an inactive Buddhist monastery that has some interesting statues in its courtyard (see above in this chapter for details).

Turn left as you exit this compound and continue down this street until you come to the bazaar street that leads south out of Durbar Square. You will hear the pounding of hammers on copper the whole time you walk along this street, and you will see in the shops what all these little workshops are making—large copper water pots. Almost directly across the T intersection with the bazaar street is a lane that leads in a few yards to:

10. **Rato Machendranath,** home to one of the most revered gods of the Kathmandu Valley for six months each year (see above in this chapter for details). Return up the little lane that leads to this temple and almost directly across the main street you will see the:

11. **Minanath Temple.** This temple dates to the 16th century and stands behind a *hiti* (sunken water fountain) that was built in the 11th century. The deity housed within this temple is associated with Rato Machendra and likewise is paraded through the city in its own chariot during the festival of Machendranath Jatra. From the Minanath Temple, walk north in the direction of Durbar Square. A block before reaching the square, turn left down a narrow lane, and you will come to the:

12. **Bishwakarma Temple.** This unusual brick temple is dedicated to the god of coppersmiths and carpenters and consequently has a facade of beaten copper. Retrace your steps up this lane, turn left, and you will shortly be back at the southern end of Durbar Square.

NEARBY TEMPLES & TOWNS

A day spent exploring the several roads that lead south from Patan, either by taxi or on a mountain bike, will provide a glimpse of rural Nepal. Though these roads lead only a few miles from the edge of the city, they pass through ancient villages that have retained many of their old buildings. There are remote temples and shrines, as well as panoramic views across the valley to the snow-capped Himalayas.

Almost due west of Patan, off the road that leads to Chovar Gorge and the Dakshinkali shrine, stands the ancient town of **Kirtipur.** Built on a hill overlooking the Kathmandu Valley, Kirtipur was once an independent kingdom. Because of its strategic hilltop location, Kirtipur was the last kingdom conquered by King Prithvi Narayan Shah when he unified Nepal in the late 18th century. Perhaps as a result of Kirtipur's legendary stubbornness, the town has been unaffected by the development of Kathmandu and Patan. For this reason, it is of great interest to visitors. The narrow streets are not clogged with smoke-belching trucks, and cement buildings have not yet replaced the traditional brick buildings of this Newari town. If you stroll through Kirtipur's streets, you will come across several small temples, but the town is more interesting simply as an insight into traditional Nepali culture. The streets are full of activity, as are the farm fields below the town. One temple of particular interest, however, is the **Bagh Bhairav Temple** near the center of town. Nailed to the facade of this temple are swords and shields once used by the soldiers who fruitlessly defended Kirtipur against the troops of King Prithvi Narayan Shah.

If you continue on this road, you will come to **Chovar Gorge, Pharping,** and **Dakshinkali,** which are all described in Chapter 4.

Heading due south from the former Tibetan Refugee Camp at Jawalakhel will take you to **Bungamati,** a town that dates back to the 16th century. It is here that the Rato Machendra statue (see above in this chapter) spends half of every year,

Walking Tour — Patan

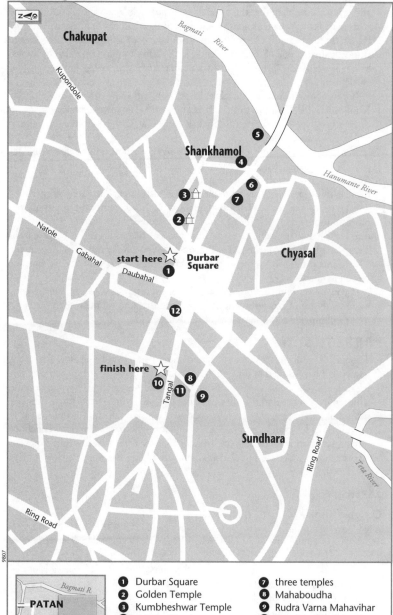

Chakupat

Bagmati River

Kupondole

Shankhamol

⑤ Sankhamul Ghat

④ Ashoka Stupa

Hanumante River

⑥ Uma Maheshwar Temple

③ Kumbheshwar Temple

⑦ three temples

② Golden Temple

Natole

Gabahal

start here ☆ **Durbar Square**
① Durbar Square

Chyasal

Daubahal

⑫ Bishwakarma Temple

finish here ☆
⑩ Rato Machendranath

Tangal

⑪ Minanath Temple

⑧ Mahaboudha

⑨ Rudra Varna Mahavihar

Sundhara

Ring Road

Tera River

Ring Road

Bagmati R.

PATAN

Walking
Tour Area

Ring Road

① Durbar Square
② Golden Temple
③ Kumbheshwar Temple
④ Ashoka Stupa
⑤ Sankhamul Ghat
⑥ Uma Maheshwar Temple

⑦ three temples
⑧ Mahaboudha
⑨ Rudra Varna Mahavihar
⑩ Rato Machendranath
⑪ Minanath Temple
⑫ Bishwakarma Temple

and it is to Bungamati that this same statue is pulled in a massive chariot every 12 years. The **Rato Machendranath Temple** in Bungamati is a shikhara-style temple rather than a pagoda. On the northern outskirts of Bungamati is the **Karya Binayak shrine,** one of the Kathmandu Valley's most important Ganesh shrines. The Ganesh of this shrine is actually a natural stone that looks only vaguely like an elephant.

If you continue north from this shrine, you will soon come to the town of **Khokana,** which is quite similar to Bungamati. This town's main temple is a three-story pagoda dedicated to Shekali Mai, one of the Kathmandu Valley's nature goddesses.

If you head south from Durbar Square and turn left at the bus park, you will pass the Patan Industrial Estate and then the Ring Road. If you continue on this road, you will eventually reach the botanic gardens at Godawari. However, if you turn right just past the Ring Road intersection instead of continuing straight, you will come to the town of **Chapagaon.** As in Bungamati and Kirtipur, the old buildings here are built of brick. In the center of town is a shrine dedicated to Bhairav. Outside of town, in a grove of trees, stands the **Vajra Varahi Temple,** which is dedicated to a Tantric goddess. The temple was built in the 17th century and today, due to its peaceful setting, is a popular picnic spot for Nepali families.

If you are traveling on a mountain bike or motorcycle, you may want to continue south from Chapagaon on the rough road that leads to the Lele Valley. This route will provide additional views of rural Nepali life.

WHERE TO STAY

Though it is really just a suburb of Kathmandu, Patan is still a separate city. Consequently I have chosen to list its hotels here rather than with the Kathmandu hotels. Should you choose to stay in Patan rather than Kathmandu, you will be quite a bit removed from Kathmandu's old city but close to the equally fascinating old section of Patan. One of the hotels listed here is among the quietest in the valley because of its location in an affluent residential neighborhood. Another benefit of staying in Patan is that the views are much better here than from the hotels in Kathmandu. In fact the Hotel Himalaya Kathmandu has the best views of any hotel in the valley.

EXPENSIVE

✪ Hotel Himalaya

Sahid Sukra Marg (P.O. Box 2141), Lalitpur, Kathmandu. ☎ **997/1-523900.** Fax 977/1-523909. 100 rms. 3 suites. A/C MINIBAR TV TEL. $131.10 double; $399 suite. Children under 12 stay free in parents' room without extra bed. AE, DC, MC, V.

Boasting the best views of any hotel in the valley, the Hotel Himalaya is one of my favorites. It's located on a hill across the Bagmati River from Kathmandu on the main road to Patan's Durbar Square. Popular with Japanese tour groups, the hotel features a glassed-in rock garden off to one side of the lobby and a partial view of the snow-covered Himalayas through the wall of glass at the back of the lobby. Unfortunately, the shrubs in the hotel's garden are beginning to block the lobby's amazing view.

Though the carpets are showing signs of wear and the halls are rather dark, the rooms are comfortable if without much character. Large windows let in lots of light. If you ask for a room on the garden side of the hotel, the fabulous view will remind you of where you are.

Dining/Entertainment: The Chalet Restaurant, upstairs from the lobby, is the hotel's main dining room. Indian, continental, Chinese, and Japanese fare is served both at lunch and dinner. On Wednesday and Saturday there is a cultural performance from 7:30 to 9:30pm with Nepali music and dancing. The stunning views of the mountains make this a good choice for lunch. Downstairs is the Base Camp Coffee Shop, open daily from 7am to 11pm. The Chautari Bar is adjacent to the coffee shop.

Services: 24-hour room service, laundry and valet service, babysitting, safe-deposit boxes, currency exchange, complimentary morning paper, complimentary city shuttle, travel desk, doctor on call.

Facilities: Swimming pool, tennis court, shopping arcade, business center, conference facilities, beauty parlor, barbershop.

Hotel Narayani
Pulchowk, Patan. (P.O. Box 1357, Kathmandu.) ☎ **977/1-525015**, 977/1-525016, or 977/1-525017. Fax 977/1-521291. 87 rms, 4 suites. A/C TV TEL. $96.90 double; $142.50 suite. One child under age 12 may stay free in parents' room without an extra bed. AE, DC, JCB, MC, V.

Located a little farther up the hill from the Hotel Himalaya on the main road from Kathmandu to Patan, the Hotel Narayani is an old luxury hotel that recently remodeled its lobby. The rooms are still a bit tired and, consequently, the hotel is overpriced. The large garden and swimming pool somewhat make up for the rooms. If you think you might spend time lounging by the pool, you might want to consider staying here.

Dining/Entertainment: The Summit Room, featuring evening buffets, and the Indreni Room, featuring Indian, Nepali, Chinese, and continental dishes, are the hotel's two main dining rooms. Both serve moderately priced, unremarkable meals. Near the swimming pool is the Café Tropicana, serving snacks and light meals. There is also a lobby bar.

Services: Room service, currency exchange, safe-deposit boxes, luggage storage, laundry service.

Facilities: Swimming pool, beauty salon, souvenir shops.

MODERATE

✪ Summit Hotel
P.O. Box 1406, Kupondole Height, Kathmandu. ☎ **977/1-521894** or 977/1-524694. Fax 977/1-523737. 61 rms (56 with bath), 4 apts. $22.20–$33.30 double without bath, $61.05–$99.90 double with bath; $138.75 apartment. Lower rates are for summer months. AE, MC, V.

Though it offers few amenities, the Summit is one of my favorite Kathmandu hotels. If you're the kind of person who prefers hotels that sacrifice a few area comforts for character, this is an excellent choice. Located down a long winding lane in a quiet residential neighborhood, the Summit incorporates traditional Kathmandu Valley architectural designs and typically Nepali crafts in its decor. The two-story brick hotel surrounds a lush garden filled with colorful flowers and shady trees. An artificial stream meanders through the garden, watering bushy papyrus plants. Ornately carved railings and pillars are reminiscent of local palaces and temples and testify to the continuing skill of local wood-carvers.

My favorite rooms are, surprisingly, the least expensive and have private baths and face the hotel's beautiful garden. Each room has two twin beds, wicker-shaded reading lamps, and rattan chairs and table that you can easily move out to the veranda. Colorful local festival masks hang from the walls. There is no air conditioning, but there are fans in every room. Floors are made of the traditional brick tiles that have been used in local homes for centuries. Bathrooms are basic but clean. The more expensive rooms are larger and have better views.

Dining/Entertainment: The hotel's small restaurant has a very Nepali feel to it with exposed brick walls, a high beamed ceiling, traditional brick-tile floors, and an old Newari-style carved lattice window. In the adjacent bar, long couches covered with pillows are a great place to relax by a cozy fire. There are dinner barbecues on Friday for Rs440 ($8.80).

Services: Currency exchange, airport transfers.

Facilities: Swimming pool, sauna, shopping arcade.

WHERE TO DINE

Other than the dining rooms of the few hotels, there aren't too many places to eat in Patan.

Café Pagode

Patan Durbar Square (in front of Bhimsen Temple). No phone. Reservations not accepted. Complete meals Rs30–Rs150 (60¢–$3). Daily 8:30am–9:30pm. INTERNATIONAL.

This restaurant on Durbar Square is the most convenient place to eat if you are spending a whole day exploring Patan. There is roof-top dining terrace and a courtyard dining area as well. Try the complete Nepali meal. Much more than just dal bhat, you get two types of curried vegetables, rice, dal, and curried chicken.

Downtown

Pulchowk. ☎ 977/1-522451. Reservations not necessary. Main dishes Rs30–Rs120 (60¢–$2.40). DC, MC, V. Sun–Fri 10am–9pm; Sat noon–9pm. INDIAN/CHINESE.

This simple restaurant is located across the street and up the hill from the Hotel Himalaya. Downtown is nondescript and off the standard tourist circuit, but it is very popular among expatriates living or working in the Kupondole district of Patan. Meals are very inexpensive, and the Indian dishes in particular are as good as you'll get at the more expensive Indian restaurants on Durbar Marg.

2 Bhaktapur

9 miles (14.5 kilometers) E of Kathmandu

The old cities of the Kathmandu Valley are often compared to medieval cities of Europe, and nowhere is this comparison more apt than in Bhaktapur. The entire heart of the city remains virtually unchanged since the 17th century, when many of the city's most beautiful buildings were erected. In recent years, the Bhaktapur Development Project, funded primarily by Germany, has done much to restore and upgrade the city's most interesting buildings. As you wander through the city you will see what appear to be brand-new buildings constructed in the old style complete with carved windows. These are the work of the BDP. As part of their renovation project, they have also included indoor plumbing for most of the houses. Unfortunately, there has been much resistance to such a radical idea, and sanitation continues to be a problem in Bhaktapur. Streets are often dirty, and

Patan Accommodations & Dining

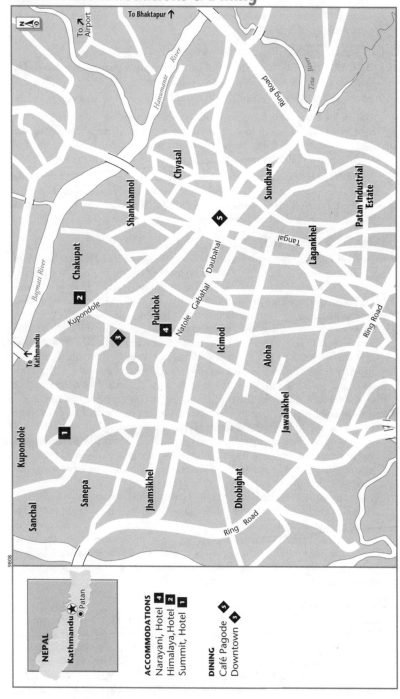

To Bhaktapur ↑

To Airport ↗

To Kathmandu ↙

Hanumante River

Ring Road

Tsta River

Chyasal

Sundhara

Shankhamol

Patan Industrial Estate

Chakupat

Daubahal

Tangal

Lagankhel

Kupondole

Pulchok

Natole Gabahal

Bagmati River

Iclmod

Ring Road

Aloha

Kupondole

Jawalakhel

Sanepa

Jhamsikhel

Dhobighat

Sanchal

Ring Road

9808

NEPAL

Kathmandu ★

Patan ●

ACCOMMODATIONS
Narayani, Hotel 🔳4
Himalaya, Hotel 🔳2
Summit, Hotel 🔳1

DINING
Café Pagode 🔶5
Downtown 🔶3

residents of upper floors often dump their garbage out their windows. Keep an eye out for falling garbage.

GETTING THERE

BY CAR You will have to hire a car and driver for the day for between Rs750 ($15) and Rs1,500 ($30). Trip time is 30 minutes.

BY TAXI A taxi will cost around Rs250 ($5) one way. Trip time is 30 minutes.

BY BUS Buses leave regularly from the old bus park on the east side of the Tundikhel near the clock tower and take 45 minutes. There is also electric bus service to Bhaktapur. These buses leave from the traffic circle beside the national stadium at the southwest corner of the Tundikhel. Tickets are Rs5 (10¢).

ESSENTIALS Bhaktapur is a compact city of narrow lanes and alleys. From the bus and taxi stop continue walking straight ahead for about five minutes to reach Durbar Square. There is currently a Rs50 ($1) admission charge for tourists visiting Bhaktapur. The money is being used to restore the city.

WHAT TO SEE & DO

Built on a hill in the eastern part of the valley, Bhaktapur is said to have been built in the shape of a conch shell, a sacred symbol of Hinduism. Today the city has grown well beyond its original size, and the conch-shell shape is no longer discernible, except perhaps from the air. However, the city is still an impressive sight when approached from the last stop on the electric bus line, which is south of the city. From here your view is of a wall of faded redbrick houses climbing a hillside. The houses seem to be stacked helter-skelter atop one another, but rising from amid this jumble is the perfect symmetry of the five-storied Nyatapola Temple. A five-minute walk past rice paddies and vegetable gardens brings you to a steep brick road leading up into the dark confines of the city. Within a block of entering the city, there is a square filled with tiny pottery dishes drying in the sun. Local potters of all ages busy themselves making simple pots and dishes. Small boys pound the clay at the foot of a shrine. Teenage boys practice spinning the heavy potter's wheels that are made from old tires. Older men shape water jars and yogurt containers with deft fingers. Women wet the gray clay dishes around the square, moving them occasionally to keep them in the sun. The scene is timeless and emphasizes the medieval atmosphere of the city.

Narrow, dark alleys lead out from this square. With overhanging windows and balconies, the houses nearly touch above these alleys, and little sunlight penetrates to the ground. Everything seems to be made of brick, wood, and stone. Vegetables and grains hang from the eaves of buildings out of the reach of rats and pigeons. If you continue uphill, you will eventually find yourself in Bhaktapur's Durbar Square. The third of the Kathmandu Valley's Durbar Squares, it is arguably the most beautiful.

DURBAR SQUARE

Large and open, Bhaktapur's Durbar Square has neither the crowds and noise of Kathmandu's Durbar Square nor the cramped feeling of Patan's. A large colorfully painted gate opens onto the square from the northwest. Just outside this gate are a number of small but interesting shrines. The gate was built about 300 years ago by King Bupathindra Malla who was responsible for erecting many of the buildings and works of art on this square. Just inside the main gate on the left is a small gate in a brick wall. Flanking this second gate are two large stone lions and smaller statues of the goddess **Ugrachandi Durga** (on the left) and the god **Bhairav** (on the right). These two statues are some of the finest stone carvings in Nepal, and legend has it that the artist, who was commissioned by King Bupathindra Malla, had his hands chopped off so he could not duplicate these works of art. The image of Ugrachandi is killing the buffalo-headed demon Mahishasur and has 18 arms. Bhairav, who is an incarnation of Shiva, is shown with 12 arms.

To the right of the gate with Ugrachandi and Bhairav is another gate flanked by two more stone lions and two more gods. These are **Narsimha** (on the right) and **Hanuman Bhairav** (on the left). Narsimha is shown tearing out the entrails of the demon Haranyakashipu. According to Hindu mythology this demon had tricked the god Brahma into making him immortal. He could not be killed by man or animal during the day or at night. When he began terrorizing the world, Vishnu manifested himself as the half-man, half-lion Narsimha and killed Haranyakashipu at twilight, which is neither night nor day. These statues guard the entrance to the National Art Gallery.

Inside two old palaces facing Durbar Square is the **National Art Gallery** (☎ 977/1-610004), one of Nepal's two collections of traditional arts. Inside is a large collection of Buddhist thangkas. These colorful and intricately detailed paintings on canvas were rolled up and carried by wandering monks to assist them with meditations and religious services. Also on display are carved stone figures of various Hindu and Buddhist deities that are even more impressive than the thangkas. The sun god at the foot of the stairs leading to the second floor is particularly beautiful. Just inside the front door is a large stone Shiva lingam with four faces on it. This phallic image is one of the most common ways of representing the Hindu god Shiva. In a large hall on the second floor are cases displaying old illustrated books that record the histories of the kings who once ruled the Kathmandu Valley. In the section of the museum that is within the Palace of 55 Windows, there are the remains of beautiful wall murals that give an indication of how richly ornamented this palace must have been when it was first built.

Admission is Rs5 (10¢), Rs15(30¢) if you bring a camera. It's open Wednesday to Monday from 10am to 5pm; it's closed on all national holidays.

To the right of the art gallery entrance is the **Sun Dhoka** or **Golden Gate.** This masterpiece of metalworking is without doubt the greatest work of art in Nepal. Erected by Ranjit Malla in the mid-18th century, the gate is made of brick and gilded bronze and was envisioned as a suitably ornate entrance to the system of courtyards that houses the Taleju Temple. The goddess Taleju, whose image is kept within the temple, was the tutelary goddess of the Malla kings and was thus highly revered. Done in the repoussé method, the gate includes an amazingly detailed figure of the fearsome goddess Kali at the center of the *torana* (the panel over the gate). Above Kali is an image of Garuda, in this case shown with the head of a bird rather than a human head. Serpents, nymphs, gods, and monsters cover every inch of the torana and the door frame. Set into either side of the gate are stone inscriptions, and on the curving gilded roof are numerous finials, including some shaped like elephants and winged lions. Through the gate are several courtyards that contain some excellent wood carvings and colorfully painted struts. In the farthest courtyard is the **Taleju Temple,** the most sacred temple in Bhatapur, said to contain the finest works of art in the valley. Unfortunately this temple is off-limits to non-Hindus, but you should be able to get a peek through the open door. Be sure to notice the large and intricate torana over the entrance to the Taleju Temple. On a pillar directly in front of the Golden Gate is a life-size **statue**

of King Bupathindra Malla. The king sits cross-legged with his hands together as a sign of respect for the goddess Taleju. Though all three of the valley's Durbar Squares have statues of past kings, this is considered the most elegant and artistic.

To the right of the golden gate is the **Palace of 55 Windows,** one of the most beautiful buildings on the square. Though there was a palace on this site as long ago as 1427, it was extensively renovated in the early 18th century by King Bupathindra Malla. It takes its name from the amazing row of carved wooden windows that line the second floor of the palace. Above each of the windows are wooden *tympana* depicting gods, goddesses, and mythological creatures. Behind this ornate facade is the palace's royal audience hall. The dark color of the carved windows is in bold contrast to the redbrick walls of the building.

To the right of the Palace of 55 Windows is a large open square bordered on two sides by an L-shaped building that was once a *dharmasala* (resting place for pilgrims). The first temple on your left as you enter this square is the **Durga Temple.** It is a small shikhara-style temple on a five-tiered base and is dedicated to Durga. Carved stone figures, including two smiling rhinos, decorate the steps that lead to the door of the temple. The 1934 earthquake leveled many of the temples on this square. Across from the dharmasala you will see the strangest evidence of the earthquake. Atop a four-tiered pyramid that once supported a large and elegant temple stands a dumpy little whitewashed shikhara-style temple erected after the earthquake. This little temple is entirely out of place on such a large base. It is a shame that the original temple has never been restored. In the middle of the courtyard are two large stone lions.

Among the buildings destroyed by the 1934 earthquake was the **Chyaslin Mandapa,** an octagonal pavilion used by kings for viewing processions and for meeting with dignitaries and ministers. In 1988, this unusually graceful structure underwent reconstruction under the auspices of the Bhaktapur Development Program and with a gift from the German government. Dedicated in late 1990, the Chyaslin Mandapa has done much to restore Bhaktapur's Durbar Square to its past grandeur. Around the stone base of the pavilion is an inscription that includes a poem to the eight seasons (thus the eight sides to the building). The reconstruction utilizes all the pieces of the original structure that could be salvaged but, in addition, a steel infrastructure has been incorporated into the design to prevent another earthquake from destroying the pavilion. Architects, construction workers, and craftspeople worked from a 19th-century drawing of the pavilion. Roof struts feature lovers embracing affectionately rather than the graphic sexual scenes on many other roof struts around the valley. The second floor of the pavilion is a pleasant place to sit and take in the activity of the square.

Behind the Chyaslin Mandapa is a stone shikhara-style temple dedicated to **Batsala Devi.** There are many excellent stone carvings of various gods and goddesses on this temple. On a platform attached to this temple is a large bell known as the **barking bell,** so named because all the dogs within hearing distance commence barking whenever the bell is rung (or so the story goes). The massive bell, erected by King Ranjit Malla in the early 18th century, is still rung every morning during worship of Taleju in the nearby Taleju Temple. Behind the temple of Batsala Devi is a large two-story pagoda-style temple that is a reproduction of the famous temple at **Pashupatinath.** Noted for its easily seen erotic carvings, this temple was constructed in the late 17th century.

Bhaktapur's Durbar Square Area

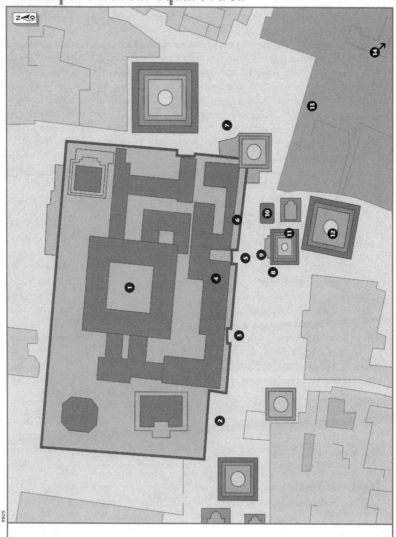

BHAKTAPUR
Bhaktapur
Area

Hanumante R.

Barking Bell **9**
Batsala Devi Temple **11**
Chyaslin Mandapa **10**
Dharmasala **13**
Durga Temple **7**
Narsimha and
  Hanuman Bhairav **3**
National Art Gallery **4**
Nyatapola Temple **14**
Palace of 55 Windows **6**
Pashupatinath Temple **12**
Statue of King
  Bupathindra Malla **8**
Sun Dhoka
  (Golden Gate) **5**
Taleju Temple **1**
Ugrachandi Durga
  and Bhairav **2**

9809

On the far side of the square from the Palace of 55 Windows, behind the Pashupatinath Temple, is a shop-lined lane leading from Durbar Square to Taumadi Square. As you step out of the narrow lane into the square, you will see towering above you on your left the tallest and what I consider the most beautiful of all Nepal's temples. The **Nyatapola Temple** is a magnificent five-roofed pagoda standing atop a massive five-tiered pyramid base. Together the roofs and base display exquisite balance and symmetry. Each level of the temple is ornately decorated with colorfully painted roof struts and windows. Hundreds of bells, tinkling in the wind, hang from the eaves. On each of the base's five tiers stands a pair of stone statues flanking the steps that lead to the temple door. These statues have a curious legend associated with them. The two lowest statues, which are nearly eight feet tall, are of a pair of famous wrestlers—Jaya Mal and Patta—who were each supposed to have the strength of 10 men. On the tier above them stand two elephants who are said to be 10 times stronger than the wrestlers. Above the elephants are two lions, which are believed to be 10 times as strong as elephants. Above the lions are two griffins that are 10 times stronger than lions. Above these stand two goddesses, Baghini and Singhini, who are part tiger and part lion, respectively. They are said to be 10 times stronger than the griffins. This progression would indicate that the deity installed within the temple must be very powerful indeed. Erected in the early 18th century by King Bupathindra Malla, the temple is dedicated to the Tantric goddess Siddhi Laxmi. However, a legend concerning the temple says that it was never dedicated, and the temple has remained locked since being erected.

To the right as you face Nyatapola Temple is a rectangular, three-roofed temple dedicated to **Bhairav.** Erected in the 18th century, the temple was destroyed by the 1934 earthquake and later rebuilt. Though it seems quite plain and uninteresting beside the towering beauty of the Nyatapola Temple, if you look closely you will notice that it has a very ornately decorated facade and is the focus of near-constant worship. The gilded repoussé work of the lower story is kept highly polished by reverent hands rubbing across it. Above the niche into which offerings to Bhairav are thrust are gilded windows similar to the wooden windows that decorate the upper floors of this temple. Atop the metal roof are seven finials, and at each corner is a small metal figure of a bird.

DATTATREYA SQUARE

If you walk down the road to the left of the Bhairav Temple, you will come to Dattatreya Square in about 15 minutes. Once the center of Bhaktapur, this square is named for the **Dattatreya Temple.** Built in 1427, this temple is the oldest structure on the square, though it was altered in 1458. The three-story temple is unique in that it has a separate little structure, complete with balcony and finial, built atop its lowest roof. A small face looks down from this little add-on room in the same way that Shiva and Parvati look down from their temple in Kathmandu's Durbar Square. The second and third floors are also surrounded by balconies. The tall stone pillar in front of the temple is crowned with a statue of **Garuda,** which indicates that this temple is dedicated to the god Vishnu, here in the incarnation of Dattatreya. Flanking the temple's entrance are statues of the famous wrestlers Jaya Mal and Patta, who are also seen on the steps of the Nyatapola Temple. Similar in design to the Kasthamandap in Kathmandu, the Dattatreya Temple is also said to have been constructed from the wood of a single tree.

Opposite the Dattatreya Temple at the far end of the square is the small **Bhimsen Temple.** Facing this temple is an ornate metal lion atop a stone pillar. The square also houses two of the city's museums, described below.

Brass and Bronze Museum

Dattatreya Square. ☎ **977/1-610448.** Admission Rs5 (10¢), Rs10 (20¢) more if you bring a camera. Wed–Mon 10:30am–4pm. Closed all national holidays.

In an old building behind the Dattatreya Temple, the Brass and Bronze Museum contains examples of Nepal's skillful metalworking history. Many of the pieces in the museum are similar to household utensils still in use today. The *gaagri* (copper water pot) is still used in villages to carry water from the local water tap. The *kala* (ritual offering pot) and *kalasha* (water pitcher) are both seen frequently around temples. In room 2, there is a collection of very ornate oil lamps. One particularly interesting lamp is a replica of the Krishna Temple in Patan.

National Woodworking Museum

Dattatreya Square. ☎ **977/1-610005.** Admission Rs5 (10¢), Rs10 (20¢) if you bring a camera. Wed–Mon 10:30 am–4pm. Closed all national holidays.

Directly across the square from the Brass and Bronze Museum, the National Woodworking Museum has a wealth of wood carvings both inside and outside of the building. The museum is housed in the Pujari Math, which was built in 1763 and for years was used as a home for Hindu priests. Down the alley to the left of the entrance is Bhaktapur's most famous wood carving—the peacock window featuring a peacock with tail feathers in full display. Nearly three dozen smaller birds are carved around the window frame. Arabesques, demons, and animals are also incorporated into the design.

Inside the museum are examples of architectural details, many with explanations in English. One small room contains 11 roof struts from a 15th-century temple. When you see a ladder in one of the main display rooms, be sure to glance up into the attic, where you will see the surprisingly cartoonlike figures of Lord Jagannath and one of his siblings. A graceful dancing Nartaki Devi in a glass case wears a quizzical look on her face. In another case there is a very ornate, three-foot-tall carving of the Buddha being tempted by Mara. Also watch for the frightening 17th-century carving of the wrathful Bhairav.

WALKING TOUR
Bhaktapur

Start: Bhaktapur's Durbar Square.
Finish: Dattatreya Square.
Time: Four hours, including lunch but not including shopping or museum visits.
Best Times: Saturday when Nepalis have the day off and visit the temples.
Worst Times: Any day around 9:30am when the tour buses arrive.

Bhaktapur is the most medieval of the three cities in the Kathmandu Valley, which means that wandering its narrow streets and dark alleys is a fascinating experience. Durbar Square is a wide expanse of brick surrounded by palaces and temples. There are also three museums along the route.

Start your tour in:

1. **Durbar Square,** the center of Bhaktapur and the largest and most open of the three Durbar Squares in the Kathmandu Valley (see above in this chapter for details). After you have explored the square, step inside the old palace which is now the:

2. **National Art Gallery,** where you can see the many styles of Nepali traditional art (see above in this chapter for details). From the museum it is just a short walk to:

3. **Taumadi Square,** the site of what is probably the most beautiful temple in Nepal—the Nyatapola Temple (see above in this chapter for details).

☕ **TAKE A BREAK**   There is no more spectacular a view from any restaurant in the valley than from the top floor of the **Café Nyatapola.** The cafe is housed in a restored pagoda-style pavilion. Try the Nepali meals or just have a pot of hot lemon.

From Taumadhi Square walk south on a wide (for Bhaktapur) and busy road. As the road heads downhill watch for a small square on your right. This square is the:

4. **Potters' Square,** where potters and their young assistants produce simple bowls, water pitchers, and other household containers. All the work is done outdoors, and you can see every step of the process.

From the Potters' Square, head down hill, and you will come to the Hanumante River. On your immediate left is:

5. **Ram Ghat,** a sacred site for bathing and cremations. It has a small temple dedicated to Rama, hero of the ancient epic *Ramayana,* but is not one of the city's more impressive *ghats* (platforms). Continuing south, you cross the river, and after a few minutes' walk you'll have an impressive view of the city. If you continue for about another half mile (1 km) on this road, passing the trolley bus stop en route, you will climb a hill and come to the:

6. **Surya Binayak shrine,** which, though hardly impressive to the uninitiated, is one of the Kathmandu Valley's four most important Ganesh shrines. Parents with a child who is slow in learning how to speak often come to ask this Ganesh's intercession on their child's behalf. Return the way you came, and after crossing the river, take your first left, walk two long blocks, and take another left. You will be at the:

7. **Mangal Ghat,** which has many old shrines and stone carvings. From here walk straight back up the hill for three blocks on a dark, dank lane and turn right on the road that leads back to Taumadi Square. Just ahead on the left is the:

8. **Jaya Varahi Temple,** which is dedicated to the *shakti* (consort) of Vishnu's incarnation as a boar. You'll see an image of Jaya Varahi on the torana of the middle second-floor window of the temple. Continuing along this road, you will come to a square devoted to Shiva. In this square is the:

9. **Jyotirlingeshwar Shiva Temple,** a shikhara-style temple that houses a stone considered a powerful Shiva lingam. The square is filled with interesting little shrines and statues.

Return to Taumadhi Square, cross the square, and take the wide road that angles northeast from the far right corner of the square. Follow this road for 10 minutes through the main market area of Bhaktapur to:

Walking Tour—Bhaktapur

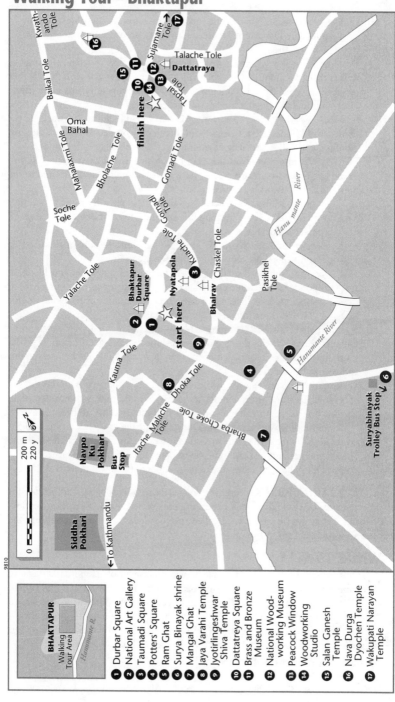

BHAKTAPUR
Walking Tour Area
Hanumante R.

1 Durbar Square
2 National Art Gallery
3 Taumadi Square
4 Potters' Square
5 Ram Ghat
6 Surya Binayak shrine
7 Mangal Ghat
8 Jaya Varahi Temple
9 Jyotirlingeshwar Shiva Temple
10 Dattatreya Square
11 Brass and Bronze Museum
12 National Wood-working Museum
13 Peacock Window
14 Woodworking Studio
15 Salan Ganesh Temple
16 Nava Durga Dyochen Temple
17 Wakupati Narayan Temple

10. **Dattatreya Square,** an ancient square that contains the oldest temple in Bhaktapur—the Dattatreya Temple. There are also two museums worth visiting. The first is the:

11. **Brass and Bronze Museum,** which houses a collection of religious statues as well as traditional household containers and utensils (see above in this chapter for details). A visit to this museum gives you an opportunity to see the inside of a traditional local home. Across the square is the:

12. **National Woodworking Museum,** housed in an old building that was once the residence of Hindu priests (see above in this chapter for details). As you face this building, you will see an alley on your left. Down this alley is the famous:

13. **Peacock Window,** an exquisite example of local wood-carving skill. If you would like to see wood-carvers at work, walk back around the corner and to the right of the woodworking museum, you will see a:

14. **Woodworking Studio,** where local Newan craftspeople still carve wood as they have for hundreds of years, keeping this ancient art very much alive (see above in this chapter for details).

    If you take the lane that leads north along the right side of the Café de Peacock, you will see on your left in just a few steps, the:

15. **Salan Ganesh Temple,** a small, attractive temple in front of the small Ganesh *Pokhari* (pond). This temple does not contain a statue or carving but a natural stone that is said to look like an elephant's head. Continue north (uphill) on this lane and you will come to the:

16. **Nava Durga Dyochen Temple,** a house-like temple dedicated to the nine Durgas, Tantric deities that are often worshiped with animal sacrifices. Head south down the street to the left of the temple; in two long blocks, take a right, and you will come to the:

17. **Wakupati Narayan Temple,** dedicated to a harvest god that is an incarnation of Vishnu. In front of the temple are several Garuda statues. From here walk west on this road, and you will soon find yourself back in Dattatreya Square.

    Before winding your way back to Durbar Square the way you came, you might want to explore the smaller side streets to the west and north of Dattatreya Square. Should you get lost, just ask someone to point the direction to Durbar Square. You will likely be escorted by one or more children (who will expect a tip).

TAKE A BREAK   After this long walk, you'll probably want to stop for some tea or a cold drink before heading back. The **Café de Peacock,** overlooking Dattatreya Square, is an excellent place to relax, cool off, and absorb the atmosphere of this medieval square.

WHERE TO STAY

Unfortunately there are only a couple of places to stay in Bhaktapur, and these are suitable only for budget travelers and backpackers. However, if you don't mind budget accommodations, I can't emphasize enough how different it is to stay in Bhaktapur than in Kathmandu. If you stay here, you are away from the crowds of Thamel, you can stay right on Durbar Square, and you can take numerous excellent day hikes that can be started or finished in Bhaktapur.

Golden Gate Guest House

Durbar Square (P.O. Box 21), Bhaktapur. ☎ **977/1-610534.** 15 rms (2 with private bath). Rs200 ($4) double, Rs500–Rs600 ($10–$12) double with private bath. No credit cards.

This guesthouse is nothing special, but it is conveniently located only steps away from Durbar Square and the famous Golden Gate from which the guesthouse takes its name. Double and triple rooms are large though very basic and contain only beds and cement floors. Some of the rooms have small balconies. From the roof, there is a nice view of Bhaktapur and the valley.

Shiva Guest House

Bhaktapur Durbar Square, Bhaktapur. ☎ **977/1-610740.** 10 rms (none with bath). Rs250 ($5) double. No credit cards.

Its ideal location overlooking Durbar Square makes this one of the best budget accommodations in the valley. Rooms are simply furnished with twin beds and little else, but they are clean. The traditional brick-tile floors of the Kathmandu Valley are cold in the winter but very attractive. On the top floor there is a cozy cafe with an international menu. It stays open as late as 9pm, which is much later than most of the other cafes in town. Suresh B. Dhaubanjar, the English-speaking manager, is very friendly and helpful.

WHERE TO DINE

Café Nyatapola

Taumadhi Tole. ☎ **977/1-610346.** Reservations not necessary. Light meals Rs50–Rs175 ($1–$3.50). No credit cards. Daily 6am–8pm. INTERNATIONAL.

Though the food is unremarkable (the standard international/Chinese/Indian/Nepali menu found in almost all budget restaurants in Nepal), the setting is superb. Housed inside an old pagoda, Café Nyatapola overlooks the Nyatapola Temple, probably the most beautiful temple in Nepal. The cafe building itself has carvings from the *Ramayana* and *Mahabharata* around the outside, and its roof struts are carved with erotic images. Take a seat on the third-floor balcony, and you can observe the activity below while you enjoy your lunch. Watch your head in here; the doorways are low.

Cafe de Peacock and Soma Bar

Dattatreya Square. ☎ **977/1-610684.** Reservations not necessary. Main dishes Rs$70–Rs150($1.40–$3). No credit cards. Daily 9am–9pm. INTERNATIONAL.

Bhaktapur seems to have cornered the market on great places to sit above the crowds and soak in the beauties and activities of a medieval Nepali square. If you didn't have lunch at the Café Nyatapola, then by all means dine here. The restaurant has a long balcony set with tables, while inside there is a large room with a high ceiling. Brick walls are hung with Tibetan carpets, and there are even brick floors. The standard please-everyone all-encompassing menu may not be memorable, but the view and general atmosphere certainly will be.

3 Nagarkot

22 miles (35.4 kilometers) E of Kathmandu, 8 miles (12.9 kilometers) E of Bhaktapur

Nagarkot is a sort of poor man's hill resort. Located on the rim of the Kathmandu Valley at an elevation of 7,200 feet, it offers a 200-mile panorama of the Himalayas from Mt. Everest in the east to Dhaulagiri in the west. It is about a 1 1/2-hour drive from Kathmandu to Nagarkot, and nearly every tour company in Kathmandu offers sunrise or sunset trips up here. At dawn and dusk, the snow-covered peaks are painted in shades of lavender, rose, pink, orange, and gold. It is a sight not to miss, though you can never be sure that the mountains will be visible, even in the usually clear winter months. Fog and low clouds often obscure the view, though seeing a single jagged, pink peak suddenly appear in the midst of clouds can be as thrilling as seeing the whole 200-mile panorama of peaks. Since mornings are usually clearer than afternoons, I recommend spending a night up here. There isn't much of a village at Nagarkot, but there are more than a dozen small lodges charging anywhere from $2 to $70 a night.

GETTING THERE

BY CAR   You will have to hire a car and driver for the day for about Rs1,200 to Rs1,500 ($24 to $30). Trip time is 2 hours. It is also possible to hire a motor-cycle in Kathmandu for about Rs350 to Rs550 ($7 to $11) plus gas.

BY TAXI   A taxi from Kathmandu will cost around Rs1,200 ($24) round trip plus a wait for you to enjoy the sunrise or sunset. Trip time is 1 1/2 hours.

BY BUS   First take a bus to Bhaktapur from Kathmandu. These leave regularly from the old bus park on the east side of the Tundikhel near the clock tower. In Bhaktapur, cross the street from the main bus park to catch the Nagarkot bus. These buses leave daily at approximately 10am and 1 and 4pm, returning from Nagarkot at the same times. Total trip time is 2 1/2 to 3 hours.

There is also now a tourist bus that leaves Thamel daily at 1:30pm and returns from Nagarkot daily at 10am. The fare is Rs75 ($1.50). Tickets can be booked at the Hotel View Point's office in Thamel. You'll find the office a couple of doors down from K.C.'s Restaurant. This bus takes about 1 1/2 hours.

ESSENTIALS   There is hardly any village to speak of at Nagarkot; it is mostly just a collection of lodges and guesthouses. Most Nagarkot lodges are above the main road about 10 to 15 minutes' walk up a rough dirt road.

WHAT TO SEE & DO

Nagarkot is also a great place for day hikes. If you have not yet been trekking or don't have time for a longer trek, you can spend a night up here and then hike down into the valley. The best part of these hikes is that, since you start at the top, everything is downhill. The best way to start a hike down from Nagarkot is to get someone who works at your lodge to point the way to the start of the trail. Banepa, Sankhu, and Changu Narayan are three possible destinations for day hikes from Nagarkot. Of these three, my favorite is the walk to Changu Narayan (see below).

HIKING FROM NAGARKOT TO CHANGU NARAYAN

The trail descends to the west along the crest of a ridge and takes about four hours to hike. From Changu Narayan it is another 1 1/2 hours to either Boudhanath or Bhaktapur. Start the hike either by descending from the Tara Gaon Resort Hotel to a saddle on the ridge where the road crosses or by walking down the road from Nagarkot to the same saddle. The saddle is about an hour from Nagarkot. From here the trail climbs up through a pine forest, part of a reforestation project, for 30 minutes. When you reach the top of this climb, you will once again have good views of the Himalayas to the north. The trail then descends gradually along the crest of the ridge. You should be able to see the gilded roof of Changu Narayan Temple off in the distance (see below for details).

There are two routes from here. Follow the steps down the west side of the hill, crossing some pastures and then descending to the south. You should be able to see Bhaktapur off in the distance as you descend. Continue on this trail in the direction of Bhaktapur. After crossing one deep valley and climbing back out, the trail makes a curve to the east before curving back around to the south. Other than this, it is almost due south to Bhaktapur.

To go to Boudhanath, descend to the northwest from Changu Narayan. At the bottom of the hill you cross a river and then wind through rice paddies to the road between Boudhanath and Sankhu. From here you can walk to Boudhanath or flag down a passing bus.

WHERE TO STAY
MODERATE

✪ The Fort
Nagarkot. (Mailing address: P.O. Box 3004, Kantipath, Kathmandu.) ☎ **977/1-290869**, or 216913 in Kathmandu. Fax 977/1-228066. 20 rms. $69.30 double. AE.

Constructed in the style of traditional Newari homes. The Fort is one of my favorite hotels in Nepal. It combines Nepali architecture with modern conveniences and makes the most of its ridge-top location. You won't find a better view from any room in Nagarkot. Tibetan tables and couches covered with colorful pillows give the lobby Himalayan flavor, and a translucent ceiling floods the room with light. The adjacent dining room has glass walls which let you enjoy the spectacular view at every meal. Guest rooms are carpeted and have Tibetan rugs, and most rooms have large windows with a view of the mountains. Watercolors of Nepali scenes and traditional *thangka* paintings decorate the rooms and halls. The dining room serves excellent food (the chicken shashlik was the best I've had in Nepal), and in the lobby, you'll find an excellent selection of books. Hikes and other excursions can be arranged at additional cost.

INEXPENSIVE

Hotel Space Mountain
Nagarkot. ☎ **977/1-290871.** Reservations in Thamel, Kathmandu ☎ **977/1-413794.** 16 rms. TEL. $48.40 double. AE, MC, V (accepted at Kathmandu office only).

Although the rooms most do not have views of the Himalayas, this is still one of the most comfortable hotels in Nagarkot. The decor in the guest rooms is rather tacky, with cheap easy chairs, wood paneling, and bright pink bathrooms, but if you spend your time in the outdoors, you may not mind. The restaurant at the top of the hotel's several terraces serves very basic meals.

BUDGET

There are quite a few small budget lodges at Nagarkot with names like Hotel Galaxy, Star Guest House, and Peaceful Cottage. Most charge around $2 per person per night. Accommodations are pretty basic, and it's a good idea to bring your own sleeping bag since the blankets they provide are not always warm enough. The best views are from the ridge above the bus stop at Hotel View Point, Peaceful Cottage, and a few others.

Hotel View Point
Nagarkot. ☎ **977/1-214444.** Reservations in Kathmandu: Thamel (P.O. Box 1285), Kathmandu ☎ **977/1-417424.** 15 rms (all with bath). $12–$20 double. No credit cards.

A 15-minute walk up a wide trail from the bus stop, Hotel View Point is the nicest of the budget hotels in Nagarkot. It is situated near the top of the ridge and consequently has one of the best views in the village. Seven of the rooms are in separate little brick cottages with tiny gardens in front, and the rest are in a motel-style building. Rooms have plaited bamboo walls, beamed ceilings, wicker furniture, vinyl floors, and twin beds. Hotel View Point operates a tourist bus between Kathmandu and Nagarkot. Contact either of the two offices for information.

WHERE TO DINE

Almost everyone who comes to Nagarkot eats at their hotel, but if you want a truly stunning view, try the following restaurant.

The Tea House Inn

Nagarkot. ☎ **977/1-290880** or 977/1-290868. Reservations not necessary. Main dishes Rs65–Rs150 ($1.30–$3). No credit cards. Daily 6am–8pm. INTERNATIONAL.

With a dizzifying ridge-top location just above the bus stop, the Tea House Inn takes full advantage of Nagarkot's views. Since there are three patio dining areas, you are almost guaranteed an unforgettable view whether you are here at sunrise, sunset, or noon. At night a crackling fire chases away the mountain cold. The menu features continental, Indian, and Nepali dishes, but I suggest you stick with the latter two. Be sure to have some of the special *masala chiya* (spiced tea); it's delicious.

4 Dhulikhel

19 miles (30.6 kilometers) E of Kathmandu

Dhulikhel is a much larger village than Nagarkot and is on the main highway from Kathmandu to Tibet, so it is easier to reach. Located at an elevation of about 5,000 feet, Dhulikhel is a 90-minute drive from Kathmandu. The view is not quite as good as the view from Nagarkot; you can only see for 130 miles. The sunrise and sunset light shows on the Himalayas are the attraction here, though most people are content to simply sit and stare all day long at the majestic row of peaks.

GETTING THERE

BY CAR   You will have to hire a car and driver for the day for about Rs1,200 to Rs1,500 ($24 to $30). Trip time is 1¹/₂ hours, one-way.

BY TAXI   A taxi from Kathmandu will cost around Rs1,200 ($24) for the round trip plus a wait for you to enjoy the sunrise or sunset. Trip time is 1¹/₂ hours.

BY BUS   Buses leave regularly from the old bus park on the east side of the Tundikhel. Trip time is 2¹/₂ hours. The fare is Rs9 (20¢).

ESSENTIALS   Dhulikhel is a small town on the rim of the Kathmandu Valley. The two tourist hotels here are both outside of town—one on the east side and one on the west side.

WHAT TO SEE & DO

Just as from Nagarkot, there are a number of interesting day hikes possible from Dhulikhel. These provide an opportunity to see the Nepali countryside away from the roads and give visitors a taste of trekking. The easiest is the hike to Namobuddha and back.

HIKING FROM DHULIKHEL TO NAMOBUDDHA

The route to Namobuddha is easy, it passes through some typical villages and ends up at a Buddhist monastery and stupa. It takes about three hours to walk to Namobuddha from Dhulikhel, so take along some food and have lunch before returning. Pass around the south side of the hill with the temple on top and climb steeply to a dirt road. Follow this road for a little more than two hours. You will be able to see the stupa and monastery of Namobuddha above you. Watch for the trail that climbs up from the road. On the hill above Namobuddha is a famous stone carving depicting a Buddha (there have been many before the historical Buddha) feeding himself to a starving tigress and her cubs. This is from a famous Buddhist tale expressing the great compassion of the Buddha. After lunch, return the way you came.

WHERE TO STAY & DINE
MODERATE
✪ Dhulikhel Mountain Resort
Dhulikhel. ☎ **977/11-61466.** Reservations in Kathmandu: Durbar Marg (P.O. Box 3203), Kathmandu. ☎ **977/1-226779** or 977/1-220031. Fax 977/1-226827. 43 rms. $81.40 double. One child under 12 stays free in parents' room without an extra bed. AE, MC, V.

Located just over the rim of the Kathmandu Valley, the Dhulikhel Mountain Resort overlooks the Panchkhal Valley and the eastern Himalayas. The thatched-roof cottages of the resort are situated on a steep hillside amid a colorful garden. Rooms are quite large and have picture windows so you can lie in bed and enjoy the sunrise over the Himalayas. The secluded feeling and lush gardens here make this one of my favorite lodges in Nepal.

Dining/Entertainment: The large dining room offers superb views to accompany Nepali, continental, and Chinese meals. There is also a bar with excellent views. Meals are also served on the garden terrace, and barbecues can be arranged for groups.

Services: Currency exchange, guided walking tours, laundry service
Facilities: Card room, TV lounge

Himalayan Horizon Hotel Sun-n-Snow
Dhulikhel. ☎ **977/11-61296.** Fax 977/11-61476. Reservations in Kathmandu: Durbar Marg (P.O. Box 1583), Kathmandu ☎ **977/1-225092.** 24 rms. $58.30 double. One child under 12 stays free in parents' room without an extra bed. AE, MC, V.

Built in traditional Newari architectural style, the Himalayan Horizon sits atop a terraced ridge overlooking hundreds of miles of mountain peaks. Older rooms have carpeting, electric heaters, fresh flowers on the bedside stand, twin beds, and large windows (you don't even have to get out of bed in the morning to enjoy the sunrise), but they are cramped. Marble-tiled bathrooms have solar-heated hot water. A newer building houses much larger rooms that have balconies, sunken seating areas, picture windows, and two double beds. Expect the price of these rooms to go up a bit in the coming year or two.

Dining/Entertainment: Both indoor and outdoor dining areas have spectacular views of the Himalayas. There is also a small, quiet bar, and if you are with a group of 15 or more, you can arrange a barbecue on the terrace.

Services: Room service, walking map of area.

INEXPENSIVE
⑤ Dhulikhel Lodge Resort
Dhulikhel (P.O. Box 6020, Kathmandu). ☎ **977/11-61494** or 977/1-61114. 16 rms. $44 double. MC, V.

Located down a dirt road before the village of Dhulikhel, the Dhulikhel Lodge Resort is built into a steep hillside and commands good views of the mountains, especially at sunrise. This hotel seems to be attempting to duplicate the Dhulikhel Mountain Resort and to that end, is busily landscaping the property. All the guest rooms face the mountains and have glass walls to capture the maximum view. Unfortunately, there are no chairs in the rooms, so you'll have to sit in bed to enjoy the view. Restaurant and bar facilities include a cozy bar with a freestanding fireplace; a large dining room with good views; a traditional dining room with low tables and pillows on the floor; a roof-top terrace where buffet lunches are served; and a garden restaurant on top of the hill behind the lodge's main building. Meals run the gamut from continental to Nepali with a little bit of everything thrown in to keep everyone happy.

BUDGET

Dhulikhel Lodge

Dhulikhel (P.O. Box 6020, Kathmandu). ☎ **977/11-61114** or 977/1-61494. 16 rms (all with shared bath). $3.30 double. No credit cards.

This is the original lodge opened by the company that operates the Dhulikhel Lodge Resort and is strictly for backpackers and those accustomed to the sort of accommodations you find along trekking routes. Housed in an old brick building in the middle of Dhulikhel, the lodge has no views, but it's a short walk to a viewpoint. There is a simple restaurant on the premises.

5 Important Valley Temples

CHANGU NARAYAN

Perched on a ridge in the eastern part of the Kathmandu Valley, Changu Narayan is one of the oldest temples in Nepal. Because it is a bit off the beaten track, this temple is little visited by tourists. Though it is possible to get here by a paved road, it is much more interesting to walk from Bhaktapur. The walk takes about two hours and is easy except for the last steep climb up to the temple. You can see the gilded roofs of the temple shining in the sun due north of Bhaktapur. To find the trail, just head north from Bhaktapur Square and aim for the temple on the ridge. Along the way people will point you in the right direction.

Originally built in the early fourth century during the Licchavi dynasty, Changu Narayan was rebuilt around 1700 after the temple was destroyed by a fire. It is a pagoda-style temple dedicated to Vishnu, also known as Narayan. Though the temple is quite beautiful, especially the repoussé doors and front facade, Changu Narayan is not known for its temple but for the stone statues, bas-relief carvings, and inscriptions that are scattered around the temple courtyard. Facing the entrance to the main temple is a large stone statue of a kneeling Garuda, the vehicle of Vishnu. This statue dates from the fifth century. Behind the statue is an inscription stone from the same century that has provided a great deal of information about the Licchavi period in the Kathmandu Valley's history. Also in front of the temple's main entrance, in an ornate little cage, are small statues of King Bupathindra Malla and his queen.

To the right of the temple entrance, there are several smaller shrines and a platform with only a carved stone atop it. This bas-relief carving, which has had its upper right corner broken off, depicts two different incarnations of Vishnu. At the bottom of the stone, Vishnu is shown reclining on a bed of snakes, the same pose that is depicted in the large statue of Budhanilkantha. Above this a 10-headed standing Vishnu is depicted. The detail in this fifth- or sixth-century stone carving is amazing.

Near the famous double Vishnu is a stone depicting another incarnation of Vishnu—the half-man, half-lion Narsimha. In the northeast corner of the courtyard is an important bas-relief that you might recognize. It depicts Vishnu riding on the back of Garuda and is the model for the image on the back of the Nepali 10-rupee note. All of the stone carvings in the temple courtyard were done between the 5th and 13th century, which makes this one of the single greatest concentrations of ancient art in Nepal.

BAJRA JOGINI

A few miles farther east than Changu Narayan along the same road is the village of Sankhu. If you continue past Sankhu another mile or so, you reach the end of the road and a stone-paved trail leading up a hill to the temple of Bajra Jogini. The temple is surrounded by sacred forests and is a very tranquil spot. Bajra Jogini is a Tantric goddess and is worshipped by Hindus and Buddhists alike. The 17th-century temple is built in the pagoda-style with three roofs. Intricately carved roof struts depict various deities, and over the main entrance to the temple is a gilded repoussé torana depicting the goddess. Outside the temple stand several chaityas, each depicting the four dhyani Buddhas. Sankhu is on the ancient road from Kathmandu to Lhasa. Legends assert that the Hindu holy man Shankaracharya was unable to spread the Hindu religion any farther north than here.

GOKARNESHWAR

This small temple is in one of the most picturesque locations of any temple in the Kathmandu Valley. On the east side of Boudha, there is a dirt road that forks off to the left and leads northeast to Sundarijal on the edge of the valley. About a mile down this road is the small village of Gokarna, located on the northern edge of the Gokarna Wildlife Reserve. The temple is on the far side of the village on the right. Walk down the flight of steps past numerous carved stone figures of various deities to the pagoda-style temple dedicated to Shiva. Watch for the carving of Parvati, Shiva's consort. She is shown holding a lotus and was carved sometime in the eighth century. Within the temple is a Shiva lingam. What makes the setting so special is that a river flows past the temple, cutting through a steep-walled gorge as it curves past. A wide flight of steps leads down to the river. It is almost a miniature version of Pashupatinath but much more tranquil.

PANAUTI

The confluence of rivers has traditionally been considered sacred by the Hindus of Nepal. Where two rivers join, you will often find temples and cremation ghats. On the east side of the Kathmandu Valley near the hills that form the valley's perimeter, the town of Panauti developed centuries ago at the confluence of two small rivers. Located 6 km south of busy Banepa, which is on the road from Kathmandu to Dhulikhel, Panauti is a Newari town surrounded by rice paddies and forested hills. Many of the town's old brick buildings are still standing, and if you wander through the narrow streets, you will get a sense of how Kathmandu must have looked not too many years ago. However, it is Panauti's extensive temple complex, which for many years has been undergoing restoration, that makes a visit here so rewarding. This project, directed by a French aid project, has so far restored many temples and other buildings in Panauti.

Located at the southeast end of town, at the confluence of the Pungamati and Roshi Khola Rivers, the temple complex is centered around the 15th-century Indreshwar Mahadev Temple, a three-story pagoda within a walled compound. Records indicate that there was a temple here as long ago as the late 13th century, but whether or not any part of the existing temple dates to that time is uncertain. However, what is certain is that this temple includes some of the most beautifully carved roof struts of any temple in the Kathmandu Valley. These struts, which date to the 14th century, depict such disparate images as willowy warriors and emaciated hags. The toranas over the temple's doors are also of stunning detail and complexity. Opposite this temple, but within the walled compound, is a house-style temple. Carved wooden statues of several gods stare from the second-floor windows.

Outside this compound stand many more smaller temples and shrines, including a pilgrims' rest house covered with colorful murals on stuccoed brick walls. Another small shrine, built in a sort of Roman–revival style during the reign of the Rana prime ministers, contains stone reliefs depicting Shiva and his consort Parvati, as well as Hanuman the monkey god. There is also a stone Shiva lingam inside this shrine. As elsewhere in the Kathmandu Valley, the striking contrast of traditional Newari architecture and borrowed European styling verges on the bizarre. Adding further to this admixture of styles is a shrine with a facade of ceramic tiles, many of which draw on classical Greek designs. Inside this latter shrine is a 5-foot tall bas relief stone carving of Vishnu standing on Garuda, his half-man, half-bird vehicle.

Across the Pungamati River from the main temple complex stands the 17th-century Brahmayani Temple, a two-story pagoda dedicated to a goddess second in importance only to Indreshwar Mahadev. Within this restored temple are some of the finest examples of traditional Newari religious paintings.

There are direct buses from Kathmandu's old bus park on the east side of the Tundikhel. Alternatively, you can take a more frequent bus from Kathmandu to Banepa and then transfer to a Panauti-bound bus.

Pokhara 6

Although Kashmir has inspired poetry, the Pokhara Valley far surpasses Kashmir for beauty and tranquillity. The view from Pokhara's Phewa Lake makes the mountains in Kashmir seem tawdry. Less than 19 miles away, rising abruptly from the valley, is one of the most beautiful mountains on earth—Machhapuchhare or, as its name translates, the Fish Tail Peak. Rising to 22,956 feet (6,997 meters) from a valley at 3,000 feet (915 meters) Machhapuchhare is a delicately tapering peak reminiscent of the Matterhorn. Twelve miles behind this peak stands a backdrop of some of the tallest mountains in the world—the Annapurna massif, with mountains more than 26,000 feet (7,925 meters) high. It is this view, seen from nearly anywhere in town that attracts visitors by the droves. Aside from this panorama, Pokhara has little to offer in the way of tourist attractions, but how could you ask for more than the most breathtaking view on earth?

For centuries Pokhara has been important as a crossroads trading center. The large bazaar has functioned as the end of the line for pony trains coming down from Tibet with salt and wool to trade for sugar and other commodities traditionally not available in Tibet. Though the trade route up the Kali Gandaki river valley is still active, trade with Tibet has decreased since that country was taken over by the Chinese.

Trekking has become a much more important part of the economy in Pokhara in recent years, and trekkers hike many of the same routes that the pony caravans once followed. Pokhara has become a trailhead and end-of-the-trail resting spot. Excited trekkers organize their trips on the streets beside the lake, while exhausted hikers, just back from a week or two or three of hiking in the Himalayas, lounge in hotel gardens drinking tea and reading in the sunshine.

1 Orientation

ARRIVING

BY PLANE Due to the poor condition of the road between Kathmandu and Pokhara, it can take as long as eight hours (and sometimes more) to cover the 124 miles (20 kilometers) by bus. For this reason, I highly recommend that you fly. **Royal Nepal Airlines**

(RNAC), **Everest Air, Necon Air,** and **Nepal Airways** all operate daily flights between the two cities for $61. The flight takes less than 45 minutes by small propeller plane and provides some spectacular scenery. The Pokhara Airport is on the east side of town, and there are always taxis waiting to meet the flights. It should cost you between Rs50 ($1) and Rs100 ($2) for a taxi to Damside or Lakeside.

Airline offices in Pokhara are all either at the airport or across the street. These include **Everest Air** (☎ 977/61-21883), **Necon Air** (☎ 977/61-20256), **Nepal Airways** (☎ 977/61-20966), and **RNAC** (☎ 977/61-20040).

If you are planning a trek, there are regular RNAC flights to Jomosom during the main trekking seasons. These flights cost around $50 one-way and are in very small planes, so make your reservation as soon as you can. Be sure to reconfirm frequently. This RNAC office is notoriously disorganized.

BY BUS   The bus terminal is on the east side of town just before the Naya Bazaar area. It is little more than a large gravel parking lot filled with battered buses. The "deluxe" tourist buses, which I highly recommend using if you must travel by bus, park in a separate, smaller parking area. When the buses arrive, passengers are immediately swarmed by touts trying to sell their hotels and guesthouses. Most touts are selling hotels that are either new, out of the way, or not very good.

From the bus terminal to either Damside or Lakeside is a 10-minute taxi ride or a 30-minute walk. The taxi will charge at least Rs50 ($1) and more likely Rs100 ($2).

At the back of the main bus parking lot is a ticket office where you can buy tickets in advance for local buses. I recommend these buses only if there is no other alternative (for example, if you are headed to Begnas Lake to start a trek around Annapurna or are going directly to Bhairawa and Lumbini). If you are going back to Kathmandu by bus, I highly recommend booking a tourist coach in advance through your guesthouse or hotel. Most tourist buses will pick you up at your hotel.

TOURIST INFORMATION

Pokhara's **tourist office** (☎ 977/61-20028) is located across the street from the airport terminal. It's open February 13 to November 16, Sunday to Thursday from 10am to 5pm (until 4pm the rest of the year) and Friday from 10am to 3pm.

The **Department of Immigration** office (☎ 977/61-21167) is located on Ratnapuri just up from the Hotel Tragopan. This office can extend your visa and issues trekking permits for the Annapurna region. They also collect fees for the Annapurna Conservation Area Project (Rs200; $4). You will have to pay this fee if you plan to go trekking in this region. There is a bulletin board here with information about the project. Office hours are Sunday to Thursday from 10am to 5pm (4pm in winter) Friday from 10am to 3pm.

CITY LAYOUT

Pokhara is a large town and sprawls over a wide area at the edge of the Pokhara Valley. Pokhara proper is actually a mile or two away from the hotel neighborhoods frequented by foreign tourists and, with nothing to attract tourists, is rarely visited. At the south, lower end of the gentle slope upon which the town is built is Phewa Lake. The lake is surrounded by high hills on the south, west, and north, and by the valley on the east. North of Pokhara (between 12 and 20 miles away) are the snow-covered peaks of the Himalayas. The city is laid out along two

Pokhara

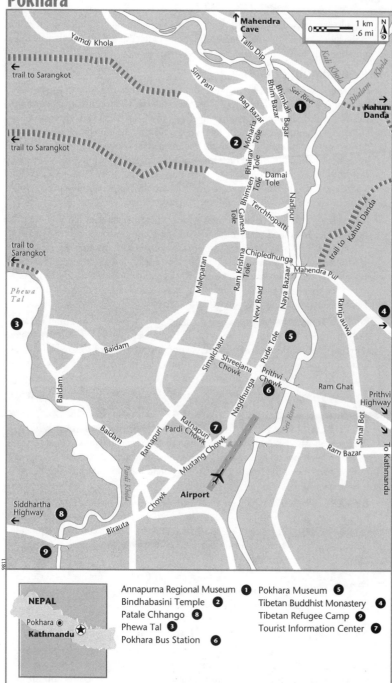

Mahendra Cave

Yamdi Khola

← trail to Sarangkot

← trail to Sarangkot

trail to Sarangkot ←

Kali Khola

Bhalam Khola

Tallo Dip

Sim Pani

Bag Bazar

Bhim Bazar

Bhimkali Bagar

Seti River

Kahun Danda →

trail to Kahun Danda

Bhairav Tole

Mohoria Tole

Damai Tole

Nadipur

Bhimsen Tole

Terchhopatti

Ganesh Tole

Chipledhunga

Mahendra Pul

Malepatan

Ram Krishna Tole

New Road

Naya Bazaar

Ranipauwa

Phewa Tal

Baidam

Baidam

Baidam

Simalchaur

Shreejana Chowk

Pude Tole

Prithvi Chowk

Nagdhunga

Seti River

Ram Ghat

Simal Bot

Prithvi Highway →

To Kathmandu →

Ratnapuri Pardi Chowk

Ratnapuri

Mustang Chowk

Pardi Khola

Chowk

Airport

Ram Bazar

Siddhartha Highway ←

Birauta

0 — 1 km
0 — .6 mi

N

NEPAL

Pokhara ⊙
Kathmandu ★

Annapurna Regional Museum	❶	Pokhara Museum	❺
Bindhabasini Temple	❷	Tibetan Buddhist Monastery	❹
Patale Chhango	❽	Tibetan Refugee Camp	❾
Phewa Tal	❸	Tourist Information Center	❼
Pokhara Bus Station	❻		

9811

roughly parallel main roads that run from the Damside neighborhood in the south to the Seti Gandaki River in the north. From end to end, the town is about 4 miles long but only half a mile wide.

NEIGHBORHOODS IN BRIEF

Lakeside   With dozens of small guesthouses and hotels charging only a few dollars a night, this is a popular spot with backpackers. Known also as Baidam, this area was once a sleepy village across the fields from Pokhara. Today there are new hotels, restaurants, and shops opening weekly. Despite the growth, though, the area retains some of its rural feel. Step off the main road and you can be surrounded by scenes of rural Nepal. As its name implies, this neighborhood is by the lake, with the largest section of the lake extending off to the west. Although Lakeside is where the king has his Pokhara palace, it is also the haunt of young people, both Western and Nepali, who have adopted a classic hippie lifestyle.

Damside   At the southeast end of the lake, where a small dam has been built, is a quieter neighborhood where the hotels and guesthouses charge slightly more than in Lakeside. This area is not as lush nor as built up as Lakeside and is therefore preferred by slightly more mature travelers who are less interested in adventure and more interested in a comfortable place to sleep. There is an attractive little park beside the dam, and the view from this area is second only to the view from Fish Tail Lodge. The lake at this point is fairly narrow.

Pokhara Town   The main town of Pokhara is uphill a mile or two from Lakeside and Damside. The older section is along the westernmost road in town, which starts in the Damside neighborhood. At the northern end of this road are some interesting old houses and a couple of temples that are worth a visit. The easternmost road through town is lined with newer businesses and the new bazaar area.

2 Getting Around

BY PUBLIC TRANSPORTATION   The public transportation system in Pokhara consists of a few battered old buses that are constantly breaking down and therefore rarely operate on anything like a regular schedule. If you decide you want to try riding one of these buses, ask at your hotel for the nearest bus stop. A ticket is Rs23 (6¢).

BY TAXI   Taxis in Pokhara are more expensive than in Kathmandu and do not have meters, so you will have to bargain for the fare. It can be as much as Rs50 ($1) or Rs100 ($2) from the airport or bus station to Lakeside or Damside. Because the bus system is so bad and because Pokhara is so spread out, taxis are the best way to get around town.

BY CAR   There are no self-drive car rentals in Pokhara. However, you can hire a car and driver for the day at nearly any hotel or tour agency (of which there are quite a few in both Damside and Lakeside). It will cost you around Rs1,250 ($25) per day.

BY BICYCLE   A bicycle is my favorite way of getting around Pokhara, especially for trips around the lake areas. If you want to go up to Pokhara proper, however, it is a long uphill pedal, so rent a mountain bike. Bikes rent for Rs25 to Rs50 (50¢ to $1) per day. You'll find numerous bicycle-rental stands in both Damside and Lakeside. Be sure to check the bell and brakes before riding off.

ON FOOT Pokhara, at least in the Damside and Lakeside areas where visitors usually stay, is a quiet town. There isn't much traffic on the narrow roads, so walking is generally quite pleasant. It will take about 30 minutes to walk between Lakeside and Damside. In the Lakeside area, there are many tranquil lanes leading off from the main road back into the fields and forests. From Damside, it is possible to walk along the river that flows out of the lake or even explore the trails of the royal wildlife preserve on the far side of the lake.

FAST FACTS: Pokhara

American Express There is no American Express office in Pokhara. Nepal's only office is in Kathmandu (see "Fast Facts: Kathmandu" in Chapter 3).

Babysitters Check with the front desk at your hotel if you need a babysitter.

Bookstores There are as many bookshops in Pokhara selling English-language books as there are in Kathmandu. You'll find them in both of the tourist neighborhoods of Lakeside and Damside, with a greater concentration in the former.

Business Hours See "Fast Facts: Nepal" in Chapter 2.

Car Rentals See "Getting Around" in this chapter.

City Code The city code for Pokhara is 61. When dialing a Pokhara number from outside of town but within Nepal, you must first dial 0 and then the city code.

Climate See "When to Go" in Chapter 2.

Currency See "Information, Entry Requirements & Money" in Chapter 2.

Currency Exchange The Nepal Rastra Bank operates a currency-exchange counter on Ratnapuri (the road that the Department of Immigration is on) across the street from the main bank and near the Hotel Tragopan. It is open daily from 10:30am to 3:30pm. The main bank across the street is a good place to stock up on small bills before going trekking. It's open Sunday to Thursday from 10am to 2:30pm and Friday from 10am to noon.

Dentist If you need a dentist, I suggest you go to Kathmandu and contact your embassy for a recommendation.

Doctor If you need medical attention, try to get to Kathmandu and contact your embassy for a recommendation. Otherwise, ask at your hotel.

Drugstores K.C. Medical Hall, Rastra Bank Chowk, Pardi (☎ 977/61-21929), is a pharmacy located across the street from the Hotel Tragopan. It is open Sunday through Friday from 7am to 7pm.

Embassies and Consulates The nearest embassies and consulates are in Kathmandu (see "Fast Facts: Nepal" in Chapter 2).

Eyeglasses Your best bet is to head back to Kathmandu before trying to have your glasses repaired or replaced.

Holidays See "When to Go" in Chapter 2.

Hospitals The Western Regional Hospital (☎ 977/61-20066) is on the east side of Pokhara near the Mahendra Pul bridge and is your only option in Pokhara if you need hospitalization. It is even more poorly equipped than the hospitals in Kathmandu. Evacuation to Kathmandu and then to Thailand or Singapore is the recommended procedure if at all possible.

Information   See "Tourist Information," above, in this chapter.

Laundry and Dry Cleaning   Your hotel will provide laundry service. If you need something dry cleaned, save it until you get home.

Lost Property   There is no lost-property office and going to the police is not likely to produce any results either. Try posting notices around the restaurants frequented by tourists.

Luggage Storage   Almost all hotels offer luggage-storage facilities if you are going off on a trek or to Chitwan and plan to return to the hotel.

Newspapers and Magazines   The *International Herald Tribune, USA Today, Newsweek,* and *Time* are all readily available at bookshops in the tourist neighborhoods.

Photographic Needs   You'll find film in shops around Lakeside and Damside, but it is even more expensive than in Kathmandu.

Police   Dial 977/61-20033 or 977/61-20412 (traffic police).

Post Office   The Pokhara Post Office is at Naya Bazaar near the Mahendra Bridge in the town's main bazaar area. It is open Sunday to Thursday from 10am to 5pm (until 4pm in winter) and Friday from 10am to 3pm.

Radio   There is only one radio station in Nepal. See "Fast Facts: Kathmandu" in Chapter 3 for details.

Restrooms   If you are in need of a restroom, you'll have to find a restaurant which will allow you to use theirs.

Safety   Pokhara is a small town, but tourists are frequently the victims of bag-snatchers. Do not be careless with your money, passport, and other valuables. I suggest always carrying tickets, money, and passport in a moneybelt or neck bag that can be worn under your clothing. Carry only as much cash as you expect to be spending during any foray out of your hotel. Keep this money separate from your moneybelt so that you don't reveal the location of your valuables to curious eyes. Most hotels will lock your valuables in a safe-deposit box.

Shoe Repairs   Head to the market area in downtown Pokhara and look for a sidewalk shoe repairman.

Taxes   Hotels charge between 10% and 13% room tax depending on the number of stars they have been given by the Hotel Association of Nepal.

Taxis   See "Getting Around," above, in this chapter.

3 Accommodations

In recent years there has been a proliferation of Pokhara hotels in the $20 to $40 range. These hotels, though far from luxurious, are generally quite clean and comfortable, and in some cases are much better deals than some of the more expensive hotels in town.

It is wise to make reservations at least six months in advance if you plan to visit in the busy trekking season during October and November, especially if you want to stay at Fish Tail Lodge, the best hotel in town. The major hotels have

Pokhara Accommodations & Dining

Mahendra
Cave

Yamdi Khola

Tallo Dip

← trail to Sarangkot

Kali Khola

Bhdam Khola

← trail to Sarangkot

Sim Pani

Bag Bazar

Bhim Bazar

Bhimkali Bagar

Seti River

→ Kahun Danda

Mohoria Tole

Bhairav Tole

Bhimsen Tole

Damai Tole

Nadipur

Terchhopatti

trail to Sarangkot

Ganesh Tole

Chipledhunga

Mahendra Pul

trail to Kahun Danda

Phewa Tal

Malepatan

Ram Krishna Tole

New Road

Naya Bazaar

Ranipauwa

Baidam

Simalchaur

Shreejana Chowk

Pude Tole

Prithvi Chowk

Ram Ghat

Prithvi Highway

Baidam

2 **3**

4 **1**

5

6 **7**

8

9

Baidam

21

20

Nagdhunga

Seti River

Simal Bot

To kathmandu

10 **11**

Ratnapuri Chowk

19

Ram Bazar

Ratnapuri

12

13

14

17

Pardi

Mustang Chowk

18

Airport

15

16

Chowk

Siddhartha Highway

Pardi Khola

Birauta

9812

ACCOMMODATIONS:
Ashok Guest House **16**
Dragon, Hotel **15**
Fairmount Hotel **2**
Fish Tail Lodge **11**
Glacier, Hotel **8**
Jharna, Hotel **15**
Meera, Hotel **6**
Mount Annapurna, Hotel **20**

Mountain Top, Hotel **1**
Mountain Villa **3**
New Hotel Crystal **21**
Pumori, Hotel **9**
Tragopan, Hotel **19**
Try Star, Hotel **18**

DINING:
Beam Beam Restaurant ◆ **4**

Fewa Park Restaurant ◆ **5**
Fish Tail Lodge Restaurant ◆ **10**
The German Bakery ◆ **12**
The Hungry Eye ◆ **7**
K.C. Restaurant ◆ **14**
Rodee Lakeview Restaurant ◆ **13**

0 ‭   ‬ 1 km
.6 mi

N

reservation offices in Kathmandu. In the low-budget end of the market, there are two areas in which you can look. The cheapest accommodations are in the Lakeside neighborhood, where dozens of new guesthouses have opened in recent years. The best thing to do here is look at a few cheap places and pick the cleanest one. In the Damside area, prices are a little higher, but rooms are slightly larger and cleaner. There isn't as much of a "scene" at Damside, but that's why many people prefer to stay in this area.

In low-budget hotels, and even in some more expensive places, you will likely encounter Asian-style bathrooms. By this I do not mean squat toilets, but showers in the middle of the bathroom with no shower curtain. This concept seems quite bizarre to most Westerners, but in a place where mildew is rampant, a shower curtain would need to be replaced several times a year.

Rates for hotels listed below include tax. All expensive, moderate, and inexpensive hotels have private bathrooms in all rooms. In the "Expensive" category, a room costs between $90 and $130 per night. In the "Moderate" category, a room costs between $50 and $90 per night. In the "Inexpensive" category, a room costs between $25 and $50 per night, and in the "Budget" category, a room costs less than $25 per night. During the monsoon season rates are usually lower, and it is always possible to bargain at hotels in the lower price categories no matter what the season.

EXPENSIVE

✪ Fish Tail Lodge
P.O. Box 10, Pokhara. ☎ **977/61-20071.** Fax 977/61-20072. In Kathmandu, contact Hotel de l'Annapurna. Durbar Marg (P.O. Box 140), Kathmandu. ☎ **977/1-221711** or 977/1-225242. Fax 977/1-225236. 50 rms. $95.20 double. Extra bed $29.15. AE, JCB, MC, V.

The *only* place to stay in Pokhara as far as many people are concerned, Fish Tail Lodge boasts the best location in town. Midway between the Damside and Lakeside neighborhoods, Fish Tail Lodge is the only hotel on the south side of the lake and is surrounded by a royal wildlife preserve. To reach the hotel you must hop aboard a tiny ferry constructed of 55-gallon drums; the boatman then pulls the ferry across a narrow section of the lake with a pair of sturdy ropes. From the garden of the lodge you can see Machhapuchhare and the Annapurnas reflected on the surface of Phewa Lake when the water is still and the sky cloudless.

The garden is gorgeous, with flowers in bloom year-round. Rooms are attractive and unusual with flagstone floors, redbrick walls, wicker furniture, and lamps with baskets for shades. Twin beds and small bathrooms with only showers are two of the drawbacks here. The main disappointment is that not everyone gets a view from their room; some face the dense forest and steep hillside in back of the hotel. When making reservations stress that you want a room with a view of the mountains, and maybe they'll save one for you.

Dining/Entertainment: There is a bar and restaurant, housed in a circular building with a curving glass wall and two levels to make the most of the view. A huge fireplace keeps the room warm in winter. Indian and continental fare receive equal treatment on the menu. A cultural program of Nepali music and dance is held daily from 6 to 7pm.

Services: Room service, currency exchange, laundry service, travel services.

Facilities: Boat rentals, hiking trail.

MODERATE

New Hotel Crystal

Nagdhunga (P.O. Box 234), Pokhara. ☎ **977/61-20035** or 977/61-20036. For reservations, contact New Hotel Crystal Pokhara Ltd., Chha 1-99 Jyatha Tole (P.O. Box 1253), Kathmandu. ☎ 977/1-228561. Fax 977/1-228028. 75 rms, 3 suites. $33.90–$76.84 double; $129.95 single suite, $141.25 double suite. Extra bed $17. AE, DC, JCB, MC, V.

Located directly across the street from the airport, the New Hotel Crystal is an old standby in Pokhara and is popular with group tours. The simple garden offers good views of the mountains, but the lake is a 20-minute walk or five-minute taxi ride away. Rooms in the main wing are showing their age. They come with old twin beds, worn carpet, Naugahyde chairs, air conditioning, and telephones. A new wing provides 20 deluxe rooms that are much nicer than any of the other rooms in the hotel. If you don't mind spending a little bit more, these are your best bet, especially in winter when the central heating is greatly appreciated. The old annex, reached by a bridge over a pond that is often empty, is an interesting looking building with parquet floors and walls that are partially made from bamboo. Rooms here are cheaper, though they are correspondingly basic in decor and amenities.

Dining/Entertainment: The hotel's main restaurant, serving an international menu, is on the second floor of the main wing. A coffee shop and bar are located in the new wing. There is a nightly cultural program featuring traditional Nepali songs and dancing.

Services: Room service, laundry service, car rentals, house doctor, safe-deposit boxes, bicycle rentals, horseback riding, boating and fishing arrangements, travel agency.

Facilities: Gift shop, luggage storage facilities.

Hotel Dragon

Damside (P.O. Box 15), Pokhara. ☎ **977/61-20052.** Fax 977/61-20391. 31 rms. A/C TEL. $56 double. Extra bed $16.80. No credit cards.

This hotel has a bit more styling than most other hotels in the area. Since nearly doubling its rates last year, however, it is no longer the bargain it once was. Before agreeing to a room here, I would insist on a substantial discount. Most rooms have large windows, and some have views of Machhapuchhare and the Annapurnas. Be sure to ask for a room with a view. Some rooms even have a separate closet and dressing area, so it is worth asking to see a few rooms before making a decision. A rooftop garden is an excellent vantage from which to watch the sunrise or sunset, and you can even have meals served up here. Down on the first floor, the hotel's restaurant is decorated to resemble a traditional Tibetan Buddhist *gompa* (temple). There is even an altar in an alcove at one end of the restaurant. Another wall is decorated with copper and brass pots.

Hotel Pumori

Lakeside, Pokhara. ☎ **977/61-21462.** 20 rms. A/C. $55 double. No credit cards.

The Hotel Pumori is one of the few lodgings in Pokhara whose design varies from the standard, characterless, concrete-box style of budget hotels here. The Pumori's guest rooms, in a rather barren garden, are contained in two single-story buildings that resemble primitive bamboo huts. However, inside, the rooms are anything but primitive and have carpeting, air conditioning, and attractive block-print bedspreads that give the rooms a bit of Nepali character. Some rooms are smaller than others but have tubs in the bathrooms to make up for the lack of space. Unfortunately all the rooms are rather dark, which will discourage you from spending any time in the room during the day. The hotel's interesting glass-walled dining room is affiliated with the Bhanchha Ghar in Kathmandu and serves Nepali and Indian meals. There is a program of Nepali music and dance here each evening at 6:30pm. You'll find the Pumori near the entrance to Fish Tail Lodge along the road leading from the airport to the Lakeside area.

INEXPENSIVE

Hotel Jharna

Pardi, Pokhara. ☎ **977/61-21925** or (in Kathmandu) 977/1-414033. 15 rms (all with bath). $26.40 double. No credit cards.

Inexpensive hotels are proliferating in Pokhara, and this is one of the better ones. It is located next door to K. C. Restaurant, and many of the rooms overlook the lake and mountains. However, some rooms have no views and actually stare into the windows of another hotel. Be sure to ask for a room with a view—Rooms 301 and 305 are the best. Guest rooms are all carpeted and have large windows. If you happen to get stuck in a room with no view, you can always spend your time on the roof terrace. Laundry and luggage-storage services are available.

Hotel Meera

Lakeside (P.O. Box 269), Pokhara. ☎ **977/61-21031.** Fax 977/61-20852. 16 rms (14 with private bath). $15 double with shared bath, $30 double with private bath. JCB, MC, V (add 5% surcharge if paying with a credit card).

Located in the middle of the busy Lakeside area, the Hotel Meera is a newer hotel offering large rooms with big picture windows. Rattan chairs are set up facing the windows so you can sit in your room and gaze out at the mountain or lake views. These rooms are carpeted and have tubs in the bathrooms. Even the rooms with shared bathroom facilities are quite comfortable and have the same rattan furniture and carpeting. These latter rooms are up on the top floor and consequently have some of the best views. Just off the lobby is the hotel's Garlic Garden restaurant, which stages a program of Nepali music and dance nightly at 6:30pm. The hotel also has a roof-top terrace dining area and a bakery across the street. Services include room service, laundry service, luggage storage, and safe-deposit boxes.

Hotel Mount Annapurna

Pokhara Airport (P.O. Box 12), Pokhara. ☎ **977/61-20037.** Fax 977/61-20027. 30 rms. TEL. $41.45 double. Extra bed $17.95. AE, MC, V.

Conveniently located across the street from the airport (which is a bit noisy these days), this hotel has seen better days. It is still popular with groups simply because it is one of the larger hotels in Pokhara. Rooms have carpets that are not too badly worn, big windows, a closet, and a desk. Bathrooms are huge, and some even come with a tub, though there isn't always enough water to fill it. The hotel's restaurant features an attractive and colorful Tibetan motif and serves the standard international fare. There is a large garden in front of the hotel, but unfortunately it is on the south side and consequently does not have a view of the mountains.

Hotel Mountain Top

Baidam, Lakeside, Pokhara. ☎ **977/61-20779.** Fax 977/61-20779. 22 rms (16 with private bath). $20 double without bath. $32–$44 double with bath. No credit cards.

This hotel, in the heart of the busy Lakeside neighborhood on the main road, rises four stories above the surrounding shophouses and shacks. The management here is usually friendly and helpful and will do what they can to make your stay a pleasant one. Most of the rooms have good views, but rooms 422 and 426 each have three walls of windows, which gives them the edge over the other rooms. Private bathrooms in the deluxe rooms can be a bit cramped, but they do have bathtubs. Rooms with shared bathrooms are as nice and almost as spacious as the rooms with private baths. Services include laundry, luggage storage, safe-deposit boxes, and travel arrangements.

Hotel Tragopan

Ratnapuri, Pardi, Pokhara. ☎ **977/61-21708.** Fax 977/61-20474. For reservations, contact Hotel Tragopan, Kantipath (P.O. Box 2388), Kathmandu ☎ **977/1-225898.** 36 rms, 4 suites. $49.50 double; $88 suite. Extra bed $16.50. Children under 12 stay free in parents' room without extra bed. AE, JCB, MC, V.

The Tragopan is not too well located (it's on a busy intersection), but the accommodations are fairly good, if a bit mildewed. It is only a few minutes' taxi ride from the airport down the road that leads both to Lakeside and Damside. The nicest rooms are the suites. They come with wall-to-wall carpeting (slightly worn), fan, air conditioning, a television, heavy wooden furniture, large windows with a superb view, and a tub in the bathroom. There are even fresh flowers and a basket of fruit upon arrival. Some of the suites even have king-size beds—a rarity in Nepal. The drawback is that the suites are on the top floor, up three flights of stairs (there's no elevator). Standard rooms are not nearly so well appointed, but they are clean and comfortable, with wall-to-wall carpeting and twin beds.

Dining/Entertainment: The Nest restaurant is open for three meals a day, serving continental, Chinese, Indian, and Nepali cuisine. The Rovers Return Pub is a popular spot for a drink.

Services: Room service, laundry service, travel agency, car rental, safe-deposit boxes.

Facilities: Shopping arcade.

BUDGET

⊗ Ashok Guest House

Damside, Pardi, Pokhara. ☎ **977/61-20374.** 10 rms (8 with bath). $22 double. No credit cards.

With its beautiful and well-maintained garden, this is my favorite budget hotel in Pokhara. It is right beside the dam spillway, and the sound of water emptying into the river can be heard from the rooms. Next door is a little park, and the view in the morning is of both the lake and the mountains. Rooms are simply furnished with twin beds, an area rug, wardrobe, table, and lamp. There is a dining room with an extensive menu. Keep your eyes peeled for colorful birds that frequent the garden.

Fairmount Hotel

Lakeside, Pokhara. ☎ **977/61-21252.** Fax 977/61-21451 (ATTN FAIRMOUNT). 20 rms (18 with private bath). $13.20 double with shared bath, $27.50–$33 double with private bath. No credit cards.

Located a hundred yards from the lake on the road from the center of Pokhara, the Fairmount provides clean rooms with a bit more style than most budget lodgings in the area. The deluxe rooms have double beds, wall-to-wall carpeting, large windows, wicker chairs, and tubs in the bathrooms. The standard rooms are not quite as comfortable and come with twin beds. If you stay in a regular room, try for one on a corner; these rooms have lots of windows, and some have good views. There is an inexpensive restaurant on the premises; services include luggage storage, safe-deposit boxes, and laundry services.

⑤ Hotel Glacier

Lakeside, Gaurighat, Pokhara. ☎ **977/61-21722.** 11 rms. $14.30–$17.60 double. No credit cards.

Located at the Damside end of Lakeside on the road from the airport, the Hotel Glacier is a rather unusual looking building with numerous balconies and arched windows. The guest rooms all have good views either of the mountains or the lake. The rooms don't have a lot of character, but they do have carpeting and tubs in the bathrooms. There is a pleasant garden as well as a rooftop terrace, and the lake is directly across the road. The rates are surprisingly low for what you get here. The hotel tends to be very popular with vacationing Indian families. Services include room service, luggage storage, and laundry service.

Mountain Villa

Lakeside (P.O. Box 202), Pokhara. ☎ **977/61-21954.** 15 rms. $20 double. MC, V.

Located a hundred yards or so up the road that leads directly from Lakeside into the center of Pokhara, this small hotel may not live up to its name, but it is certainly a good value. The best rooms are those on the top floor of each of the hotel's three-story buildings. These rooms are larger than the others here and have their own large terraces. However, all the rooms have large windows, and many have good views. There's an attractive, quiet garden where you can sit and read or write postcards.

Hotel Try Star

Lakeside, Pardi (P.O. Box 13), Pokhara. ☎ **977/61-20930.** 12 rms (all with bath). $15 double. No credit cards.

If you want to stay in Damside, but don't want to spend $5 to $10 extra for a waterfront room, try the Try Star. It's only a hundred yards or so from the lake on the road that leads from Damside toward the airport and still has an excellent view of the mountains. Ask for a room in back if you want to enjoy the view without going up on the roof. Guest rooms, which are larger than most in this price category, are all carpeted and have tiled bathrooms. There is a small garden in back of the hotel and a dining room on the ground floor. Services include laundry, safe-deposit box, and travel arrangements.

4 Dining

You don't have many choices when it comes to dining in Pokhara. Basically, you can dine at your hotel dining room or take a walk to one of the restaurants mentioned below. There are quite a few other budget restaurants in the Lakeside area, though none distinguishes itself in any way. They all serve the same international menu, and most have seating outside as well as in the dining room. You can have the best meal in Pokhara at the most expensive restaurant in town (which is still in the "Moderate" category) and spend less than $10.

✪ Fish Tail Lodge Restaurant

Fish Tail Lodge. ☎ **977/61-20071.** Reservations recommended. Main courses Rs125–Rs580 ($2.50–$11.60); set meals Rs600 ($12). AE, MC, V. Daily 7–9am, noon–3pm, and 7–9pm. INDIAN/CONTINENTAL.

Pokhara's best and most expensive restaurant, the dining room at Fish Tail Lodge is a great place for lunch. The circular room has a glass wall that faces the distant mountains so that most seats in the house have an outstanding view. The cozy, comfortable bar is on a level above the dining area. At night in the winter, there is always a roaring fire in the large fireplace in the bar area. Service is excellent by Nepali standards, and so is the food. For set meals there is always a choice of continental or Indian cuisine. I prefer the Indian meals. Dinners in the busy season often consist of a buffet that might include roast duck with garlic, barbecued spareribs, lamb crêpes, potatoes, rice, veggies, consommé, and desserts such as apple cake and souffles.

Beam Beam
Lakeside. No phone. Reservations not required. Main dishes Rs78–Rs230 ($1.60–$4.60). No credit cards. Daily 11am–10pm. INTERNATIONAL.

This garden restaurant near the shore of the lake has a variety of seating areas, including tables in the garden, tables under thatched-roof shelters, and traditional floor–pillow style seating in the main dining room. In one corner of the garden there is a tandoori oven that turns out good Indian dishes. However, many people come for the Mexican and continental dishes rather than for the tandoori chicken. The loud music doesn't quite fit with the marigolds and bamboo, but no one seems to mind. You'll find Beam Beam about midway between the king's palace and the turn-off into the center of Pokhara.

✪ Fewa Park Restaurant
Lakeside. ☎ **977/61-201669.** Reservations not required. Main dishes Rs65–Rs150 ($1.30–$3). No credit cards. Daily 7am–10pm. INTERNATIONAL.

There are only a couple of places in Pokhara where you can dine on the lakeshore, and this is by far the most pleasant. Linger over a long lunch or spend the afternoon snacking, sipping tea, and writing postcards. There may be better food in town, but you won't find a more tranquil atmosphere; after dark you can sit by a fire and watch the moonlight shimmering on the lake.

The German Bakery
Damside, Pardi. No phone. Reservations not accepted. Pastries and sandwiches Rs10–Rs65 (20¢–$1.30). No credit cards. Daily 6am–8pm. PASTRIES/SANDWICHES.

Bakeries have long been popular with budget travelers in Nepal, so the Nepalis have had plenty of time to perfect the art of baking. Whole-wheat rolls, flaky cheese croissants, banana bread, cinnamon rolls, and apple strudel are the specialties here, and they're all done very well. There's a covered patio with a few tables, but no indoor dining.

The Hungry Eye
Lakeside, Baidam. ☎ **977/61-20908.** Reservations recommended for groups. Main courses Rs59–Rs165 ($1.20–$3.30). AE, MC, V. Daily 6am–10pm. INTERNATIONAL.

This has long been the most popular restaurant in town with the backpack crowd, and over the years, the Hungry Eye has had to spread from its one small dining room to additional rooms, a porch, and a large patio to accommodate the throngs that flock here. It is located across from a large old banyan tree and the king's Pokhara palace. The sizzling steak is one of the restaurant's most popular dishes. I once watched a table of eight order eight sizzling steaks. What a racket when they all came out.

K. C. Restaurant

Damside, Pardi. ☎ **977/61-21560.** Reservations not necessary. Main courses Rs50–Rs230 ($1–$4.60). No credit cards. Daily 9am–10pm. INTERNATIONAL.

With a pleasant garden set with tables for the daytime and a warm circular dining room with a fireplace in the middle for the nighttime, K. C. has long been popular with people staying in the Damside area. Located near the Ashok Guest House, K. C. even has an unusual shrine in its garden, so you'll be dining with the gods. You'll certainly find many familiar dishes on the menu, but one bite of something like bean enchiladas will tell you that something was lost when Mexican food crossed the Pacific and climbed into the Himalayas. Nonetheless, the food is tasty if unrecognizable. Service, however, can be glacially slow.

Rodee Lakeview Restaurant

Damside, Pardi. ☎ **977/61-21706.** Reservations not necessary. Main courses Rs75–Rs195 ($1.50–$3.90). No credit cards. Daily 7am–10pm. INTERNATIONAL.

Built right on the edge of the lake in the Damside neighborhood, the Lakeview restaurant has tables in an open-air dining area. The clientele is mostly young, and the rock music loud, but the sunsets are gorgeous. The menu is extensive, and contains everything from Japanese to Mexican, with an emphasis on big-is-better cakes and pies prominently displayed in the front window to lure weary trekkers in for some serious carbo-loading.

5 Attractions

THE TOP ATTRACTIONS

Pokhara's single greatest attraction is its view. The view of the Himalayas from the valley floor is one of the world's most awe-inspiring vistas, especially at dawn and dusk when alpenglow paints the peaks in shades of pink, rose, mauve, and lavender. The best spot for observing this natural light show is usually your hotel roof. Nowhere else on earth can you get so close (25 miles) to so many peaks that exceed 22,000 feet while relaxing in a tropical valley. Starting from the left the mountains are Dhaulagiri (26,795 feet; 8,167 meters), Annapurna I (26,545 feet; 8,091 meters); Machhapuchhare (22,956 feet; 6,997 meters), Annapurna III (24,787 feet; 7,555 meters), Annapurna IV (24,688 feet; 7,525 meters), Annapurna II (26,041 feet; 7,937 meters), and Lamjung Himal (22,909 feet; 6,983 meters).

Phewa Tal (Lake) is Pokhara's next most important attraction. Legend has it that there was once a beautiful city in the valley now filled by the lake. When a god disguised as an old man came to the city asking for a little food, none of the city's wealthy residents would give him a bite to eat. At last a poor old couple invited him to share their meager meal. When the god had finished his meal, he advised the couple to abandon their home and flee to high ground. Shortly after leaving home, the old couple glanced back to find their city covered with a shining lake.

Sailboats and paddleboats can be rented at various places around the lake. One of the most popular excursions is to paddle out to the little island offshore from Lakeside. On this island is a small temple. Be careful of the unpredictable winds if you should rent a sailboat. See "Sports," below, for more information on boat rentals. In the warmer months, many visitors go swimming in the lake, though due to the pollution in the lake, I don't advise this.

Patale Chhango, south of town on the right-hand side of the Siddhartha Highway, is one of Nepal's most amazing natural phenomena. Known by numerous names, including David's Falls, Devin's Falls, Devil's Falls, and Devi's Falls, this small waterfall mysteriously disappears into a dark chasm after coursing through a narrow gorge. There are small natural bridges, strange potholes carved by the river, and beautiful growths of ferns along the steep rock walls. There is a Rs5 (10¢) admission fee, and several trinket vendors set up outside the entrance to the falls.

Tibetan Refugee Camp, located almost directly across the street from Patale Chhango, contains a carpet factory that is worth a tour. Here you can see all the stages involved in making a hand-knotted wool carpet, from dying the wool to trimming the finished carpet with huge shears. Large rooms are almost entirely filled with huge wooden looms at which young women sit tying knots. The women's flying fingers make it almost impossible to discern how they tie the knots. The carpet factory and showroom, where you can buy one of the carpets, are open daily from 10am to 6pm. There is no charge for looking around the factory, but photography is not permitted.

Pokhara Museum, on Pode Tole north of the airport (☎ 977/61-20413), is a small museum housing displays of the different tribal groups living in the Pokhara region. Each group has a display of mannequins in traditional dress. Murals depict village life, and the tableaux show what a typical home is like. There are also displays of musical instruments, old weapons, and old photos. However, the best reason to visit is to learn how to recognize different ethnic groups by their styles of dress. The museum is open in summer, Wednesday to Monday from 10am to 5pm, and in winter from 10am to 4pm. Admission is Rs5 (10¢).

MORE ATTRACTIONS

The **Annapurna Regional Museum** (☎ 977/61-21102) is on the university campus at the far north end of Pokhara. This is a natural history museum with poorly stuffed animals and badly painted murals on the wall. However, there is an amazing collection of butterflies, and lepidopterists will be interested in visiting. The Annapurna Conservation Area Project also has a very informative display in the museum. Anyone planning to go trekking should be sure to stop by and learn about the effects of trekking on this region. The museum is free and is open Sunday to Friday from 9am to 5pm (closed for lunch from 1 to 2pm).

The **Bindhabasini Temple,** in Mohariya Tole at the north end of Pokhara, is a small temple dedicated to the goddess Bhagwati, who is also known as Bindhabasini. The temple is at the top of a small hill just off the bazaar. Stone steps lead up from a sunny square to the shady hilltop where the shrine is located. Chickens and other domestic animals are sometimes sacrificed to Bindhabasini.

There is a **Tibetan Buddhist Monastery** a mile or so to the east of Pokhara. It is surrounded by trees and is on top of a low hill. Though the monastery itself is not very impressive, there is a nice view. Tall slender prayer flags flutter from poles beside the main building of the monastery, framing the view of the mountains. Remember to take off your shoes before entering the prayer hall. Take the road that crosses the Mahendra Bridge. The road to the monastery is on the left about one mile from the bridge.

The **Seti River gorge,** best seen from the Mahendra Bridge, is similar to Patale Chhango. The river has cut a narrow gorge less than 15 feet wide, but the water is nearly 50 feet below the level of the bridge. As you first begin to cross the bridge,

> ## ⭐ Frommer's Favorite Pokhara Experiences
>
> **Watching the Sunrise on the Himalayas.**   This is the only reason you need to come to Pokhara. When the morning light rises, the peaks change from a deep blue to lavender to pink to orange to gold. It's a sublime experience.
>
> **Exploring Patale Chhango.**   Viewing this mysterious disappearing waterfall is fascinating enough, but the adventurous can go rock-hopping up the ravine to find tiny natural bridges and strange potholes gouged by the river. Botanists will love the growths of ferns on the walls of the ravine.
>
> **Trekking out of Pokhara.**   Pokhara is the best place in Nepal to start a trek. You can simply walk out the door of your hotel and begin hiking into the mountains (although most people take a taxi to the trailhead).
>
> **Boating on Phewa Lake.**   Whether you want to paddle yourself, be paddled by a boatman, or sail, there is no more relaxing way to spend a morning or afternoon than boating on the emerald-green waters of Phewa Lake.

you will see nothing but vegetation (and garbage) in the wide valley below you. As you approach the middle of the bridge, you begin to hear the sound of water. With no warning you are looking down into a dark, mossy gorge. Every time I look into the Seti River gorge, I want to raft through it just to see what it is like down there.

ORGANIZED TOURS

Though most of the attractions—the mountains and the lake—in Pokhara are natural and readily visible from almost anywhere in the valley, you can book a tour that will take you around to all of the other main attractions. **Fishtail Sightseeing Service,** Mahendra Pul (☎ 977/61-21870), offers a tour that visits virtually all of the valley's natural and cultural attractions in one long day. The cost of the eight-hour tour is 400($8); hotel pickup is at 9:30am. **Pokhara Sight Seeing,** Damside (☎ 977/61-21943), offers similar tours and prices.

6 Sports

Outdoor activities are the main pastime in Pokhara. There isn't much in the way of cultural offerings, so people go off on day hikes, rent boats, bicycle, and even go fishing.

BICYCLING   Bicycling is the best way to get around in Pokhara (if you are in good enough shape to pedal uphill on a one-speed bike). Bicycles rent for about Rs25 to Rs50 (50¢ to $1) per day and are readily available in Damside and Lakeside. Just look for a row of bicycles beside the road. One of the easiest bicycle destinations is Devil's Falls and the Tibetan Refugee Camp. For a real workout, try pedaling up to Mahendra Cave north of town. It's all uphill going, but the ride back is a breeze.

BOATING   Boating is a major pastime in Pokhara. There used to be dugout canoes available, but these have almost all been replaced by wooden rowboats. You can hire a boat for Rs30 to Rs80 (60¢ to $1.60) per hour if you want to paddle it yourself. If you are feeling lazy, boatmen will gladly paddle you around for an additional Rs60 to Rs70 ($1.20 to $1.40) per hour. There are boats available in Damside near the spot where women do their laundry in the lake and in Lakeside past the royal palace. The most popular destination for boaters is a little island with a temple on it just offshore from Lakeside. There are also sailboats available in Lakeside for Rs150 to Rs200 ($3 to $4) per hour. Look for these at Hotel Fewa, near the fish hatchery.

HIKING   The Pokhara Valley is a rural valley surrounded by hills and mountains, and there are numerous opportunities for hiking. Most of the popular hikes are to hills overlooking the valley. If you stop by the tourist office (see "Tourist Information," above, in this chapter) with your Pokhara map in hand, someone there can show you where to find the trails for various valley hikes.

To Sarangkot   This 5,200-foot hill is a popular destination for day hikers who want to get a panorama of Phewa Lake and the Pokhara Valley in one direction and of the Annapurnas in the other. At the top of the hill there are the remains of an old fortress built by King Prithvi Narayan Shah in the 18th century. It was this king who unified Nepal by conquering the many tiny kingdoms that controlled the Himalaya's valleys. The hike takes two to three hours to the top and another one to two hours to descend so you need to have a full day. The trail starts near the Bindhabasini Temple at the north end of Pokhara, where there is a sign pointing the way to Sarangkot. The trail climbs a long ridge passing through a small village, forests, and brushy slopes. A steep alternative route back to Pokhara descends directly toward the lake. You can also hire a taxi to drive you part way to the top for about Rs600 ($12) and then walk back. I recommend spending the night up here at Sarangkot so you can enjoy the sunset and sunrise. There are a couple of very basic trekking-style lodges up here charging Rs20 (40¢) per person for a room.

To Kahun Danda   Northeast of Pokhara is Kahun Danda, a 5,000-foot-high hill overlooking the valley. It is about a five-hour hike to the top of the hill and back. The trail begins east of the Mahendra Bridge at the intersection where the telecommunications office is located. Take the road heading north from here following the trail that leads up the hill when the road ends. About halfway up the hill, take the left fork. When this trail meets another major trail, turn right and continue climbing the hill. There is an old observation tower at the top of the hill.

To Dhungesangu   This may be the most interesting short hike in the valley. The trail follows a gravel road that begins south of the airstrip. The road, which heads east then south, leads to a large natural bridge over the Seti River. From the bridge, you can look down into the deep narrow gorge. Across the bridge, a trail to the left leads up to the top of a bluff. A crack in the earth forms a natural gateway to the top. There is a great view of the valley, river, and snow-covered peaks along the way. A campsite here is a good place for a picnic. It is less than two miles from the airport to the natural bridge. The entire hike can easily be done in a morning.

HORSEBACK RIDING   Pokhara is the southern end of a centuries-old trading route between Tibet and India, and the town is still plied by caravans of sturdy mountain ponies laden with heavy bags. If you'd like to ride one of these ponies, **Pokhara Pony Trek** (☎ 977/61-20339) offers a number of different trips around the valley. Prices range from Rs750 ($15) for a half-day ride (with guide) to Rs1,500 ($30) for a full-day ride.

WHITE-WATER RAFTING   Any of the small travel agencies around Lakeside or Damside can arrange a rafting trip for you. These trips start at the same place that rafting trips from Kathmandu start. Rates are also comparable. See "Alternative/Adventure Travel" in Chapter 2 for details.

7 Easy Excursions from Pokhara

Most people are content to just take it easy while in Pokhara, but if you are full of energy and wondering what else you might do while in town, try a day-trip out to **Begnas Tal** and **Rupa Tal.** Tal means lake in Nepali, and these two lakes at the east end of the valley are more remote and less developed than Phewa Lake. You can spend the day hiking around one or the other of the two lakes before catching the bus back to Pokhara. Be sure to ask upon arrival what time buses return to Pokhara. With three large lakes in the valley, it is not surprising that this is called the Nepali lake district.

For three other hiking excursions, see "Sports," above.

Pokhara also makes a good base for overnight visits to a couple of other rarely visited hill towns. One is of historic interest as the birthplace of modern Nepal, and the other offers one of the widest panoramas of the Himalayas.

GORKHA

Located a little less than halfway to Kathmandu, Gorkha was the seat of power for King Prithvi Narayan Shah who, in the 18th century, united Nepal by conquering dozens of tiny Himalayan kingdoms, including those of the Kathmandu Valley. So legendary did the soldiers of Gorkha become that the British began recruiting men from this region to serve in the British army. These soldiers are known today as the Gurkhas, some of the most feared soldiers in the world. Today, though there is a good road to Gorkha, the town is rarely visited by tourists. To reach Gorkha from Pokhara, you can take a tourist bus as far as the turnoff at Kaireni for around Rs150 ($3), and from here catch a local bus the rest of the way for around Rs10 (20¢). The local bus from Pokhara costs only Rs45 (90¢), but it takes an hour or so longer to reach the turnoff. Alternatively you could hire a taxi for the day for around Rs3,000 ($60) or a motorcycle for Rs350 ($7) plus gasoline.

WHAT TO SEE & DO

Though Gorkha is an excellent town for starting a trek into the little visited surrounding hills, its main claim to fame is its old fort from which King Prithvi Narayan Shah launched his conquest of Nepal. This fort sits 1,000 feet above the city on a forested hilltop and commands a nearly 360-degree view of the surrounding countryside—an excellent spot from which to conquer everything in sight. There are two routes from town up to the fort—the steep route and the steeper route. Either way, it's going to be a sweaty uphill slog. If you're a fast walker, you can be at the fort in 30 minutes, but 45 minutes is a better estimate. At the bus turnaround, if you look up at the fort, one route will start on your left, and one route will start on your right. The former circles around to the west of town before turning back east on a well-constructed stone stairway. This is the steep route. The steeper route climbs through the center of the town and plows straight up the hillside on a vertiginous stairway. This was the path that visiting vassals were forced to walk when they came to pay respects to their conquerer.

After such a strenuous hike, you'll probably be expecting Camelot, but what you'll actually find is a rather modest brick building that is only loosely a fort. "Palace" might be a better term for the building, but it is a rather humble palace. Newari craftsmen from the Kathmandu Valley were brought in to build the fort, and the similarity to the palaces of the Kathmandu Valley is immediately evident. The building is constructed of red brick with intricately carved latticework windows and is surrounded by several stone-paved terraces. The fort has been restored and is still frequently visited by the current king.

The fort is also a pilgrimage spot and houses a temple to Kali. The statue inside this temple is considered so holy and powerful that only priests and the king of Nepal are allowed to view it. Common folks must be content to sacrifice goats and chickens at the front door of the temple, and the steps leading up to the shrine are often stained with fresh blood.

In front of and below the main palace building is a shrine surrounding the cave in which a famous holy man named Gorkhanath meditated. It is from this holy man that Gorkha takes its name. Around to the east of the fort are several *stelae*, carved stones that record historical events from Gorkha's heyday.

Down in town there is another palace that is known as the Lower Palace. This building was more of an administrative center and was built around 1750. A parade ground in front of the palace gives the building a very imposing appearance. Look for the peacock windows that are almost identical to the famous peacock window in Bhaktapur.

WHERE TO STAY & DINE

Gorkha Hill Resort
Laxmi Bazaar, Shikhar Danda, Gorkha. In Kathmandu Durbar Marg (P.O. Box 1759) Kathmandu. ☎ **977/1-271329.** Fax 977/1-471630. 24 rms (all with bath). $44 double. MC, V.

Located 2¹/₂ miles downhill from the town of Gorkha, this small lodge sits on a hill overlooking valleys and mountains and also has a good view of Gorkha's old fort. Rooms are comfortable, though simply furnished. Gardens and lawns create a pleasantly relaxing atmosphere for gazing up at snowcapped peaks. If you'd like to get away from the crowds and noise during your trip to Nepal, this is a great place. Meals are an additional $22 per person per day.

Hotel Gorkha Bisauni
Gorkha Bazaar, Gorkha. ☎ **977/64-20107.** 20 rms (14 with bath). $1.60 double without bath, $3–$10 double with bath. No credit cards.

This is the backpacker's first choice in Gorkha, and as you can guess by the prices, the accommodations are Spartan and only marginally clean (slightly better than you might find in a trekkers' lodge on the trail). There are a dark restaurant and shady garden. You'll find the lodge back downhill from the bus turnaround.

7 The Terai

The Terai, Nepal's lowland area along the Indian border, is primarily an agricultural and industrial region. Its vast flat plains, an extension of the fertile plain created by the Ganges River, are a striking contrast to the jagged peaks that most foreigners associate with Nepal. However, it is also here that the foothills of the Himalayas begin. Until the 1960s, when a program to eradicate malaria-carrying mosquitoes with DDT was instituted, the Terai was covered with dense forests of hardwoods, primarily *sal* trees. The Tharu people, who have a natural resistance to malaria, were among the few inhabitants of the region. When malarial mosquitoes were brought under control, people from the higher regions of Nepal began migrating to the Terai. Since that time, much of the forest has been cut down for building materials and firewood, and much of the region has come under cultivation.

Fortunately, several areas of the Terai have been set aside as national parks and wildlife preserves, for it is here that Nepal's greatest concentrations of wildlife live. Tigers, one-horned rhinoceroses, wild elephants, bears, monkeys, deer, antelope, crocodiles, and many other rare and endangered species make their homes in the Terai. No visit to Nepal is complete without a visit to either Royal Chitwan National Park or Royal Bardia Wildlife Reserve to see some of these wild animals in their native habitats.

The Terai was also the birthplace of Prince Siddhartha Gautama, better known as the Buddha. What is today the small town of Lumbini was once a garden in the kingdom of Kapilvastu. It was in that garden that the Buddha was born more than 2,500 years ago. Today Lumbini is one of the world's most important pilgrimage sites.

1 Royal Chitwan National Park

103 miles (166 kilometers) SW of Kathmandu, 127 miles (204 kilometers) SE of Pokhara, 194 miles (312 kilometers) E of Lumbini

There are only a few places on earth where you can still see a Bengal tiger in the wild, and Royal Chitwan National Park is one of these. Located along the Indian border in the Terai, Chitwan is Nepal's premier wildlife-viewing area. The park, formerly a royal hunting reserve, covers nearly 400 square miles of dense forest and

What's Special About the Terai

Natural Attractions
- Royal Chitwan National Park is home to tigers, one-horned rhinoceroses, leopards, crocodiles, and many other endangered species.

Activities
- Riding an elephant through Chitwan Park in search of tigers and rhinos.

Religious Shrines
- Lumbini is the birthplace of the Buddha and is an important pilgrimage site for the world's Buddhists.

Offbeat Oddities
- Tiger Tops Jungle Lodge holds an annual elephant polo tournament that is attended by the world's rich and famous (the only folks who can afford to compete).

riverine grasslands and is home to nearly 60 Bengal tigers and a large population of Indian one-horned rhinoceroses. Other wildlife includes the *gaur* (Indian bison), sloth bear, leopard, several species of deer, wild boars, several species of monkeys, two species of crocodile, the freshwater Gangetic dolphin, and more than 400 species of birds.

Contrary to what you may be led to believe by agents trying to sell you a package trip to the park, Chitwan is not a jungle or a rain forest. This area has two very distinct seasons—the wet monsoon season (June through September) and the dry winter months. The best time of year to visit the park is March through May, when the elephant grass that can grow 20 feet tall is too short to provide cover for rhinos, which prefer this riverine environment. In January each year, the local Tharu villagers, who have traditionally built their homes from various grasses gathered along the rivers, are allowed to enter the park and cut as much grass as they want. This grass will later form the walls and roofs of their houses. After the grass has been cut, the stubble is set on fire to fertilize the soil. Though there are hundreds of villagers in the park during grass-harvesting season in January, this can often be a good time to see wildlife. I have been to Chitwan during harvest season on two occasions and have seen many rhinos, deer, monkeys, and even a tiger.

GETTING THERE

BY PLANE There are two airports in the Chitwan area, Meghauli and Bharatpur, and there are regularly scheduled flights to both. Meghauli airport is used primarily by Tiger Tops, Temple Tiger, and Island Jungle Resort. A round-trip ticket is $144. The airport at Bharatpur is used primarily by Gaida Wildlife Camp, Chitwan Jungle Lodge, and Machan Wildlife Resort. A round-trip ticket costs $100. Airlines flying to these airports include **RNAC, Everest Air, Necon Air,** and **Nepal Airways.**

BY BUS If your budget only allows you to travel by bus, at least you have the option of taking a tourist bus from Kathmandu or Pokhara. These buses take slightly less time than the regular bus and are slightly more comfortable. The fare is between Rs120 and Rs140 ($2.40 and $2.80) one-way. Tickets are available at hotels and travel agencies in either city. In Kathmandu the buses leave from in

Royal Chitwan National Park

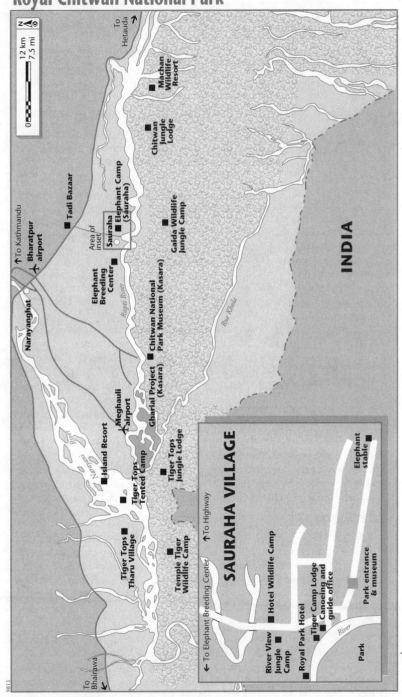

front of the Department of Immigration, while in Pokhara, the buses usually will pick you up at your hotel. If you want to travel by regular bus, plan on at least a 10-hour ride. You will probably have to change buses in Bharatpur or Narayan Ghat. Be sure to tell the driver of the second bus that you want to get off at Tadi Bazaar if you are going to Sauraha. Buses leave Kathmandu from the new bus park north of Thamel. Buses also leave daily from the main bus terminal in Pokhara. A bus to Tadi Bazaar costs Rs50 ($1).

When you get off the bus, whether it is a tourist bus or a regular bus, you will be in Tadi Bazaar, and you will immediately be assaulted by touts screaming at you and grabbing your bags. If you are on a prepaid package tour, just wave your travel voucher at them, and they'll leave you alone. There will be a representative of your lodge waiting to pick you up. If, however, you don't have a reservation, you're fair game for the touts.

If you can fight off the touts, you can try to find a Jeep going to the lodge you have chosen. However, if your preferred lodge does not have a Jeep meeting the bus, you'll have to negotiate passage on another Jeep for Rs30 (60¢). No doubt a tout will climb into the vehicle with you and convince you that you should have a look at his excellent, hygienic, and homey lodge.

BY CAR   If you are coming to Chitwan on a package tour, you will almost certainly be given the option of traveling by car or minivan. A car can carry one to three people, and for a minivan, you will need to have a group of at least five people. A round-trip ticket by car is between $50 and $70.

DEPARTING

If you are on a package trip, this will be taken care of for you; otherwise, you will need to arrange with your lodge to transport you the four miles out to the highway where you can catch the tourist bus or a regular bus to Bharatpur. In Bharatpur, there are buses to Pokhara, Kathmandu, or the Indian border.

ESSENTIALS

Chitwan is a remote park surrounded by small villages, and park admission is Rs650 ($13). Only Sauraha village, which consists of four sandy lanes through the rice fields, has any amenities, and these are fairly Spartan. Be sure to bring a flashlight, batteries, sunscreen, insect repellent, a long-sleeve shirt, and long pants. Sunglasses are also a good idea. If you are staying in Sauraha, you can rent bicycles for Rs80 ($1.60) per day. This is a good way to get to the elephant breeding center.

WHAT TO SEE & DO

If you are on a package tour, you won't have any choice about what you see and do, but if you are a budget traveler on your own, you should know which excursions are the most worthwhile. The very first thing you should do is get your name on the list for an **elephant ride** (or elephant safari as it is called). The best and safest vantage point for viewing rhinos is from the back of an elephant, and this elevation also makes it easier to spot other wildlife. Even if you don't see any wild animals (and some people don't), riding through the forest on the back of an elephant is great fun. A one- to two-hour elephant ride costs Rs650 ($13) per person.

If you are in good physical shape and don't mind being exposed to a little danger, a **half-day or full-day walk** through the park with a trained naturalist/guide is one of the best ways to see wildlife up close. You may, however, have to spend some time up in a tree if you get *too* close to a rhino. These lumbering behemoths have poor eyesight and so to protect themselves will charge almost anything that moves. Should one charge you, the best thing to do is climb a tree. If there is no tree, run in a curve and throw down some article of clothing; this will usually distract a rhino. On a walk through the park you are likely to see gharial (fish-eating crocodiles) and marsh-mugger crocodiles, deer, rhinos, and monkeys. A full-day hike will cost around Rs300 ($6) per person.

The **dugout canoe trip** is pleasant, but you aren't likely to see much but a few birds. If you're especially lucky, you might see a few marsh-mugger crocodiles sunning themselves on the banks of the river. This species of crocodile is known as a man-eater throughout India and Nepal and is best given a wide berth. The canoe ride, if booked near the park entrance, will cost Rs50 ($1) per person.

There are two **elephant camps** in the area, both worth a visit. The camp in Sauraha is primarily a working camp and is where most of the elephants that give rides are stabled. Here you can watch men making elephant power pills (dietary supplements) by filling a grass cup with rice and sugar and then shaping the cup into a ball. An hour's walk away down the river is the elephant breeding camp where you may be lucky enough to see a baby elephant or two.

In the past, **jungle drives** have been offered, but floods in 1993 made driving across the river impossible. If it is possible once again to cross the river into the park when you visit, you will likely find lodges offering this trip again. These drives are not likely to turn up much wildlife, since the truck's engine generally scares away everything in the area, but the trip's final destination, the gharial breeding center, is interesting. Gharials are a type of fish-eating crocodile with a long thin snout that gives them a supercilious appearance. Floods several years ago swept away much of the region's population of gharials so this center was set up to help restore the population to its previous levels. You can see tiny baby gharials that look like they belong in terrariums and 12-foot-long adults that look like dinosaurs. The 3-hour jungle drive costs around Rs650 ($13) per person.

Another possible excursion while in the area is to take an **all-day guided bike ride.** These rides sometimes turn up wildlife and usually stop at a nearby Tharu village. The rides cost around Rs250 ($5).

No matter which activities you choose, please remember that many of the animals that live in this park are very dangerous. You visit at your own risk.

WHERE TO STAY

Accommodations at and in the vicinity of Chitwan National Park are all very similar. Most people who come to Chitwan are on two- or three-day package tours that include transportation, accommodations, all meals, park entrance fees, and activities such as elephant rides, canoe trips, birdwatching walks, and jungle drives. The major difference is in price. Outside the park, prices are generally much lower, while inside the park's boundaries prices skyrocket. All lodges include the same excursions, and your chances of seeing rhinos and tigers (usually the main objective of anyone coming here) are generally the same no matter where you stay. The rates listed below are for all-inclusive package tours. At the lodges within the park the lower price generally includes transportation by car or minivan, and the higher price includes transportation by plane. At the least expensive lodges, the lowest rates include transportation by tourist bus.

It is also possible to travel part of the way by car and part of the way by raft on the Trisuli River. This method of getting to the park is less expensive than flying but more expensive than taking a car all the way.

One more thing you should know is that all the rates listed here are *published* rates. In actuality Chitwan lodges almost never charge these prices, not even in the high seasons. It is not unusual to walk into a lodge office and immediately be offered a 50% discount, so in effect there are many more moderately priced lodges than it would seem. It is always worth asking for a discount.

IN THE PARK
Very Expensive

☉ Chitwan Jungle Lodge
Durbar Marg (P.O. Box 1281), Kathmandu. ☎ **977/1-228918**, 977/1-222679, or 977/1-228458. Fax 977/1-228349. 32 rms (all with bath). 2-night, 3-day package $520–$620 double. Pokhara pickup $30 extra per person. Additional nights $90 per person. Children 2 to 10 pay 50% of above rates. AE, MC, V.

Located deep in the forest at the eastern end of the park, Chitwan Jungle Lodge is one of the largest jungle lodges. Traditional Tharu-style mud-walled huts with thatch roofs are built around a sunny garden where guests lounge in the sun when they aren't busy viewing wildlife. Rooms have twin beds with wool blankets and locally made cotton quilts. Though there is no electricity, wood fires heat the water for your afternoon shower. In the evening, the resident naturalists who lead hikes, elephant rides, and dugout-canoe trips also give slide presentations on the park's wildlife.

The dining hall, where Nepali and continental meals are served, is as rustic as the rest of the lodge, with a thatch roof and elephant-grass walls. A local dance troupe provides evening entertainment with its performances of the traditional Tharu stick dance.

Island Jungle Resort
Durbar Marg (P.O. Box 2154), Kathmandu. ☎ **977/1-220162** or 977/1-225615. Fax 977/1-223814. 16 rms (all with bath), 20 tents (none with bath). 2-night, 3-day package $540–$620 double at tented camp, $580–$660 double at lodge. Children under 3 stay free. Children 3 to 12 pay 50% of above rates. AE, MC, V.

This lodge is located on an island in the Narayani River near the western end of the park. The Narayani River is much larger than the Rapti River, which most of the other lodges are near, and consequently, you are more likely to see marsh-mugger and gharial crocodiles. You may also see the rare freshwater Gangetic dolphin in the waters near the camp. Rhinos and tigers are sometimes seen crossing between the many islands in this part of the river. Naturalist-led excursions are available. Tents are spacious, with windows, twin beds, and local wool felt rugs, and a small veranda out front. The resort can be reached only by boat, giving it a very isolated feel.

A round, open-air dining room with a warm fire in the hearth serves Nepali and continental meals. There is also a small bar.

✪ Machan Wildlife Resort

Durbar Marg (P.O. Box 78), Kathmandu. ☎ **977/1-225001** or 977/1-227099. Fax 977/1-220475. 28 rms (all with bath), 12 tents (none with bath). 2-night, 3-day package $370–$480 double at tented camp, $490–$600 double at resort. Children under 12 pay 50% of above prices. AE, MC, V (add 3%–5% surcharge).

Located at the eastern end of the park, Machan is one of the newest lodges in the park. Though the accommodations are the same rustic-but-comfortable mud-walled huts found at most of the other jungle lodges at Chitwan, Machan has a rock-lined swimming pool made by widening a stream that flows across the property. There's also a well-stocked library containing books and films on wildlife, ecology, and culture of the Indian subcontinent. Naturalist-led excursions are available. The resort takes its name from the wildlife-viewing blinds (*machans*) that are scattered around the park.

Though there is no electricity at the lodge, hot showers are provided daily by heating the water tanks over wood fires. Rooms are in mud-walled thatch-roofed duplex huts with hardwood floors and wicker furniture. There are even sleeping lofts for children. At the tented camp, deeper inside the park than the resort, the tents are sheltered under thatch roofs and have shared toilet and shower facilities. Your chances of seeing wildlife are slightly better at the tented camp since it is farther from the villages on the edge of the park.

Temple Tiger Wildlife Camp

Pratap Bhawan, Kantipath (P.O. Box 3968), Kathmandu. ☎ **977/1-221585**, 977/1-225780, or 977/1-227559. Fax 977/1-220178. 25 rms, 25 tents (all with bath). 2-night, 3-day package $794–$982 double. Children 3 to 12 pay 50% of above rate. Children under 3 stay free. AE (add 5%) MC, V (add 4%).

Located at the far western end of the park, Temple Tiger provides accommodations in a rustic lodge and large two-room tents that have a sleeping area and a dressing area. Traditional Nepali gray felt rugs and twin beds provide a certain level of comfort, and a thatch roof over the tents keeps them cool in the day. Bathrooms have hot showers, though there is no electricity at the lodge. Reaching the lodge is an adventure in itself. Whether you travel from Kathmandu by car or plane, you will transfer to a dugout canoe to cross the Narayani River, and once on the far shore, you will be met by elephants that will take you to the camp. It is also possible to spend three days rafting from Kathmandu. There are four tigers living in the immediate vicinity, so your chances of seeing one of these majestic and elusive big cats is quite good if you stay here, though there are no guarantees. The camp's location 80 feet above the grasslands along the Narayani River makes it an excellent vantage point for observing rhinos, especially in January and February when the tall grasses have just been cut by local villagers. Naturalist-led excursions are available.

Tiger Tops Jungle Lodge

Durbar Marg (P.O. Box 242), Kathmandu. ☎ **977/1-222706** or 977/1-223328. Fax 977/1-414075. 27 rms at lodge, 12 tents at tented camp, 12 rms at Tharu Resort (all with bath). 2-night, 3-day package $988 double at Tharu Resort, $1,020 double at tented camp, $1,146 double at Tiger Tops Lodge. Children under 5 accepted only with prior arrangement. Children 5 to 12 pay 50% of above rates, including airfare. AE, MC, V.

Tiger Tops was the first lodge to open at Royal Chitwan National Park, and today it is still the most expensive and exclusive. Its astronomical rates assure that the guests here are among the world's wealthiest citizens, and during the annual elephant polo matches, celebrities abound. Accommodations at the Jungle Lodge, Tiger Top's original facility, are in buildings constructed on stilts and made from local materials. Plaited bamboo walls and a thatch roof provide a rustic atmosphere, while the rooms are comfortably furnished. Hot water is provided by solar panels. Though there is no electricity, a generator is turned on at night so that slide presentations can be given. The tented camp is in a picturesque valley three miles east of the main lodge. Tents are roomy, with two twin beds and a table. A covered vestibule area is carpeted and has a couple of stools and another table. Though the accommodations at Tiger Tops Tharu Safari Resort are the least expensive, they are by far the most luxurious. This lodge is actually outside the park but is close to the Narayani River and has good wildlife viewing nearby. The lodge is designed to resemble a traditional Tharu village longhouse, but it actually looks a lot like a Mexican hacienda. Rooms are spacious with high ceilings. The decor includes wall paintings, traditionally done by unmarried Tharu women, and local artifacts, such as ceramic water pots used as lamp shades. Wicker furniture and colorful bedspreads, curtains, and rugs give the resort an exotic feel that is a perfect counterpoint to the exotic locale outside the door. Activities here include a swimming pool, horseback riding, elephant rides, horse-drawn buggies, and ox-cart rides. Naturalists also give tours.

Note: Tiger Tops also operates a lodge at the Royal Bardia Wildlife Reserve in western Nepal. Though there are fewer rhinos in Bardia, there is more wildlife of other types such as wild elephants, black buck (a type of antelope), and deer. Also in western Nepal, there is the Silent Safari Tented Camp in the Royal Sukilaphanta Wildlife Reserve. Should you wish to visit either of these lodges rather than one of the lodges at Chitwan, ask about Tiger Tops Karnali Lodge and Tented Camp.

OUTSIDE THE PARK
Expensive
River View Jungle Camp
15/79 Thamel, Kathamandu. ☎ **977/1-410418,** or (in Sauraha) 977/56-60165 or 977/56-29363. Fax 977/1-419361. 11 rms (5 with private bathroom). 2-night, 3-day package $187–$286 double without bath, $231–$330 double with bath. MC, V (at Kathmandu office only).

Although the view of the river isn't much to speak of, this lodge is conveniently located on tree-shaded grounds. The rooms with private bathrooms are definitely the best accommodations. These rooms are built of brick, have vinyl (rather than cement) floors, and feature large porches with chairs. The rooms with shared bathrooms are built in traditional Tharu style with grass-and-mud walls and are rather musty. The quoted rates here are rather high for what you get at this basic lodge, so be sure to ask for a discount.

✪ Royal Park Hotel
Sauraha. ☎ **977/56-29361,** or (in Kathmandu) 977/1-414939. 12 rms. 2-night, 3-day package $264 double. No credit cards.

Set on the banks of the Rapti River amid a spacious well-manicured garden, the Royal Park Hotel is the best of the Sauraha lodges. Flagstone walkways lead to the guest rooms, which are housed in several buildings. The rooms are all large and have brick floors, high ceilings, Tibetan carpets on both the floor and the chair seats, and attractive bathrooms with slate floors and walls. You won't find a nicer room even at the most expensive Chitwan jungle lodges. There's a large dining hall with screen walls and brick-and-flagstone floors. In the garden, you'll find an open-air bar and a few shaded tables where you can watch for rhinos as you sip your cocktail. The lodge even has its own little bakery just outside the front gate.

Note: The rates quoted above do not include the park admission fee, which you should arrange to pay yourself. Do not pay through the lodge, which charges much more than the official rate for park admission.

Tiger Camp
Sauraha (P.O. Box 2506, Kathmandu). ☎ (in Kathmandu) **977/1-522641** or 977/1-227567, or (in Pokhara) 977/61-21435. 16 rms (12 with private bath). 2-night, 3-day package $242–$275 double. Children ages 3 to 10 pay $93.50 for the package, and children under age 3 stay free. MC, V (in Kathmandu only).

This small lodge is not very attractive, but it is right on the bank of the Rapti River near the park entrance and museum. From the lodge's rooftop dining room, you can sometimes spot rhinos. If you don't mind using a shared bathroom, you can stay in one of the two *machan*-style huts, which are built on stilts and are designed to resemble traditional wildlife-viewing blinds. The other rooms, though less interesting and without views, are comfortable and have large bathrooms. All rooms have mosquito nets over the beds.

Hotel Wildlife Camp
Thamel (P.O. Box 2525), Kathmandu. ☎ **977/1-228784.** 13 rms (9 with bath). 2-night, 3-day package $100–$280 double. Children under 3 pay 10% of above rates; children 3 to 10 pay 50% of above rates. Extra nights $30 per person, excluding activities. AE, MC, V (in Kathmandu only).

Located in the village of Sauraha, Hotel Wildlife Camp consists of new brick buildings and older duplex huts constructed in typical Tharu fashion from local materials such as elephant grass, thatch, bamboo, and mud. There is a circular thatch-roofed dining hall in the middle of the compound. It is only a short walk to the park entrance. The staff is friendly, and there are guides available to answer your questions and lead you on your wildlife-spotting excursions. The standard package tour includes jungle walk, birdwatching walk, canoe trip, elephant ride through the forest, Tharu stick dance performance, and a visit to a nearby Tharu village.

Budget
Budget accommodations for backpacking visitors abound in Sauraha village. At last count there were more than 50 lodges, most charging only a few dollars a night, in this small village. Nearly all of these lodges offer accommodations in the same Tharu-style huts, which have mud walls and floor and a thatch roof. Low-budget lodges usually have shared bathrooms, no electricity, and solar- or wood-fire-heated shower water, just like the more expensive lodges. As elsewhere in Nepal, the newest budget hotels are always the best because maintenance is rarely a priority at such places.

2 Lumbini

155 miles (249 kilometers) W of Kathmandu, 125 miles (201 kilometers) S of Pokhara, 13 miles (21 kilometers) W of Bhairawa

More than 2,500 years ago Prince Siddhartha Gautama, who would later become the Buddha, was born in Lumbini, a town that is now part of Nepal. At the time of his birth Lumbini was part of the kingdom of Kapilvastu, which had its capital 17 miles west on the site of modern Tilaurakot. Today Lumbini is just a small town, but it is very important as a Buddhist pilgrimage site. Emperor Ashoka of India, one of the earliest pilgrims to visit Lumbini, erected an inscribed stone pillar here in 250 B.C. When this pillar was discovered late in the 19th century, it helped archaeologists to uncover many other ruins in the area.

GETTING THERE

BY PLANE   There are daily flights from Kathmandu taking 45 minutes. The fare is $72 one way.

BY BUS   There are daily buses to Bhairawa from Kathmandu taking 8 to 12 hours and daily buses from Pokhara taking 8 to 10 hours. Both trips cost about Rs80 ($1.60) one way. These buses leave from Kathmandu's new bus park and the Pokhara main bus terminal, respectively. From Bhairawa local hourly buses costing Rs6 (12¢) cover the 13 miles to Lumbini and take 45 minutes. It is also possible to hire a taxi for Rs500 ($10) or a three-wheeled taxi called a tempo for Rs300 ($6).

BY CAR   From Kathmandu take the Prithvi Rajmarg east to Mugling and then south to Bharatpur and west to Bhairawa and Lumbini.

DEPARTING

Buses for Kathmandu and Pokhara leave from the main bus terminal in Bhairawa early in the morning. It is best to buy your ticket at the bus terminal the night before departing.

ESSENTIALS

There are several very basic hotels in Bhairawa.

WHAT TO SEE

Today you can see the Ashoka pillar, the temple of Maya Devi (Buddha's mother), the pond where Maya Devi is said to have taken a bath before giving birth, and other ruins. In the gardens that surround the ruins, there is a bo tree, and it was under such a tree that Siddhartha Gautama gained enlightenment and became the Buddha. There are also two modern monasteries—one Nepali and one Tibetan. Within these two monasteries are interesting paintings and large statues of the Buddha. The Lumbini Development Trust is in the process of developing Lumbini as a major pilgrimage site with tourist facilities, a library, a visitors center, and a museum. It is impossible to say when this project will be completed.

WHERE TO STAY

Lumbini is not a major tourist destination and does not have much in the way of accommodations. There is a high end and a low end and nothing in between.

Lumbini Hokke Hotel

Lumbini Sacred Garden, Rupandehi. ☎ **977/71-20236.** Fax 977/71-20236. In Kathmandu: Kupondole (P.O. Box 5136), Kathmandu. ☎ and fax 977/1-521348. 24 rms (all with bath). $135.60 double; $161.60 triple. AE, JCB, MC, V.

Built and managed by the Japanese primarily for Japanese Buddhist pilgrims, the Lumbini Hokke has the best rooms in Nepal. Twenty of these rooms are done in Japanese style with tatami floors and sliding shoji screens between the bedroom and sitting area. For a room such as this you would have to spend a small fortune in

Japan. Among the amenities here are a pilgrim's gift shop, Japanese bathhouse, meditation room, and large dining room. It's too bad that such comfortable accommodations are so far off the main tourist routes.

Hotel Himalaya Inn

New Road, Siddhartha Nagar-7 (Bhairawa). ☎ **977/71-20347.** 20 rms (all with bath). $13.20 double. No credit cards.

This is a very basic hotel, but if you can't afford to stay at the Lumbini Hokke, this is your next best choice. The rooms are Spartan, but they do have fans. Be sure to have some mosquito coils with you since the window screens aren't always in such good shape. About half the rooms have Asian squat toilets, and these are actually preferable to the rooms with Western toilets.

Planning a Trek 8

The Himalayas are the highest and most spectacular mountains on earth, and among their peaks and valleys wind thousands of miles of trails—the human highways of the Himalayas. For centuries the people of Nepal, Tibet, and India have traveled these trails as farmers, traders, and pilgrims. Today thousands of foreigners from around the world are also walking these trails, discovering the countless wonders of the Himalayas.

WHAT IS TREKKING?

To trek—the word is Afrikaans and originally meant a journey by ox cart across South Africa—is to do far more than hike through beautiful mountains. Trekking is very different from backpacking; it is an outdoor experience, but it is also a cultural experience. There are villages nearly everywhere in Nepal—in the remotest arid valleys and on the steepest terraced mountainsides—and these villages are what make a trek in Nepal unique. However, despite the many villages along the trail in Nepal, treks do venture into very remote regions.

To gain the greatest enjoyment from trek, it is necessary to plan carefully beginning six months to a year before the trek depending on the intended duration and destination. You must take care of immunization, passports, or permits and you must get into good shape. Choosing the right trek and the right mode of trekking for you is of primary importance and can take time. What are your interests—people, mountains, birds, wildlife? When should you, or can you, go trekking? These are some of the questions that this chapter answers as it helps you prepare for one of the most memorable experiences of your life.

1 Booking a Trek

BOOKING YOUR TREK AT HOME

If you have more money than time or if you like to have everything arranged before starting out on a trip, you will probably want to book your trek through an agency in your home country. By booking your trek this way, you will let someone else take care of all the arrangements; all you need do is show up in good health with your bag.

All of the major trekking companies in Nepal have overseas agents, and that is how they get most of their business. Agencies in the United States that offer treks in Nepal usually call themselves adventure-travel specialists or something of that nature. The largest of these companies tend to advertise in such magazines as *Outside* and *Sierra*. Among the largest and best U.S. and U.K. companies offering treks in Nepal are the following (quoted rates include ground costs within Nepal but do not include airfare to and from Nepal):

IN THE U.S.

Above the Clouds, P.O. Box 398, Worcester, MA 01602-0398 (☎ 508/799-4499 or 800/233-4499; fax 508/797-4779). Rates for 1995 treks ranged from $1,150 for an 8-day trip to $2,450 for a 30-day trip.

Adventure Center, 1311-63rd St., Suite 200, Emeryville, CA 94608 (☎ 510/654-1879 or 800/227-8747; fax 510/654-4200). Rates in 1995 ranged from $599 for a 4-day trek to $2,166 for a 22-day trip to Mustang.

InnerAsia Expeditions, 2627 Lombard St., San Francisco, CA 94123 (☎ 415/922-0448 or 800/777-8183). Rates for 1995 ranged from $1,790 for a 10-day trek to $3,320 for a 28-day trek.

Journeys, 4011 Jackson Rd., Ann Arbor, MI 48103 (☎ 313/665-4407 or 800/255-8735). Rates for 1995 ranged from $895 for a 4-day trip to $3,585 for a 22-day trip.

Lute Jerstad Adventures International, P.O. Box 19537, Portland, OR 97280 (☎ 503/244-6075; fax 503/244-1349). Founded by famed mountaineer Lute Jerstad, this company is the U.S. representative for Mountain Travel in Nepal, the oldest trekking company in Nepal. Rates in 1995 ranged from $1,795 for a 17-day trip to $3,525 for a 22-day trip.

Mountain Travel Sobek, 6420 Fairmount Ave., El Cerrito, CA 94530-3606 (☎ 510/527-8100 or 800/227-2384; fax 510/525-7710). This company is a merger of the two oldest adventure-travel companies in the United States. Treks in 1995 ranged in price from $1,895 for a 10-day trek to $3,190 for an 18-day trek.

Overseas Adventure Travel, 349 Broadway, Cambridge, MA 02139 (☎ 617/876-0533 or 800/221-0814; fax 617/876-0455). Rates (including airfare from the U.S.) for 1995 ranged from $3,490 for a 17-day trip trip that includes a 9-day trek to $3,990 for 27-day trip that includes a 19-day trek.

Wilderness Travel, 801 Allston Way, Berkeley, CA 94710 (☎ 510/548-0420 or 800/368-2794; fax 510/548-0347). Another of the largest and most reliable adventure-travel companies in the U.S., Wilderness Travel treks for 1995 ranged in cost from $1,695 for an 18-day trip with a 10-day trek to $2,595 for a 22-day trek.

IN THE U.K.

Classic Nepal, 33 Metro Ave., Newton, Alfreton, Derbyshire DE55 5UF (☎ 01773/873497; fax 01773/590243). Rates for 1995 (airfare from London included) ranged from £1,445 for a trip that includes a 7-day trek to £2,395 for 15-day trek to Mustang. Several mountain-climbing treks are also offered. In 1993, this company organized a reunion trek for Sir Edmund Hillary and the other members of his 1953 Everest expedition.

Exodus, 9 Weir Rd., London SW12 0LT (☎ 081/675-5550; fax 081/673-0779). Rates for 1995 ranged from $1,650 for a 16-day trek to $2,550 for a 15-day trek to the Mustang region.

Explore, 1 Frederick St., Aldershot, Hampshire GU11 1LQ (☎ 01252/319448; fax 01252/343170). Rates for 1995 ranged from $1,120 for a 12-day trek to $1,745 for a 22- or 23-day trek. Note that these prices are in U.S. dollars.

Himalayan Kingdoms, 20 The Mall, Clifton, Bristol BS8 4DR (☎ 0117/923-7163; fax 0117/974-4993). Rates in 1995 (airfare from London included) ranged from £1,695 for a 15-day trek to £2,695 for a 14-day trek to the Mustang region. This company also offers several mountain-climbing expeditions.

Karakoram Experience, 32 Lake Rd., Keswick, Cumbria CA12 5DQ (☎ 017687/73966; fax 017687/74693). This company specializes in treks that include mountain climbing. Rates in 1995 ranged from £1,480 to £2,130 for 24-day treks.

Sherpa Expeditions, 131a Heston Rd. Hounslow, Middlesex TW5 0RD (☎ 081/577-2717; fax 081/572-9788). Rates for 1995 ranged from £1,325 for a 15-day trek to £1,945 for a 23-day trek.

SOCIALLY RESPONSIBLE TREKKING

There are a number of ways that you can make your visit to Nepal socially responsible. By doing what you can to reduce your use of firewood (showering less often, eating local foods, dressing warmly instead of sitting by a fire), you will be helping preserve the forests of the Nepali Himalayas. Respecting local customs, packing out nonbiodegradable garbage, and avoiding the purchase of bottled water will all help minimize your personal impact on the Himalayas. However, there are ways to do more than just minimize your impact.

Journeys (see "Booking a Trek," above, for address) offers several tree-planting trips that allow trekkers to assist in a reforestation project.

The Center for Himalayan Research & Studies, 14600 SE Aldridge Rd., Portland, OR 97236-6518 (☎ 503/658-6600 or 800/225-4666), offers treks that include volunteer-assisted service projects to distribute school supplies to remote schools in the Himalayas. **Sagarmatha Environmental Expedition,** 2216 38th Place East, Seattle, WA 98112 (☎ 206/726-0575), has in the past mounted expeditions that combined climbing Mt. Everest with picking up garbage left behind by past mountain-climbing expeditions. Contact this organization for more information on their trips.

BOOKING YOUR TREK IN NEPAL

If you have more time than money, you should consider booking your trek after you arrive in Nepal. Trekking rates when you book this way can be as low as $15 a day for a teahouse trek or up to $65 a day for an organized group trek with porters, guides, and cooks. Before visiting a Kathmandu trekking agency, decide which type of trek you prefer—a teahouse trek or an organized trek using tents.

On a teahouse trek you will be staying in village lodges used primarily by independent trekkers. This type of trek is the least expensive type of trek you can book through a trekking agency. Basically what you are doing is hiring a guide and a porter to walk with you from village to village.

An organized trek, on the other hand, includes a large entourage of Sherpas, porters, cooks, and kitchen boys and is not restricted to staying near villages. On this sort of trek you can camp wherever there is water. However, on the more popular routes, these group treks almost always use lodge gardens as their campgrounds, which seems a bit silly. More remote and less traveled routes provide a truer glimpse of life in the hills of Nepal and also give you a greater feeling of adventure because you see fewer other trekkers. I highly recommend asking about treks that do not follow the popular teahouse trekking routes.

When arranging a trek, it is almost always cheaper per person if you have four or more people in your group. In fact, some companies will not arrange treks for fewer than three or four people. Treks in the Annapurna region and north of Kathmandu in Helambu and Langtang are less expensive than treks in other areas. The price that a trekking agency will quote you most likely will not include such additional costs as trekking permits, Annapurna Conservation Area Project entrance fees, national park entrance fees, porter insurance, or transportation costs. Be sure to ask about these charges so that you will know what your total costs will be.

The following Kathmandu trekking agencies are known for well-organized treks and are highly recommended. The rates listed with each company include the cost of a guide, porters, cooks, tent, sleeping bag, mattress, kitchen equipment, food, transportation within Nepal (though sometimes domestic flights are extra), trekking permit, and visa extensions but do not include national park entrance fees.

Before booking your trek, you might want to stop by the **Kathmandu Environmental Education Project,** Potala Guest Home (☎ 977/1-410303), which is located up the lane from the Tilicho Hotel on Tridevi Marg near the Department of Immigration. Here you can learn about altitude sickness, register with your embassy, read other trekkers' comments about various treks, find out which are the most environmentally conscious trekking companies, and learn how you can minimize your impact on Nepal's environment and culture. This information center is open Sunday through Friday from 10am to 5pm.

Mountain Travel, Lazimpat (P.O. Box 170), Kathmandu (☎ 977/1-414508; fax 977/1-414075). Though they cater primarily to groups who make reservations through foreign agents, it is possible to arrange a trek with Mountain Travel after you arrive in Nepal. Rates are about the highest in the country, but their years of experience make them the best in the business. Rates average around $65 per person per day. You'll find their office on the road behind the Royal Palace.

Asian Trekking, Keshar Mahal (P.O. Box 3022), Thamel, Kathmandu (☎ 977/1-413732; fax 977/1-411878). Rates range from $45 to $120 per person per day. You'll find their office up the first road to your right as you walk from the Department of Immigration toward Thamel.

Ganesh Himal Trekking, Thamel (P.O. Box 3854), Kathmandu (☎ 977/1-416282). Current rates are $50 to $55 per person per day for a minimum of two people, depending on what region is trekked. Teahouse treks cost around $20 to $40 per person per day depending on where you trek. You'll find their office up the street that leads north from Thamel's main square.

Eco Trek, Thamel (P.O. Box 6438), Kathmandu (☎ 977/1-417420; fax 977/1-413118) offers a wide variety of treks in different regions at different budgets. The company tries to be as environmentally conscious as possible. Among other things, it publishes *Everest Voice,* a quarterly journal focusing on environmental issues in Nepal. Trekking rates range from $32 to $50 per person per day. You'll find this office on the main road into Thamel on the same side of the street as the Department of Immigration.

Himalayan Encounters, Kathmandu Guest House Courtyard (P.O. Box 2769), Thamel, Kathmandu (☎ 977/1-417426; fax 977/1-417133), became known for its white-water rafting trips but now offers treks as well. Most of the treks offered by this company are fairly short, though many are through areas not normally traveled by independent trekkers. The rate for most treks is $45 per day.

Himalayan Expeditions, Thamel Chowk (P.O. Box 105), Kathmandu (☎ 977/1-226622 or 977/1-229031; fax 977/1-526575 or 977/1-228890), is a small trekking company offering well-organized trips and very reliable service. Treks in all regions of Nepal can be arranged. Daily rates range from $35 to $50 per person per day. You'll find this office about 100 yards down the street from the Kathmandu Guest House on the same side of the street.

Mountain Way Trekking, Nepal Rastra Bank Chowk (P.O. Box 59), Pokhara (☎ 977/61-20316; fax 977/61-21240). In Pokhara, there are only a handful of trekking agencies. This is one very reliable company that organizes both teahouse treks for individuals and group treks. Rates range from $30 to $75 per person per day. You can hire a guide and porter for about $21 per day.

INDEPENDENT TREKKING

If you are an experienced traveler and backpacker, you will probably want to hit the trail on your own. This is by far the cheapest trekking option, and there are several different ways to go about it. Unless you have brought your own tent, you will be staying in lodges along the trail. You will probably meet plenty of other independent trekkers along the way. In fact, during the busy October-November trekking season, you may meet far more trekkers than you ever imagined you would encounter. If you don't want to see many other trekkers, I suggest that you arrange a trek through a trekking agency.

ON YOUR OWN

It is no longer a good idea to trek alone. In the past few years, crime on the trail has been increasing. Each year a few trekkers are murdered or simply disappear, and others are robbed. Individuals should either find some trekking companions or hire a porter or guide. Those seeking trekking partners often put up notices on the bulletin board at the Kathmandu Environmental Education Project office near the Department of Immigration. This is also an excellent place to learn more about altitude sickness and about how to lessen your impact on the environment and culture of Nepal. Even if you don't need to find a trekking companion, you should stop by here.

Restaurants around Thamel and Freak Street also have bulletin boards that you can check. Try Pumpernickel Bakery in Thamel. Another option is simply to strike up a conversation with someone interesting while standing in line for your trekking permit. Just look for someone carrying the same color papers that you have. If this fails, you can always leave for the trailhead and hope to meet someone in transit (very likely, especially on busy routes). If this fails and you reach the trailhead without a companion, you can either wait around for a while to see if anyone shows up who doesn't mind your joining their trek or start asking around for a porter. I have found excellent trekking companions this way.

WITH A GUIDE

Trails can be difficult to follow even with the best trekking guidebook. Trails change with every monsoon, and more hotels are built every year. Therefore, it is worth having a guide who is familiar with the year-to-year changes or who can ask local residents about trail conditions or for directions. I once trekked without a guide and was forced to spend Christmas Eve in a half-constructed building when, in a thick fog, I missed a village that was slightly off the trail. In the clear skies of dawn, I saw less than a quarter of a mile away a newly opened trekkers' lodge to which a guide could have directed me.

Traditionally trekking and mountaineering guides have been Sherpas, who come from the high elevations of the Solu-Khumbu region near Mt. Everest. Their knowledge of the mountains has made them legendary, and the term "Sherpa" is often used interchangeably with guide.

Guides who speak English well are always more expensive than those who do not, and it is sometimes possible to hire what is called a porter–guide, which is a guide in training. This type of guide will carry your pack and will help you stay on the right trail but usually speaks only a few words of English. A porter–guide costs more than a porter but less than a guide.

Daily rates for hiring a guide range from around $8 to $20, which may or may not include the guide's room and board along the trail. Most smaller trekking companies will quote you a rate that does not include food and lodging. In this case, you can expect to pay an additional $7 or so per day for your guide's room and board. A porter–guide can usually be hired for around $6 to $10 per day. Guides can be hired at smaller trekking companies around Thamel and in Pokhara. It is not advisable to hire someone off the street. Larger trekking agencies that deal primarily in group treks may or may not be willing to arrange a guide for you.

WITH ONLY A PORTER

If you need to cut costs, you may want to head out with only a porter. A porter will carry your pack for $3 to $6 a day (plus room and board) but rarely speaks English. Though porters are not expected to inquire about trail conditions or lead the way, they will often perform this duty simply to avoid getting lost. Porters are inexpensive to hire, and by carrying your pack, they make it much easier for you to walk up and down steep mountain trails.

Despite carrying your pack, your porter is likely to travel faster than you do. It is always a good idea to carry whatever things you might need during the day, such as a water bottle, first-aid kit, and camera, in a day pack that you carry yourself. Before setting out in the morning, you should make it clear where you plan to stop next, whether it is for tea or lunch or for the day. That way your porter will know where to stop and won't get too far ahead of you. At other times, your porter may lag a ways behind you, especially if you are a particularly fast walker. If this is the case, try to keep in mind that your porter may have had only tea for breakfast and will want to stop for lunch around 10am, the traditional Nepali time for the midday meal.

Though I have not met anyone who has had anything stolen by a porter, it does happen. The best way to avoid this is to hire your porter through an established and trustworthy trekking agency. I have listed the names of a few such companies (see "Booking Your Trek in Nepal," above), but you can also ask around once you reach Kathmandu. People who have just returned from trekking may be able to recommend the company they used.

If you plan to trek in the winter months or at very high elevations, it is your responsibility to provide your porter with adequate shoes, jacket, sleeping bag, sunglasses, and other sundries. Your responsibilities should all be clarified before leaving Kathmandu or Pokhara. With the exception of Namche Bazaar near Mt. Everest, there are few places on any trail where you can rent or buy appropriate gear for your porter.

WITH A PORTER AND GUIDE

Even if you are not going on a group trek, you can have a traditional trekking experience by hiring both a porter and a guide. The porter carries your pack, and the guide shows the way, acts as interpreter, and explains things along the trail. Though it costs a bit more, this arrangement can be very beneficial. Not only are you freed from the burden of carrying a pack, but you also learn more about Nepal, and your porter and guide have someone to talk to other than you. This may sound strange, but you can easily tire of carrying on minimal conversations with a porter or guide. This is not so important if you are traveling with a companion, but if you are traveling alone, it is tiresome always to be struggling to communicate in a smattering of English and Nepali.

2 Preparing for a Trek

PREPARING PHYSICALLY

Though it is possible for someone who is completely out of shape to go trekking, it is a much more pleasurable experience if you are physically prepared for the rigors involved. While almost anyone can go trekking, hiking in the Himalayas does entail a good deal of physical exertion, sometimes at altitudes higher than any you may have been at before. The best way to prepare for a trek is to begin or maintain a regular program of aerobic exercise several times a week. This will develop the cardiovascular system and give you more stamina. However, trekking in the Himalayas presents challenges for which a simple exercise regimen cannot prepare you. On several of the most popular treks there are ascents and descents of 2,000 to 6,000 feet at a time. This is usually on trails that have been made into seemingly endless stairways by the locals who prefer a steep, but direct, route over an indirect route with switchbacks. Legs, especially knees, take a real beating on these unrelenting stairways. The best way to prepare yourself for these trails is to find a tall building and walk up and down the fire escape stairs with a loaded backpack. This is only a simulation of how difficult a trail in Nepal might be since you will be climbing such stairs at elevations likely to deprive you of your normal intake of oxygen, which will cause additional fatigue. Remember also that even the most physically fit person can develop altitude sickness, and some people claim that those people who are slightly less fit and who are a bit overweight are *less* likely to develop altitude sickness. Should you prepare yourself physically, however, you will enjoy your trek far more than if you had come totally unprepared for the difficulties that may lay ahead.

One other piece of advice I want to share: Don't spend too much time in Kathmandu before going trekking. Kathmandu has a bad reputation for giving people gastrointestinal and respiratory problems. The sooner you get onto the trail the more likely you are to have all your strength for your trek. Even the most physically fit person can become too weak to trek after a several-day bout with diarrhea or a bad chest cold.

INSURANCE & HELICOPTER RESCUES

While trekking you may be many days' walk from the nearest medical facility or doctor. In the event of an emergency, it is possible to be evacuated by helicopter. The cost of a helicopter evacuation is $600 to $1,400 per hour. A rescue operation will usually take two to three hours, so you can expect to pay as much as $1,200 to $4,200. Before the helicopter will take off, there must be proof of ability to pay. Neither a trekking agency nor your embassy nor the Nepali government will pay the bill. If you happen to have enough cash on you, then you won't have a problem, but most people don't carry this much money with them while trekking. The best solution is to take out travel-assistance insurance that provides evacuation coverage. This insurance is not available in Nepal, so it is very important that you get it before leaving home. If you are going on a group trek, you will most likely have to show proof that you have such insurance before you will be allowed to participate in the trek. Adventure-travel companies outside Nepal will be able to arrange such insurance for you. If you are traveling on your own, you should let your embassy know that you are going trekking and that you have evacuation insurance. See "Health, Insurance & Other Concerns" in Chapter 2 for a list of insurance companies that provide this type of insurance.

If you or someone in your party needs to be evacuated by helicopter, here is the procedure you must follow. First, locate the nearest two-way radio, telegraph, or telephone and contact Kathmandu. You will need to relay the following information to your embassy or trekking agent: injured person's name, passport number, location, nature of emergency, whether a medical team needs to be on board the helicopter, and identification of the person supplying the information to the authorities in Kathmandu. Before the helicopter will leave Kathmandu, your trekking agent or embassy must guarantee payment for the rescue.

HEALTH & OTHER CONCERNS
WATER

Never drink untreated water. It's that simple. All water, whether from a village water tap, stream, or spring, should be considered contaminated. Though this is not always the case, taking chances while trekking can lead to extreme complications. However, even if you do treat your water, you will not be able to know whether your tea is safe to drink. It is questionable whether tea has been boiled long enough to kill any bacteria or protozoa that might be present, but this is an unavoidable risk of trekking. You should always carry a water bottle and a means of treating water, such as a bottle of iodine or a two-stage filter. Be especially wary of cold water or lemonade that is handed to you on a group trek. In their desire to please you, porters and cooks will sometimes tell you that cold water has been treated when it has not. It is best to only drink cold water that you have prepared yourself. See "Health, Insurance & Other Concerns" in Chapter 2 for details on ways of treating water.

It is also important to drink plenty of fluids when trekking at higher elevations. It is very easy to become dehydrated above 9,000 feet, even if you are not exercising heavily. Frequent stops for tea are one of the best ways to avoid dehydration, and such stops also prevent you from overexerting yourself. To avoid dehydration, drink enough fluids to maintain a normal output of urine. If you do feel that you are dehydrated, it is a good idea to mix some rehydration salts (electrolyte powder) into your water bottle, especially if you have been sweating a lot.

FIRST-AID KIT

Your first-aid kit is one of the most important pieces of equipment in your pack. On the trail you will often be several days' walk from the nearest clinic and even farther from the nearest hospital or doctor. You must be prepared for a wide variety of possible illnesses and accidents. You may find that your first-aid kit seems excessively large, but over the years, I have used almost every item I carry. Your first-aid kit should include the following supplies and medications. This should be enough for two people.

- thermometer
- scissors—for cutting bandages and tape
- tweezers—for removing splinters, etc.
- needle and thread—for stitching wounds
- 4 butterfly bandages—used in place of stitches
- 1 roll of surgical tape—for taping down gauze pads and cotton bandages
- 3 small gauze pads—for covering wounds and infected eyes
- 3 large gauze pads—for covering larger wounds
- 2 rolls of cotton bandages—for dressing large wounds
- 1 triangular bandage—for a sling
- 20 adhesive bandages in an assortment of sizes—for protecting cuts
- 1 dropper bottle of antiseptic such as iodine—for sterilizing cuts. Best purchased at home because those sold in Nepal tend to leak.
- 1 Ace Bandage (elastic bandage)—for sprains, strains, and twists, especially of the knee
- 1 package Moleskin—used to prevent blisters. Not available in Nepal.
- 1 package Second Skin—used to protect blisters after they form. Not available in Nepal.

Medications

The medications listed below are just a recommendation of what to include in your first-aid kit. Consult your doctor for any necessary prescriptions, dosages, and warnings. For further advice on immunizations and medications, contact the nearest International Health Care office in your area.

- Acetaminophen—for fever, aches, and pain. Unlike aspirin, this drug will not reduce swelling or inflammation. Sold as Paracetamol in Nepal.
- antibiotics—useful in treating a variety of bacterial infections including diarrhea, urinary-tract infections, bronchitis, inner-ear infections, sinusitis, strep throat, and skin infections
- antidiarrheal or antimotility drug—will stop diarrhea but will not treat the cause of the diarrhea. Antidiarrheal agents should not be taken if food poisoning is suspected.
- antihistamine and nasal decongestant—used for treating symptoms of colds and hay fever
- antiprotozoal drug—treats giardiasis and amoebas
- anti-itch cream—used to stop the itching of mosquito, flea, and bedbug bites
- aspirin—for aches, pain, fever, cold symptoms, inflammation, and swelling
- codeine—useful in suppressing a cough and in reducing diarrhea
- Diamox (acetazolamide)—to relieve minor symptoms (headaches, nausea, insomnia) of altitude sickness. This is not a cure, and signs of acute mountain sickness should not be ignored.
- eardrops—for treatment of outer ear canal infections
- eyedrops—to treat bacterial eye infections (conjunctivitis) that are very common in Nepal
- hydrocortisone cream—used to stop itching caused by rashes and insect bites
- Mycostatin—for treatment of vaginal yeast infections. Yeast infections frequently develop after a course of strong antibiotics.

- Pepto-Bismol tablets—your first line of defense against upset stomach and diarrhea. Pepto-Bismol is not sold in Nepal.
- rehydration salts—oral rehydration salts (electrolyte solution) should be added to a quart or liter of treated water and drunk by those suffering from severe diarrhea. Oral rehydration salts are sold as Jeevan Jal in Nepal and are very inexpensive. In the United States they are available at outdoor-equipment and sporting-goods stores.
- sore-throat lozenges—sore throats are a fact of life in Nepal where the winds pick up a lot of dust. Trekkers, especially in the winter months, often have chronic sore throats from all the dust.
- sunscreen—despite the cool temperatures you are likely to encounter during the prime trekking seasons, Nepal is a subtropical country, which means that the sun is probably stronger than in your home country. It is very easy to get sunburned while bicycling in the Kathmandu Valley, and at high elevations, the sun is particularly intense. If you keep your arms and legs covered, you will need only enough sunscreen to keep your face and hands protected.

WHAT TO PACK BEFORE YOU LEAVE HOME

The key to staying comfortable on a trek is layering. Temperatures can vary 30° or 40° between night and midday, so you need to be prepared with a variety of clothing. During the day, you will generate a lot of heat just walking, especially if you are carrying a pack. Even in November, shorts and a T-shirt are adequate attire in the middle of the day, but at night, you'll need thermal underwear, wool socks, and a down jacket. Even a stop for tea or lunch will require a change into dry warm clothes, so keep these items handy. In December or January, I start the day wearing shorts and loose pants, a T-shirt or thermal undershirt, cotton shirt, wool sweater, and down jacket. Within a few minutes of setting out, I usually have the jacket off. In another 30 minutes or so the sweater and long pants usually come off. When I stop for lunch, I put the sweater and sometimes the jacket back on. At the end of the day I change into my dry evening layers, including thermal underwear, top and bottom. All this layering, however, is only necessary at higher elevations and during the winter months (late November to early February). In October and early November, you normally won't need so much warm clothing, but it's still a good idea to have it along.

Boots   The single most important item to pack for trekking in Nepal is a good pair of hiking boots. To avoid developing blisters while trekking, boots should be broken in thoroughly before leaving. Since you can easily walk 150 miles or more on a two-week trek, it is crucial that your boots are sturdy, rugged, and well-made so that they stand up to the strain of steep trails. I have worn lightweight nylon hiking boots, leather boots, and leather-and-nylon boots and still prefer the heavier leather boots because of the ankle support they offer. Nylon boots also tend to have thinner soles, which do not adequately protect your feet from stones on the trail. A few days of feeling pebbles through the soles of your boots is sure to make your feet tender and sensitive. Although a wide assortment of hiking boots, both new and used, is now available in Kathmandu, it is a much better idea to get your boots before arriving so that you can break them in.

Sneakers   It's a good idea to carry some sort of lightweight athletic shoe with you for switching into at night, because your boots are likely to be quite damp from sweat after a day of hiking. Also, should your hiking boots give you blisters or give out on you entirely, you can hike in your athletic shoes. A nylon running shoe with a sole that provides good traction is the best choice.

Socks   Good boots should be accompanied by appropriate socks. Polypropylene sock liners and wool outer socks are still the best combination for keeping your feet dry and free from blisters. I like to carry three pairs of each type of sock. I keep one pair of wool socks for changing into at night and alternate between the other two pairs during the day. Wool socks take a long time to dry. Try to put them near the cooking fire after washing them.

Down jacket   Though it can be hot in Kathmandu in October and November, higher up in the mountains, you might find yourself caught in a snowstorm. Down jackets are the best choice because they offer warmth without a lot of weight. Some people prefer fiber-filled jackets because, although they are heavier than down, they provide warmth even when wet. However, you are not likely to encounter much rain in Nepal during the normal trekking seasons. Down jackets can be rented in Kathmandu.

Wool sweater or synthetic fleece jacket   Despite its weight, wool is still one of the best materials to have on a trek. It will keep you warm even if it's wet. The wool sweaters sold in Kathmandu, though pretty, are neither tightly woven enough nor durable enough for life on the trail. In the past few years, synthetic fleece jackets have surpassed wool sweaters in popularity. These jackets offer the same benefits of wool.

Shorts   Men (and women who don't mind being stared at) will want a sturdy pair of walking shorts. Even in late November, long pants can be too hot during the day. By wearing your shorts while you hike, you can keep your long pants dry for the evening.

Long skirt   Most Nepali women hike in long skirts. Though this idea may seem strange to most Western women accustomed to wearing shorts or pants, it is not such a bad idea. A spacious, midcalf length skirt provides room for long strides yet makes it easy to relieve oneself by the side of the trail when it is almost impossible to find any privacy.

Wool or synthetic fleece pants   If you plan to hike in December or January, wool or synthetic fleece pants are a good idea, especially above 9,000 feet, where nights and early mornings are cold.

Loose cotton or nylon pants   Pants that you can pull on over your shorts make it easy to change from warm pants to shorts as you are walking along the trail. The cotton drawstring pants available for a few dollars in Kathmandu are excellent for this, as are nylon warm-up pants.

Down pants   These are really only necessary if you are planning to spend several days above 12,000 feet in midwinter. At other times of year and at lower elevations they are simply too hot. These can be rented in Kathmandu.

Thermal underwear   Silk or polypropylene thermal underwear is a necessity at night from November through January, and at higher elevations even during the day. Above Jomosom strong winds can cut right through a single layer of pants or through a sweater and shirt.

Rain gear   Though you are not likely to encounter more than one or two days of rain while trekking (if any at all), it is still a good idea to be prepared for it. A simple plastic or coated nylon poncho that you can wear over your pack is the best choice, since it keeps your pack dry as well and won't cause you to sweat excessively in warm weather. Goretex rain gear is the high-tech solution. This expensive clothing keeps the rain off while allowing moisture from your skin to get out. Consequently, you don't end up soaked with sweat as you might with rain gear that doesn't breathe.

Wool or synthetic fleece hat   I usually carry a beret that I can pull over my ears, while others prefer a balaclava or ski hat. There are also good wool hats with earflaps available in Kathmandu. Some people also like to bring a sun hat to keep the glare out of their eyes.

Gloves or mittens   Wool gloves or mittens are necessary at night at high elevations and in the winter. Since you aren't likely to need your fingers for much, mittens are the better choice. A combination of polypropylene glove liners and wool mittens or ski gloves are the best choice for high-elevation winter treks.

Sunglasses   If you expect to be crossing any snowy areas, sunglasses are essential to prevent snow blindness. Sunglasses also come in handy during dust storms, which are frequent around Manang and Jomosom.

Sleeping bag   Either a down or a fiber-filled bag designed to keep you warm at temperatures below freezing is the best bet. If you are planning to trek in the Everest region or anywhere else above 11,000 feet in December or January, you can expect temperatures well below freezing at night. Be prepared.

Backpack or duffel bag   If you plan to carry your own load, you'll want a comfortable backpack. There are hundreds of different models available in several different basic styles. I prefer an internal-frame travel pack that can be converted into a suitcase for airplane travel. If you get one of these packs, make sure it is a backpack that can be converted rather than a suitcase that can be put on the back. A good travel pack has all the hip, shoulder, and neck adjustment straps of a good backpack. Many people still prefer an external-frame pack, but these are bulky and difficult to get into crowded buses. If you are going on a group trek, a large duffel bag is really all you need since whatever bag you are using will likely be crammed into a porter's large basket.

Day pack   A small pack is essential if you plan to trek with a porter. You should keep your water bottle, camera, snacks, rain gear, and some warm clothing in your day pack.

Flashlight   A good flashlight is an absolute necessity when trekking since you will only rarely be in a village with electricity, and even then, the power is only on for a few hours at night. The best choice is a miner's-type headlamp that is worn on an elastic headband. These lights leave your hands free for reading and, more importantly, balancing yourself in dirty outhouses. This type of flashlight is available at most outdoor-equipment stores. Only large flashlights requiring heavy D-cell batteries are available in Nepal, but they are available almost anywhere. Be sure to bring spare batteries.

Water bottle   A one-quart (liter) water bottle is a necessity while trekking. Never drink water that has not been treated. I carry a small bottle of iodine to treat my water. This saves firewood since it is not necessary to boil the water if you treat it with iodine. If you have no iodine, ask to have your bottle filled with boiled water whenever necessary. However, this method is not guaranteed because you have no assurance that the water has been boiled long enough to kill any bacteria or protozoa. This is the same risk you take when drinking tea on the trail and is, unfortunately, unavoidable.

Playing Cards   Card playing is very popular along the trail, especially when cold weather keeps people indoors for a good part of the day.

TREKKING PERMITS

For some people the most difficult part of trekking is acquiring a trekking permit. In fact, I'm one of those people. Securing your trekking permit can be a frustrating ordeal that tries your patience, or it can be a chance to practice a bit of that newfound Eastern philosophy you picked up since your arrival in the country. First let it be said that you will need the better part of a day to get a trekking permit in Kathmandu. Secondly, it is slightly easier to get a trekking permit in Pokhara.

If you are going on an organized trek with a trekking company, you won't have to deal with any of these hardships, but if you are the adventurous type setting out on your own for a teahouse trek, here is the lowdown.

First you will need your passport and two extra passport-size photos of yourself. If you forgot to bring some spare photos with you, you can have some made directly across the street from the Department of Immigration office in Kathmandu. In Pokhara you can have photos made next door to the currency-exchange counter down the street from the Department of Immigration. Instant photos cost the most and overnight photos the least. Either way, it is cheaper to have photos made here than in the United States. If you are traveling to other countries in Asia, get a bunch made. You will probably need them.

You must next fill out the trekking-permit request form and the trekking permit itself. These two forms are available at the counter just inside the front door of the Department of Immigration in Kathmandu. In Pokhara, you can get these forms at the window on the left side of the Department of Immigration.

Permits are color coded according to regions. For instance, the trekking permit (heavy card) and trekking-permit request form (flimsy tissue paper) for Langtang, Gosainkund, and Helambu are both blue. Simple. Make sure that you have the right color for the region in which you will be trekking and that your two pieces of paper are the same color. If you have time, I suggest picking up your forms one day, filling them out at your leisure, and coming back the next morning to turn them in.

Once you have filled out both forms, it is time to stand in line. If you did as I suggested and filled out your forms in advance, you might get to go to the head of the line. Regardless, if it is the busy trekking season of October and November, you can count on a line forming at least two hours before the office opens. Once inside, make sure you are in the correct line. Some of the lines are for visa extensions, and some are for trekking permits. When you finally get to the window, hand over your passport, passport photos, trekking permit, and trekking-permit request form. The man at the counter will check your passport to make sure that your visa is valid. He will also check to see if you have been trekking already in the same calendar year. Trekking fees increase after your first four weeks of trekking in one calendar year. Currently the fees are $5 per week for the first four weeks and then $10 per week for the next eight weeks after that. You have to pay for an entire week, so even if you are only going for 10 days, tell them you are going for 14, just in case something happens or you decide to extend your trek. You are allowed a maximum of 90 days trekking per calendar year.

Packing in Nepal for a Trek

If you decide after arriving in Kathmandu that you want to go trekking, it is possible to rent jackets, sleeping bags, and other essentials. There are numerous shops around Thamel in Kathmandu and in the Lakeside and Damside neighborhoods of Pokhara that rent trekking equipment. Most rental items such as down sleeping bags and jackets rent for between Rs20 and Rs30 (40¢ and 60¢) per item per day. You will also have to leave a deposit of between $20 and $100 per item. Other items to pick up before hitting the trail are toilet paper, oral rehydration salts, and iodine.

If you plan to be trekking beyond the 30 days of your visa, you will have to get a visa extension in addition to your trekking permit. In the past a trekking permit could serve as a visa extension, but this is no longer the case. Visa extensions cost $1 per day.

The Department of Immigration office in Kathmandu is located on Tridevi Marg (☎ 977/1-412337), the road leading into Thamel from the top of Durbar Marg. It is on the north side of the street across from a small temple and a shopping mall. In Pokhara, the office (☎ 977/1-21167) is north of the Hotel Tragopan on Ratnapuri. Though both offices are open Sunday to Thursday from 10am to 4 or 5pm and Friday from 10am to 3pm, the Kathmandu office only accepts permit applications from 10am to 1pm (noon on Friday).

MAPS

Maps of various qualities and with different contour intervals are available at bookshops in Kathmandu and Pokhara. The best are German Schneider maps, but these are expensive and hard to find. The next best maps are the Italian-designed Nepa Maps, which cost around Rs125 ($2.50) and are available at many bookstores in Kathmandu and Pokhara. More common are the maps published by Mandala Trekking Maps in Kathmandu. These sell for about Rs30 (60¢) and are fairly accurate. Some of these maps now include route descriptions printed on the back. These are quite helpful and cost only a few cents more than maps without route descriptions.

3　When to Trek

Because Nepal is subject to monsoon rains from June through mid-October, the trekking season is effectively limited to October through May. However, the favored period is the six weeks immediately following the monsoon between mid-October and the end of November. During this time the skies are usually clear for most of the day, there is rarely any rain or snow, and temperatures are warm by day and cool at night. At lower elevations it is even too hot for vigorous exercise, and trekking at such elevations can be quite unpleasant. Though many people arrive in the first week of October, I have found that there is usually rain as late as the 18th of the month, so it is best to arrive around October 20th. Because this is the busiest season of the year, there are long lines for trekking permits, and you will encounter hundreds of other trekkers on the more popular trails.

From the end of November through the end of January, my favorite time to trek, the weather is cold and clear with temperatures going below freezing at night at altitudes above 3,000 feet. During the day, however, the cool temperatures make trekking very pleasant. You can expect one or two days of rain sometime during this period. Fewer people choose to trek in this season so lines are shorter and there are fewer trekkers on the trail.

By the end of January, the weather begins to warm up again, making February and March the next most popular trekking months. The sky is clear most of the time, though haze begins to obscure the views of the mountains. By April it is very hot in Nepal at elevations below 3,000 feet, and even above this elevation it can be too hot to trek comfortably. Also, the haze obscures the mountains almost entirely.

4 What the Trekking Routes Have to Offer

VIEWS

For most people who have never been to Nepal, the chance to view the Himalayas is the primary reason for trekking in Nepal. The Himalayas, the highest mountain range on earth, are by far the most spectacular mountains as well. Imagine hiking at elevations above 13,000 feet (almost as high as the highest mountains in North America) and gazing up at mountain peaks that are another 13,000 feet higher. Mt. Everest is more than twice as high as the highest mountain in North America. There are, however, no treks with nonstop views since all the trails ascend and descend. Often you will have no view until you reach the crest of a ridge. Also keep in mind that the Himalayas are often obscured by clouds in the afternoon. Try to be at spots with particularly good views early in the day.

Some of the best views in Nepal include the view from Poon Hill on the Jomosom trek, the view inside the Annapurna Sanctuary, and the views from Namche Bazaar, Thyangboche Monastery, Gokyo, and Kala Pattar in the Khumbu region near Mt. Everest.

ECOLOGICAL DIVERSITY

For viewing ecological diversity, a trek that crosses to the north side of the Himalayas is the best choice. The trek around Annapurna and the trek from Jiri to Everest Base Camp provide the greatest ecological diversity because you start at around 3,000 feet in regions where bananas and papayas grow and rise to more than 17,000 feet where the climate is dry and harsh. If you do not care to climb to such high elevations, it is possible to experience as much diversity simply by trekking as far as Manang or Muktinath.

CULTURAL DIVERSITY

Nepal is an ethnic mosaic. Different ethnic groups inhabit different regions, whose composition often varies with elevation. Each ethnic group has its own cultural identity, which is often most evident to trekkers by the different styles of dress and architecture. The trek from Pokhara to Muktinath offers the greatest cultural diversity of any in Nepal. Along this route you will pass through Thakali, Gurung, and Magar villages, and in the higher elevations, the people are closely related to Tibetans.

TREKKING PEAKS

If simply hiking through the beautiful scenery of Nepal's mountains is not enough to assuage your thirst for adventure, you may want to look into climbing a trekking peak. These are peaks that have been designated by the Nepali government as easy enough to be climbed without the aid of a full-scale expedition. However, don't get the idea that a trekking peak is just another easy stroll in the hills. Most of these peaks are over 20,000 feet high and require technical climbing experience and equipment. The best way to climb one of these peaks is with an organized trek. Many of the major trekking companies offer trips to various trekking peaks each year (see "Booking a Trek," above, in this chapter). In addition to a trekking permit, you must also secure a climbing permit from the Nepal Mountaineering Association on Nagpokhari, Naxal (P.O. Box 1435), Kathmandu (☎ 977/1-411525 or 977/1-416278). Permits cost $150 to $300 depending on the height of the mountain you intend to climb.

MOUNTAIN-CLIMBING EXPEDITIONS

Trekking should not be confused with mountain climbing, which requires long and serious planning, large amounts of equipment and supplies, and usually dozens of porters, cooks, and Sherpas as support. The peaks of Nepal are so popular that many of them are booked years in advance by expeditions from all over the world. Even a small expedition can cost thousands of dollars, and the expedition permit alone can cost as much as $50,000. For more information on mountain climbing in Nepal, contact the Nepal Mountaineering Association, Nagpokhari, Naxal, Kathmandu (☎ 977/1-411525 or 977/1-416278). Most adventure-travel companies also arrange mountain-climbing expeditions and can steer you in the direction of more information.

5 Hitting the Trail

What you can expect on the trail varies considerably depending on whether you participate in an organized group trek or go on an independent teahouse trek.

HYGIENE

It is especially important to make every attempt to maintain personal hygiene on the trail. Unfortunately, you will not find much in the way of facilities along the trail. Toilets are generally tiny outhouses equipped with a hole in the ground and nothing else. Often these outhouses are rarely if ever cleaned and can be pretty disgusting. No wonder the locals never use them. Traditionally Nepalis use the fields and bushes to ensure that their lands remain fertile.

If you are staying in a village off the beaten track, you may find that there is no toilet in the entire village. The best thing to do in this case is try to locate the communal toilet area on the edge of the village and use it before sunrise or after sunset, which is what Nepalis do. If you know you will be off the normal trekking routes, carry a trowel and bury your feces. Organized group treks will have a latrine tent set up somewhere near camp.

Washing your hands before eating is one of the best things you can do to avoid developing diarrhea, but water is not always available. When it is available, it may be only a stream or perhaps a communal spigot. It is a good idea to carry some moist towelettes with you to clean your hands when water is not available for washing. Don't expect hot showers while trekking either. If you can live with being dirty for longer than usual, you will be helping to preserve the natural environment of Nepal. Water for showers is usually heated with firewood, and in some areas frequented by trekkers, such as Poon Hill on the Jomosom trek, the hillsides have rapidly become deforested to provide trekkers with the hot baths and showers they demand. Cold showers, though not very comfortable, will get you clean without doing nearly as much damage to the environment as will a small bucket of warm water. Some lodges now have solar showers or water-heating systems that do not require the burning of extra wood for shower water. Several of the treks pass by natural hot springs that are the ideal way to clean up while trekking. Just remember not to use soap in the bathing pools themselves.

You will also need to wash socks and clothes while you are trekking. This is usually done in the nearest stream or at a village water spigot, though it is a good idea to try to avoid using soap in streams. It is a good idea to always keep a set of dry clothes that you only wear in the evening. The clothes you wear while walking during the day are likely to get sweaty, and when you stop walking will become quite cold.

LODGES & TEAHOUSES

When the first independent trekkers began exploring the hills of Nepal, they took their meals and lodging in tea stalls or teahouses called *bhattis*. The term "teahouse trek" is still common for this sort of trek, though the teahouses have graduated into full-scale lodges and hotels on the more popular trails. A trekking lodge is generally constructed in whatever the local style of architecture might be, with a restaurant on the first floor and rooms above. In the past few years most lodges have offered private double rooms, but you will still encounter smaller and older lodges that have only dormitory rooms. These rooms are sometimes directly above the kitchen area and smoke from the open cooking fire may fill the upstairs. If this is the case, about the only thing you can do is stay in the kitchen or dining room until your host family puts out the fire and goes to bed.

Occasionally you may stumble upon a local village celebration or perhaps a family gathering that will likely go on all night with much drinking and noise. If this happens, your only recourse is to join the party, which you will invariably be invited to do. Coughing, crying babies, crowing roosters, family arguments, and the inescapable Radio Nepal broadcasts are other noises that you can expect when staying in a trekking lodge. Though these disturbances may interrupt your sleep, they are all part of the cultural experience of a teahouse trek. In fact, most trekkers are so tired at night that once they fall asleep they never hear a thing.

Whereas traditional bhattis usually serve only tea, dal bhat, and chang or rakshi and cater primarily to porters and traveling Nepalis, newer lodges are built specifically for trekkers. The menus at trekking lodges are amazingly extensive, listing Nepali, Indian, Chinese, English, American, Italian, Swiss, German, and even Mexican meals. However, whatever you order is likely to end up tasting pretty much like anything else on the menu since the ingredients used are basically the same. Order meals as far in advance as possible (order breakfast before you go to sleep and dinner when you first arrive at a lodge for the night) to give the cook enough time to prepare your order. In a crowded lodge it can often take hours for everyone's meals to be prepared, and orders are often mixed up. Please be patient and understanding. The meals at such lodges are often prepared by older men or women who speak no English and must rely on their children or grandchildren for translations of orders. Occasionally you may find yourself at a lodge where the cook has taken sick. If this is the case, you may find no food available or perhaps young and inexperienced children will be doing the cooking. I have seen trekkers become irate and abusive when it took several hours for their meal to arrive for one reason or another. This sort of behavior does no good and only presents Nepalis with a bad image of trekkers. You can speed the preparation of your meal by ordering the same menu items if you are with several people. This will avoid the time-consuming process of preparing several different meals on a stove that has only two or three burners.

In the busy October-November trekking season, you will find that lodges get very crowded. It is often necessary to stop by 2 or 3pm in order to get a room. However, if you keep walking until later in the day, you won't be turned away, you will just have to sleep wherever there is space available.

MONEY

If you are trekking on your own, you'll need to carry enough money for your entire trek. Although there are banks in a few large villages such as Namche Bazaar and Jomosom, you can't count on their being open when you need money. If you are staying in local lodges, plan on spending around $10 per day during your trek. Carry more money if you like to have a beer or two at the end of the day, and if you are paying for a porter or guide's meals and lodging, be sure to carry sufficient rupees to pay these costs. Small change is hard to come by on the trail, so carry plenty. I usually get the bulk of my money in 50- and 100-rupee notes, plus several hundred rupees in smaller bills.

If you are on a group trek on which everything is catered, you need not carry much money. Since you will be passing through villages that sell soft drinks, beer, and domestic liquors, you might want to carry some change for such purchases. In Helambu and on the Jomosom trek you are likely to encounter traders with goods for sale or trade. Prices out here on the trail are not necessarily any better than they are in Kathmandu, so don't let anyone tell you you're getting a great deal. However, occasionally these traders do have unusual and rare pieces from Tibet or from Nepali mountain villages, and these items may be real bargains.

MINIMIZING YOUR IMPACT ON THE ENVIRONMENT

Before heading out on a trek, or before even booking a trek if you are arranging a catered trek after you arrive in Nepal, you should be sure to stop by the Kathmandu Environmental Education Project information center off Tridevi Marg near the Hotel Tilicho (☎ 977/1-410303). You can learn about the impact trekking is having on Nepal's environment and pick up a copy of *Trekking Gently in the Himalaya,* a booklet on trekking responsibly and reducing your impact on the environment. This booklet sells for only Rs50 ($1) and should be in everyone's backpack.

In the past few years trekking companies have begun offering environmentally conscious treks. These include treks to plant trees as part of reforestation projects and to pick up garbage left by previous mountaineering and trekking expeditions. However, it is important to take care of the sensitive Himalayan environment on any trek. The most salient thing to remember is that deforestation is one of the greatest problems facing Nepal today. Each year during the monsoon vast amounts of soil washes away from deforested hillsides, causing landslides, destroying villages, and eliminating productive cropland. The great numbers of trekkers visiting Nepal have played a big part in deforestation in recent years. Food is prepared almost exclusively over wood fires, as is tea and bath water. If at all possible try to use kerosene for cooking and patronize lodges that use kerosene. By reducing the number of hot showers you take while trekking you will be doing a great deal to save the trees of Nepal. Instead of demanding a roaring fire to sit around at night, put on more clothing or climb into your sleeping bag.

Don't litter the trails and in villages try to be sure that there is some sort of garbage pit for biodegradable garbage. All nonbiodegradable garbage should be carried out, especially batteries, which are becoming an insidious form of toxic pollution throughout the hills of Nepal. If there are no toilet facilities where you are staying, burn your toilet paper or store it in a plastic bag until you can dispose of it in a garbage pit. Don't use soap or shampoo in lakes, streams, or hot springs. Instead take a bucket or pail and wash the soap off away from the water source.

TIPPING & BEGGING

Guides, porters, and other trek personnel have traditionally been tipped at the end of treks. In the past well-funded mountaineering expeditions have been very lavish in their tips because they didn't want to pay to ship unneeded gear back home. Sleeping bags, hiking boots, down jackets, and the like became tips, and consequently trekkers often think they must tip in an equally lavish fashion. This is not so. The most appropriate tips are warm clothing that you no longer need. Good socks are difficult to get in Nepal and make a good tip for porters. If you have room in your bag for some warm clothes that you no longer need, stuff them in and hand them out as tips. Sherpas and sirdars, the people who organize and lead treks, usually deserve larger tips. The best way to know what is appropriate is to ask the agency with whom you book your trek.

Begging has, unfortunately, become a fact of life along Nepal's more popular trekking routes. It is done primarily by small children who greet trekkers with cries of "Hello, one pen. Hello, one rupees. Hello, *mithai* (sweet)." This begging is a direct result of previous trekkers passing out gifts indiscriminately along the trail. The damage has already been done, and an entire generation is growing up expecting the rich foreigners to give them whatever they demand. Please do not further encourage begging by passing out candies, pens, balloons, or other gifts.

A more subtle form of begging is practiced by adults who corner trekkers and explain that their local school is in need of supplies or desks or whatever. These people will show you books signed by other generous donors, and the amounts of previous donations may startle you. Though some of these people are legitimate, you have no way of telling, so it is better not to make any donations.

9

The Trekking Routes

Imagine walking all day every day for a week or two or three. Imagine covering 150 miles on your own two feet and doing it in two weeks. This is what it means to trek. The first thing you need to decide after you have made up your mind to go trekking is which route to trek. This chapter includes descriptions of the seven most popular teahouse trekking routes. Because there is not enough room in this book for detailed descriptions of each route, descriptions are rather broad. Use them to get an idea of what to expect on a particular route, not as your only source of information on a trail.

I have broken the descriptions into days, and these days reflect my normal pace in most cases (some days are a bit longer than I prefer because of the lack of suitable lodgings at an easy stopping point). I prefer to walk between five and six hours a day with a one- to two-hour lunch break. Some trekkers prefer to get up at dawn, toss down a cup of tea, and hit the trail, making use of all the sunlight the day offers. These people finish their treks quickly, but they often miss one of the most important reasons for going on a trek— to slow down from the hurried pace of late-20th-century life. If you are one of these types or simply someone who walks quickly, I have included information on lodges and teahouses in villages the route passes through between the morning departure point and the day's stopping point.

Perhaps the most important information to note in these descriptions is the elevations. A trek that sounds easy at first may include a 6,000-foot ascent in one day (the Jomosom trek) or three ascents and descents of 3,000 to 5,000 feet over three days (the trek to Namche Bazaar from Jiri). It is always a good idea to prepare yourself mentally for such difficult days. Also some treks ascend to very high elevations where altitude sickness is a very real danger. Many people have died over the years in Nepal because they ignored signs of altitude sickness. Check the elevations and make sure you spend the required numbers of days acclimatizing at high elevation.

If you are going on an organized trek, you may find that you do not follow any of the treks described here. More and more trekking agencies are trying to take groups to less traveled areas. However, it is still possible to do one of these very popular treks with a group. If you have chosen to go on a group trek on a popular trail, the route description here will give you an idea of what to expect. Organized treks usually spend only four hours a day walking, so there is lots of time to relax. Compare your trek itinerary to my route description to get an idea of what you will be covering each day.

Every year at the end of the monsoon season, thousands of adventurers descend on Nepal from all over the world. They set off for the hills with trekking guidebooks in hand only to find that the trail they are supposed to take no longer exists. Landslides are a constant problem in Nepal, and frequently they cause trails to be rerouted. Flooding washes away bridges and makes it impossible (or at least very difficult) to cross rivers. These are the unforeseen problems inherent in any trek. Please keep this in mind as you follow the route descriptions in this chapter.

1 Solu-Khumbu & the Everest Trek

For many trekkers, nothing else will do but to trek as close to Mt. Everest as possible. However, there are a number of aspects of this trek that may cause you to have second thoughts. First is its length. The best way to do this trek, if you have both time and money, is to hike from Jiri to Kala Pattar or Gokyo and then fly out of Lukla. This itinerary will take 18 to 20 days. It is also possible to shorten the trek by flying into Lukla. By flying in and out of Lukla, you can trek up to Kala Pattar for a view of Everest and be back in Kathmandu in 15 days. Should you choose to hike both to Everest Base Camp and Gokyo, you'll need an extra 5 or 6 days. If you walk in and out from Jiri, you'll need around a month.

If you do plan to walk in from Jiri, keep in mind that the trail climbs and descends three major ridges before beginning the steady climb up the valley of the Dudh Kosi to Namche Bazaar. This is a grueling and unrewarding section of the trail with few mountain views. However, it will get you in shape for trekking higher up and will allow you to trek through terraced fields, pastures, meadows, and different types of forests. Also, remember that beyond Namche Bazaar the trek remains quite high at elevations where altitude sickness is a very real danger. For a close-up view of Mt. Everest, it is necessary to climb as high as 17,000 or 18,000 feet (5,185 or 5,490 meters). Quite a few trekkers abandon their quest to see Everest close up because they cannot handle the elevation. Lastly, don't make Everest Base Camp your ultimate goal unless you have a very good reason. Despite the name, you cannot see Mt. Everest from Everest Base Camp.

All this said, this is still a very rewarding trek. The high peaks surrounding Namche Bazaar are spectacular. The terrain and vegetation change dramatically between Jiri and the glaciated regions in the immediate vicinity of Mt. Everest. The Sherpa people, in whose lodges and homes you will be staying, are generally the friendliest in Nepal. If you have plenty of time to spare, this might be the best choice for you. There are also quite a few day and overnight hikes possible from Namche Bazaar that make a stay of several days or a week there worthwhile. Also the Mani Rimdu festivals at Tengboche in November and Thami in May are reason enough to make the long journey up here. During these Buddhist festivals, masked and costumed monks perform various dances in the courtyards of their monasteries. The November festival has become particularly popular with trekkers and attracts large crowds that strain the facilities at Tengboche.

TO KALA PATTAR
DAY 1: KATHMANDU TO JIRI

It is a 12-hour bus ride from Kathmandu to Jiri, which is the trailhead for the route to the Everest region. The bus to Jiri costs Rs108 ($2.20) and leaves from the old bus park on the east side of the Tundikhel. This bus is usually so crowded that many people ride on the roof, and pickpocketing and theft of or from backpacks have become all too common on this route. Take all possible precautions and never let your backpack out of your sight.

Also, landslides during the monsoon often wash our sections of the road, adding hours to the journey and making a real adventure. **Jiri** (6,250 feet; 1,906 meters) is an unappealing town with a wide main street lined with shops, teahouses, and lodges.

Day 2: Jiri to Bhandar

The trail begins climbing immediately at the end of the main road into Jiri. It is about 1 1/2 hours through scrubby rhododendron forest to the crest of this first ridge (7,875 feet; 2,402 meters). From this ridge, which is topped by a small cairn, the trail drops quickly to a bridge over the Yelung Khola. After crossing this first small river, the trail then crosses the larger Khimti Khola and enters the village of **Shivalaya** (5,900 feet; 1,800 meters). From Shivalaya, the trail begins climbing again, this time quite steeply. **Sangbadanda** (7,200 feet; 2,196 meters) is reached in about 2 hours. Here the trail forks. Take the right fork, which passes through the small village of **Kasourbas,** to reach the pass (8,900 feet; 2,715 meters) in about 2 hours. At first the trail climbs gradually, but after leveling off for a while, it climbs steeply through a forest to the pass. There are several lodges at this windy pass, so if you just can't take another step, you can stay the night up here. They all sell cheese from the cheese factory at Thodung, which is another 1 1/2 hours and 1,250 feet (381 meters) above the pass on the trail leading north up the ridge. There are also several large mani walls at this pass, an indication that you are now in Sherpa country. The trail descends the far side of this ridge, cutting across the ridge toward the village of Bhandar, which can be seen from the pass. Just below the pass, the trail forks. Take the left fork and continue descending steadily toward Bhandar.

Bhandar (7,200 feet; 2,196 meters) is a picturesque Sherpa village in a wide valley. The path, almost a road, passes two large *chortens* before entering the village itself. A chorten is a Buddhist shrine similar to the huge stupas in Kathmandu. It incorporates the same elements and symbols as a stupa, only on a much smaller scale. The two chortens of Bhandar have very colorful eyes painted on them. There is also a gompa beside the chortens, which you are welcome to visit if it happens to be unlocked when you pass by. There are several hotels in town, which you will find very welcome after this long and exhausting day.

Jiri to Shivalaya: 3 1/2 hours; Shivalaya to Sangbadanda: 2 hours; Sangbadanda to Deurali Pass: 2 hours; Deurali Pass to Bhandar: 1 hour.

Day 3: Bhandar to Sete

From Bhandar the trail continues across the wide valley, crossing a small covered wooden bridge at the edge of the fields before entering a dark and damp forest. The trail then drops steeply through an even more lush forest full of ferns and mosses. Long ribbons of water cascade down the opposite wall of the narrow valley the trail passes through. At the bottom of this valley, the trail crosses to the opposite side of the stream and heads north up the valley of the Likhu Khola, a much larger river. Don't take the first bridge you see but continue up the west bank to the second bridge (5,180 feet; 1,580 meters), crossing to the east bank there. The trail continues on this bank to the village of **Kenja** (5,350 feet;

1,632 meters). There are quite a few teahouses and lodges here. If you have any mending that needs to be done, local tailors who set up their hand-cranked sewing machines in the village streets will fix you right up. You should eat a big lunch, heavy on carbohydrates, before continuing the day's trek.

From Kenja it is a long, steady, and steep climb up to the Lamjura Pass. Luckily you reach the village of **Sete** (below the pass) in about 3 hours, which makes it a good place to stop for the night. There are a couple of lodges in Sete, as well as a small gompa. There is a good view down into the valley of the Kenja Khola, and sunsets can be spectacular here even though you can't see any snow-clad peaks.

Bhandar to Kenja: 3 hours; Kenja to Sete: 3 hours.

DAY 4: SETE TO JUNBESI

Before leaving Sete, be sure to fill all your water bottles. There is little, if any, water available between here and the far side of the pass. From Sete the trail continues climbing steadily toward the Lamjura Pass. At first you walk through oak forest, but as you gain more elevation, the vegetation changes to fir trees and eventually to rhododendron. About two hours above Sete, there are a couple of teahouses where you should have lunch. At a mani wall 2^1/$_2$ to three hours from Sete, take the left fork. You will reach the **Lamjura Pass** (11,580 feet; 3,532 meters) about four hours after leaving Sete. The forests leading up to this pass are quite magical (straight out of *The Wizard of Oz*), and it is easy to imagine lions and tigers and bears lurking in the shadows. The trunks of the rhododendrons below the pass are often covered with growths of moss almost a foot thick, which gives you some indication of how often this pass is socked in with clouds. At the pass itself there is an amazing jumble of sticks and stones that have been assembled into several cairns and festooned with prayer flags and marigolds. These are all offerings left by travelers as they crossed this place that is just a little bit closer to the gods.

From the pass it is a steep and slippery descent through a damp forest. However, as the trail leaves the forest it becomes much less steep and enters a green pasture crisscrossed with wooden fences. The forest is left behind as the hills become covered with meadows. Before reaching the village of **Tragdobuck** (9,400 feet; 2,867 meters), the trail passes under an impressive outcropping of rock. In Tragdobuck there are two more huge boulders, both of which have been carved with Buddhist prayers. One of the boulders even has a wind-driven prayer wheel on top of it. The trail continues across the meadows until it rounds a notch in the ridge and reveals the village of Junbesi ahead and below. The snow-covered mountain you see above Junbesi is Numbur (22,825 feet; 6,962 meters). Its Sherpa name means God of Solu, which is the lower region inhabited by Sherpas. From here it is about an hour to **Junbesi** (8,775 feet; 2,676 meters), a very attractive Sherpa village. There are quite a few large new lodges in Junbesi, so you might want to check them all out before making a choice. The Junbesi Guest House is popular. Junbesi has the first water-driven prayer wheel of this trek. It is built atop a stream that flows through the middle of the village. There is also a monastery above the village on the trail from Tragdobuck and an older monastery in the middle of town. Another 1^1/$_2$ hours up the valley from Junbesi is the large Thubten Chholing Gompa, which has nearly 200 Buddhist monks and nuns. This monastery is well worth a visit. If you don't want to backtrack to Junbesi, it is possible to take a little-used trail up and over the ridge to the east of the monastery, joining the main trail from Junbesi just before the village of Ringmo. It should take 3 or 4 hours to cross this way.

Sete to teahouses: 2 hours; teahouses to Lamjura Pass: 2 hours; Lamjura Pass to Tragdobuck: 2 hours; Tragdobuck to Junbesi: 1 hour.

DAY 5: JUNBESI TO MANIDINGMA

To reach the onward trail, head south out of the village past several stone chortens. Just after crossing the river on a wooden bridge, the trail forks. The right fork goes to Phaphlu, which has a hospital and an airstrip, while the left fork continues toward Khumbu and the Everest region. The trail climbs through different types of forest. Near the top of the ridge, the forest gives way to open pastures, and at the crest (10,000 feet; 3,050 meters) you get your first glimpse of Everest (called Sagarmatha by the Nepalis and Chomolungma by the Tibetans). The trail then descends through forest again heading northeast up a wide valley. In 2 hours you reach **Sallung** (9,750 feet; 2,974 meters), where there is a lodge. The trail continues descending to the Beni Khola (8,700 feet; 2,654 meters), crosses the river, and then climbs to the village of **Ringmo** (9,200 feet; 2,806 meters). Be sure to stop here for some apple pie or apple cider from the large orchard. The trail widens here, but it is still a steep climb up to **Tragsindho Pass** (10,075 feet; 3,073 meters), which is marked by a large chorten, mani walls, and prayer flags. On the way up from Ringmo you will see signs for a cheese factory below the pass. The cheese factory has a lodge and serves excellent food with the emphasis on cheese, of course. There are also several lodges at the pass itself.

Descending from the pass, you reach the village of **Tragsindho** in about 20 minutes. There are more lodges here and a large Buddhist monastery. It is an hour's descent through lush forest alive with birds to the village of **Manidingma** (7,600 feet; 2,318 meters), where there are quite a few lodges.

Junbesi to Sallung: 2¹/₂ hours; Sallung to Ringmo: 2 hours; Ringmo to Tragsindho Pass: 1 hour; Tragsindho Pass to Tragsindho: 20 minutes; Tragsindho to Manidingma: 1¹/₂ hours.

DAY 6: MANIDINGMA TO KHARTE

Continue descending through forests to the valley of the **Dudh Kosi** (Milk River), which gets its name from the pale blue color of its water and from its many rapids. This large river flows south from the glaciers of Khumbu. Cross the river on a suspension bridge (4,900 feet; 1,495 meters) and head north to the village of **Jubing.** The trail passes through the terraced fields surrounding this village. Jubing is inhabited by people of the Rai ethnic group who are found primarily in eastern Nepal. You may notice that the houses look different from Sherpa homes and are often decorated with garlands of marigolds. The trail continues north up the valley of the Dudh Kosi to the village of **Khari Khola.** There are quite a few good hotels here, so if you are ready for an afternoon of rest, make this a short day. If you are full of energy and want to continue onward, walk through Khari Khola, cross the bridge, and begin climbing to the village of **Kharte,** which you can see from Khari Khola. There are a few small lodges here.

Manidingma to Dudh Kosi: ¹/₂ hour; Dudh Kosi to Jubing: 1 hour; Jubing to Khari Khola: 2 hours; Khari Khola to Kharte: 1¹/₂ hours.

DAY 7: KHARTE TO CHAUNRIKARKA

From Kharte, continue climbing through forest with the river far below you in a steep-walled valley. The trail climbs to the top of a ridge at about 10,000 feet

Solu-Khumbu Trekking Routes

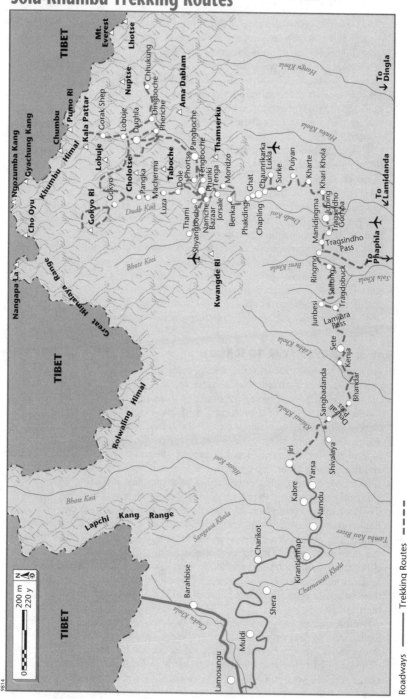

Roadways ——— Trekking Routes ------

(3,050 meters) before descending through the canyon of a tributary. The trail through this canyon is often icy and at times is very narrow with a steep drop-off. Use extreme caution. At the head of the canyon, you cross a landslide area that can be unstable in the first weeks after the end of the monsoon. After crossing this stream, it is a short walk with a gentle slope to **Puiyan** (9,300 feet; 2,837 meters) where there are a couple of lodges. The trail continues climbing to another ridge (9,650 feet; 2,943 meters) beyond which it is possible to see Lukla and its airstrip. You may even get to see a plane make the hair-raising landing on this postage-stamp field.

The trail descends through shady forest to another tributary of the Dudh Kosi. In the little valley beside this stream is the village of **Surkhe,** which has a couple of lodges. The trail climbs steeply out of Surkhe to a junction with a trail to Lukla. If you are hoping to fly back to Kathmandu, it is worthwhile to hike up to Lukla and put your name on the waiting list for the day you want to return. Remember, getting on a flight out of Lukla can take days of waiting, so leave yourself plenty of time. Passing this junction, the trail continues climbing steeply on a path blasted out of the mountainside. The trail then crosses a rocky pasture strewn with giant boulders, several of which have been turned into very finished-looking caves. These caves are used by porters as a resting and camping spot on their way to the Saturday market in Namche Bazaar. **Chaunrikarka** (8,700 feet; 2,654 meters) is shortly beyond these caves. There are several hotels here.

Kharte to Puiyan: 2 hours; Puiyan to Surkhe: 2¹/₂ hours; Surkhe to Chaunrikarka: 2 hours.

DAY 8: CHAUNRIKARKA TO JORSALE

Leaving Chaunrikarka, you pass several mani walls and a large chorten. The trail passes through attractive fields. At the top of a low ridge this trail joins with the trail from Lukla. If you have hiked up from Jiri, you will be shocked to suddenly find yourself in the company of dozens and possibly hundreds of trekkers. The trail up to Namche Bazaar becomes a human highway with trekkers and porters often blocking the trail as they stop to rest. The village of **Chapling** is just down from this ridge. Beyond Chapling, the trail crosses a tributary stream and descends to **Ghat.** There are a few lodges here. Keep to the east bank, climbing, descending, and climbing again before reaching **Phakding** (8,600 feet; 2,623 meters). There are several hotels in Phakding. Cross over the Dudh Kosi to the west bank and continue north, passing a lodge along the way, to the village of **Benkar** (8,850 feet; 2,699 meters), where there are a couple of lodges. Beyond Benkar, you cross back to the east bank of the river and climb to Chumoa, where there are several lodges. The trail continues climbing then descends to a stream and climbs to **Mondzo** (9,300 feet; 2,837 meters), which also has several lodges. Sagarmatha National Park has its entrance here in Mondzo, and you will have to show your park permit (purchased in Kathmandu at the Department of Immigration) and sign the register.

Because the trek now leads through a national park, all trekking groups are prohibited from cooking with firewood; consequently, kerosene must be carried. There is a kerosene depot in Namche Bazaar, and containers for kerosene can also be purchased. This rule does not, however, apply to lodges catering to trekkers. Lodges still use wood to cook and heat water for showers. Though a few lodges have begun using kerosene (and even propane) stoves, these are still the exception.

If you ask a few lodge owners whether they use kerosene and if you express an interest in staying at a lodge that does use kerosene, maybe things will begin to change. Using kerosene may add a little bit to the cost of a meal, but saving the forests of the Himalayas is well worth the expense.

Beyond the park entrance the trail descends a stone stairway, crosses back to the west bank of the river, and continues to **Jorsale** (9,100 feet; 2,776 meters). There are quite a few lodges here, and I suggest staying here for the night. Though it is possible to reach Namche Bazaar on the same day, it is still a very steep 3-hour hike away. It is better to make this climb in the morning when you are rested and full of energy.

Chaunrikarka to Chapling: 45 minutes; Chapling to Ghat: 45 minutes; Ghat to Phakding: 1 hour; Phakding to Benkar: 1¼ hours; Benkar to Mondzo: 1 hour; Mondzo to Jorsale: 1 hour.

DAY 9: JORSALE TO NAMCHE BAZAAR

From Jorsale, there are two possible routes onward toward Namche Bazaar. The preferred route is to cross the river on the long suspension bridge and follow a flat trail upriver for 20 minutes or so to a bridge that crosses back over the river. The alternate route never crosses the river but instead climbs high on the forested valley wall. This trail is steep and muddy and is used primarily by yak herders who cannot take their animals across the smaller of the two bridges on the other route. The two trails merge just below the confluence of the Dudh Kosi and Bhote Kosi rivers.

The path now climbs above the valley floor to one of the highest suspension bridges I have ever seen in Nepal. The trail then continues climbing steeply through forest to a teahouse with a partially obscured view of Mt. Everest. This is a steep climb, and the teahouse is a welcome resting spot.

You have probably been encountering yak caravans since passing Lukla. These caravans are a constant source of danger. Yaks can be bad tempered, so always be prepared for a nudge from one. Keep to the uphill side when passing these slow-moving beasts to avoid being pushed or accidentally knocked off the trail. Luckily this steep section of trail is not very long. Beyond the tea stall, take the right fork, which leads into Namche Bazaar through the area used as a market on Saturdays. You'll need to spend a full day acclimatizing in Namche Bazaar before continuing to higher elevations, so this is a short day. Find a lodge and spend the afternoon exploring the village or relaxing in the sun.

Namche Bazaar (11,300 feet; 3,447 meters) is the largest village and the administrative center of the Khumbu region. Situated in a horseshoe-shaped valley high above the Bhote Kosi and surrounded by steep hills, it faces the impressive north face of Kwangde peak (20,285 feet; 6,187 meters). There is a police checkpost here, a bank where it is possible to change money, and a post office. A small hydroelectric project provides electricity for lights at night. There are also dozens of lodges and hotels here. Currently the Khumbu Lodge and the Himalayan Lodge are considered the best in town. The village shops sell an amazing variety of imported foods—the leftovers of international mountain-climbing expeditions. You can also buy hand-knitted wool sweaters, socks, and gloves and rent down jackets and sleeping bags. The Sagarmatha National Park headquarters and visitors center are above the police checkpost on the hill to the east of the village. This hill has a spectacular view up the valley to

Mt. Everest and all its surrounding peaks. Sunrises and sunsets from this ridge are worth all the grueling days it takes to get here.

Jorsale to Namche Bazaar: 2¹/₂ to 3 hours.

DAY 10: DAY HIKES FROM NAMCHE BAZAAR

The best way to acclimatize is to hike to higher elevation and then return to Namche Bazaar for the night. There are numerous day hikes possible from Namche. One you might find interesting is to climb the hill north of town to the **Shyangboche** airstrip area. From the east end of this little-used airstrip, a trail leads to the Hotel Everest View, a deluxe hotel built by the Japanese in the 1970s. The hotel was closed for many years due to problems with the water supply. It is now open again on a limited scale with undeservedly deluxe prices. The long, low stone and glass building is so incredibly out-of-place in this remote landscape that it is fascinating. Stop by for a very expensive pot of tea and enjoy the view of Everest from the dining room or terrace. For more information on the hotel, contact Hotel Everest View, Durbar Marg (P.O. Box 1694), Kathmandu (☎ 977/1-224854; fax 977/1-227289). Rates are around $375 per night for a double (with meals included).

Another possible day hike is to walk west toward the village of Thami, and in **Thamo,** 1¹/₂ hours out of Namche Bazaar, climb the steep slope to a small gompa built by the English-speaking lama who helped found Kopan monastery in Boudha. This gompa is frequently used as a retreat for Western Buddhists who come from all over the world to get away from it all. The Sherpa caretakers of the gompa are always happy to have guests, and even the Westerners staying here may be willing to talk with you about Buddhism if you are interested.

From Thamo, continue up the valley to **Thami,** which you should reach in about 2 hours. After exploring Thami, you can visit the monastery outside of the village before heading back to Namche Bazaar.

DAY 11: NAMCHE BAZAAR TO TENGBOCHE

The route to Everest Base Camp is probably the most popular trail originating in Namche Bazaar. Climb the hill to the park headquarters and then level off. The Dudh Kosi is far below, and the view from here is spectacular with Thamserku (21,675 feet; 6,608 meters) directly across the valley, Kwangde to the south across the Bhote Kosi valley, and Everest (29,028 feet; 8,848 meters), Nuptse (25,845 feet; 7,879 meters), Ama Dablam (22,488 feet; 6,856 meters), Cholotse (21,125 feet; 6,440 meters), and Khumbila (18,900 feet; 5,761 meters) all ahead of you up the valley. Keep your eyes open for pheasants along this stretch of trail. The wide path descends slowly through steep pastures. Within 1¹/₄ hours you pass **Sanassa** and the trail up to Khumjung, a large Sherpa village in a desolate valley. Continue descending on the main trail, entering a forest, to reach the Dudh Kosi and the village of **Phunki Tenga** (10,660 feet; 3,251 meters) with its water-driven mills and prayer wheels. There are a couple of lodges here. Cross the river and climb steeply through a dense forest.

Tengboche (12,679 feet; 3,867 meters), the largest monastery in Khumbu, perches on the saddle of a ridge and commands an outstanding panorama with peaks in every direction. The monastery is especially beautiful with Ama Dablam rising up behind it. This is one of the most memorable sights anywhere in Nepal. Tengboche monastery, which was rebuilt after a fire a few years ago, is the site of the annual Mani Rimdu festival held at the November full moon. During the festival monks wearing masks and colorful costumes act out traditional dances in the courtyard of the monastery. It is an amazing sight, though it has become very crowded with trekkers in recent years. Stay at the excellent Tengboche Trekkers Lodge or the Gompa Lodge, which is operated by Tengboche's monks. If you are camping, you will be asked to pay a small charge for pitching your tent on monastery land. While in Tengboche, you can visit the Sherpa Cultural Center, a small museum with informative displays about the Sherpa people. It's in a building behind the gompa. Because the monastery has banned hunting in the vicinity, you may see pheasants, musk deer, Himalayan *tahr* (mountain goats), or jungle cats along the nearby trails.

Namche Bazaar to Sanassa: 1 hour; Sanassa to Phunki Tenga: 1 hour; Phunki Tenga to Tengboche: 1 hour.

DAY 12: TENGBOCHE TO PHERICHE

Descend a steep trail through a damp rhododendron forest to the village of Deboche which has a long mani wall and a nunnery. There are two lodges here. Continue descending through rhododendrons until you cross the Imja Khola (12,400 feet; 3,782 meters). Across the river you have an excellent view of Ama Dablam as you begin climbing past chortens and mani walls. At a fork in the trail keep to the right to reach lower **Pangboche** village. The left fork climbs to Pangboche Monastery and upper Pangboche village, which once claimed to have the partial remains of a yeti. Unfortunately, in 1991, these relics were stolen from the monastery and were never recovered. Upper Pangboche is the more interesting section of the village and is surrounded by large cedar trees. Try the Pangboche Gompa Lodge here, or, in lower Pangboche, the Ama Dablang Lodge or the Shiri Dewa Lodge.

On the far side of the lower village, cross a stream and ascend through terraced fields, eventually climbing above the treeline. The trail proceeds up a gentle slope and passes the small village of Somare, where there are some teahouses. Beyond Somare, the trail flattens a bit and passes a lodge at Orsho.

Past here there is a fork in the trail. The right fork leads to Dingboche, but you should take the left fork. Climb a ridge before dropping down to a wooden bridge across the stream flowing from Khumbu Glacier. **Pheriche** (13,900 feet; 4,240 meters) is about 10 minutes beyond the stream. There are many small lodges in Pheriche, none of which is much better than any other. There is also a Trekkers' Aid Post staffed by Western physicians and sponsored by the Himalayan Rescue Association. If you have not yet learned about altitude sickness, it is a good idea to stop by this post and learn more.

Tengboche to Pangboche: 2 hours; Pangboche to Pheriche: 2 hours.

DAY 13: PHERICHE

It is necessary to spend a day in Pheriche acclimatizing. Try to make a day hike up to higher elevation and then return to Pheriche for the night. Wherever you choose to hike today, if it is much higher than Pheriche, you are likely to be rewarded with amazing views of the peaks.

DAY 14: PHERICHE TO LOBUJE

From Pheriche head up the valley to Phulong Karpo, a grassy pasture used for grazing yaks in the summer. The mound of rocks in front of you is the terminal moraine of Khumbu Glacier. Climb up and over the moraine and down to a stream that flows from beneath the glacier. Cross the stream and ascend to **Dughla** (15,100 feet; 4,606 meters), which has several lodges. Not far beyond Dughla there is a collection of memorials to Sherpas and climbers who have died scaling nearby peaks. At this point the trail descends a little then levels off and continues up the valley to **Lobuje** (16,170 feet; 4,932 meters). There are several lodges here, but the National Park Lodge is probably the best choice. Lobuje is very crowded during the prime trekking seasons, so it is a good idea to get here as early as possible.

Pheriche to Dughla: 2 hours; Dughla to Lobuje: 2 hours.

DAY 15: LOBUJE TO GORAK SHEP

Continue up the valley along a level path with Khumbu Glacier to your right. The trail then climbs a moraine, from which there is a view of Gorak Shep (a sandy flat area with a frozen lake) and Kala Pattar (a rocky hill that provides the best view of Everest). Descend the moraine to the sandy flats and skirt the lake to the two stone huts of **Gorak Shep.** There are a few simple lodges here. If you are fully acclimatized and full of energy, you might want to go ahead and climb Kala Pattar this afternoon. However, most people take the afternoon off to further acclimatize. It is about a 1¹/₂-hour steep climb to the top of **Kala Pattar** (18,190 feet; 5,548 meters), and from the top you have not only a stunning view of Everest, but a 360-degree panorama of peaks including Nuptse, Ama Dablam, Kantenga, Thamserku, Tawetse, Pumo Ri, and Changtse.

Lobuje to Gorak Shep: 2¹/₂ hours; Gorak Shep to Kala Pattar: 1¹/₂ hours.

DAY 16: GORAK SHEP TO LOBUJE

If you haven't already climbed Kala Pattar, do so early in the morning and then return to Lobuje in the afternoon. Unless you have some intense motivation for continuing to the area known as Everest Base Camp, I would head back down today. Everest Base Camp is not a single specific area; it is many different spots located about an hour apart and 3 hours beyond Gorak Shep. So count on a 6-hour round-trip. You will not be allowed to enter an expedition camp if there happens to be one here, and otherwise all you will see is the garbage left by previous expeditions. You probably get the picture that I'm not too keen on going to base camp.

From Gorak Shep back down to Lobuje takes about 2 hours on the same trail you came up. Spend the night here again.

DAY 17: LOBUJE TO CHHUKUNG

If you don't mind backtracking, continue back down to Pangboche or even Tengboche. It is faster going back down to Namche Bazaar, and you can make better time than you did coming up. From Gorak Shep to Namche Bazaar will take only 3 days.

If you prefer to return by a different route, you can take the high trail down the east side of the valley to **Dingboche.** The Dingboche trail leaves the main trail at the bridge below Dughla and climbs up the hill to the north side of the valley. There are couple of lodges in Dingboche.

From Dingboche, it is possible to continue up the valley of the Imja Khola to the yak pastures at **Chhukung** (15,525 feet; 4,735 meters), where there are several lodges operating during the main trekking seasons. Explorations in this valley provide close-up views of Ama Dablam from the north, which is a much different perspective than from elsewhere on this trek. There are also good views of many other peaks including Cholatse, Taboche, Kongde, and Numbur. This is the route taken by expeditions headed for Island Peak, one of Nepal's most popular trekking peaks.

Lobuje to Dingboche: 4 hours; Dingboche to Chhukung: 3 hours.

DAYS 18–19: DINGBOCHE TO NAMCHE BAZAAR

To continue back toward Namche Bazaar, backtrack back down the valley to **Dingboche.** From Dingboche, the trail descends steadily to cross the Khumbu Khola on a wooden bridge. You then climb steeply to meet the **Pangboche-Pheriche** trail. Continue on to spend the night in **Tengboche.** The following day return to Namche Bazaar. Though there is a trail from Pangboche that bypasses Tengboche and leads to Phortse for the trek up to Gokyo, most people choose to go either to Gokyo or Kala Pattar, not both, since the objective of either trek is a view of Everest. Consequently, I will describe the Gokyo trek from Namche Bazaar.

Chhukung to Dingboche: 2 1/2 hours; Dingboche to Pangboche: 2 hours; Pangboche to Tengboche: 1 1/2 hours; Tengboche to Namche Bazaar: 4 hours.

DAYS 20–21: NAMCHE BAZAAR TO LUKLA

Though it is possible to hike from Namche Bazaar to Lukla in one long day, the journey is better split into two short days. Phakding makes a good stopping point on the day you leave Namche Bazaar. The next day, you should reach Lukla by lunchtime. Keep in mind that you need to reconfirm your ticket before 4pm the night before departing. **Lukla** (9,200 feet; 2,806 meters), because it has an airstrip, has become a very busy town in recent years. There are dozens of lodges, hotels, teahouses, and shops catering to the thousands of trekkers who pass through yearly. Of the many lodges in town, the Sagarmatha Resort (charging $55 double) and the Himalaya Lodge (charging $2) are probably the best. Despite the many hotels, the village can become very crowded. Accommodations and tempers are frequently strained when several days of bad weather cause a human logjam of trekkers waiting to catch flights out. RNAC planes don't fly if there are too many clouds, because, as they say, the clouds in Nepal have rocks in them. I have seen as many as 12 flights a day out of Lukla after a few days without any flights. Still, there were more people waiting to get on flights the next day. Waiting in Lukla for a flight is not a pleasant pastime. There is little to do but sit around hoping that your name will be called. Many people spend their time drinking beer or local home brew. The combination of alcohol and elevation often leads to violent outbursts from people who *absolutely must* be on the next flight out. If you are planning to trek in the Everest region and fly out of Lukla, be sure to leave at least a week between flying out of Lukla and flying out of Kathmandu. This buffer will give you time to hike out if necessary. Now that Asian Airlines and Nepal Airways fly helicopters into Lukla, flights out of here are more reliable (helicopters can fly in worse weather than fixed-wing planes). I recommend trying to make your reservation on a helicopter if at all possible.

There are also airstrips at Tumlingtar, about 4 days from Kharte, and Phaphlu, 4 hours south of Ringmo. You may be able to get a flight out of either of these places, though whether it will get you back to Kathmandu faster than if you walked all the way back to Jiri and caught the bus is questionable.

DAY 22: LUKLA TO KATHMANDU

If you are very lucky and have a confirmed return ticket out of Lukla and arrived in Lukla early enough the previous day to reconfirm your ticket, you can be back

in Kathmandu today. Unfortunately, even people with reconfirmed tickets sometimes get bumped from flights. Alternatively you can hike from Lukla back to Jiri
in 6 days or from Namche Bazaar in 7 days.

TO GOKYO

The following is a route description of the trek to Gokyo. This trek can be done
in addition to or instead of the trek to Kala Pattar and Everest Base Camp. There
are several picturesque lakes along this route, including Gokyo Lake, on the
waters of which someone once sailboarded. It also takes 2 days less to get a
spectacular view of Everest, which makes this route a good choice if you are short
on time but still want to see Everest up close. If you choose this route alone, you
can be back in Lukla in only 14 days. If you choose to visit both Gokyo and
Kala Pattar, plan on 24 to 28 days.

This route has come to be known as "the valley of death" because of the many
trekkers who develop (and ignore) symptoms of altitude sickness as they trek up
to Gokyo. It is very easy to gain too much elevation too quickly on this route, so
be particularly watchful for signs of altitude sickness in both yourself and the other
members of your trekking party.

DAY 1: NAMCHE BAZAAR TO DOLE

There are two routes out of Namche Bazaar to Phortse Tenga. You can climb the
steep hill directly behind the village to Shyangboche airstrip and continue from
there, through fields and forests of dwarfed pines, to Khumjung, a large Sherpa
village in a wide gray valley (at least outside of the monsoon season it's gray). The
trail then joins the main route below Khumjung. The other route begins by following the route described in the trek to Everest Base Camp. Climb to the national
park headquarters and head north up the valley. This is a much easier trail than
the trail through Shyangboche and passes through open pastures. After about
1¼ hours minutes, you will come to **Sanassa,** where there are several lodges and
teahouses. It is here that the trail divides, with the lower trail leading to Tengoche
and Kala Pattar and the upper trail leading toward Gokyo. Watch for musk deer
and danphe pheasants (the national bird) in the vicinity of Sanassa. From here the
trail leads up to the **Mon Pass** (13,000 feet; 3,965 meters). The trail then descends
steeply to **Phortse Tenga** (11,950 feet; 3,645 meters), where there are two very
basic lodges. I don't recommend staying here unless it is too late in the day to continue. From Phortse Tenga, the trail stays on the west side of the valley and climbs
through dense forest to the yak pastures at **Dole** (13,400 feet; 4,087 meters). Here
there are two more lodges and good views across the valley. Because the elevation
gain from Namche Bazaar to Dole is a bit more than is recommended for a single
day at this altitude, be particularly watchful for symptoms of altitude sickness, both
in yourself and in others. If anyone in your party is experiencing difficulties with
the altitude (headaches, loss of appetite, dizziness, nausea), it may be wise to take
an acclimatization day in Dole.

*Namche Bazaar to Sanassa: 1¼ hours; Sanassa to Mon Pass: 2 hours; Mon Pass to
Phortse Tenga: 45 minutes; Phortse Tenga to Dole: 2 hours.*

DAY 2: DOLE TO PANGKA

At Dole, the forest ends and the trail becomes easier and more gradual. Past the
stone huts at Gyele (13,150 feet; 4,010 meters), you enter high pastures in a narrow valley. Climbing again, you reach the pastures and huts of **Lhabarma** (14,200

feet; 4,331 meters). Here the trail levels off for a while before climbing gradually again. Just past **Luza** (14,400 feet; 4,392 meters) the trail tops a low ridge from which you can see Macherma (14,650 feet; 4,468 meters) across a side valley. There are several lodges in Macherma.

Climb from Macherma to crest a ridge. The view from this ridge is quite good, with Cho Oyu (26,750 feet; 8,153 meters) ahead of you and Kangtenga (22,226 feet; 6,779 meters) behind you. Across the valley to your right are Cholotse (21,125 feet; 6,440 meters) and Taboche (21,460 feet; 6,542 meters). From this ridge the trail descends to Pangka (14,689 feet; 4,480 meters), which has one lodge. Looming ahead of you is the terminal moraine of Ngozumba Glacier.

Dole to Luza: 1 1/2 hours; Luza to Macherma: 30 minutes; Macherma to Pangka: 30 minutes.

DAY 3: PANGKA TO GOKYO

Continue descending from Pangka to a stream flowing down the west side of the valley. Cross the stream and climb up the steep, rocky moraine to the source of the stream, a small glacial **lake** (15,350 feet; 4,682 meters). This is the first of five lakes that often take on a startling shade of blue that is in brilliant contrast to the gray and brown of the surrounding hills. Continue past this lake, reaching a second lake in less than an hour. Continue up the valley to Dudh Pokhari, the third lake. Passing a mani wall, you arrive in Gokyo (15,574 feet; 4,750 meters). There are numerous lodges in Gokyo. The most comfortable is the Gokyo Resort Lodge, which has a sun room for lounging in during the day.

Pangka to first lake: 1 1/2 hours; first lake to Gokyo: 1 1/4 hours.

DAY 4: GOKYO

Though the view from Gokyo is spectacular enough, you will want to climb just a bit higher for a truly memorable sight. There are two choices for this higher view. You can climb to the top of another peak called Gokyo Ri (17,990 feet; 5,483 meters), the peak above Gokyo and Dudh Pokhari, in about 2 hours. Alternately, you can hike up the valley to the fourth or fifth lake; above the lake you will find good views. From either of these locations, you will be treated to a breathtaking view that includes Cho Oyu, Everest, Nuptse, Lhotse, Makalu, and many other peaks. Below you in the valley are the shimmering turquoise lakes and the convoluted gray bulk of Ngozumba Glacier. Remember to take it easy as you climb these peaks. Though the skies are usually clearer in the morning, you might want to wait until afternoon to climb above Gokyo so your body has time to acclimatize.

DAYS 5-6: GOKYO TO NAMCHE BAZAAR

Since you will be descending and won't have to worry about altitude sickness, you will make much better time on the return to Namche Bazaar. You should be able to reach Phortse Tenga in 1 day from Gokyo. The next day you should reach Namche Bazaar with no trouble.

TO GOKYO VIA PHORTSE
DAY 1: GORAK SHEP TO PANGBOCHE

If you have plenty of time and want to see as much of this region as possible, you may want to trek up to both Kala Pattar and to Gokyo. There are a couple of options for linking up the Kala Pattar trek and the Gokyo trek. The easier route is to head back down the valley through **Lobuje** and **Pheriche** to **Pangboche,** which will likely take around 7 hours.

Gorak Shep to Lobuje: 2 hours; Lobuje to Pheriche: 3 hours; Pheriche to Pangboche: 1 hour.

DAY 2: UPPER PANGBOCHE TO PANGKA

Leaving upper Pangboche, follow the trail that contours high above the Imja Khola. Do not take the trail that leads down to the river, as this will take you to Tengboche, which would add two ascents and two descents to your trek. About 2 hours from Pangboche, the trail rounds a ridge into the valley of the Dudh Kosi and reaches the spread-out village of **Phortse,** where many of the homes are surrounded by walled fields. There are a couple of lodges here.

From Phortse there are two possible routes—the east valley route and the west valley route. The east valley route, which is on the same side of the valley as Phrortse, is rarely used by trekkers and consequently has few lodges and may sometimes be difficult to follow. However, if you are doing this route in reverse, you can make good time descending the east valley route. You should be able to walk from Gokyo to Phortse in a day.

The west valley route, though it entails descending to the **Dudh Kosi** and then climbing the far side to regain lost elevation, is preferable. It is only 45 minutes down to the river and another 10 minutes up to the main trail from Namche Bazaar to Gokyo. From this point on, there are lodges and teahouses every hour or two. You can probably reach Macherma or Pangka on the same day. See above for a description of this route.

There is also a trail that connects Phortse and Tengboche. This trail climbs to the ridge above Phortse before descending precipitously down a shadeless slope. This section of trail is steep and covered with loose rock. A slip could be fatal. It takes less than an hour to reach the valley floor from Phortse. From the river, the trail climbs even more abruptly than it descended, though luckily it is through a cool, moist forest. Tengboche is about an hour from the river.

Dudh Kosi bridge to Dole: 1^1/$_2$ hours; Dole to Luza: 1^1/$_2$ hours.

TO GOKYO VIA THE CHO LA (PASS)
DAY 1: GORAK SHEP TO DZONGLA

It is now possible to cross the 17,377-foot (5,300-meter) Cho La during the main trekking season. However, this strenuous route is difficult to follow. I recommend trying it only if you have a guide.

From Gorak Shep, return down the main valley through **Lobuje** toward Dughla. About 30 minutes below Lobuje, watch for a trail that contours around a ridge and heads up the valley to the northwest. Below this trail you will see Tshola Lake. Continue up this valley to the yak-herding huts and simple lodge at **Dzongla** (15,879 feet; 4,843 meters). The views from here are stupendous.

Gorak Shep to Lobuje: 2 hours; Lobuje to Dzongla: 3 hours.

DAY 2: DZONGLA TO DRAGNAG

From Dzongla, the trail ascends a bit then descends before starting the climb up to the pass. The trail, which is not very distinct, heads in the general direction of a glacier, passing to the east of the glacier for a while before actually crossing the glacier itself. For much of the year crampons and an ice axe are essential when crossing the glacier. The glacier crossing is quite steep at the beginning but then levels out as you approach the **Cho La** (17,377 feet; 5,300 meters).

Dropping down from the pass, you cross snow at first and then reach a slope of loose rocks. Footing can be precarious through this section. After descending the pass, you cross a lateral moraine; keep to the right as you go. The trail follows a valley down to Dragnag, where there is a very basic lodge operating during the main trekking seasons.

From Dragnag, the trail leads across the Ngozumba Glacier and winds around quite a bit. Each year, many trekkers get lost on this section of trail. It is primarily this stretch that requires a guide. Crossing the lateral moraine, you reach the main trail from Namche Bazaar to **Gokyo,** just below the second of the Gokyo lakes.

Dzongla to Cho La: 3 hours: Cho La to Gokyo: 4 hours.

FLYING TO LUKLA

This is currently the most popular way of starting a trek in the Mt. Everest region. By flying in, you shorten the trek by a week, but you also bypass a week's worth of interesting villages that provide a broader look at Nepali hill life than do the few villages between Lukla and the higher elevations.

R.N.A.C. (☎ 977/1-220757 or 977/1-226574) operates fixed-wing planes into Lukla. **Asian Airlines** (☎ 977/1-417753) and **Nepal Airways** (☎ 977/1-418214) both operate helicopters to the remote airstrip. R.N.A.C. charges $83 one way and the two helicopter companies charge $90 one way. The steeply angled airstrip at Lukla provides one of the most hair-raising landings in the world, a memorable beginning to a trek.

DAY 1: KATHMANDU TO LUKLA

Lukla (9,200 feet; 2,806 meters) has become a very busy village since the opening of the airstrip. There are more than a dozen lodges and as many general stores and trekking supply shops. Because the altitude here is about as high as you should fly into if you don't want immediately to suffer from altitude sickness, it is advisable to spend the rest of the day here acclimatizing. The best way to acclimatize is to do a bit of walking, preferably above the village. If you want to hire a guide, porter, or both, ask at your lodge. Avoid dealing with any touts that might approach you as you get off the plane or helicopter. The Himalaya Lodge just above the airstrip is a popular lodge and charges $2 for a double. However, if you aren't quite ready to give up private bathrooms, you could stay at the Sagarmatha Resort, which charges $55 for a double.

DAY 2: LUKLA TO MONDZO

The trail from Lukla begins at the far end of the village from the airstrip and leads gradually downhill to **Chapling** (8,767 feet; 2,674 meters). This section of the trail is mostly without any shade, so it's a good idea to start while it is still cool. As in Lukla, there are views down into the valley of the Dudh Kosi. Several hundred feet below, you can see the village of Chaunrikarka. Shortly before reaching Chapling, the trail from Lukla joins the trail up from Jiri. See "Day 8: Chaunrikarka to Jorsale," above, to continue this trek onward toward Namche Bazaar. You should be able to reach Mondzo or Jorsale today.

Lukla to Chapling: 45 minutes.

2 Around Annapurna

Though the Pokhara-to-Jomosom half of this trek is much more popular than the entire 18- to 20-day route, this huge loop covering more than 150 miles is still one of the more popular treks in Nepal. Offering amazing variations in topography, vegetation, and culture, the trek around the Annapurna massif is fascinating from beginning to end. Starting in the tropical Pokhara Valley, the trek climbs to the arid valley of Manang, which is in the rain shadow of the Himalayas. Crossing over the Thorong La (pass) at 17,770 feet; 5,400 meters, the route descends to Muktinath, a pilgrimage site sacred to both Buddhists and Hindus. In the main shrine here, you can even see the sacred flames that burn on bare rock (a natural gas leak). On either side of the pass are several fascinating villages built almost entirely of stone and populated by people akin to Tibetans. These villages offer anyone who has never been to Tibet a chance to see what village life is like across the border. Descending from Jomosom, the trail passes through villages inhabited by various ethnic groups, giving the trekker a chance to observe different Nepali life styles. In Tatopani there is a hot spring that usually provides a long-anticipated hot bath after 2 weeks on the trail. Above Tatopani at Poon Hill, there is one last opportunity for spectacular mountain views, though the views from the Manang Valley and from around Jomosom are far more spectacular.

Much of this trek's popularity stems from the fact that there are many lodges along the entire route, which makes carrying a tent and food unnecessary. Lodges vary from bamboo-walled huts to three-story stone chalets. The food available on this trek is also quite good, especially on the Jomosom side. Hardly a day goes by without apple pie. The major drawbacks of the trek are, of course, the crowds of trekkers and the Thorong La. Quite a few people have died trying to cross this high pass. You must be very watchful for signs of altitude sickness in yourself, your companions, porters, and guides. If you become ill, *do not* attempt to cross the pass. Descend immediately to lower elevation.

Aside from the altitude, the main drawback of this trek is its popularity. During the main trekking season, thousands of trekkers take to the trail here, and you are likely to see as many trekkers as Nepalis. If you have come to Nepal expecting to be the only foreigner on the trail, avoid this trek in October and November. Another drawback of this trek's popularity is the changes that have been brought on by the numbers of trekkers descending on the region. Lodges all along the Jomosom trek have lost much of their unique Nepali character, and many now have electric generators, satellite TVs, and VCRs. If you have come here expecting an escape from civilization, these modern "conveniences" can be an unwelcome surprise.

There are several ways to start this trek. Most people take a bus to Dumre, either from Kathmandu (6 hours) or Pokhara (2 hours) and then take a truck to Besi Sahar. I don't recommend this route, however, because the trucks that operate between Dumre and Besi Sahar are notorious for breaking down and crashing. These trucks take at least 4 hours and usually much longer. So if you start the day from Pokhara, you can usually be in Besi Sahar by nightfall, but if you start from Kathmandu, you will probably have to spend the night in Dumre. About a 1¹/₂–hour walk up the valley from Besi Sahar brings you to the trail junction with the route I describe below. Taking the bus and truck to Besi Sahar cuts 1 to 1¹/₂ days off the trek.

DAY 1: POKHARA TO KARPUTAR

The main advantages of following this route are that you spend only 1 hour on a bus before beginning trekking and you avoid the hair-raising, heart-stopping truck ride from Dumre to Besi Sahar. From the main bus park in Pokhara, take a bus to the village of **Sisuwa** between Begnas Tal and Rupa Tal, two lakes to the east of Pokhara. Sisuwa is the end of the line, and the bus usually stops right at the beginning of the trail, which leads uphill from the collection of shops at the east end of the village. The trail climbs moderately up a ridge, from the top of which there are views of both Rupa Tal and Begnas Tal with the Annapurna Himal in the background and reflected in Begnas Tal. The trail descends the ridge at the far end of Rupa Tal and heads up the terraced river valley to the village of Tarbensi, where there is a teahouse. From Tarbensi the trail ascends gradually to the east through a narrow, rocky valley and then climbs steeply and steadily through forest to a pass at **Sakra Bhanjyang,** where there are more teahouses. The trail then descends very steeply, still in forest, on an eroded trail paved with stone steps. Leaving the forest, you continue descending gradually across a rocky dry riverbed, eventually crossing the shallow river itself. The trail then enters the forest again and descends through the beautiful Achari Bhanjyang, a village of stucco and thatch houses that are painted orange and white, with black trim. There are shady pastures surrounding the village giving it a very idyllic atmosphere. Reaching the valley floor, the trail cuts across rice paddies to Bagwa Bazaar and the long suspension bridge across the Madi Khola. Just across this bridge, the trail enters the village of **Karputar** (1,600 feet; 488 meters), which is shaded by several large pipal trees. Karputar has a large stone lodge just before the suspension bridge and a couple of very basic bamboo-walled teahouses right in town.

Pokhara to Sisuwa: 1 hour; Sisuwa to Sakra Bhanjyang: 3 hours; Sakra Bhanjyang to Karputar: 2 hours.

DAY 2: KARPUTAR TO BAGLUNGPANI

Get an early start because it is a long day to Baglungpani. From Karputar, head northeast up the wide valley of the Midim Khola to Laxmi Bazaar. Just as you enter this little village on the edge of the rice paddies, there is a small shrine beneath a banyan tree. Turn right at the shrine to follow a canal out of the village. Walk alongside the canal, which eventually is separated from the river only by large cages full of stones. This trail brings you to to Shyauli Bazaar, where there are a few simple teahouses. The valley here is below 1,600 feet (488 meters) which makes it lower and hotter than Pokhara. Be prepared to sweat profusely all day. Beyond Shyauli Bazaar, the trail enters the woods again and winds up and down the steep walls of the narrowing valley. At times the trail is very steep. In the dry season, when the river is low, it is possible to walk up the riverbed. On the high route, you will cross a suspension bridge and come to a teahouse perched high above the valley floor. If you have walked up the riverbed, you must climb to the teahouse when you see the suspension bridge. This teahouse is called **Phedi,** which means "foot of the hill." From here it is nearly 4,000 feet up to Baglungpani.

From this teahouse, you begin climbing in earnest up a steep forest trail. When you finally reach the ridge crest, the trail becomes much less steep and crosses terraced fields to the village of **Nalma.** This picturesque Gurung village is scattered along the crest of the ridge and has several teahouses. You could probably stay here for the night, though there is no real trekkers' lodge. From Nalma, the trail climbs steeply up a stone stairway. This ridge trail climbs and levels off three times before descending through a damp forest and then ascending to **Baglungpani** (5,315 feet; 1,621 meters), a small village on a saddle. There is a spring here and also a large school. Baglungpani has only one small and poorly run lodge. It is located where the trail reaches the crest of the ridges and heads down the opposite side. Sunsets and sunrises from Baglungpani are stunning.

Karputar to Phedi: 3 hours; Phedi to Nalma: 1$\frac{1}{2}$ hours; Nalma to Baglungpani: 3 hours.

DAY 3: BAGLUNGPANI TO NGATTI

The trail descends steeply from Baglungpani through forests full of birds. Slightly more than halfway to the valley floor, you come to the village of Samrong. The trail now descends toward the river with **Lama Gaon** village on both sides. At the far end of the suspension bridge across the river, the trail drops down a large boulder and continues east along the riverbank. The trail then angles away from the river, crosses through terraced fields, and passes a few hundred yards to the north of Sera village. Beyond Sera, you enter the wide valley of the Marsyangdi River, which you can see below you. The trail continues descending gradually until you come to a tributary of the Marsyangdi. On the far side of this tributary is the village of **Khudi** (2,300 feet; 702 meters). There are several teahouses and lodges here. From Khudi you have a view up the Marsyangdi valley to Ngadi Chuli (25,820 feet; 7,875 meters) and Manaslu (26,755 feet; 8,156 meters). The trail continues up the west bank of the Marsyangdi, passing Khudi's school in about 10 minutes. You pass through two small villages and then cross the Marsyangdi on a suspension bridge. On the east bank is **Bhul Bhule** (2,700 feet; 824 meters), which has quite a few hotels and teahouses. The trail continues up the east bank past an impressive waterfall and through a wide expanse of terraced fields to Ngatti, a small village inhabited by people from Manang. Pony trains often stop here for the night and load up rice to be carried up to Manang. There are a couple of teahouses and lodges here.

Baglungpani to Lama Gaon: 1$\frac{1}{2}$ hours; Lama Gaon to Khudi: 1 hour; Khudi to Bhul Bhule: 1 hour; Bhul Bhule to Ngatti: 1 hour.

DAY 4: NGATTI TO JAGAT

The path crosses a stream at the edge of Ngatti and continues across terraced fields before crossing the Ngatti Khola, a major tributary of the Marsyangdi. After crossing the bridge, head straight across the wide flat area to pick up a new trail to Bahudanda. Do not take the old trail to the right. The old trail does considerably more climbing than the new one. The new trail contours around the hill that the old trail climbed over. On the far side the two trails join again before starting a steady climb toward the next large hill, atop which is the village of **Bahudanda.** After the village of Lampata, the trail becomes steeper and very dusty. If you follow this switchbacking trail all the way to Bahudanda (4,300 feet; 1,312 meters), you will enter the village through a combination dump and open latrine. Watch for the nearly vertical shortcut that climbs directly to the teahouses on the crest of the hill. There are several teahouses and lodges here, as well as a police checkpost and some small shops. After the hot, sweaty climb up to the top, the shade of Bahudanda is a welcome spot for a rest.

The trail out of the village passes a bamboo grove before descending rapidly on a dusty eroded path worn into soft rock. After 15 minutes the trail levels off, crosses

The Annapurna Region Trekking Routes

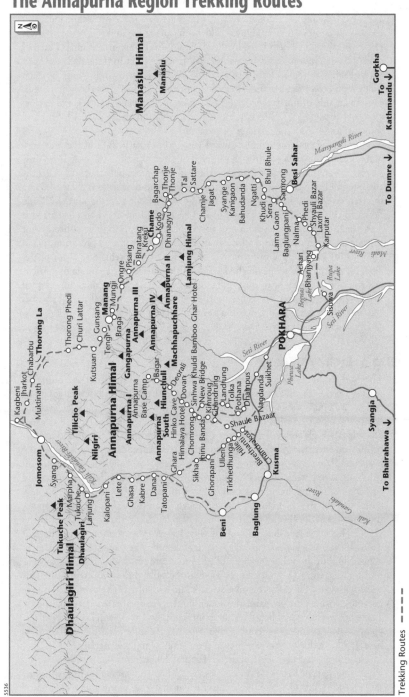

Trekking Routes – – –

a stream, and contours through terraces. The valley narrows above Bahudanda, and the walls become very steep. Down below you can see the milky, turquoise waters of the Marsyangdi, which is fed by the glaciers of the Annapurna Himal. The trail crosses a steep mountainside where the trail is actually cut into the rock and then enters Kanigaon (3,870 feet; 1,180 meters). The trail then winds along the steep valley walls before descending rapidly to a suspension bridge over the Marsyangdi. On the far side of the bridge, wedged between the river and a cliff, is the narrow village of **Syange** (3,725 feet; 1,136 meters), where there are several lodges and some teahouses.

From Syange the trail climbs toward Jagat on the steep walls of the now very narrow canyon. Much of this trail is carved out of cliff walls with steep drop-offs. In places water and stone stairs make the trail even more nerve-racking. Eventually the trail begins to descend again, though almost as quickly as it climbed. Here the trail often becomes a streambed because water from a spring on the hillside flows down the eroded path. **Jagat** (4,230 feet; 1,290 meters) looks like a Stone Age village with dark houses built of rocks. There are huge boulders throughout the village that further emphasize the ancient feel. The village's precarious perch on a jutting cliff high above the river only adds to the prehistoric atmosphere. There is a large new lodge on the far side of the village and a couple of smaller, less appealing ones right in the middle of the village. Jagat has an annual festival in mid-January. If you happen to be passing through on festival day, it's worth staying to see what goes on, but don't expect to get any sleep.

Ngatti to Bahudanda: 2 hours; Bahudanda to Syange: 2 hours; Syange to Jagat: 1¹/₂ hours.

DAY 5: JAGAT TO THONJE

The trail descends steeply from Jagat almost to the river before ascending an equally steep path. The opposite bank is almost a sheer cliff with several long ribbonlike waterfalls streaming down its face. After this next climb, the trail levels off before reaching **Chamje** (4,700 feet; 1,434 meters). Chamje, like Jagat, is situated precariously high above the river on a steep mountainside. There is a lodge just before you enter the village. After Chamje the trail descends again and crosses the Marsyangdi on a long suspension bridge (4,625 feet; 1,411 meters). Again the trail climbs on a very steep path with drop-offs. Pass through the village of Sattare and continue climbing steeply. Looking down to the valley below you, you may notice that the river is no longer visible, though it can still be heard. Above Sattare, the river flows under the giant boulders of a landslide that once blocked the valley. This same landslide formed the wide flat valley surrounding the village of **Tal.** Tal means "lake," as this valley is a dry lakebed. The same steep cliffs rise up above you, but the valley has been filled in to create this wide plain. It is a beautiful sight as you top a hill and see Tal and the valley below you with waterfalls streaming down the cliffs. It is an easy walk into the village. The town itself is very attractive with colorfully painted wooden houses, many of which have balconies. There are several lodges here. Try the Himalchuli Lodge. As you leave the village, you pass by a beautiful waterfall with a large white chorten and prayer flags at its base. If you are lucky, you might even see a rainbow in the waterfall.

There is an excellent trail between Tal and Dharapani that avoids the steep climb and descent that were once necessary. When you come to a fork with one trail ascending steeply, take the fork to the left that leads along a level trail past a reforestation nursery. Cross the river and continue up the valley on the west bank.

This trail is quite steep in places and is often blasted out of rock. It rejoins the old trail near a suspension bridge below Dharapani. Stay on the west bank, and you will soon come to **Dharapani,** a dark and dirty village. Though there are a few lodges here, you'll do better to continue another 10 minutes to the Hotel Dhorje above the village of Thonje. There is a police checkpost beside this three-story stone lodge overlooking the confluence of the Dudh Khola and the Marsyangdi. **Thonje,** about 10 minutes below the lodge and across a bridge, is well worth a visit. It is a fascinating little village built almost entirely of stone. The people here are very friendly, and there are also many mani walls and chortens.

Jagat to Chamje: 1¼ hours; Chamje to Tal: 2 hours; Tal to Dharapani: 2 hours; Dharapani to Thonje: 10 minutes.

DAY 6: THONJE TO CHAME

At Thonje, the Marsyangdi, which has been flowing from the north, makes a wide bend to the west. As you round this bend, you see far ahead of you Annapurna II (26,035 feet; 7,937 meters). You soon come to **Bagarchap** (7,100 feet; 2,166 meters), a sunny village with a network of small canals winding through it. There are several teahouses and lodges here. Above the village is a Buddhist monastery of the Nyingmapa sect. Be sure to have a look at the amazing selection of goods available at Bagarchap's Fancy Store. The trail enters a thick rhododendron forest where you might see gray langurs, a long-tailed monkey that frequents the higher elevations. The trail passes the small village of **Dhanagyu,** which has several teahouses but which is almost always cold and dark due to its location on the north side of a steep ridge.

Beyond Dhanagyu the trail crosses a bridge in front of a powerful waterfall. Beyond this waterfall, the trail becomes a steep stone stairway that is almost always wet and icy. Be especially careful. The trail continues through enchanting forests for several hours, passing only a few scattered houses along the way. From the rhododendron forest of the lower elevations, you climb to forests of fir and pine. Finally the forest gives way to a flat cultivated area, and you enter the village of **Kodo,** where there is a police checkpost. Entering the forest again the trail climbs gradually to **Chame** (8,900 feet; 2,715 meters), a government administrative center with many offices, lodges, and shops. None of the lodges right in town is very appealing, but you can try the Kamala Lodge or Pratap Lodge. The New Tibetan Lodge is the best choice in town. Almost directly in front of this lodge, on the bank of the river, is a small hot spring that is used by locals as a combination laundry and public bath. There is an excellent view of Manaslu back down the valley to the east.

Thonje to Bagarchap: 30 minutes; Bagarchap to Dhanagyu: 1½ hours; Dhanagyu to Kodo: 3 hours; Kodo to Chame: 30 minutes.

DAY 7: CHAME TO PISANG

The trail crosses the river in Chame and climbs through an older section of the village. After leaving Chame, the trail traverses cultivated fields and apple orchards to the few houses of Kreku village. The far side of the valley becomes a very steep wall as you hike through forests toward **Bhratang** (9,575 feet; 2,920 meters). There is now a trail that bypasses the actual village of Bhratang, which is on the south bank of the river. The new trail on the north bank has a couple of teahouses at the foot of a sheer cliff. Just beyond these teahouses, the trail is blasted out of a vertical rock wall with the river several hundred feet below.

After this vertiginous section, the trail climbs through a rocky, and often icy, forest to a bridge over the Marsyangdi. As you approach this bridge you begin to see, above you on your right, an awesome solid rock slope that rises nearly 5,000 feet (1,525 meters) and curves from south to west. High on this rock face you can even see a tiny shrine. This marks the beginning of the glaciated reaches of the Marsyangdi valley.

Continue climbing through quiet forests. The trail crests a hill and descends slightly into a wide valley with meadows scattered among the trees. Ahead of you, on a brown hillside on the opposite side of the river, you see the stone houses and prayer flags of upper **Pisang** (10,800 feet; 3,294 meters) and soon reach lower Pisang (10,450 feet; 3,187 meters), on this side of the river. Lower Pisang is surrounded by barren rocky hills and has a long wall of prayer wheels as you enter the village. The people of the Manang region are closely related to the Tibetans, which is reflected in their faces and architecture. The homes are all tiny stone fortresses with flat roofs for storing fodder and for sunning in the cold winter months. A trip up the steep slope to upper Pisang affords a glimpse of a fascinating Manangi mountain village. If you stay at one of the family-run lodges in lower Pisang you will avoid the necessity of climbing the steep path to upper Pisang with your pack on. There are several lodges in both lower and upper Pisang. If you cross the bridge in Pisang and follow the stream that leads upstream, you will come to an unbelievably beautiful mountain lake in about 20 minutes. The waters of the lake are turquoise and reflect Annapurna II. Don't miss this little excursion.

Chame to Bhratang: 2¹/₂ hours; Bhratang to Pisang: 2¹/₂ hours.

DAY 8: PISANG TO MANANG

Keeping to the south bank of the Marsyangdi River, cross a tributary stream as you leave lower Pisang. Pass a mani wall and several small chortens and then enter the forest again. The trail climbs steeply to the top of a ridge bedecked with many prayer flags. From this ridge a rugged panorama spreads before you with Tilicho Peak (23,400 feet; 7,134 meters) at the far end of the valley. This is the Manang Valley, and directly below you is the Manang airstrip. There are sometimes flights to this airstrip, so should you decide to return from here, you can check on your flight out. These flights also offer an option for anyone who is unable to cross the Thorong La because of altitude sickness. It is possible to fly back to Pokhara and then fly to Jomosom and continue the trek.

The trail descends to the flat valley, passing the airstrip and a few teahouses at **Ongre** (10,800 feet; 3,294 meters). There is also a police checkpost here. Beyond the airstrip, at a wide valley opening up to the south, you will see a large building. This is the Trekkers' Aid Post of the Himalayan Rescue Association and a mountaineering school. Should you have any questions about altitude sickness or should you begin suffering from it as you climb higher, you can get information and help from the doctors here.

The landscape has now become very barren, with rocky brown mountains rising all around. In the monsoon months, however, this valley is green with barley fields. Cross the Marsyangdi to the tiny village of **Mungji** (11,425 feet; 3,485 meters). Ahead of you on the right you can see, on an eroded brown hillside, the village of **Braga** (11,500 feet; 3,508 meters). The homes of this village are built one on top of the other with the roof of one serving as the front yard of the one above. Steep paths wind up through the village to a large old gompa. Above the gompa are the eroded rocky pinnacles that line both sides of the windswept Manang Valley. Just past Braga there are several chortens and a prayer wall with many carved slates depicting various Buddhist deities. Crossing a barren and rocky stretch, you come to a small stream with two small flour mills. Cross the stream on a log and climb the hill trail to enter **Manang** (11,600 feet; 3,538 meters). The Hotel Yak and the Annapurna Lodge are two of the better choices in Manang.

Pisang to Ongre: 2 hours; Ongre to Manang: 2 hours.

DAY 9: MANANG

Because of the elevation that will be gained in the next 2 days, it is necessary to spend at least 1 day acclimatizing in Manang. The best way to do this is to hike to a higher elevation and then return to Manang the same day. Though the view across the valley to the Annapurna Himal is spectacular, you can get an even better view by hiking up the ridge to the north of Manang. From this ridge, you can see (from east to west) Annapurna II (26,035 feet; 7,937 meters), Annapurna IV (24,685 feet; 7,525 meters), Annapurna III (24,787 feet; 7,555 meters), Gangapurna (24,450 feet; 7,455 meters), and Tilicho Peak (23,400 feet; 7,134 meters). From this point you should also be able to walk back down the valley to a large red gompa on a ridge between Manang and Braga. You probably saw this building as you walked up the valley from Braga yesterday. Another good choice would be to continue up the main trail to Tengi (12,000 feet; 3,660 meters), the last permanent village before the ascent of Thorong La.

Manang itself is also a fascinating place to explore. Perched on the edge of a high ridge overlooking a glacial lake and the Gangapurna icefall, the village is a maze of narrow alleyways, some of which actually go under houses. Each home is a multilevel compound with a stable on the first floor, living quarters on the next floor, and storage on the roof or the third floor. The people of Manang are primarily farmers and goatherders. Each afternoon the children herd the goats back into the village, and the tinkling of bells and bleating of goats fill the air. There is also a small gompa, which is usually kept locked, toward the west end of the village. You should be able to see the murals on the exterior walls of the gompa's porch.

DAY 10: MANANG TO (THORONG) PHEDI

From Manang, the trail climbs through Tengi, beyond which there are only summer villages used by herders who bring their flocks up to the high pastures. Above Tengi, the trail leaves the valley of the Marsyangdi and turns northwest up the Jargeng Khola. In the village of Gunsang there is a lodge beside the trail. After this village cross a stream and continue to Kutsuan and cross another stream. The trail climbs steadily to a wide alluvial plain at **Lattar** (13,700 feet; 4,179 meters), where there are two simple lodges. Be sure to find out whether the lodges at Phedi are operating and have food before continuing.

From Lattar climb a ridge and then descend and cross the Jareng Khola. The trail climbs on the west bank of the river and then descends once again to cross back to the east bank of the river. The trail stays in the riverbed for 10 minutes before climbing to a flat area called **Phedi** (14,450 feet; 4,407 meters) or Thorong Phedi. This is not a village but simply the last inhabited outpost before crossing over the Thorong La. The one lodge is often very crowded. Phedi translates as "Foot of the Hill," and from here it is a long steady climb to Thorong La.

Manang to Lattar: 3 hours; Lattar to Phedi: 2 hours.

DAY 11: (THORONG) PHEDI TO MUKTINATH

Do not attempt to continue over Thorong La if the weather is bad. It is very easy to lose the trail in snow. This is a long day to begin with, and fresh, unbroken snow can make it impossible to reach Muktinath before nightfall. Even when there is no snow, the strong winds blowing over the pass make every footstep difficult. After Phedi, the trail immediately begins switchbacking up a steep hill. For the next several hours the trail climbs and descends several moraines and hills (false passes that will make you think the true pass will never appear) before beginning a steady but gradual climb up to the pass. **Thorong La** (17,765 feet; 5,418 meters) is marked by a chorten, several cairns, and prayer flags.

The descent of more than 5,000 feet (1,525 meters) is gradual at first, but after about an hour, it becomes steeper and crosses a scree slope and a steep cliff. Be very careful through this section if there is snow on the ground. Below this steep section is the lone stone lodge at **Chabarbu** (14,200 feet; 4,331 meters). From Chabarbu to Muktinath, the trail is less steep. Crossing two streams near Chabarbu, you descend gradually across grassy slopes to **Muktinath** (12,475 feet; 3,805 meters). As you descend, you can see Dhaulagiri (26,790 feet; 8,167 meters) and Ilukuche (22,700 feet; 6,920 meters) to the southwest down the Kali Gandaki Valley. Before reaching the lodges at Muktinath, the trail passes a police checkpost and the several temples of this remote pilgrimage site. Within the main temple here are the sacred flames that were mentioned 2,000 years ago in the Indian epic *Mahabharata.* These flames, caused by natural gas leaks, burn on water, rock, and earth. If you give a small donation, the keeper will gladly open the temple and show you the flames, which are hidden behind curtains. There are also 108 waterspouts, through which flow holy waters. Because one of the temples here is dedicated to the Hindu god Vishnu, and because Buddha is considered an incarnation of Vishnu, the shrine is sacred to both Hindus and Buddhists. The annual pilgrimage and festival takes place during the full moon of late August or early September. There are several lodges in Muktinath. Try the Hotel Muktinath or the Himalaya Hotel.

Phedi to Thorong La: 4 hours; Thorong La to Chabarbu: 3 hours; Chabarbu to Muktinath: 1 hour.

DAY 12: MUKTINATH TO KAGBENI

From Muktinath, the trail continues descending gradually across barren, grassy slopes to **Jharkot,** an ancient fortress village surrounded by a grove of poplar and apricot trees. Below Jharkot is the Jhong Khola, named for the even older fortress village of Jhong, visible on the opposite side of the river. There are a couple of lodges in Jharkot. The Himali Hotel incorporates a passive solar–heating system into its design. The path leads along a stone wall as it leaves Jharkot and, after crossing through terraced fields, strikes out across the barren sloping hillside.

After passing through a grove of trees, you reach the small village of Khinga. Beyond Khinga the trail forks. The right fork leads to Kagbeni, while the left fork leads straight to Jomosom. From here it is about 3 hours to Jomosom, with only a single teahouse at the bottom of this slope where the trail reaches the floor of the Kali Gandaki valley. However, I strongly recommend that you take a detour down to Kagbeni, since it is one of the most interesting villages on the entire trek.

The trail to Kagbeni gradually descends a long slope. On the far side of the Jhong Khola, you can see caves in the hillside. Some of these caves can be reached by climbing up from Kagbeni. Crossing through terraced and walled fields, you reach **Kagbeni** (9,200 feet; 2,806 meters), where the stone and mud houses are packed together on a steep hillside. Narrow, muddy alleys wind between, over, and under the flat-roofed houses. Prayer flags sprout from every roof, and prayer wheels line many walls. In the middle of this village are the remains of an old castle, and out at the far end is a huge cube-shaped gompa painted ocher. The gompa is a striking contrast to the barren brown hills and brilliant blue sky. Try the Red House or the Nilgiri Lodge for food and lodging.

Muktinath to Jharkot: 1 hour; Jharkot to Kagbeni: 2¹/₂ hours.

DAYS 13–19: KAGBENI TO POKHARA

Trekking from Kagbeni down the Kali Gandaki to Pokhara takes about 7 days. See "The Jomosom Trek," below for details on this segment of the trek. Follow the Jomosom route descriptions in reverse. Because you will be descending for most of the trip, your trekking times will probably be shorter than those listed for the uphill journey.

3 Annapurna Sanctuary

In the past few years, this trek has become extremely popular because of the amazing scenery in the Annapurna Sanctuary. The sanctuary is a huge amphitheater surrounded by 10 peaks that are more than 20,000 feet (6,100 meters) tall, including Annapurna I, Annapurna South, Annapurna III, and Machhapuchhare. Enterprising Nepalis have opened very basic trekkers' lodges between Chomrong and the sanctuary. However, these lodges are only open during the peak trekking seasons of October to November and February to March. During December and January, innkeepers move back down to Chomrong because of deep snows. In the spring, frequent avalanches close down the sanctuary and make trekking very dangerous. If it has been raining at low elevations, you can be sure that snow has been building on the slopes above and that avalanches are likely to follow. Be sure to ask anyone you meet coming from the opposite direction about trail conditions. This is a remote area a day or two beyond the last village and is as close to a wilderness as you are likely to find on a trek in Nepal.

As part of the Annapurna Conservation Area Project, there is a kerosene depot at Chomrong village, which is between the large village of Ghandrung and the sanctuary itself. Though kerosene is not always available here, you should stop at the depot and try to secure enough for your journey into the sanctuary if you are doing your own cooking. The use of firewood is prohibited beyond Chomrong, and all lodges are required to use kerosene for cooking. Consequently, the price of meals goes up considerably beyond here, making this the most expensive teahouse trek you can do. The numbers of trekkers on this route has had a heavy toll, worsening deforestation and increasing amounts of trailside litter and garbage in the sanctuary. It was in part due to the abuse of such a pristine area that the Annapurna Conservation Area Project was begun.

Pokhara is the starting point for this trek, and you should allow at least 10 or 11 days and preferably 2 weeks to allow for avalanches interrupting your trek.

DAY 1: POKHARA TO LANDRUNG

Take a taxi from Pokhara to the trailhead at Phedi for around Rs300 ($6). The ride takes about 30 minutes. **Phedi** (3,700 feet; 1,129 meters), which means

"Bottom of the Hill," is at the foot of a moderately steep trail that climbs through scrubby forest to the ridge-top village of **Dhampus** (5,700 feet; 1,739 meters). This 2,000-foot (610-meter) climb is a tough way to start a trek, but after you reach Dhampus, the trail becomes easier. There are excellent views of Machhapuchhare and Annapurna from along the trail near Dhampus. Should you decide to stop in Dhampus, try the Basanta Lodge. From Dhampus, the trail climbs slowly as it contours around a forested ridge with only a few simple teahouses. Just below the crest of this ridge is the village of **Pothana** where there are several lodges with glassed-in rooftop dining rooms that make the most of the mountain views.

From Pothana, the trail first climbs a bit and then, after cresting the ridge, descends very steeply, passing the hamlet of Beri Kharka, to the small village of **Tolka** (5,900 feet; 1,800 meters) where there are more lodges with rooftop dining rooms. The trail continues descending through forest and, after leveling off at Medigala, enters **Landrung** (5,450 feet; 1,662 meters), a fairly large village with lots of unremarkable lodges. If you don't mind having a slightly longer walk tomorrow, you'd do better to stay in Tolka. The large village across the valley from Landrung is Ghandrung.

Pokhara to Phedi: 30 minutes; Phedi to Dhampus: 1¹/₂ hours; Dhampus to Pothana: 1¹/₂ hours; Pothana to Tolka: 1¹/₂ hours; Tolka to Landrung: 1¹/₂ hours.

Day 2: Landrung to Chomrong

From Landrung, there are two possible routes. If you take the trail that descends steeply from Landrung to the floor of the Modi Khola valley, you will be headed for Ghandrung, the largest village in the area. The trail is a steep 1,000-foot (305-meter) descent followed by an equally steep 2,000-foot (610-meter) ascent. To avoid this grueling stretch of trail, I suggest you take an alternate route that descends slowly to the valley floor. Watch for this trail on the right at the lower end of Landrung. This is the trail that leads up the valley of the Modi Khola on the east bank. The trail finally crosses the river at a spot known as **New Bridge** or Himal Kyu (4,975 feet; 1,517 meters). There are a couple of teahouses at the bridge.

From here the trail climbs steeply to **Jhinu Danda** (5,775 feet; 1,761 meters), where there are a couple of lodges. A 30-minute walk from Jhinu Danda will bring you to a very relaxing hot spring on the banks of the Modi Khola; unfortunately, it is a steep climb back up to the lodges after bathing. From Jhinu Danda, the trail continues climbing steeply, and without shade, to a few lodges on the shoulder of a ridge. These lodges mark the junction of the trail to Ghandrung, which I will describe on the return trip. In 30 minutes you will reach **Chomrong,** a medium-size village about 600 feet (183 meters) below this trail junction. For the first 15 minutes the trail descends gradually, but for the last 15 minutes, you will be walking on steep stone steps. At the point where the steps begin, there are several very comfortable lodges with flagstone terraces, gardens, solar showers, and sun rooms. These lodges also have a better view than the older lodges down in the village. From Chomrong, there are good views of Machhapuchhare, Annapurna South, and Hiunchuli. The Captain's Lodge, in the village, and the Moonlight Lodge, above the village, are the two trekkers' favorites here. There are no more villages beyond this point, so, before continuing, find out whether lodges in the sanctuary are open.

Landrung to New Bridge: 1¹/₂ hours; New Bridge to Jhinu Danda: 1¹/₂ hours; Jhinu Danda to Chomrong: 1¹/₂ hours.

DAY 3: CHOMRONG TO DOVAN

This is a short and fairly easy day. From Chomrong, the trail descends and crosses the Chomrong Khola (6,200 feet; 1,891 meters), a tributary of the Modi Khola, before beginning the long climb to Khuldi Ghar. The first part of this section of trail is up the side of the tributary valley, but at about 7,000 feet (2,135 meters) you contour around a ridge into the main valley of the Modi Khola. As this section of trail rounds a shoulder of the ridge at **Sinuwa,** you'll find a couple of lodges. The trail continues climbing and passes a couple of more lodges at Tibesa before finally reaching **Khuldi Ghar** (7,800 feet; 2,379 meters). Here you'll find another lodge and, just above the trail a bit, the buildings of an old British sheep-breeding station that is now a government lodge. This section of trail is paved with tight-fitting paving stones and even has gutters on either side of the path. From here, the trail descends steeply, sometimes along rock outcroppings that have had steps set into them. At the bottom of this steep stretch, the trail enters a dark, damp bamboo forest where the trail is almost always muddy. The next rest spot you come to is known as **Bamboo Hotel** (7,500 feet; 2,288 meters), although there are now several very basic lodges here. Bamboo Hotel makes a good lunch stop. Beyond Bamboo, the trail continues through dense, damp forest to Tiptop Lodge, another basic lodge that is often packed by early afternoon. This stretch of trail can be extremely slippery, and it is easy to trip on muddy roots and fallen bamboo trunks. Continuing past Tiptop, you soon come to the two lodges of **Dovan** (8,500 feet; 2,593 meters).

Chomrong to Sinuwa: 1 1/2 hours; Sinuwa to Khuldi Ghar: 1 hour; Khuldi Ghar to Bamboo Hotel: 30 minutes; Bamboo Hotel to Tiptop Lodge: 1 hour; Tiptop Lodge to Dovan: 30 to 45 minutes.

DAY 4: DOVAN TO BAGAR

Dovan is little more than a clearing in the forest, and after passing the second lodge, you enter a forest of giant rhododendrons. These are not the shrubs you have in your garden at home, but trees with trunks of several feet in diameter. The valley is extremely steep-walled at this point and because of its north-south orientation gets little sunlight but plenty of rain. Streamers of water plunge hundreds of feet down the opposite valley wall and can occasionally be glimpsed through breaks in the forest. Due to the lack of sunshine and the clouds that roll up the valley daily around noon this section of trail is almost always cool and damp. Parts of the trail are also subject to avalanches, so be very cautious. Tree roots and loose gravel on the trail make the footing treacherous. Finally, shortly after the **Himalayan Hotel,** you climb above the forest and get back on dry trail again. You are now hiking through scrubby grasslands. A steep climb brings you to **Hinko Cave** (9,900 feet; 3,020 meters), an unusual and very basic lodge built into an overhanging cliff. Unfortunately, the cave is rather unprotected and doesn't make a very pleasant place to stop. The trail descends a bit before climbing again to the lodges at **Deorali** (10,600 feet; 3,233 meters) and **Bagar** (10,825 feet; 3,302 meters). Most people are feeling the elevation by the time they reach Hinko Cave, and it is a good idea to stop early and make this an acclimatization day. Though it would be possible to reach Annapurna Base Camp today, you would be risking altitude sickness since the base camp is at 13,000 feet (3,905 meters).

Dovan to Himalayan Hotel: 1 hour; Himalayan Hotel to Hinko Cave: 30 minutes; Hinko Cave to Deorali: 30 minutes; Deorali to Bagar: 30 minutes.

DAY 5: BAGAR TO ANNAPURNA BASE CAMP

The trail descends to the bed of the Modi Khola after Deorali with good views of Machhapuchhare to the east and Gangapurna to the north. Between Bagar and Machhapuchhare Base Camp, you pass through the natural gateway to the sanctuary. This gateway is formed by Machhapuchhare on the east and Hiunchuli on the west as they pinch the Modi Khola into a steep-walled valley. This is another avalanche area, so be careful. The trail is sometimes obliterated by these avalanches. If you lose the trail, just continue following the riverbed. **Machhapuchhare Base Camp** (12,100 feet; 3,691 meters) is a wide grassy area scattered with gigantic boulders about 1¹/₂ hours beyond Bagar. There are three lodges here and an excellent view of Machhapuchhare, Annapurna III, Fang, and Annapurna South. From here the trail leads almost due west at the base of the north slope of Hiunchuli. To the north of the trail are South Annapurna Glacier and the moraine formed by this impressive glacier.

It is 2 hours to **Annapurna Base Camp** (13,000 feet; 3,965 meters), where there are four lodges. The Hotel Garden Paradise has no garden and is hardly a paradise, but it is the best of the lodges here. The view from Annapurna Base Camp is by far the most spectacular of the trek and is arguably the most spectacular in Nepal. It is this spot that is rightfully known as Annapurna Sanctuary. The 360-degree panorama here includes (starting on the south side and moving clockwise) Hiunchuli (21,130 feet; 6,441 meters), Annapurna South (23,680 feet; 7,219 meters), Fang (25,089 feet; 7,647 meters), Annapurna I (26,545 feet; 8,091 meters), Annapurna III (24,787 feet; 7,555 meters), and Machhapuchhare (22,942 feet; 6,993 meters). This was the location of the base camp for the 1970 ascent of Annapurna I led by famed mountaineer Chris Bonnington. Bonnington scaled the nearly vertical south face of Annapurna I, which is the massive peak you see to the northwest of Annapurna Base Camp. Three peaks within the sanctuary, Tharpu Chuli (Tent Peak, 18,580 feet; 5,663 meters), Singu Chuli (Fluted Peak, 21,315 feet; 6,501 meters), and Hiunchuli (21,130 feet; 6,441 meters), are open to trekking parties, though you must have a permit to climb Hiunchuli. All three require extensive equipment and mountaineering skills.

Bagar to Machhapuchhare Base Camp: 1¹/₂ hours; Machhapuchhare Base Camp to Annapurna Base Camp: 2 hours.

DAY 6: EXPLORING ANNAPURNA SANCTUARY

If it is not too cold and windy, you may want to spend a day exploring the sanctuary, hiking up higher for better views, or perhaps hiking back for a night at Machhapuchhare Base Camp. Since the whole sanctuary area is above 12,000 feet, it is very important to be aware of altitude-sickness symptoms. You will almost certainly be short of breath and find exercising much more difficult than at lower elevations. You can also expect the lodges up here to be crowded and food to be very basic and relatively expensive. These two factors are enough to prevent most people from spending more than a day or two in the sanctuary.

DAYS 7-8: ANNAPURNA BASE CAMP TO CHOMRONG

Before heading back down, be sure that there is no danger of avalanches. The route back is the same as the route up for most of the way, though you can expect to make better time going out since it is mostly downhill.

Annapurna Base Camp to Himalayan Hotel: 4 to 5 hours; Himalayan Hotel to Khuldi Ghar: 3 to 3¹/₂ hours; Khuldi Ghar to Chomrong: 2 to 3 hours.

DAY 9: CHOMRONG TO GHANDRUNG

Rather than retracing your steps from Chomrong to the road, I suggest returning by way of Ghandrung, a prosperous Gurung settlement that is the largest village in the area. From Chomrong, the trail climbs a bit to a spur ridge (6,650 feet; 2,028 meters) that looks down on Jhinu Danda and the lodge near the hot springs. Be sure to glance back over your shoulders for one last close-up glimpse of Machhapuchhare, Hiunchuli, and Annapurna. Take the trail to the right at this point and contour up the valley of the Kimrong Khola. This stretch of trail is quite level and offers easy walking. Parts of the trail are in forest, but most of it is through terraced millet fields and is open to the warmth of the sun, a welcome change from the cold and damp of the Modi Khola. Above the village of **Kimrong** (6,000 feet; 1,830 meters), the trail suddenly drops in short, steep switchbacks to the village, which itself is 200 feet (61 meters) or so above the river. There is a shortcut that descends steeply to a teahouse on the banks of the river, but it is worthwhile to take the longer route through the village. On the opposite bank of the river, the trail follows a stream through terraced fields before entering a rather open forest. It is a steep climb up to the **Kimrong Pass** (7,320 feet; 2,233 meters), but luckily it is in the shade and does not take too long. At the pass, there are a couple of lodges. You can see Ghandrung below you across a sparsely wooded hillside. Drop quickly and then contour through open rock-strewn fields to Ghandrung.

Ghandrung, a Gurung village, has grown large and prosperous on the pensions of retired Gurkha soldiers. Two- and three-story stone houses with slate roofs and flagstone terraces are crammed tightly together in a maze of narrow paved alleys. The village is broken up into three sections, and coming from Chomrong, you first reach the oldest section of town. Here you might stay at the Excellent View Lodge, which is run by a woman who has spent time in the United States. Passing through this section of the village, you will come to a smaller grouping of old homes. Continuing on around the hill will bring you to the newest part of town, which is where you will find the newest lodges, including the Himalaya Hotel, which charges around $10 a night for a double room with private bathroom. This is also where you'll find the headquarters of the Annapurna Conservation Area Project (ACAP). Stop by to learn more about what ACAP is doing to preserve the culture and natural beauty of this spectacular region.

Chomrong to Kimrong: 2¹/₂ hours; Kimrong to Kimrong Pass: 1 hour; Kimrong Pass to Ghandrung: 1¹/₂ hours.

DAY 10: GHANDRUNG TO BIRETHANTI

From Ghandrung, the trail descends gradually at first on a wide flagstone-paved trail that is the superhighway of this trek. The trail crosses open hillsides and consequently is usually warm and sunny. Shortly before the small village of Kimche, you pass the trail that leads down to the river and back up to Landrung. Keep to the ridge and continue descending slowly. Eventually the trail becomes steeper as it heads for the valley floor just below **Shaule Bazaar.** The trail finally reaches the river at a couple of lodges known as Riverside. From here the trail is once again quite level, but the going is rather difficult because you are walking on river rocks. Along this stretch of trail, you will pass the Sanctuary Lodge, which, with its spacious gardens and cathedral-ceilinged dining hall, may seem at first like a mirage. Attractively decorated spacious rooms and tiled private bathrooms do nothing to dispel this belief. This lodge may well be pointing toward the future of lodge-to-lodge trekking in Nepal as more affluent trekkers demand more and more comforts. Despite a comfort level high above that of most trekking lodges, this place costs around $10 per night for a double room. It is definitely worth a stay if they have a room available.

In another 30 minutes or so you will be in **Birethanti** (3,500 feet; 1,068 meters), which is the last village before the road. Birethanti stands at the confluence of the Bhurungdi Khola and the Modi Khola and is a busy bazaar village on the trekking route to Jomosom. This is the most popular trekking route in the country, and consequently, there are plenty of comfortable lodges in Birethanti including the upscale Lakshmi Lodge, which charges around $10 for an attractive room with a shared bathroom. From here it is only a 30- to 45-minute walk to the road where you can catch a truck or bus back to Pokhara.

Ghandrung to Shaule Bazaar: 3 hours; Shaule Bazaar to Birethanti: 2 hours.

DAY 11: BIRETHANTI TO POKHARA

Because Biretanti is an attractive village in a picturesque setting, I suggest staying here for the night and catching a bus or truck back to Pokhara early the next morning. The trail crosses the suspension bridge and forks to the right, staying on the valley floor. Be sure to glance back over your shoulder at the excellent view of Machhapuchhare. The trail soon reaches the new road, which connects Pokhara with Baglung. Here there will be buses or trucks waiting to carry people to Pokhara. It can be a wait of an hour or more before a bus or truck leaves, so be patient and claim your spot.

An alternative to this easy route is to climb from Birethanti to **Chandrakot** (5,125 feet; 1,563 meters). This is a more rigorous trail, but it cuts off almost an hour of the bus or truck ride and gives you a chance to visit one last village before ending your trek. Why rush back to the noise and pollution of civilization? To take this route, cross the suspension bridge and keep to the left; the trail immediately begins climbing steeply to Chandrakot, which is about 1,500 feet (458 meters) higher than Birethanti. From Chandrakot, it is just a few minutes downhill to the road where you can wait for a bus or truck. If you are full of energy, you might just start walking along the road and flag down the next vehicle headed toward Pokhara.

Birethanti to the road: 30–45 minutes (Birethanti to Chandrakot: 1 1/2 hours); trailhead to Pokhara: 2–3 hours.

4 The Jomosom Trek

This is by far the most popular trek in Nepal. I have heard it referred to as a highway by people who have trekked more remote routes, and in the peak October to November trekking season, it is indeed overrun with trekkers. However, there is good reason for this popularity. Except for one long climb a day or so out of Pokhara, the trip is relatively easy. It does not climb above 13,000 feet (3,965 meters), so most people will not be bothered by altitude sickness. The trail to Jomosom begins just outside Pokhara and includes spectacular views of Annapurna, Dhaulagiri, and Machhapuchhare. The trail passes through picturesque villages inhabited by different ethnic groups and climbs from lush lowland forests to the arid wastelands of the upper Kali Gandaki, which is similar in many ways to the Tibetan Plateau.

DAY 1: POKHARA TO ULLERI

This first day is a long one, so try to get an early start. From Pokhara, you can take a taxi, bus, or truck to the trailhead near Chandrakot. A taxi will likely cost around Rs500 ($10) and a bus or truck Rs50 ($1) or less. It takes a couple of hours to reach this trailhead and then it is just a few minutes uphill to **Chandrakot** (5,125 feet; 1,563 meters). This village sits atop a ridge overlooking the village of Birethanti and the confluence of the Modi Khola and the Bhurungdi Khola.

There is an excellent view of Annapurna South (23,680 feet; 7,219 meters) and Machhapuchhare (22,940 feet; 6,993 meters) up the Modi Khola valley. There are several lodges here. The Hungry Eye Lodge is one of the better ones and takes full advantage of the view up the valley. If you have time, it is possible to hike up this valley to the Annapurna Sanctuary (see "Annapurna Sanctuary," above, for details). From Chandrakot it is a fast steep descent to **Birethanti** (3,500 feet; 1,068 meters) on the banks of the Modi Khola, and much of the trail is on stone steps. Birethanti is a very attractive and prosperous-looking village with a stone-paved street and several comfortable lodges. The first lodge on the left as you enter the village has a terrace overlooking the river and the suspension bridge. This terrace is an excellent place to have lunch.

From Birethanti, the trail climbs northwest up the valley of the Bhurungdi Khola, passing a waterfall just as you leave the village. Stay on the north bank of the river and follow the trail. During the dry season the trail may be in the riverbed, while in the wetter months, it is likely to climb high on the slope above the river. Pass through the small villages of Ramghai and Sudame, beyond which the trail becomes wider and easier to follow. Crossing terraced fields, you enter the village of **Hille** (5,000 feet; 1,525 meters) where there are a few lodges. Continuing through Hille, you reach Tirkhedhunga (5,175 feet; 1,578 meters), where there are a couple more lodges, in another 20 minutes.

Beyond Tirkhedhunga, the trail crosses first a stream and then the Bhurungdi Khola. Here begins the climb up the infamous Ulleri staircase, a switchbacking stairway of stone steps that climbs 1,600 feet (488 meters) up a south-facing slope with no trees for shade. At the top of this stairway is **Ulleri** (6,800 feet; 2,074 meters), an attractive Magar village with slate-roofed houses and several good lodges. From Ulleri you can see Annapurna South and Hiunchuli (21,130 feet; 6,441 meters).

Pokhara to Chandrakot: 2 hours; Chandrakot to Birethanti: 1 hour; Birethanti to Hille: 2¹/₂ hours; Hille to Ulleri: 2¹/₂ hours.

DAY 2: ULLERI TO GHORAPANI

Above Ulleri, you leave the terraced hillsides for oak forest. In the middle of this forest is the tiny village of Banthanti, which has several teahouses. Above Banthanti, you enter a dense forest that is almost perpetually enshrouded in clouds. Mosses and ferns grow on the twisted, gnarled branches of huge old rhododendron trees. At one point the trail passes a tiny narrow gorge with bamboo growing from the walls and beautiful pools of water down below. This trail is almost always either muddy or snowy or both, so watch your step. Continue climbing to the village of **Nayathanti,** which has several lodges. Ascend through forest to the village of Ghorapani (9,365 feet; 2,856 meters), which is just 10 minutes below **Ghorapani Pass** (9,600 feet; 2,928 meters). At the pass itself there are more than half a dozen lodges. The Super Lodge is a good choice, though you might want to continue climbing above the pass to one of the lodges higher up on Poon Hill (10,475 feet; 3,195 meters). The sunrises and sunsets from Poon Hill are one of the highlights of this trek, and the higher you climb to a lodge, the less you have to climb before or after dark to see the light shows. It is about an hour from Ghorapani Pass to the top of **Poon Hill.** From west to east, the view from Poon Hill encompasses Dhaulagiri (26,790 feet; 8,167 meters), Tukuche (22,700 feet; 6,920 meters), Nilgiri (22,765 feet; 6,940 meters), Annapurna I (26,540 feet; 8,091 meters), Annapurna South, Hiunchuli, Tarke Kang (23,595 feet; 7,193 meters) and Machhapuchhare.

All the hotels at Ghorapani Pass are recent constructions. There was no village here until trekkers began traveling this route in large numbers. Ghorapani village is back down the mountain a few minutes. Since the opening of all these lodges, the deforestation of Ghorapani Pass has been rapid. The massive old rhododendrons that make this area so beautiful are disappearing at an alarming rate. Please do your part to reduce your impact on this already badly impacted area. Don't demand a large fire to sit by at night and wait until you get to the hot springs at Tatopani for a hot bath. These two simple measures will do much to ensure the future beauty of this pass.

Ulleri to Nayathanti: 2 hours; Nayathanti to Ghorapani Pass: 1¹/₂ hours; Ghorapani Pass to Poon Hill: 1 hour.

Day 3: Ghorapani to Tatopani

From Ghorapani, the trail descends almost 6,000 feet (1,830 meters)—all of the elevation gained climbing up from Birethanti. It is this 6,000-foot ascent and 6,000-foot descent that many inexperienced and out-of-shape trekkers find so difficult and discouraging. Many trekkers make it as far as Tatopani and give up on the trek altogether. By breaking the ascent to Ghorapani into 2 days, it is much easier to descend all the way to Tatopani in 1 day. However, if you climb to Poon Hill from Ghorapani Pass for sunrise you will be adding almost 1,000 feet (305 meters) of extra climbing and descending, which means you might want to split up the descent as well.

From Ghorapani Pass, a steep, muddy (often icy) trail descends through rhododendron forests that are home to gray langurs. Lower down, the forest changes to oak trees before terraced fields take over above the village of Chitre (7,600 feet; 2,318 meters). In Chitre there are a couple of lodges and a good view of Dhaulagiri. Continue descending through extensively terraced hillsides, crossing a landslide area, to **Sikha** (6,300 feet; 1,922 meters), a Magar village with picturesque slate-roofed houses and several lodges. There is a fantastic view of Dhaulagiri from here. From Sikha, the trail descends more gradually, crossing another landslide area before reaching **Ghara** (5,800 feet; 1,769 meters), where there are teahouses and lodges. In winter when the mustard plants bloom bright yellow, the brick-red houses of Ghara make a beautiful contrast with them. Beyond Ghara, the trail climbs slightly up a rocky slope to a teahouse and then begins descending again. From this teahouse, the trail descends 1,600 feet, (488 meters) mostly on a stone stairway. After reaching the left bank of the Kali Gandaki, the trail turns upstream and crosses a suspension bridge over the Ghar Khola. A little farther, the trail crosses the Kali Gandaki on another suspension bridge. About 20 minutes up the right bank you come to **Tatopani** (3,900 feet; 1,190 meters), which means "hot water" in Nepali. There are indeed hot springs here, and consequently Tatopani is a favorite resting spot for both trekkers and Nepali caravan drovers.

The main hot springs are just below the center of the village and are always busy with people bathing and washing clothes, which detracts immensely from their appeal. However, if you are desperately in need of a hot bath, this is the best place to get clean. In addition to the developed hot springs with its cement-walled pool, there are some natural springs alongside the river downstream toward Beni about 45 minutes. Nudity is not acceptable at either of these springs. There are many lodges here, some of which even have VCRs and TVs and offer nightly videos. The town's electricity comes from numerous sources including hydroelectricity and biogas generators. The Namaste Lodge and the Kamala Lodge are good choices here. Be sure to show your trekking permit at the police checkpost just south of the village.

Ghorapani to Sikha: 2½ hours; Sikha to Tatopani: 3 hours.

DAY 4: TATOPANI TO GHASA

From Tatopani, head up the west bank of the Kali Gandaki. Near the village of Jhartare, you pass through orange groves, which give you an idea of how low you are here. The mountains all around give the deceptive impression that you are quite high. In the winter months there are always people selling oranges along this stretch of trail. It's a good idea to stock up for the higher altitudes. The trail ascends slowly. After passing the Miristi Khola, a large river flowing into the Kali Gandaki on the opposite bank, you pass through a small tunnel. After two small villages you cross a stream and enter **Dana** (4,700 feet; 1,434 meters), a long village surrounded by orange groves. Dana has several lodges and teahouses, as well as a police checkpost.

Beyond Dana you pass a suspension bridge across the Kali Gandaki, but you should stay on the west bank. Continuing up the valley, you climb steadily and pass a beautiful waterfall, at the base of which are terraced fields abloom with yellow mustard flowers in the winter. In the nearby village of Rukse Chhara there is a teahouse. Here the trail divides into an east-bank route and a west-bank route. The west-bank route, leading through Kabre, is the favored trail. To take this route, switchback up the hillside behind the teahouse. After this initial steep section the climb becomes more gradual. As you continue north, the valley becomes narrower and steeper until the trail is traversing rocky cliffs. Though this trail is cut into the cliff face, it is quite wide. Descend again to the bank of the river and pass a suspension bridge across the river. This is the bridge you would be using to cross back to the west bank if you took the east-bank trail. From the bridge, the trail climbs to **Ghasa** (6,600 feet; 2,013 meters), a large Thakali village. Try the Kali Gandaki Lodge or Mustang Lodge.

Tatopani to Dana: 2 hours; Dana to Kabre: 2 hours; Kabre to Ghasa: 2 hours.

DAY 5: GHASA TO TUKUCHE

Above Ghasa, the trail climbs steadily through forests. Cross a stream and then pass through Kaiku. The next village, Gomanek, has a couple of teahouses. Continue climbing to cross the Lete Khola on a suspension bridge. There are also a couple of teahouses here. Climb a bit more to reach the village of Lete (7,800 feet; 2,379 meters) where there are some lodges. From just before Lete you begin to have an excellent view of (from west to east) Dhaulagiri, Tukuche, Annapurna I, and Nilgiri.

Beyond Lete the trail ascends very gradually through pine forests as the valley becomes wide and flat. It is about 30 minutes to **Kalopani** (8,300 feet; 2,532 meters). In Kalopani the See You Lodge and Kalopani Guest House are both good choices. The Kali Gandaki valley is said to be the deepest river valley on earth. Just past Kalopani, you pass between Dhaulagiri (26,790 feet; 8,167 meters) and Annapurna I (26,540 feet; 8,091 meters), two of the tallest mountains on earth. It is nearly 3^1/$_2$ miles from the riverbed at Kalopani to the top of Annapurna I.

Just past Kalopani, cross a tributary and then cross to the east bank of the Kali Gandaki on a suspension bridge. The trail climbs up above the river through dry pine forests interspersed with pastures before descending again to the wide valley floor. Continue up the rocky riverbed to a teahouse. From the teahouse the trail crosses back to the west bank to the village of **Larjung** (8,400 feet; 2,562 meters). In Larjung there are mani stones and a gompa, signs that you are now in a region inhabited by Buddhists. There are several lodges in Larjung.

The village of Khobang just beyond Larjung is architecturally similar, with the trail winding through the village in a narrow, covered alley. As the trail leaves Khobang, it also leaves the riverbed and climbs slightly through terraced hillsides to the Thakali village of **Tukuche** (8,500 feet; 2,593 meters). This large village was once an important trading center. Tibetan traders would come down the Kali Gandaki (also known as the Thak Khola above this point) with salt and wool and exchange it for rice and barley from Nepal. When the salt trade was stopped in 1959, Tukuche began to decline in regional importance. When trekking became popular, the Thakali people, who dominated the salt trade here in Nepal, turned to operating lodges, which they now do very successfully all up and down the Kali Gandaki. There are several very comfortable lodges in Tukuche. Most of the lodges are in old homes that were built on the profits of the salt trade. Try the Sunil Lodge, which has an intricately carved large window opening onto its courtyard. Most of the houses in this region are built with central courtyards to block the fierce winds that blow down the Kali Gandaki. In the winter when it is sunny but cold and windy, a courtyard can be very cozy, while outside the windchill makes it very uncomfortable. As you wander through the village admire the carved and brightly painted wooden balconies. Tukuche, Marpha, and Jomosom all have electricity at night provided by a small hydroelectric generator near here.

Ghasa to Kalopani: 3 hours; Kalopani to Larjung: 2^1/$_2$ hours; Larjung to Tukuche: 1^1/$_2$ hours.

DAY 6: TUKUCHE TO KAGBENI

As you leave Tukuche, the trail passes through the last bits of juniper forest. Ahead lie the barren upper reaches of the Kali Gandaki where annual rainfall is less than 10 inches. This is high desert, and thorny shrubs begin to dominate the vegetation. However, before reaching Marpha, you cross terraced and irrigated fields, which are part of an agricultural project. There are apple and apricot groves in this area, and all up and down the valley you will find apple pie on lodge menus. Passing a long whitewashed mani wall, you enter the handsome village of **Marpha**. While most villages along the trekking route have had muddy streets strewn with garbage, Marpha has a system of stone-covered canals that act as a sewer system, giving the village a very tidy appearance. You enter and exit the village through gateway chortens known as *kanis*. On the inside walls and ceiling of the kanis are paintings of various Buddhist deities. There is also a gompa in Marpha. If you have time to spare, Marpha is actually a much nicer place to stay than Jomosom. The Hotel Yak is a good choice. You will likely encounter Tibetan traders near Marpha. They live across the river in Chhairo and come over here to sell curios to the trekkers. These vendors are often willing to trade for anything you want to get rid of, but prices are not always better than in Kathmandu.

From here you can take a shortcut up the rocky riverbed during the dry season, or you can follow the main trail through the small village of Syang. **Jomosom** (8,900 feet; 2,715 meters) is a very large village. You first come to the airstrip where there are several comfortable lodges. Beyond this are a police checkpost and a collection of houses on the west bank of the Kali Gandaki. After crossing the river on a bridge, you come to the town's main section, which includes more lodges, a bank, a post office, and an army base. The view from Jomosom is dominated by Tilicho Peak (23,400 feet; 7,134 meters) which rises up from the south side of the valley. To the right of Tilicho is Nilgiri, and down at the west end of the valley is Dhaulagiri. Though there are plenty of good lodges here serving some of the best food on the trek, Jomosom still has the feel of a military town, which makes it rather unpleasant. The Alka Guest House is one of the better lodges here.

If you feel up to it and the winds are not too strong, I recommend continuing on to **Kagbeni**. In the winter months, the winds in this valley can be ferocious, making it almost impossible to be outside in the afternoon. If the winds are not blowing it is an easy, though rocky, hike up the valley to Kagbeni. Most of the way you are walking in the middle of the dry riverbed and are exposed to the winds. Luckily the winds blow up the valley toward Kagbeni, so even if you set out on a windy day you would have the wind at your back.

The trail leaves Jomosom on the west bank of the Kali Gandaki, passing beneath steep cliffs. After almost 1 1/2 hours, you cross the river on a wooden bridge and continue up the east bank to a teahouse called Eklai Bhatti at Chyancha-Lhrenba. Here the trail forks. The right fork climbs up a rocky slope and continues to Muktinath. Take the left fork, which follows the riverbed to **Kagbeni** (9,200 feet; 2,806 meters). This is a fascinating warren of mud-and-stone houses piled one on top of the other. Narrow alleyways wander through the village sometimes under houses, sometimes across their roofs. In the middle of the village are the ruins of an old fortress that guarded the two valleys above this point. There is also a large, though decrepit, gompa in Kagbeni. Across the valley and on the steep hillside above the village are numerous caves once used by Buddhist hermits. It is possible to climb to these caves, but please do not disturb any of their contents. Further up the Kali Gandaki, near the Tibetan border, is the Mustang region. The Red House and the Nilgiri Lodge are two of the better lodges in town.

Tukuche to Marpha: 1 1/2 hours; Marpha to Jomosom: 2 hours; Jomosom to Kagbeni: 2 1/2 hours.

DAY 7: KAGBENI TO MUKTINATH

To continue up to the pilgrimage site of Muktinath, cross back over the stream you crossed just outside Kagbeni and turn southeast up the valley. This trail climbs a barren hillside to meet the direct trail from Jomosom to Muktinath in 2 hours. Across the valley you can see more caves and the ruins of an ancient fortress village. Pass the village of Khingar and enter a grove of trees. Climb across terraces to enter **Jharkot** (11,850 feet; 3,614 meters), where there are more castle ruins. Jharkot sits atop a small hill; around the flanks of the village, you will see the locally favored yak-cow crossbreed. These animals are shaggy and stocky but have a better temperament than a purebred yak. They are used both for producing milk and as a beast of burden. Jharkot is very similar in architecture and design to Kagbeni and also has a gompa. Try the Hotel Jarkot or the Himali Hotel. The latter is on the east side of the village and has a passive-solar heating system.

From Jharkot, the trail continues climbing past some more trees and across terraced fields to the small village of Ranipowa. Beyond Ranipowa a few minutes are the shrines of Muktinath in a glade of trees. Within the main temple are the sacred flames that were mentioned 2,000 years ago in the Indian epic *Mahabharata*. These flames, caused by natural gas leaks, burn on water, rock, and earth. If you give a small donation, the keeper will gladly open the temple and show you the flames, which are hidden behind curtains. There are also 108 waterspouts here, through which flow holy waters. Because one of the temples here is dedicated to the Hindu god Vishnu and because Buddha is considered an incarnation of Vishnu, the shrine is sacred to both Hindus and Buddhists. The annual pilgrimage and festival takes place during the full moon of late August or early September. There are several lodges in Muktinath. Try the Hotel Muktinath or the Himalaya Hotel.

Kagbeni to Jharkot: 3¹/₂ hours; Jharkot to Muktinath: 1 hour.

DAYS 8–13: MUKTINATH BACK TO POKHARA

Since Kagbeni is the most interesting village on this entire trek, I would go back and spend another night there. However, if you are in a hurry to get back to Pokhara or you need to catch a plane in Jomosom, you can bypass Kagbeni and go directly from Muktinath, via Jharkot, to Jomosom. This direct trail continues past the junction with the trail from Jharkot to Kagbeni, descending a long slope to the floor of the Kali Gandaki valley at Eklai Bhatti, which was mentioned on the trip up. I suggest continuing on to Marpha unless you are planning to fly out of Jomosom. From Muktinath to Jomosom should take about 3 hours.

There are a number of options available for the return trip from Jomosom to Pokhara. If you don't have much time or you have the cash handy, you can fly back to Pokhara. The flight takes only 45 minutes and costs about $50. Another choice is to retrace your steps as far as Tatopani and instead of making the grueling climb up to Ghorapani and back down the other side, you can follow the Kali Gandaki to Beni. From Beni the trail goes to Baglung, which is the end of a recently completed road. In Baglung you can get a bus or truck to Pokhara. There is also an airstrip in Balewa near Baglung, but flights are not reliable.

If you are full of energy and feel up to making the climb to Ghorapani and down the other side in only 2 days, you can get back to Pokhara in 6 days, rather than the 7 days it took to reach Muktinath. An alternate route worth considering is to leave the main route at Ghorapani and take the trail to Ghandrung, a large Gurung village on the main route to the Annapurna Sanctuary. If you want to extend your trek, you could then continue up to the sanctuary (see "Annapurna Sanctuary," above). If you return to Pokhara through Ghandrung, you have three choices of routes. One trail goes from Ghandrung to Birethanti, and one goes to Chandrakot. The third route from Ghandrung avoids any backtracking by crossing the Modi Khola to Landrung and then goes on to Dhampus. From Dhampus the trail leads to Phedi where you can get a bus, truck, or taxi back to Pokhara (see "Annapurna Sanctuary," above).

5 The Langtang Valley

Due primarily to the crowds on the Everest and Annapurna treks, this trek has been gaining in popularity in the past few years. You certainly won't see as many other trekkers here as you will on the more popular routes, but likewise the accommodations are fewer, farther between, and less comfortable. There are few teahouses between villages, which means you frequently will have to hike for 3 hours to reach the next village that has food and accommodations. However, what makes this trek appealing are its long stretches of undisturbed forest where birds are plentiful; high-altitude meadows where you may see wild sheep; excellent mountain views; and Tibetan-like culture. If you bring along your own tent, stove, and food, you can even strike out on your own and do a bit of exploring at the upper end of the Langtang Valley, which is only a few miles from Tibet.

DAY 1: KATHMANDU TO DHUNCHE

Buses to Dhunche, the Langtang trailhead village, leave from the new bus park on the north side of Kathmandu. Buses leave daily between 6 and 8am and normally take between 8 and 9 grueling hours to reach Dhunche. However, it is not unheard of for this trip to take 14 hours or even longer. Be psychologically prepared. The fare is Rs72 ($1.45), and it is a good idea to buy your ticket the day before you intend to travel. Also, be sure to arrive early enough to find your bus amid the chaos of the bus park.

About 45 minutes out of Kathmandu, you pass through the town of Kakani, where there are great views of the Ganesh Himal, a grouping of peaks only partially visible from Kathmandu. Trisuli, on the river of the same name, is a busy bazaar town, often called Trisuli Bazaar. The river, which flows southwest, is very popular with rafting companies, and you may see a group getting ready to put in here.

For many years, this was the start of the Langtang trek, but there is now a road to Dhunche that bypasses the old trail and cuts the number of days necessary for this trek. It is a rough road to Dhunche, and during the rainy season there are frequent landslides, which may keep the road closed until sometime in mid-October. For part of the way the road clings to the edge of a steep mountain.

Between Trisuli and Dhunche, you will be required to show your trekking permit at least once and possibly twice. Because you will be trekking through Langtang National Park, you will also have to check in at the park headquarters near the outskirts of Dhunche and show your park permit, which you should have acquired for Rs650 ($13) at the Department of Immigration office in Kathmandu. You will also likely be subjected to an unexplained military inspection of your belongings. It is unclear what sort of contraband the soldiers are searching for, but only trekkers' bags are searched. Finally, on the edge of Dhunche, you will once again have to show your trekking permit.

Dhunche (6,400 feet; 1,952 meters) is an attractive village with large stone houses. The older part of the village is below the road and is almost completely hidden from view by newer buildings constructed to take advantage of road traffic. Along the road you will find several lodges. The most comfortable are the Hotel Langtang View and the Namaste Lodge. Be sure to take time to explore the narrow, winding stone footpaths of old Dhunche. Most of the houses here have stone-walled first floors and second floors of wood, often with ornately carved walls and window frames. The view from Dhunche, which is high above the Trisuli River, is breathtaking.

Kathmandu to Dhunche: 8–9 hours.

DAY 2: DHUNCHE TO SYABRU

The first 90 minutes of today's hike is clearly visible from Dhunche; it is the road that angles across the far side of the valley to the north of town. Luckily, there is little traffic on this road, and it follows a much easier route than the old trail. To begin the trek from Dhunche, follow the gravel road out of town heading north. The road descends to a bridge over the Trisuli Khola, a stream flowing from the Gosainkund Lakes, which are a 2-day walk from here. The road then climbs steadily to round a ridge, at which point you lose sight of Dhunche. Ahead and below lies the village of **Bharkhu,** which is much smaller than Dhunche but which features the same sort of attractive architecture. Both Dhunche and Bharkhu are Tamang villages. The Tamang people are primarily Buddhists and are often farmers or porters.

Pass through Bharkhu, and on the far side of the village, watch for a trail leading uphill to the right. It climbs a steep slope to the top of a ridge (7,550 feet; 2,303 meters) where there is a good area to rest. You have now entered the Langtang Valley, and there are views of Ganesh Himal to the west, Tibet to the north, and Langtang Lirung to the east. After an hour, you will also be able to see, on a ridgetop below you, the village of **Syabru** (7,000 feet; 2,135 meters). The trail contours around the ridge at first before descending a short steep slope into this village. There are several lodges in Syabru, which is scattered across the ridge. If you are planning on trekking to Gosainkund and on to Helambu, take the trail that climbs the ridge to the south of Syabru. This trail leads to Shin Gompa in about 5 hours.

If you got an early start and feel like walking farther, you could continue on today to the lodges at Landslide or the single lodge at Bamboo. However, Syabru makes a much more interesting place to spend the night.

Dhunche to Bharkhu: 2 hours; Bharkhu to Syabru: 3 hours.

DAY 3: SYABRU TO LAMA HOTEL

Descend through the village of Syabru and continue down the ridge until you come to a trail to the east that drops sharply off the ridge and through a dense forest. Cross a bridge (6,400 feet; 1,952 meters) over a tributary of the Langtang Khola and then climb for a short distance through a dry forest. After rounding the ridge, you will come to a teahouse, beyond which the trail suddenly begins a steep and slippery descent to the floor of the Langtang Khola valley. This section of trail skirts the edge of a huge landslide until you are almost to the river and then cuts across the unstable slope to reenter a lush, damp forest. Not far beyond the landslide, you come to two very basic lodges, which are known collectively as **Landslide.**

The valley, which runs east-west at this point, is very narrow and rarely receives much sunlight on the south bank, which is where the trail is located. However, the valley walls on the north bank receive considerably more sunshine and support a landscape of striking contrast to other parts of the valley. Instead of ferns, mosses, and tall trees, there are only grasses and cactuses. Such contrasts are typical of the Himalayas, where the orientation of the mountains plays a crucial role in modifying the climate.

An hour beyond Landslide, you will pass another small lodge deep in the forest at a spot known as **Bamboo.** Thirty minutes beyond this lodge, you cross a **bridge** (6,700 feet; 2,044 meters) to the drier north side of the Langtang Khola. There are a couple of small lodges at this bridge.

The trail begins climbing up from the river at this point, and in an hour, shortly after the trail levels off, you join the old Langtang trail (7,800 feet; 2,379 meters) from Syarpagaon and Syabrubensi. Another hour from this trail junction brings you to the **Lama Hotel** in the tiny village of Chongong (7,800 feet; 2,379 meters) There are also several lodges and teahouses and a camping site here. Another hour or so beyond the Lama Hotel, there is another lodge at Gumnachowk. If you don't feel like stopping yet, you can continue.

Syabru to Landslide: 2 hours; Landslide to Bamboo: 1 hour; Bamboo to bridge: 30 minutes; bridge to Lama Hotel: 1 hour.

DAY 4: LAMA HOTEL TO LANGTANG VILLAGE

From the Lama Hotel the trail climbs steadily to Ghora Tabela with glimpses of Langtang Lirung (23,763 feet; 7,248 meters) through the trees. Midway between Lama Hotel and Ghora Tabela, you pass by the simple lodges at **Gumnachowk** and Chhunama.

At times the trail becomes very steep, but only for short distances. At **Ghora Tabela** (9,850 feet; 3,004 meters) the trail leaves the forest, and a spectacular view of Langtang Lirung appears. Ghora Tabela was once a Tibetan resettlement camp but is now an army post. There is a good lodge where you can get lunch or stop for the day if you like. You must show your trekking permit at the police checkpost. Continue up the valley, leaving the forests behind.

In 30 to 45 minutes, you come to **Thangshyap** (10,754 feet; 3,280 meters), where there are two very basic lodges and good views both up and down the valley. The trail climbs steadily up to **Langtang** village (11,475 feet; 3,500 meters), passing below a monastery about 30 minutes before reaching the village. Langtang is another Tamang village with stone-and-wood houses and pastures in which you just might see yaks. There are several trekkers' lodges here.

Lama Hotel to Gumnachowk: 1 hour; Gumnachowk to Ghora Tabela: 3 hours; Ghora Tabela to Langtang: 3 hours.

DAY 5: LANGTANG TO KYANJIN GOMPA

You may notice that the valley above this point is U-shaped, which indicates that it was carved by a glacier. Below Langtang, the valley has the characteristic V-shape of a river-carved valley. Leaving Langtang, you climb gradually to a chortens behind which are several very long mani walls. You are now above the treeline, and low-growing shrubs dominate this alpine environment. As the valley widens, the trail passes the three villages of Mundu, Sindum, and Yamfu, all of which have small lodges.

You cross several streams and a moraine before arriving at **Kyanjin Gompa** (12,450 feet; 3,797 meters). Between Langtang and Kyanjin Gompa, the views get better and better. You can see Yansa Tsenji (21,452 feet; 6,543 meters) and Kimshun (22,123 feet; 6,745 meters) to the north and the Langtang Himal to the northwest. Kyanjin Gompa is a small Buddhist monastery, but there are also numerous lodges and a cheese factory here. The Himalaya Lodge and the Tibet Hotel are currently the two most popular lodges in Kyanjin. Since you will probably arrive before lunch, you will have time to do some exploring in the afternoon, though you may be experiencing some discomfort from the altitude. One possibility is to climb the steep hill to the north of Kyanjin Gompa. This hill is more than 13,000 feet(3,965 meters) high and provides an excellent view of Langtang Lirung.

Langtang to Kyanjin Gompa: 3 hours.

DAY 6: KYANJIN GOMPA

A day hike farther up the valley past the airstrip will provide more spectacular views that include Langtang Lirung, Ganchenpo (20,950 feet; 6,387 meters), Langshisa Ri (21,072 feet; 6,427 meters), Dorje Lakpa (22,839 feet; 6,966 meters), Lenpo

Gang (22,882 feet; 6,979 meters), and Urkinmang (20,175 feet; 6,151 meters). Other possibilities are to climb the lateral moraine north of Kyanjin for a close view of the Lirung Glacier and icefall. There is another cheese factory in the village of Yala, which can be reached in about 3 hours if you are acclimatized. Another 2 hours above Yala is 16,500-foot (5,033-meter) Tsergo Ri. If you start early in the morning and are acclimatized, you should be able to climb this peak and return to Kyanjin Gompa in 1 long day. If you have some mountaineering experience and have come equipped for a difficult climb, it is possible to cross the Ganja La, a 16,800-foot (5,124-meter) pass, to Helambu. This crossing is not possible in the winter months when the pass is closed by snow. You will need a guide, tents, food, and fuel to cross the Ganja La, and it is essential that you spend a day acclimatizing at Kyanjin Gompa.

DAY 7: KYANJIN GOMPA TO LAMA HOTEL

Since you will be acclimatized and will be descending, you should be able to reach the Lama Hotel in a short day's walk from Kyanjin Gompa. If you reach Lama Hotel by lunch and don't feel like stopping so early, consider continuing to Bamboo or Landslide.

Kyanjin Gompa to Lama Hotel: 5 hours.

DAY 8: ONWARD FROM LAMA HOTEL

Beyond Lama Hotel there are several possible routes, depending on where you are headed and how much time you have. If your goal is to reach Dhunche as fast as possible, you should be able to get there after a long day hike from Lama Hotel. This route can be shortened by continuing to Landslide or Bamboo on the day you leave Kyanjin.

There are also two routes to the village of **Syabrubensi,** which is on the road north of Bharkhu. To reach Syabrubensi in a long day, take the old trail that forks off the main trail at Rimche, 15 minutes below Lama Hotel. This route stays high above the river and does a bit of climbing. A newer alternate route to Syabrubensi leaves the main trail beyond Landslide. This latter route takes about 2 hours less than the old route. From Syabrubensi, you can either catch the bus to Kathmandu or hike along the road to **Dhunche** and then catch the bus.

If you are on your way to Gosainkund, you would definitely do better to continue past Lama Hotel on the day you leave Kyanjin. From Lama Hotel, it would be a long day's hike to **Shin Gompa,** but this day would be a bit more bearable if you started from Bamboo or Landslide. See the "Gosainkund" section, below, for details on continuing the trek through that region.

Lama Hotel to Syabrubensi (old route): 7 hours; Lama Hotel to Syabrubensi (new route): 5 hours; Lama Hotel to Dhunche: 8 hours; Lama Hotel to Shin Gompa: 8 hours.

DAY 9: DHUNCHE (OR SYABRUBENSI) TO KATHMANDU

Since you will arrive in Dhunche too late to catch a bus to Trisuli, you will have to spend the night in either town and take the bus the next morning. Alternatively, if you can't bear the thought of riding back down that hair-raising road, you can hike the old trail through Bokajundo, Thare, Garang, Ramche, Manigaon, Banwa, Bhotal, and Betrawati or return to Kathmandu via Gosainkund and Helambu.

Dhunche to Kathmandu: 8–9 hours.

6 Gosainkund

This trek connects the Helambu and Langtang treks by way of the trail over the Surjakund pass. Each summer during the August full moon, Hindu pilgrims from all over Nepal and India make the trek up to Gosainkund's sacred high-altitude lakes. It is said that they were formed when the god Shiva pierced a glacier with his trident. There is a large white stone in the middle of the lake that is believed to be the remains of a Shiva temple, and on the lakeshore, there is a shrine containing a large stone Shiva lingam. Local legends also claim that the water from Gosainkund, the main lake, flows underground to emerge from a spring at the Kumbeshwar Temple in Patan. For a truly fascinating experience, try making the trek during the annual pilgrimage. August is the middle of the monsoon, so you can expect to stay wet for most of the trek. This trek can be done in either direction, but it is a good idea to have a guide.

During the warmer months of the main trekking seasons, there are lodges all along the route over Surjakund Pass, so it is no longer necessary to carry a tent and food as it once was. However, after late November when snow begins to accumulate at the higher elevations, the lodges shut down. If you are planning to do this trek anytime in the colder months, be sure to find out about trail conditions and whether lodges are open.

I describe the trek starting on the Langtang side and proceeding to Tharepati on the Helambu trek. (See "Langtang" above, and "Helambu," below, for descriptions of these two treks.)

DAY 1: DHUNCHE (OR SYABRU) TO SHIN GOMPA

The trail to Shin Gompa leaves the road through Dhunche on the far side of town from the police checkpost. The trail crosses through terraced fields before descending to the Trisuli Khola, a stream that has its origin in Gosainkund Lake. The path keeps close to the right bank for a while but then begins climbing steadily through forests of oak and, at higher elevations, fir and rhododendron. This is a long, steep climb with only one teahouse and a couple of lodges between Dhunche and Shin Gompa, so carry plenty of water and some snacks. This stretch of trail is so sparsely populated, so it is the most likely place for you to spot wildlife. I've seen families of langurs (long-tailed monkeys) and many species of birds through here.

It is a sweaty 3 hours before you reach the first teahouse and another hour or so to the lodges at **Dimsa,** which is above the point where a trail from Bharkhu joins this trail. In another hour of climbing through forest from Dimsa, you come to the small Buddhist monastery of **Shin Gompa** (10,950 feet; 3,340 meters) in a large clearing on the side of a steep slope. This clearing was caused by a fire more than a decade ago, and the skeletal tree trunks that rise from the hillside frequently serve as perches for large hawks. Shin Gompa is also the site of a large government cheese factory and a couple of good lodges. The Evergreen Hotel is my favorite.

If you are coming from Syabru, walk uphill through the village; just past the army post, take the trail that forks to the right. This trail leads very steeply uphill and continues to climb sharply for several hours. For the first 2 hours, the trail is up an open hillside with good views. There are three teahouses along this stretch of trail. The trail then enters a thick wood filled with huge old trees. After hiking through this forest for an hour or more, you come to a teahouse on a cleared ridge (10,492 feet; 3,200 meters). There are excellent views from here, and this makes a great lunch spot.

Beyond this teahouse, the trail is much less steep. Short climbs alternate with fairly flat sections of trail, and forests alternate with pastures. After passing through the last bit of enchanting forest, you come to **Shin Gompa.**

Dhunche to Dimsa: 4 hours; Dimsa to Shin Gompa: 1 hour; Sybaru to Shin Gompa: 4 hours

DAY 2: AT SHIN GOMPA

Because you will be crossing a 15,100-foot (4,606-meter) pass, it is essential that you spend a day acclimatizing to the high elevation. If you do not do this, you risk developing altitude sickness. Rather than spending the day sitting around, you should be active and try climbing higher than Shin Gompa. This will help your body acclimatize.

DAY 3: SHIN GOMPA TO GOSAINKUND

From Shin Gompa the wide, well-trodden trail continues climbing steadily through rhododendron forest with the Trisuli Khola far below. The trail crosses over to the Langtang side of the ridge you are climbing shortly before you reach the two lodges at **Cholang Pati** (11,751 feet; 3,584 meters).

Above Cholang Pati, you leave the forest and pass through a landscape of rhododendron shrubs. You are now above the treeline, and as you continue to climb, the vegetation becomes more and more stunted.

An hour and a half above Cholang Pati, you come to the two stone lodges at **Laurebina Yak** (12,787 feet; 3,900 meters). This is a barren ridgeline with no protection from the fierce winds and is always cold, but it offers one of the most stunning vistas in Nepal. Visible are Langtang Lirung (23,718 feet; 7,234 meters) to the north; a mountain range in Tibet to the northwest; and the Ganesh Himal (24,357 feet; 7,429 meters), Himalchuli (25,879 feet; 7,893 meters); and Manaslu (26,764 feet; 8,163 meters) all to the west. For this reason, it is worth spending a night here if you can adjust your hiking times. The views are best in the early morning, when the skies are free of clouds. By late afternoon, this ridge is often socked in by dense clouds and consequently can be very cold and damp.

Above Laurebina Yak, the trail climbs steeply to a grassy ridge where there is a small Buddhist shrine just off the trail. Beyond this shrine, the trail ascends more gradually but clings to a vertiginous mountainside. This area is used in the summer months as high-altitude grazing land for flocks of sheep and goats. You will finally be able to see the Gosainkund lakes from here. The first two lakes lay far below the trail, but when the third lake comes into view, the trail begins to descend. This third lake is the holy **Gosainkund Lake** (14,350 feet; 4,377 meters), which is evident from the Shiva shrine and the four guesthouses on its shores.

Shin Gompa to Cholang Pati: 1¹/₂ hours; Cholang Pati to Laurebina Yak: 1¹/₂ hours: Laurebina Yak to Gosainkund Lake: 2 hours.

DAY 4: GOSAINKUND TO GOPTE

The trail skirts the north shore of Gosainkund Lake before climbing toward the pass. As you climb this easy slope, you will see four more lakes. You will know you have reached **Suriakund Pass** (15,100 feet; 4,606 meters) when you see the many cairns that have been built over the years. The trail now descends, steeply at first but then more gradually, to the southeast on a rocky path. In about an hour you will come to an area known as Phedi, where during the trekking seasons there is usually a primitive lodge. From here the trail descends another ridge, crossing several streams and passing two waterfalls. After passing another stone hut, the trail climbs to another ridge and to **Gopte** (11,700 feet), where overhanging rocks form a cave that is also used as a trekkers' lodge.

Gosainkund to Surjakund Pass: 1¹/₂ hours; Surjakund Pass to Gopte: 4 hours.

DAY 5: GOPTE TO MALEMCHIGAON OR KUTUMSANG

From Gopte, the trail descends to more caves and enters a thick forest of rhododendrons. The trail crosses a stream, which is dry for part of the year, before climbing through the forest to **Tharepati** (11,500 feet; 3,508 meters), a grouping of small stone huts used in the summer months by herders. During trekking season, there is usually a very basic lodge at Tharepati.

From the ridge above Tharepati there are two choices for your onward path. Both trails will get you back to Kathmandu in 3 days if you are a fast walker. The trail through Tarke Gyang is the more interesting route, though the first day of this trail entails a steep and difficult descent and an equally steep ascent. To take this route, head southeast and descend to **Malemchigaon** near the floor of the Malemchi Khola valley. You will be able to see Tarke Gyang high up on the far side of the valley. The other route back to Kathmandu stays high on a system of ridges that leads from here to the Kathmandu Valley. This trail follows a ridge to the south and leads to **Kutumsang.** (For detailed descriptions of these two routes see "Helambu," below in this chapter.)

Gopte to Tharepati: 2 hours; Tharepati to Malemchigaon: 4 hours; Tharepati to Kutumsang: 5 hours.

7 Helambu

The Helambu trek, though not the easiest or most spectacular, is the easiest to begin because the trailhead lies within the Kathmandu Valley. You can be on the trail within an hour of leaving your hotel in downtown Kathmandu. Perhaps because of its proximity to Kathmandu, the trail is rarely traveled by trekkers. The existing trails are badly eroded, poorly maintained, and often difficult to follow. Consequently, hiring a guide is highly advisable if you plan to do this trek.

DAY 1: KATHMANDU TO PATI BHANJYANG

You should be able to hire a taxi to take you all the way to the trailhead at Sundarijal, which is beyond Boudha on the north side of the Kathmandu Valley. Alternatively, you can take a taxi just to Boudha and then take one of the minibuses that operate from there to Sundarijal. If there is no minibus making the trip any time soon, you can walk to Sundarijal (and the trailhead) from Kathmandu in 2 to 3 hours.

Sundarijal (4,800 feet; 1,464 meters) is at the foot of Shivapuri Ridge, the long hill that forms the north side of the Kathmandu Valley. The trail begins at the north end of town near a water treatment plant and parallels a large water pipe that brings water down to the treatment plant. In about 45 minutes you cross a small dam. The trail climbs alternately through forest and terraced fields to the village of Mulkharka (5,800 feet; 1,769 meters). After 2 hours on a steep and badly eroded trail you reach the top of the Shivapuri Ridge and the small village of **Borlang Bhanjyang** (8,000 feet; 2,440 meters), which is just over the pass on the north side of the ridge. From the pass you get your first view of the Langtang and Jugal Himal, the mountains you are hiking toward.

The trail descends through sparsely populated scrubby forests. After an hour or so you cross a newly constructed dirt road in a closely cropped pasture near the village of **Chisapani.** About 100 yards beyond the road, there is a small trekkers' lodge that takes good advantage of the view from here. This is a better place to stop than the village of **Pati Bhanjyang** (5,800 feet; 1,769 meters), which is in a ridge saddle another 1¹/₂ hours farther down the trail and which doesn't have such a spectacular view. There are a couple of lodges in Pati Bhanjyang and a police checkpost where you must show your trekking permit.

Kathmandu to Sundarijal by taxi and bus: 1 hour; Sundarijal to Borlang Bhanjyang: 4 hours; Borlang Bhanjyang to Chisapani: 1 hour; Chisapani to Pati Bhanjyang: 1¹/₂ hours.

DAY 2: PATI BHANJYANG TO TALAMARANG

From Pati Bhanjyang you have a choice of two routes. One stays high on the ridge, while the other descends steeply to the valley floor. I prefer the lower route, since it makes the trek a bit easier and gives you a few days to develop your trekking muscles before making the ascent to Tharepati. The trail to the Malemchi Khola and Talamarang begins north of town near the top of a hill with a few houses on it. Take a right to head east at these houses, and you will see the trail ascending to a notch in a ridge. It is about 1 hour to the notch and another 30 minutes to the village of **Thakani.** The trail stays above the village and shortly passes through a meadow. In another hour you will come to **Batache.** Here the trail turns northward and begins its steep descent to the river. This trail may be difficult to find. If you are trekking without a guide, ask directions frequently. It is 3 hours to **Talamarang,** which has several lodges and shops.

Pati Bhanjyang to Thakani: 1¹/₂ hours; Thakani to Batache: 1 hour; Batache to Talamarang: 3 hours.

DAY 3: TALAMARANG TO THIMBU

The trail from Talamarang to Thimbu is fairly flat and easy to walk, a welcome relief after the previous 2 days' steep ascent and descent. The villages along the Malemchi Khola are prosperous and attractive, and all of them have lodges. If you decide you'd like to stop early, you should have no problem. The elevation here is quite low, only about 3,000 feet (915 meters), so bananas line the trail. It can be warm hiking even in December. It is about 2 hours to the lodges in **Mahankal** village, beyond which the trail crosses the Malemchi Khola on a suspension bridge. In another hour from Mahankal you reach **Kiul,** where there are several lodges and teahouses. From Kiul, it is 1¹/₂ hours to **Thimbu,** which is a scattered village covering a very steep hillside. There are two lodges (4,500 feet; 1,373 meters) beside a stream at the foot of the mountainside on which Thimbu is built. These are your only choices for a place to stay in Thimbu, and they are not very luxurious accommodations, even by trekking standards.

Talamarang to Mahankal: 2 hours; Mahankal to Kiul: 1 hour; Kiul to Thimbu: 1¹/₂ hours.

DAY 4: THIMBU TO TARKE GYANG

The day starts out with a grueling climb up from the river on a bad trail that seems to go straight up the mountainside. However, once the trail gets above upper Thimbu (5,150 feet; 1,571 meters), it is a fairly gradual ascent, with a few short climbs, to Tarke Gyang. There are few houses or villages along this section of trail,

so it is a good idea to carry some food with you for lunch. Chapati and egg sandwiches, made up in the morning at your lodge, are an easy trail meal. In 2^1/$_2$ hours
you pass through the village of **Kakani** (7,850 feet; 2,394 meters), where there are
several lodges and teahouses.

You are now entering the region inhabited by the Helambu Sherpas, who are
only distantly related to the famous Sherpas of the Solu-Khumbu region. As in
Solu-Khumbu, the Sherpas of this region build both mani walls covered with
stones that have had prayers carved onto them and *chortens*—small stupalike
shrines. Remember to keep these mani walls and chortens on your right side as you
pass them. It is considered disrespectful to have your left side to one of these
structures. There is a gompa (Buddhist monastery) in Kakani.

Beyond Kakani, the trail enters a large valley created by a tributary of the
Malemchi Khola. There is a hydroelectric project in this valley and electric power
lines running to Tarke Gyang. From Kakani it is about 3 hours to the hydroelectric project and another hour to **Tarke Gyang** (9,000 feet; 2,745 meters), the
largest and most important village in the region. After the many small and scattered villages you pass on the way here, Tarke Gyang is like an oasis. There is a
large gompa surrounded by the densely packed stone houses of the village. On the
steep slopes above the village there is a dark forest of rhododendrons and fir trees.
Five minutes before town, there is a large trekkers' lodge, but I prefer the smaller
Lama Lodge beside the gompa. This latter lodge is run by the family of the local
lama. Beware of local entrepreneurs who want to sell you local curios. Most of the
items they have for sale can be gotten in Kathmandu at lower prices, and the genuinely valuable pieces offered for sale carry genuinely steep price tags.

Thimbu to Kakani: 2^1/$_2$ hours; Kakani to Tarke Gyang: 4 hours.

DAY 5: TARKE GYANG TO THAREPATI

If you are feeling lazy you might want to spend a few days in Tarke Gyang,
making day trips up to some of the high pastures above the village. There are
excellent views to the north from within a few hours of Tarke Gyang. It is a
long and arduous trek up to Tharepati.

From Tarke Gyang, descend to the river (6,200 feet; 1,891 meters) in about
2 hours. Cross the bridge and climb steeply to **Malemchigaon** (8,300 feet; 2,532
meters), which takes about 2 hours also. Here in Malemchigaon, you will have to
show your Langtang National Park entry permit (which you purchased for Rs650
[$13] when you got your trekking permit at the Department of Immigration in
Kathmandu), before continuing on to Tharepati, which is within this large national
park.

From Malemchigaon, the trail leads up a very steep mountainside. This trail
is often hard to follow and can be slippery. It takes at least 4 hours to
reach **Tharepati** pass (11,500 feet; 3,508 meters). This climb of more than 5,000
feet (1,525 meters) in 1 day is grueling. In the winter snow makes the going
even more difficult, and the trail becomes even harder to follow. Prayer flags mark
the pass.

*Tarke Gyang to Malemchi Khola: 2 hours; Malemchi Khola to Malemchigaon:
2 hours; Malemchigaon to Tharepati: 4 hours.*

DAY 6: THAREPATI TO KUTUMSANG

From Tharepati, there are two possible routes. The trail north climbs up to the
15,100-foot (4,606-meter) Surjakund Pass and links the Helambu trek with

the Langtang trek by way of Gosainkund. This route is usually not passable in winter and is quite difficult the rest of the year. Though it is possible to cross the Surjakund Pass without a guide, it is not recommended. See "Gosainkund," above, for details about that trekking route.

If you are only making a circuit of Helambu, follow the ridge to the south, and in an hour you will pass the stone huts of **Mangegoth,** which are usually only inhabited in the summer months. This is a very remote area of high pastures and oak and rhododendron forests. If you are going to see any wildlife at all other than birds, this is probably the most likely area. For the first 3 hours the trail descends gradually, but the second half of the day's trek is a steep descent to **Kutumsang,** a small village on a windy ridge saddle. The Langtang National Park office here will probably check your national park permit. There are a couple of lodges beside the park office and several more as you head south out of the village and up the ridge.

Tharepati to Mangegoth: 2 hours; Mangegoth to Kutumsang: 4 hours.

DAY 7: KUTUMSANG TO PATI BHANJYANG

From Kutumsang, the trail climbs the ridge before making a steep descent to **Gul Bhanjyang,** which has a few teahouses and is also in a saddle. Climb up the ridge from Gul Bhanjyang, continuing to head south, and in 2 hours you will reach **Chipling,** where there are some teahouses and a lodge. A steep and rocky trail descends from Chipling to another saddle where there are a few houses and a tea stall. The trail then ascends another ridge before dropping down to the saddle on which **Pati Bhanjyang** is built.

Kutumsang to Gul Bhanjyang: 2 hours; Gul Bhanjyang to Chipling: 2 hours; Chipling to Pati Bhanjyang: 2 hours.

DAY 8: PATI BHANJYANG TO KATHMANDU

From Pati Bhanjyang, retrace your steps back to **Sundarijal.**
Pati Bhanjyang to Sundarijal: 5¹/₂ hours.

8 Less-Traveled Treks

If you have already done the more popular treks in Nepal, you might want to consider one of these lesser–traveled routes. For the most part, these are not treks that can be done on your own. On the Mustang, Dolpo, around Manaslu, and Kanchenjunga treks, the Nepali government requires that you trek with an official trekking company. Special, high-priced trekking permits are also levied on people who wish to trek these routes. The reasons for these restrictions are to limit the number of trekkers descending on these regions. Hordes of trekkers have made lasting changes on areas such as Annapurna and Solu-Khumbu, and these changes are not necessarily good. These restrictions mean that if you do one of these treks, you will be experiencing Nepali culture that has been less tainted by contact with the outside world. If you're lucky you won't see a single Madonna T-shirt on a trek through Mustang or Dolpo, but then that might be wishing for too much. In my opinion, the costs (financial, physical, and time required for these treks) are far outweighed by the benefits of trekking through regions rarely visited by foreigners.

The last three treks—Kathmandu to Pokhara, Rara Lake, and Gorkha—do not require special permits, but the lack of lodges along these routes almost necessitates

Langtang, Gosainkund & Helambu Trekking Routes

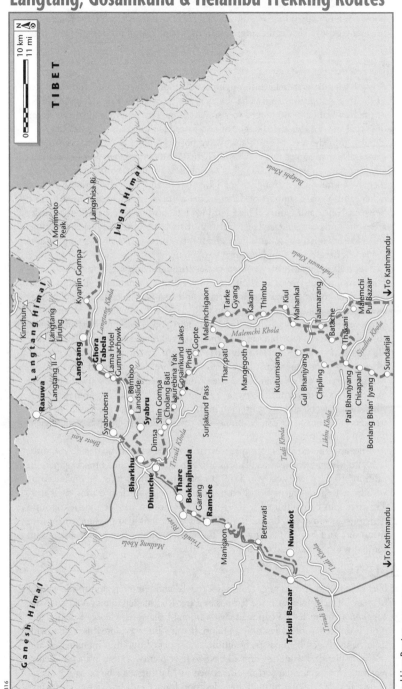

Trekking Routes ----

booking an organized trek. Again, you will see few trekkers along these routes, and for many people, that is the single most important reason for doing one of these treks.

MUSTANG

Anyone who has ever trekked through the village of Kagbeni on the Jomosom trek or the trek around Annapurna has likely gazed toward Tibet up the barren valley of the Kali Gandaki and longed to visit Mustang. This remote and barren region of Nepal was for decades thought of as a forbidden kingdom. No trekkers were allowed into the area due to its sensitive position along the Tibetan border. A glance at a map shows that this region actually juts into Tibet, and both culturally and geographically Mustang has far more in common with Tibet than with Nepal. Mustang was a stronghold of Tibetan resistance after the Chinese invaded Tibet, and Nepal's support of Tibet in the conflict with China caused tension between Nepal and China. These tensions left most of Nepal's Tibetan border areas off-limits to trekkers. Today relations between China and Nepal are stable, and Nepal is opening up its border areas to trekkers. In 1992, Mustang became the last of these once-forbidden areas to open up.

The Kali Gandaki valley, which passes through Mustang, has been a trans-Himalayan trading route for thousands of years and is a natural route into Tibet. Trade along this route was very important, and anyone who could control passage along the Kali Gandaki could become very wealthy. Consequently, several small kingdoms developed throughout the Mustang region. *Dzongs* (castles) and *gompas* (Buddhist temples) were built in the densely packed earth-and-stone villages. These villages still stand and are today little changed by the passing of centuries. Mustang is what Tibet must have been like before the coming of the Chinese. Meager harvests of barley are still coaxed from the barren rocky soil with the help of irrigation waters from the river. Yaks and goats and stocky ponies provide labor, butter, wool, and transportation in the region. These are the reasons so many trekkers have longed to visit Mustang—to catch a fleeting glimpse of an ancient Tibetan Buddhist culture.

A fleeting and expensive glimpse is what it will be should you decide you must trek into Mustang. Special regulations apply to this region, and a trekking permit, valid for 10 days, will cost you $700 per person. All treks must be organized by an official trekking agency, and groups must be self-sufficient during their trek. This trek can be combined with either the Jomosom trek or the trek around Annapurna. However, if you have limited time, it is also possible to fly into Jomosom and begin trekking from there. It is only a few hours' hike from Jomosom to the trailhead of the Mustang trek.

DOLPO

Nearly as fabled as Mustang, Dolpo is a rugged and remote region to the west of Mustang. The region was made famous by Peter Matthiessen in his book *The Snow Leopard,* a chronicle of a trip made with animal-behaviorist George Schaller. Remote is the key word in describing Dolpo. If you wish to explore this region, with its ancient villages, high passes, beautiful lakes, isolated Buddhist monasteries, and relatively plentiful wildlife, you will have to have plenty of time available. Before reaching the spectacular settings described in Matthiessen's book, you'll spend quite a few days hiking through low-elevation forests with few views. Most treks into Dolpo take 20 to 30 days, and because winter comes early to the high passes, the best time to trek in Dolpo is toward the end of the monsoon season, since heat and leeches can be a problem during the monsoon season at lower elevations. Shorter Dolpo treks are possible by flying into the airstrip at Jumla.

Trekking permits for lower Dolpo cost $10 per week for the first month and $20 per week after that. To visit the more spectacular region of upper Dolpo, you will have to pay the same $70 per day charged for permits to visit Mustang. You will also have to arrange a fully organized trek with an established trekking company. If you book your trek in Nepal, you will have to pay between $30 and $40 per day of your trek.

Appendix

A Basic Phrases & Vocabulary

CONVERSATIONAL PHRASES

Hello/Good-bye *Na*masto

How are you? *Kasto* chha

Fine *San*chaai

Please (give me) *Khaa*nuhos

Thank you *Dhany*abad

Yes (it is) **Ho**

Yes (it exists) **Chha**

OK *Hun*chha

No (it is not) *Hoi*na

No (it does not exist) *Chaai*na

Excuse me *Ha*jur

Give me *Ma*laai . . . *di*nos

Where is? . . . *ka*haa chha?

a hospital *aas*pital

a hotel *ho*tel

the toilet *chhar*pi

Straight ahead *Sojhai jaa*nus

Turn left *Baa*yaa *mod*nos

Turn right *Daa*yaa *mod*nos

Do you have a? *Tapaai* . . . *san*ga?

room *ko*thaa

How much is this? *Yesko kati*?
(or *Ka*ti *parch*ha?)

When? *Ka*hile?

Where? *Ka*haan?

How? *Ka*sari?

Why? *Ki*na?

What? **Ke?**

How much? *Kati*?

Today *Aa*ja

Tomorrow *Bho*li

Yesterday *Hi*jo

Minute *Mi*nut

Hour *Ghan*taa

Day **Din**

Good *Raam*ro

Bad Na*raam*ro

May I please take your picture? *Ta*paai*ko photo khi*chu?

How old are you? *Ta*paai*ko umer ka*ti *bha*yo?

What is your name? *Ta*paai*ko* naam ke ho?

My name is . . . *Mer*o naam . . . ho.

Where are you from? *Ta*paai*ko* ghar *ka*ha ho?

I come from . . . *Mer*o ghar . . . ma.

What is the name of this? *Yes*ko naam ko ho?

I don't speak Nepali. **Ma** Ne*paa*li bol*di*na.

I only speak a little Nepali. **Ma** *al*i *al*i Ne*paal*i maatrai bolchhu.

I don't understand. *Mai*le bu*jhi*na.

What time is it? *Ka*ti *baj*yo?

It is four o'clock. **Char** *baj*yo

I will stay for one day. **Ek din** bas*ne.**

Trekking Phrases

Which is the way to . . .? **. . . *jaa*ne *baat*o kun ho?**

How much for one night? **Ek raat ko *ka*ti?**

How many hours to . . .? **. . . *ka*ti *ghan*taa *laag*chha?**

Is there a lodge in . . .? **. . . maa *bhaa*tti chha?**

Can we get food in . . .? **. . . maa *khaa*naa *paain*cha?**

Is food available? ***Khaa*na *paain*chha?**

Please give me . . . **. . . *di*nos.**

food **khaa*na***

tea ***chi*yaa**

shelter **baas**

Where is the . . .? **. . . *ka*haa chha?**

inn ***bhat*ti**

village **gaau**

Where are you going? **Ta*pai ka*haa *janne*?**

Numbers

1 **ek**
2 **dui**
3 **teen**
4 **char**
5 **panch**
6 **chha**
7 **saat**
8 **aath**
9 **nau**
10 **das**
11 ***e*ghaara**
12 ***baah*ra**
13 ***teh*ra**
14 ***chau*dha**
15 ***pan*dhra**
16 ***soh*ra**
17 ***sat*ra**
18 ***a*thaara**
19 ***un*naais**
20 **bis**
21 ***ek*kaais**
22 ***baa*is**
23 **teis**
24 ***chau*bis**
25 ***paa*chis**
26 ***chha*bis**
27 ***satt*haais**
28 ***at*thaais**
29 ***un*antis**
30 **tis**
40 **chaa*lis***
50 **pa*chaas***
60 ***saa*thi**
70 ***sat*tari**
80 ***ash*i**
90 ***nab*be**
100 **ek say**
101 **ek say ek**
200 **dui say**
1000 **ek *ha*jaar**

B Menu Items

Bhat Rice usually served with dal—the mainstay of the Nepali diet

Chang Home-brewed rice, barley, or millet beer

***Chi*ya** Tea

Dal Watery lentil soup served over rice; the mainstay of the Nepali diet

Hot lemon Usually listed as a tea but consists only of lemon and water

***Ko*thay** Tibetan fried dumpling similar to a Chinese potsticker

***Mo*mos** Tibetan steamed dumplings stuffed with either meat or vegetables

Si*kar*ni Dessert made from yogurt and spices

***Thuk*pa** Tibetan noodle and vegetable soup

C Glossary of Terms

ARCHITECTURAL TERMS

Bahal   Buddhist monastery
Chaitya   Small stupa
Chorten   Tibetan Buddhist term for "chaitya" (see above)
Dharmasala   Resting house for pilgrims
Ghat   Stone platform used for performing cremations beside rivers
Gompa   Tibetan Buddhist temple or monastery
Hiti   Bathing and washing fountain, usually with ornate water spouts
Jhya   Carved window
Mandir   Temple
Math   Hindu priest's house
Pagoda   Tower-shaped building, usually a temple, with several roofs
Stupa   Large hemispherical Buddhist shrine
Torana   Semicircular and ornately decorated panel usually found over temple entrances; depicts the deities housed within the temple
Tympanum   Similar to a torana, but not as large; usually hangs above windows, leaning out slightly from the building
Vihara (Viharn)   Buddhist monastery

RELIGIOUS SYMBOLS

Ghanta   Buddhist ritual bell representing wisdom and the female aspect; used in conjunction with the vajra, it is always held in the left hand
Dorje   Tibetan name for "vajra" (see below)
Lingam   Phallic symbol that represents the Hindu god Shiva
Lotus   Called also *padma*, the lotus is associated with the Buddha and symbolizes self-creation
Kailash   Holy water pitcher
Mandala   Tantric symbol representing meditation; it consists of circles enclosing squares and is used in meditation
Prayer Wheel   Wheels filled with prayers that are spun by hand, by the wind, or by water, thus saying the prayers housed inside the wheel
Sankha   Conch shell symbolizing the Hindu god Vishnu and used as a trumpet at religious services
Shirivasta   Endless knot; one of the eight primary Buddhist symbols, it is a symbol of luck
Swastika   Symbol of the law in both Hindu and Buddhist doctrine; also a symbol of well-being
Trisul   Trident, a symbol of Shiva
Vajra   Buddhist symbol (called *dorje* in Tibetan) that represents the thunderbolt or diamond that destroys all ignorance and is itself indestructible; it represents power (or method) and the male aspect; used in conjunction with the *ghanta* (bell) and always held in the right hand
Yoni   Represents the female genitals and is used in conjunction with the lingam to symbolize Shiva

MYTHOLOGICAL FIGURES

Ashta Matrikas   The eight mother goddesses

Avalokiteshwara   A bodhisattva and the Buddhist deity of compassion (known as Chenrezig in Tibet)

Bhairav   Ferocious aspect of Shiva

Bodhisattva   Enlightened being or Buddha who chooses to remain on earth to help others become enlightened

Brahma   One of the Hindu trinity of the most powerful gods; the creator

Buddha   Prince Siddhartha Gautama, born in Lumbini, which is now in Nepal; he became the Buddha after meditating under a boddhi tree and discovering the way to transcend all suffering

Dhyani Buddhas   Five Buddhas, symbolic of five aspects of Buddhahood that are found on stupas

Durga   Frightening incarnation of Parvati

Ganesh   The elephant-headed son of Shiva and Parvati; a widely worshiped god said to bring good luck and remove impediments

Garuda   Half-man, half-bird vehicle upon which the Hindu god Vishnu travels

Green Tara   Buddhist goddess who embodies all that is good in women and who is credited with introducing Buddhism to Tibet

Hanuman   White-monkey god who helped rescue Sita, Rama's wife, from Ravana in the epic *Ramayana*

Indra   Hindu god of rain and king of heaven

Kali   Another wrathful incarnation of Parvati, worshiped at Dakshinkali in Kathmandu Valley

Krishna   Well-loved incarnation of Vishnu; his skin is usually blue

Kumari   The living goddess; the most famous kumari lives on Kathmandu's Durbar Square

Laxmi   Hindu goddess of wealth

Macchendranath   Incarnation of Avalokiteshwara and a highly revered god in Kathmandu Valley

Maitreya   Future Buddha

Manjushri   Buddhist god of knowledge who, according to legend, drained the lake that once filled the Kathmandu Valley by slicing through the surrounding mountains with his sword

Milaropa   Famous 12th-century Buddhist monk who wrote thousands of songs and is always depicted with his right hand to his ear

Naga   Guardian serpent

Nandi   Bull upon which Shiva rides; stands in front of temples containing statues of Shiva lingam

Narayan   Most common incarnation of Vishnu in Nepal; considered the creator of life

Narsimha   Half-man, half-lion incarnation of Vishnu who killed the demon Hiranya Kashiapu

Padmasambhawa   Buddhist saint of northern India who brought Buddhism to Tibet

Parvati   Shiva's wife

Saraswati   Hindu goddess of learning and Brahma's consort

Shiva   One of the Hindu trinity of most powerful gods; the destroyer of all things

Vishnu   One of the Hindu trinity of highest gods; the preserver

White Tara   Consort of Avalokiteshwara and Buddhist goddess who protects human beings as they cross the ocean of existence

Index

Key to Abbreviaitons B=Budget; E=Expensive; I=Inexpensive; M=Moderate; *= Author's
Favorite; $=Super-Value Choice.

Now Save Money on All Your Travels by Joining

Frommer's

T R A V E L   B O O K   C L U B

The Advantages of Membership:

1. Your choice of any **TWO FREE BOOKS.**

2. Your own subscription to the **TRIPS & TRAVEL** quarterly newsletter, where you'll discover the best buys in travel, the hottest vacation spots, the latest travel trends, world-class events and festivals, and much more.

3. A **30% DISCOUNT** on any additional books you order through the club.

4. **DOMESTIC TRIP-ROUTING KITS** (available for a small additional fee). We'll send you a detailed map highlighting the most direct or scenic route to your destination, anywhere in North America.

Here's all you have to do to join:

Send in your annual membership fee of $25.00 ($35.00 Canada/Foreign) with your name, address, and selections on the form below. Or call 815/734-1104 to use your credit card.

Send all orders to:

FROMMER'S TRAVEL BOOK CLUB
P.O. Box 473 • Mt. Morris, IL 61054-0473 • ☎ 815/734-1104

YES! I want to take advantage of this opportunity to join Frommer's Travel Book Club.

[ ] My check for $25.00 ($35.00 for Canadian or foreign orders) is enclosed.
   All orders must be prepaid in U.S. funds only. Please make checks payable to Frommer's Travel Book Club.

[ ] Please charge my credit card: [ ] Visa or [ ] Mastercard

   Credit card number: _____

   Expiration date: ___ / ___ / ___

   Signature: _____

   Or call 815/734-1104 to use your credit card by phone.

Name: _____

Address: _____

City: _____ State: _____ Zip code: _____

Phone number (in case we have a question regarding your order): _____

Please indicate your choices for TWO FREE books (*see following pages*):

   Book 1 - Code: _____   Title: _____

   Book 2 - Code: _____   Title: _____

For information on ordering additional titles, see your first issue of the *Trips & Travel* newsletter.

Allow 4–6 weeks for delivery for all items. Prices of books, membership fee, and publication dates are subject to change without notice. All orders are subject to acceptance and availability.

AC1

The following Frommer's guides are available from your favorite bookstore, or you can use the order form on the preceding page to request them as part of your membership in Frommer's Travel Book Club.

FROMMER'S COMPLETE TRAVEL GUIDES

(Comprehensive guides to sightseeing, dining and accommodations, with selections in all price ranges—from deluxe to budget)

Acapulco/Ixtapa/Taxco, 2nd Ed.	C157	Jamaica/Barbados, 2nd Ed.	C149
Alaska '94-'95	C131	Japan '94-'95	C144
Arizona '95	C166	Maui, 1st Ed.	C153
Australia '94-'95	C147	Nepal, 3rd Ed. (avail. 11/95)	C184
Austria, 6th Ed.	C162	New England '95	C165
Bahamas '96 (avail. 8/95)	C172	New Mexico, 3rd Ed.	C167
Belgium/Holland/Luxembourg,		New York State, 4th Ed.	C133
4th Ed.	C170	Northwest, 5th Ed.	C140
Bermuda '96 (avail. 8/95)	C174	Portugal '94-'95	C141
California '95	C164	Puerto Rico '95-'96	C151
Canada '94-'95	C145	Puerto Vallarta/Manzanillo/	
Caribbean '96 (avail. 9/95)	C173	Guadalajara, 2nd Ed.	C135
Carolinas/Georgia, 2nd Ed.	C128	Scandinavia, 16th Ed.	C169
Colorado '96 (avail. 11/95)	C179	Scotland '94-'95	C146
Costa Rica, 1st Ed.	C161	South Pacific '94-'95	C138
Cruises '95-'96	C150	Spain, 16th Ed.	C163
Delaware/Maryland '94-'95	C136	Switzerland, 7th Ed.	
England '96 (avail. 10/95)	C180	(avail. 9/95)	C177
Florida '96 (avail. 9/95)	C181	Thailand, 2nd Ed.	C154
France '96 (avail. 11/95)	C182	U.S.A., 4th Ed.	C156
Germany '96 (avail. 9/95)	C176	Virgin Islands, 3rd Ed.	
Honolulu/Waikiki/Oahu, 4th Ed.		(avail. 8/95)	C175
(avail. 10/95)	C178	Virginia '94-'95	C142
Ireland, 1st Ed.	C168	Yucatán '95-'96	C155
Italy '96 (avail. 11/95)	C183		

FROMMER'S $-A-DAY GUIDES

(Dream Vacations at Down-to-Earth Prices)

Australia on $45 '95-'96	D122	Ireland on $45 '94-'95	D118
Berlin from $50, 3rd Ed.		Israel on $45, 15th Ed.	D130
(avail. 10/95)	D137	London from $55 '96	
Caribbean from $60, 1st Ed.		(avail. 11/95)	D136
(avail. 9/95)	D133	Madrid on $50 '94-'95	D119
Costa Rica/Guatemala/Belize		Mexico from $35 '96	
on $35, 3rd Ed.	D126	(avail. 10/95)	D135
Eastern Europe on $30, 5th Ed.	D129	New York on $70 '94-'95	D121
England from $50 '96		New Zealand from $45, 6th Ed.	D132
(avail. 11/95)	D138	Paris on $45 '94-'95	D117
Europe from $50 '96		South America on $40, 16th Ed.	D123
(avail. 10/95)	D139	Washington, D.C. on $50	
Greece from $45, 6th Ed.	D131	'94-'95	D120
Hawaii from $60 '96 (avail. 9/95)	D134		

FROMMER'S COMPLETE CITY GUIDES

(Comprehensive guides to sightseeing, dining, and accommodations in all price ranges)

Amsterdam, 8th Ed.	S176	Minneapolis/St. Paul, 4th Ed.	S159
Athens, 10th Ed.	S174	Montréal/Québec City '95	S166
Atlanta & the Summer Olympic		Nashville/Memphis, 1st Ed.	S141
Games '96 (avail. 11/95)	S181	New Orleans '96 (avail. 10/95)	S182
Atlantic City/Cape May, 5th Ed.	S130	New York City '96 (avail. 11/95)	S183
Bangkok, 2nd Ed.	S147	Paris '96 (avail. 9/95)	S180
Barcelona '93–'94	S115	Philadelphia, 8th Ed.	S167
Berlin, 3rd Ed.	S162	Prague, 1st Ed.	S143
Boston '95	S160	Rome, 10th Ed.	S168
Budapest, 1st Ed.	S139	St. Louis/Kansas City, 2nd Ed.	S127
Chicago '95	S169	San Antonio/Austin, 1st Ed.	S177
Denver/Boulder/Colorado Springs,		San Diego '95	S158
3rd Ed.	S154	San Francisco '96 (avail. 10/95)	S184
Disney World/Orlando '96 (avail. 9/95)	S178	Santa Fe/Taos/Albuquerque '95	S172
Dublin, 2nd Ed.	S157	Seattle/Portland '94–'95	S137
Hong Kong '94–'95	S140	Sydney, 4th Ed.	S171
Las Vegas '95	S163	Tampa/St. Petersburg, 3rd Ed.	S146
London '96 (avail. 9/95)	S179	Tokyo '94–'95	S144
Los Angeles '95	S164	Toronto, 3rd Ed.	S173
Madrid/Costa del Sol, 2nd Ed.	S165	Vancouver/Victoria '94–'95	S142
Mexico City, 1st Ed.	S175	Washington, D.C. '95	S153
Miami '95–'96	S149		

FROMMER'S FAMILY GUIDES

(Guides to family-friendly hotels, restaurants, activities, and attractions)

California with Kids	F105	San Francisco with Kids	F104
Los Angeles with Kids	F103	Washington, D.C. with Kids	F102
New York City with Kids	F101		

FROMMER'S WALKING TOURS

(Memorable strolls through colorful and historic neighborhoods,
accompanied by detailed directions and maps)

Berlin	W100	Paris, 2nd Ed.	W112
Chicago	W107	San Francisco, 2nd Ed.	W115
England's Favorite Cities	W108	Spain's Favorite Cities (avail. 9/95)	W116
London, 2nd Ed.	W111	Tokyo	W109
Montréal/Québec City	W106	Venice	W110
New York, 2nd Ed.	W113	Washington, D.C., 2nd Ed.	W114

FROMMER'S AMERICA ON WHEELS

(Guides for travelers who are exploring the U.S.A. by car, featuring a brand-new
rating system for accommodations and full-color road maps)

Arizona/New Mexico	A100	Florida	A102
California/Nevada	A101	Mid-Atlantic	A103

FROMMER'S SPECIAL-INTEREST TITLES

Arthur Frommer's Branson!	P107	Frommer's Where to Stay U.S.A.,	
Arthur Frommer's New World		11th Ed.	P102
of Travel (avail. 11/95)	P112	National Park Guide, 29th Ed.	P106
Frommer's Caribbean Hideaways		USA Today Golf Tournament Guide	P113
(avail. 9/95)	P110	USA Today Minor League	
Frommer's America's 100 Best-Loved		Baseball Book	P111
State Parks	P109		

FROMMER'S BEST BEACH VACATIONS

*(The top places to sun, stroll, shop, stay, play, party, and swim—with each
beach rated for beauty, swimming, sand, and amenities)*

California (avail. 10/95)	G100	Hawaii (avail. 10/95)	G102
Florida (avail. 10/95)	G101		

FROMMER'S BED & BREAKFAST GUIDES

*(Selective guides with four-color photos and full descriptions of
the best inns in each region)*

California	B100	Hawaii	B105
Caribbean	B101	Pacific Northwest	B106
East Coast	B102	Rockies	B107
Eastern United States	B103	Southwest	B108
Great American Cities	B104		

FROMMER'S IRREVERENT GUIDES

*(Wickedly honest guides for sophisticated travelers
and those who want to be)*

Chicago (avail. 11/95)	I100	New Orleans (avail. 11/95)	I103
London (avail. 11/95)	I101	San Francisco (avail. 11/95)	I104
Manhattan (avail. 11/95)	I102	Virgin Islands (avail. 11/95)	I105

FROMMER'S DRIVING TOURS

*(Four-color photos and detailed maps outlining
spectacular scenic driving routes)*

Australia	Y100	Italy	Y108
Austria	Y101	Mexico	Y109
Britain	Y102	Scandinavia	Y110
Canada	Y103	Scotland	Y111
Florida	Y104	Spain	Y112
France	Y105	Switzerland	Y113
Germany	Y106	U.S.A.	Y114
Ireland	Y107		

FROMMER'S BORN TO SHOP

*(The ultimate travel guides for discriminating
shoppers—from cut-rate to couture)*

Hong Kong (avail. 11/95)	Z100	London (avail. 11/95)	Z101